THE CURE OF THE PASSION
ORIGINS OF THE ENGLIS

This new study examines the role of the passions in the rise of the English novel. Geoffrey Sill locates the origins of the novel in the breakdown of medical and religious dogmas prior to the eighteenth century, leading to a crisis in the regulation of the passions which the novel helped to address. He examines medical, religious, and literary efforts to anatomize the passions, paying particular attention to the works of Dr. Alexander Monro of Edinburgh, Reverend John Lewis of Margate, and Daniel Defoe, novelist and natural historian of the passions. He shows that the figure of the "physician of the mind" figures prominently not only in Defoe's novels, but also in those of Fielding, Richardson, Smollett, Burney, and Edgeworth. The "rise" of the novel comes to an end when the passions give way at the end of the century to the more modern concept of the emotions.

GEOFFREY SILL is Associate Professor of English and Chair of his department at Rutgers University in Camden, New Jersey. He is the author of *Defoe and the Idea of Fiction* (1983) and the editor of *Walt Whitman of Mickle Street* (1994) and other books. He is the Defoe editor of *The Scriblerian* and an active member of the American Society for Eighteenth-Century Studies.

THE CURE OF THE
PASSIONS AND THE ORIGINS
OF THE ENGLISH NOVEL

GEOFFREY SILL

CAMBRIDGE
UNIVERSITY PRESS

CAMBRIDGE UNIVERSITY PRESS
Cambridge, New York, Melbourne, Madrid, Cape Town, Singapore, São Paulo

Cambridge University Press
The Edinburgh Building, Cambridge CB2 2RU, UK

Published in the United States of America by Cambridge University Press, New York

www.cambridge.org
Information on this title: www.cambridge.org/9780521808057

First published 2001
This digitally printed first paperback version 2006

A catalogue record for this publication is available from the British Library

ISBN-13 978-0-521-80805-7 hardback
ISBN-10 0-521-80805-7 hardback

ISBN-13 978-0-521-02790-8 paperback
ISBN-10 0-521-02790-X paperback

Contents

Illustrations

Acknowledgments

A scholarly project that requires over a decade to complete is, in the end, the work of many hands besides the author's. I gratefully acknowledge the assistance I received from the students in my courses at the Camden campus of Rutgers University, whose willingness to hear about the passions as a way of reading the eighteenth century helped sustain my own interest in the subject; my colleagues at Rutgers, who gave me the freedom and security necessary to see me through a long period of research and writing; the administrators at Rutgers who approved sabbatical leaves in 1992, 1996, and 1999, during which substantial progress was made; my colleagues in the American Society for Eighteenth-Century Studies (ASECS), and particularly the East-Central ASECS, who listened to a dozen versions of this book in the form of short papers and talks; and Peter Jones, director of the Institute for Advanced Studies in the Humanities, and Dr. Michael Barfoot, director of the Medical Archive Centre, both at the University of Edinburgh. I also owe thanks to the librarians at Rutgers University, the College of Physicians of Philadelphia, Edinburgh University Library, the Bodleian Library at Oxford University, the British Library, Dr. Williams's Library in London, the Royal College of Physicians and the Royal College of Surgeons of Edinburgh, the Royal College of Physicians of London, the Wellcome Institute for the History of Medicine, the National Library of Scotland, the Dean and Chapter of Canterbury, the Kent County Council Library at Margate, and the London Public Record Office, all of which opened their treasures to me. I am grateful to Richard Gilder for his interest in the passions and humours, and for many other kindnesses; Linda Bree of the Cambridge University Press, for her interest in this project and safeguarding of it; Heather Bosence, for showing me St. Mary's in Minster and reading my chapter on John Lewis; John T. Williams of the Margate Local History Museum and Penny Ward of the Kent County Council for information on Margate; and Henry L. Fulton, Yvonne Noble,

Peter Sabor, and the anonymous readers at Cambridge University Press who offered many useful suggestions. I am grateful for the work of Rachel De Wachter, Lesley Atkin, and Pamela Mertsock Wolfe, who produced, copyedited, and indexed the book, respectively. I thank David Blewett, editor of *Eighteenth-Century Fiction*, for allowing me to use portions of "Crusoe in the Cave: Defoe and the Semiotics of Desire," *ECF* 6 (1994), 215–32; Suzanne Poirier, editor of *Literature and Medicine*, for the use of "Neurology and the Novel: Alexander Monro *primus* and *secundus*, *Robinson Crusoe*, and the Problem of Sensibility," 16 (1997), 250–65; and Timothy Erwin and Ourida Mostefai, editors of *Studies in Eighteenth-Century Culture*, for "*Roxana*'s Susan: Whose Daughter is she Anyway?," *SECC* 29 (2000), 261–72. Finally, I owe more than I can acknowledge or repay to the members of my extended family, particularly my son Ian, daughter Maggie, and my wife Susan, who taught me everything there is to know about the passions. This book is dedicated affectionately to her.

Introduction: the passions and the English novel

In the two decades that followed the appearance of *Robinson Crusoe* in 1719, the most popular form of literary discourse was not prose fiction, but conduct books that addressed what J. Paul Hunter describes as the "ethical issues of behavior in daily life."[1] One such conduct book was the Reverend Isaac Watts's *Doctrine of the Passions, Explain'd and Improv'd*, in which Watts sought to explain the necessity of regulating or "improving" the passions. The passions, Watts declared, are designed for "valuable Ends in Life, when put under due Government"; if, however, "they are let run loose without controul, or if they are abused, and imployed to wrong Purposes, they become the Springs and occasions of much Mischief and Misery."[2] Passions suffered to "run loose" would soon "break all the Bonds of human Society and Peace, and would change the Tribes of Mankind into brutal Herds, or make the World a mere Wilderness of Savages" (iv). Where, however, "these vehement Powers of Nature are reduced to the Obedience of Reason," they will "go a great way to procure our own Ease and Happiness, so far as 'tis attainable in this Life," and will "make our neighbours happy as ourselves" (v).

The art of regulating the passions requires some understanding of their nature. "It requires a good skill in Anatomy, and long and watchful Observation" to understand their workings, he cautions (10). The passions are a "sensible Commotion" of both the animal powers and the volitional soul of mankind. They arise "either from the Impressions or Commotions which the animal Powers receive by the Soul's Perception of that Object which raises the Passion, or from the Impression or Sensation which that Soul receives by this Commotion of the animal Powers, or perhaps from both of these" (3). These commotions may be accompanied by "some Ferments of the Blood, or natural Spirits, or some Alterations which affect the Body, as well as . . . special Impressions of the Mind," which leads Watts to conclude that the passions belong "partly to the Soul or Mind, and partly to the animal Body, i.e. the Flesh and Blood" (9–10).

I

What is most striking in Watts's doctrine of the passions is its ambiguities. Where a philosopher or physician in classical antiquity would have had little trouble determining the location, uses, and effects of the passions, Watts has many uncertainties: the passions may be part of the mind, the body, or both; they may be used for "valuable Ends" or for "Mischief and Misery," or both; they may form the bonds of affection between neighbors that bring peace and happiness to human society, or they may reduce the tribes of mankind into "brutal Herds" in a Hobbesian "Wilderness of Savages." Even the number and form of the passions are unknown: "The Motions of the Heart of Man are infinitely various: The different Forms and Shapes in which our Passions appear, the sudden and secret Turns and Windings of them through the Heart, with the strange Mixtures and Complications of them in their Continual Exercise, are innumerable and nameless" (i). And Watts has similar difficulties describing the mechanism by which passions are conveyed through the body: "What I call here *natural Spirits*, are sometimes called *animal* or *vital* Spirits, which are supposed to be the Springs or Mediums of animal Motions, both inward and outward: But whether these be some refined spiritous Liquids, or Vapour drawn off from the Blood, or whether they be nothing else but the elastick or springy Parts of the Air drawn in by Respiration, and mingled with the Blood and other Animal Juices, is not yet entirely agreed by Philosophers" (10n).

My purpose in thus exposing the ambiguities in Watts's doctrine of the passions is not to diminish him as a philosopher, but rather to present textual evidence of the unsettled state of knowledge – or, as we might say, the *crisis* of thought and opinion – about the passions that waxed and waned through much of the eighteenth century. "Passion unbridled would violate all the sacred Ties of Religion, and raise the Sons of Men in Arms against their Creator. Where Passion runs riot, there are none of the Rights of God or Man secure from its Insolences," Watts warns – a sentiment that would resonate in the works of Edmund Burke, Thomas Paine, and Mary Wollstonecraft before the century was over. The sense of crisis in Watts's doctrine is directly related to the uncertainties it reflects: the feeling that the nature, function, and ends of the passions, once thought to have been permanently settled (along with other anatomical questions) by the works of Galen, have been rendered ambiguous by seventeenth-century discoveries and innovations in science, medicine, and religion. And in his call for "good skill in Anatomy, and long and watchful Observation" on the part of those who would respond to this crisis, Watts identifies the essential quality that such novelists as Richardson,

Fielding, and Smollett would share with physicians, philosophers, and essayists in the collective effort to "cure" the passions over the coming decades.

Richardson, Fielding, and Smollett were of course by no means the first or the only novelists who anatomized the passions. Some four hundred "novelistic" works of fiction were published between 1700 and 1739, and nearly three hundred more in the 1740s.[3] Aphra Behn, Delarivier Manley, Elizabeth Haywood, Mary Davys, Jane Barker, Penelope Aubin, and Elizabeth Rowe have all been scrutinized in recent searches for the origins of the early modern novel, searches that have confirmed William McBurney's observation, forty years ago, that "the main lines of eighteenth-century fictional development" were already in place when the male novelists named above were still apprentices in their craft.[4] Though the works of Behn, Manley, and the early Haywood gave their authors the reputations of being more interested in arousing the passions than in disciplining them, Davys professed that the correction of the passions informed the "whole design" of her work.[5] In her preface to *The Accomplished Rake* (1727), she argued that the advantage of the novel over other forms is its "invention," which "gives us room to order accidents better than Fortune will be at the pains to do, so to work upon the reader's passions." The work to be done is "to restore the purity and empire of love, and correct the vile abuses of it," a task of paramount importance because, "since passions will ever have a place in the actions of men and love a principal one, what cannot be removed or subdued ought at least to be regulated."[6] These sentiments, which agree perfectly with those in Watts's conduct manuals, provide a clear intersection between the perceived crisis in the management of the passions and the emerging mission of the novel.

After the success of Richardson's *Pamela*, which as Margaret Doody has shown was indebted to these "feminine love-novels" for some of its thematic if not its formal elements, the reformation of the passions was a secure part of the agenda of the novel.[7] The distortion of character by passion is the principal subject matter of such novels as Sarah Fielding's *The Adventures of David Simple* (1744), Eliza Haywood's *Life's Progress through the Passions: or, the Adventures of Natura* (1748), and Charlotte Lennox's *The Female Quixote* (1752), all of which demonstrate the necessity of restraining a predominant passion, while such later works as Frances Sheridan's *The Memoirs of Miss Sidney Bidulph* (1761), Frances Burney's *Evelina* (1778), and Maria Edgeworth's *Belinda* (1811) present dramatically the importance of subordinating passion to manners or even of extirpating it from character altogether. The confusion that marked Watts' treatises on the passions is replaced in these novels by a remarkably clearsighted sense of the dangers to which both heroes and heroines were exposed by errors and false opinions arising from passion, as well as of the equanimity and goodness of heart that alone could vanquish it. The ambiguities that remain only serve to assist the "invention" that, for Mary Davys, was the essential formal quality of the novel. As Doody has said, the "natural passion" of love in Richardson's work plays on just such an ambiguity, presenting itself first as erotic, next social, and then divine, teasing us to ask ourselves what form of passion the text arouses in us. "The 'answer,'" she says, "is the novel, in short" – that is, the novel is defined as a genre by the reader's imaginative exploration of passion in all its complexity and ambiguity.[8]

This book extends into new areas the debate on the origins of the novel begun in Ian Watt's *The Rise of the Novel* (1957) and often reconsidered, most recently in two published colloquia. For Watt, the defining characteristic of the early modern novel is the formal realism of its presentation, which reflects the philosophical realism of the age. This philosophical realism, in turn, is explained by the rising rate of literacy, the rising middle class, and the rising spirit of individualism in English culture generally.[9] Though critics have identified many problems inherent in this "triple rise" thesis, most important contributions to the theory of the novel since Watt have studied the transformation of the genre in a social context of some sort. Well-known books by Nancy Armstrong, G. J. Barker-Benfield, John Bender, Terry Castle, Robert A. Erickson, Jean H. Hagstrum, J. Paul Hunter, and John Richetti, among others, have shown that the novel emerged in connection with larger social and intellectual changes.[10] G. S. Rousseau, to take one example, suggests that, while developments in seventeenth-century science did not cause the rise of the novel, they "deflected" the complacent acceptance of the theory of humours and temperaments toward an empirical interest in the question of sensibility, a subject that the novel was eminently well suited to examine.[11] The connection between the rise of the novel and events in philosophy, science, and religion was one of parallel developments between loosely associated fields, rather than a directly causal relation, but philosophers, physicians, and theologians undoubtedly drew some of their knowledge of the passions from novelists, and novelists drew a sense of the urgency and legitimacy of their task from moral philosophy, religion, and medicine. One of the premises of this book, then, is that the search for the "cure" – or the regulation and improvement – of the passions depicted in many novels of the period reflects a crisis that energized widely disparate fields of thought in the eighteenth century, which can best be traced through an interdisciplinary study of their relations.

Ian Watt extended his own thesis about the origins of the novel in his final book, *Myths of Modern Individualism* (1996), which examines the ways in which the myth of individualism has shaped Western civilization since the Renaissance. Four mythic figures – Faust, Don Quixote, Don Juan, and Robinson Crusoe – exhibit the distinctive qualities of individualism: "exorbitant egos," a desire to do "something no one else has done," a freedom to choose his own fate, and a single-minded will to pursue this choice at all costs.[12] The first three of Watt's mythic figures fall victim or martyr to the powerful forces of the Counter-Reformation, that league of Church and secular authority that, in regarding individualism as a threat to social order, created an intellectual climate in which the triumph of the individual was unthinkable. The last figure, Robinson Crusoe, is the first individualist hero to emerge intact; he is "an articulate spokesman of the new economic, religious, and social attitudes that succeeded the Counter-Reformation" (xi). Even the religion that Crusoe acquires during his twenty-eight years of solitude on the island is individualistic: the "collective and sacramental" elements of both Roman Catholicism and Calvinist Protestantism are absent from his forms of belief, which consist entirely in "trying to see how the most minute or unnoticed event of daily life may contribute to his place in the divine scheme of reprobation or salvation" (162). According to Watt, Crusoe is not even a Puritan, which would make him part of the collective response to the Counter-Reformation, but an entirely self-sufficient entity, the first representative of the modern myth of individualism.

Watt's description of the rise of individualist ideology is similar in some respects to the account of the Protestant Reformation given by Roland Bainton, who sees it as a product of "the philosophy of individualism undercutting the great unities" of the Roman Catholic Church.[13] Foremost among these unities was the dogma of the Holy Trinity, which had been adopted in principle at the Council of Nicaea in 325 A.D. The Nicene Creed held that the deity consists of three persons – Father, Son, and Holy Ghost – in one substance, a paradox that is at once a test of faith and an emblem of the corporate nature of the Church. This doctrine was undercut, according to Bainton, when some fifteenth-century theologians accepted the principle that reality consists of unrelated particulars, because "if reality consists of unrelated individuals, then the three persons of the Trinity must be three gods" (16). Despite the loss of the Trinity's philosophical underpinning, the Church maintained the doctrine on the basis of authority alone, thus prompting struggles over the rights of the individual to believe or not to believe in the Trinity that continued throughout the eighteenth century.

According to J. G. A. Pocock, the process of individuation that broke the unity of the Christian church had a comparable effect on the teaching and practice of medicine. As Pocock observes, medicine had since the time of Plato been subject to the charge that it was unphilosophical – that it was based not in universals, but in particular cases, which could be learned only through empirical experience.[14] Galen had endeavored to systematize this body of empirical knowledge, showing how the uses of the parts of the body could be comprehended in terms of a unifying teleology, though he emphasized the value of observation and experiment in the practice of medicine.[15] By the fifteenth century, the aspiration of medicine to prove itself a system based on rational principles had led to an emphasis on Aristotle and Galen in medical education to the exclusion of empirical knowledge, with the result that Galenism had become a dogma comparable in some respects to the doctrine of the Trinity for the church.[16] In medicine as in theology, the discovery that reality is not subject to a unifying teleology, but consists of unrelated particulars – or at least, that the particulars are related in ways not consistent with rational theory – led first to cracks in the structure of the institution, and then to a reformation according to new principles. This anti-Galenist reformation was the work of many hands in the sixteenth and seventeenth centuries, among whom Paracelsus, William Harvey, Thomas Willis, Thomas Sydenham, Herman Boerhaave and others are often counted.[17] It was not accomplished without some severe penalties for the prophets of reform; what Roland Bainton said of Roman Catholic theology also proved true of scholastic medicine: as the philosophic undergirding of the institution weakened, there was a "recourse . . . to authority when the grip on truth relaxed."[18] One such prophet of individualism who suffered the severest penalties was the sixteenth-century heretic Michael Servetus, a Spanish physician whose writings challenged the dogmas of both the church and the medical establishment. This book will repeatedly examine eighteenth-century references to Servetus as a way of invoking this problematic tension between individual passion and institutional authority which lay at the origins of the novel. In this way, Servetus figures as the godfather of the novel, even though, so far as is known, he neither wrote nor even read one.

The question of the novel's origins – rather than its rise – has previously been addressed most systematically in Michael McKeon's *The Origins of the English Novel* (1987), which describes what Alistair Duckworth has called an "elegantly simple model of [the] epistemological and social crisis" that prompted the transformation of the genre.[19] McKeon examines two major questions (or as he variously describes them, "instances of categorical instability") that together compose a dialectic in the period of his study: questions of truth, and questions of virtue. The instability of truth – which is, in effect, the narrative problem of choosing among different ways of *telling* the truth – posed an epistemological crisis, while the instability of virtue – which presented "a cultural crisis in attitudes toward how the external social order is related to the internal, moral state of its members" – was essentially social in nature.[20] The genre of the novel, in his view, was adapted from earlier literary materials in order to mediate this crisis. As we have seen in Isaac Watts, however, there was a third category of instability that was of equal importance to truth and virtue in the eighteenth century: the question of passion, which resulted from the uncertainty of the age over the nature, function, and uses of mankind's irrational, individualistic self. The chapters that follow this introduction assume the proposition that McKeon's thesis should be broadened to include another primary category (despite the damage thereby done to the notion of a dialectic), which is the question of passion.

Passion appears in *The Origins of the English Novel* as an aggravating factor to questions of truth or virtue, but not as a category of instability in itself. For example, McKeon discusses Robinson Crusoe's capacity to understand the signs given him by God in the form of "secret Intimations of Providence" as essentially an epistemological and cultural problem, complicated by Robinson's passions – in this case, a complex of guilt, fear, and desire centered around his hope of physical deliverance from the island (*Origins*, 330–33). Though Robinson had previously enjoyed the "Calm of Mind" that came with resignation to the will of Providence in placing him on the island, his obsession with leaving the island brings about a "transvaluation of desire" that allows him, through a dream, to re-signify the language of God to accord with the "logic of inner conviction" that would authorize his escape. By this means, the will of Providence, which he previously understood as counseling resignation, becomes transvalued into a command to engage in "impassioned activity" directed at leaving the island. Many readers see religious hypocrisy in Robinson's manipulation of the meaning of Providential signs to suit inner desires, but McKeon defends the passage as ironic, arguing that Defoe's intent is to show through the incident the contradiction between the religious forms of language that Robinson uses and the underlying basis of his actions. For McKeon, the passage exhibits Defoe's "unparalleled penetration and candor" in exposing the "absurdity" of Robinson's effort to make an epistemology based in religion consist with values derived from an expansive, exploratory, entrepreneurial age. But it might very well be argued, on the basis of other works written by Defoe before and after *Robinson Crusoe*, that no irony is intended: that the principal "instability" that concerns Defoe in this book is neither epistemological nor social, but what we would now call psychological – that is, the conflict between desire and restraint. Robinson's goal, in writing the history of his life, is to show his readers how he accomplished the task of mediating that conflict – in effect, how he cured his passions. For Defoe, the passions are a category of instability in human nature that must be addressed *before* questions of truth and virtue can be raised. *Robinson Crusoe*, like *Moll Flanders*, *Roxana*, and his other fictional biographies, is an experimental laboratory in which Defoe worked out the operations of fear, anger, and desire, and considered the ways in which they may lead us to good as well as betray us into the hands of the Devil. Robinson Crusoe's history might well be discounted as hypocritical if that book were meant to define a standard of either truth or virtue, but if its purpose was to provide a guide to conduct through Hunter's "ethical issues of behavior in daily life," it succeeds on purely pragmatic grounds. Learning to know the difference between passions and the will of God, as McKeon has shown, leads eventually to questions that are epistemological and moral in nature. The origins of the English novel, then, are to be found not only in the generic transformations through which questions of truth and virtue are worked out, but also in the question of passion that raises and problematises them.

Of the nine chapters in this book, the first three establish a historical and intellectual context for the "cure" of the passions. We begin by examining one such cure, that of Matt Bramble in Tobias Smollett's last novel, *The Expedition of Humphry Clinker*, in which the novelist pays Dr. John Arbuthnot the compliment of using him as the model for his fictional physician, Dr. Lewis. Smollett's reader soon learns that Bramble's maladies are mostly mental, and that Lewis is a physician for the mind as well as the body. The physician of the mind is a familiar figure in Stoic philosophy, which developed therapeutic methods ranging from extirpating the passions to training them with the assistance of an elder friend or physician. Such "cures" for the passions, which entered literary tradition through the works of Cicero, Seneca, Galen, Aquinas, Augustine and others, assumed the form of a narrative centered around a philosopher-physician whom Henry Fielding formally identified in both *Tom Jones* and *Amelia* as the "Physician of the Mind." Depending on the occupation of this philosopher-physician, the cure could assume the metaphorical form of a surgeon performing an amputation, a cleric tending to his curacy, or even a country gentleman improving the raw products of the land, as Robinson Crusoe discovers when he cures the tobacco on his island. The narrative of the cure of the passions thus came more or less fully formed to the hand of the eighteenth-century novelist, who found in it both a proven formal element capable of resolving the story and a link to a classical heritage for a genre with a questionable pedigree.

From the classical period to the mid-seventeenth century, the heart, whose triangular shape was held to validate the dogma of the Trinity, was widely considered to be the seat of the passions. The discovery of circulation by William Harvey in 1628 severely challenged these Galenist and Christian orthodoxies. Galenists such as Robert Burton and Tobias Venner, following the ancient tradition, regarded the passions as "an epidemical disease, that so often, so much, crucifies the body and mind," while the "modern" philosopher Thomas Hobbes held the passions to be the stimuli that initiate all "Animall Motions," and were thus indispensable to life itself.[21] William Wotton's revelation in 1694 that the first steps toward Harvey's discovery had been taken in the mid-sixteenth century by the heretic Michael Servetus only deepened the philosophical divisions about the nature and function of the heart, nerves, and passions, making their examination in both the anatomical theatre and the laboratory of the novel a matter of greater urgency.

In their common interest in the cure of the passions, the eighteenth century doctor and novelist share what we might call the anatomist's gaze. Anatomists such as Dr. Alexander Monro of Edinburgh sought, like their predecessors Democritus, Galen, Vesalius, Servetus, Harvey and others, to clarify the function of the heart and nerves in order to understand (among other purposes) whether passions are, as the ancients held, the handmaidens of disease, or, as the moderns believed, the sources of sensibility and motion. Much as the anatomist drew back the skin and muscles of a cadaver to reveal the nerves, organs, and bones below, the novelist looked beneath the visible signs of character for the invisible, immaterial, yet vital motions of the passions in his or her subjects. The novel is a cultural by-product of the explorations of the natural historian, probing the body and case history of mankind for the origins of disease.

The middle third of this book focuses on several books by Daniel Defoe which have since come to be read as novels, but which were written to be read as natural histories of the passions – case studies of the perturbation of human nature by desires of various sorts, including youthful lusts for selfhood, irrational curiosities about death in the midst of a plague, and ambitions for a place in society to which one has no legitimate claim. What makes these case studies work as novels is not only their "philosophical realism," as Ian Watt put it, nor even, as he later said, their connection with one of the most powerful and empowering myths of Western civilization, but the humanity of their narrators as they repeatedly fall into the snares laid for them by their own passions. Though Robinson Crusoe is able to effect a partial cure through reflection and the mediation of his Bible, and Moll Flanders finds a helpful physician of the mind in the minister who befriends her in Newgate, Defoe's narrators are trapped by their own individualism into a dark pit of memory and despair. This pit, which Defoe first described in *The Consolidator* as "Nature's strong Box, the Memory, with all its Locks and Keys," is the warehouse where the passions are stored, and the Devil keeps the keys. From this pit Robinson and Moll are able to escape, but Roxana's deep-rooted passion proves an incurable disease. Defoe's works occupy a major portion of this study of the origins of the novel not because of his contributions to narrative form, but because he made curing the passions – rather than just arousing them – the focal point of the emerging genre of English prose fiction.

The last third of this book examines a few – though it leaves aside many more – narrative representations of the cure of passion in works written after 1740. The first case is that of the Reverend John Lewis, the author of many published works on the history of the English Reformation, but also of some unpublished manuscripts, including an autobiography, a "History of the Life of Servetus," and perhaps a letter to a young woman named Betty, advising her against an elopement with a Quaker. Lewis's manuscripts illuminate a lifetime of struggle to cure his passions and those of his parishioners, with limited success. His "Life of Servetus," suppressed by his friend Peter Thompson on Lewis's death in 1747, is an artifact of the Church of England's campaign to hold in check the religious passions set free by the individualist tendencies of the Protestant Reformation. In this manuscript, Lewis questions the sovereignty of private judgment and endeavors to define the limits of passion in the pursuit of freedom, questions that were being addressed at the same time by Fielding, Richardson, and other novelists.

Rather than compare Fielding and Richardson straight up, as is often done in studies of the novel, this book proceeds by contrasting two ways of curing the passions: one that assumes some inherent goodness of heart in the subject of the novel and seeks to restore it to health by removing or moderating the passions that have distempered it; and another that seeks to reform behavior by subjecting the passions to a disciplinary code of manners, or, should that cure fail, by extirpating them. In the former kind of cure, which is consistent with the moral system devised by Francis Hutcheson in the 1720s and '30s, a corrupted sensibility is shown regaining its natural function, often through the intervention of a friend, such as Tom Jones' intervention in the tragic circumstances of Nightingale and Nancy Miller, or with the assistance of a physician of the mind, such as *Amelia*'s Dr. Harrison. In the second kind of cure, the affected passions must be chastised or rooted out and replaced by softer sentiments that reflect an idealized and often feminized code of behavior. The novels of Richardson and Frances Burney epitomize this latter sort of cure, but the most powerful instance is Burney's narrative of her own mastectomy, in which an "evil" that is "so deep" that it "could only with life be extirpated" is removed from her breast.

As Alan Downie points out, it is difficult to terminate the discussion of the origins of the novel at 1740, as McKeon does, because the "making" of the English novel was still in process at least through the 1770s.[22] But an even better reason for not terminating the study at 1740 is that the most interesting developments in the "cure" of the passions were still to come. Adam Smith's *The Theory of Moral Sentiments* (1759) and Edmund Burke's *A Philosophical Enquiry into the Origin of our Ideas of the Sublime and Beautiful* (1759) completed the integration of the passions into moral and aesthetic philosophy that had begun earlier in the century in the work of Hutcheson and David Hume, while Robert Whytt in his *Essay on the Vital and other Involuntary Motions in Animals* (1751) and Alexander Monro *secundus* in his *Observations on the Structure and Functions of the Nervous System* (1783) consolidated the theory of nervous sensibility that had begun with Newton and the anatomical studies of his father, Alexander Monro *primus*, among others. Though none of these developments may have had a direct influence on the transformation of the novel, it is plain that philosophy, medicine, religion, and literature were, particularly in the eighteenth century, different ways of talking about the same set of questions. Questions of truth, questions of virtue, and perhaps especially the question of the passions dominated all fields of discourse through the eighteenth century; the goal of this book is to show how the connections between those discourses of passion are illuminated by the search for a cure.

CHAPTER I

The physician of the mind from Zeno to Arbuthnot

Of the many relationships between physicians and patients represented in eighteenth-century British fiction, perhaps the best example is that of Dr. Lewis and the hypochondriacal Matthew Bramble in Tobias Smollett's epistolary novel, *The Expedition of Humphry Clinker*. Three weeks into his tour of the British Isles, which his doctor has ordered him to take for his health, Matt Bramble writes a letter of complaint to Dr. Lewis. He apologizes for troubling his physician with a long list of grievances, but he asserts that it is a doctor's traditional function to treat his patient's mental, as well as physical, health:

I cannot help thinking, I have some right to discharge the overflowings of my spleen upon you, whose province it is to remove those disorders that occasioned it; and let me tell you, it is no small alleviation of my grievances, that I have a sensible friend, to whom I can communicate my crusty homours, which, by retention, would grow intolerably acrimonious.[1]

Always the amateur physician, Bramble adopts what he believes is suitably Hippocratic language to diagnose his disease and prescribe his own cure: his spleen being filled with bile, he must empty the resulting ill humours into the vessel of his doctor's care in order to avoid further encrustation of his temperament. In asserting that he has a "right" to do so, and that it is the "province" of his "sensible friend" to listen to his complaints, Bramble defines the unique relation between himself and his physician in terms of an ancient tradition, one in which the doctor is not just a medical practitioner, but also a counselor, a philosopher, a friend, and a man of sensibility. This philosopher-physician cures his patient not with hellebore or peruvian bark, but by listening sympathetically to the outpouring of his patient's disturbed passions – which are often the source of the malady – and providing some "hints" through which the patient may cure himself.

The dialogue between Bramble and his philosopher-physician appears one-sided, in that only letters to Lewis are presented to the reader, but the nature of Lewis's responses may be inferred from several letters in which Bramble thanks Lewis for the "hints" through which the doctor has set his patient's mind at ease. In the first letter of the novel, Bramble quarrels with his physician over the remedy for his ailments, which appear to include constipation and related forms of bloating ("The pills are good for nothing . . . I have told you over and over, how hard I am to move"), for which Lewis has recommended laxative pills and generous use of the mineral waters at Bristol Hot-Well and Bath (5). In his answer, Lewis evidently reproves Bramble, reminding him of the dangers of self-diagnosis and self-treatment by lay persons, because Bramble replies, "I understand your hint. There are mysteries in physick, as well as in religion; which we of the profane have no right to investigate." Despite this admission, Bramble maintains that he has studied medicine as thoroughly in the "hospital" of his own body as if he had been trained in "regular courses of physiology *et cetera et cetera*" (21). One of these mysteries, which the doctor seems to understand much better than the patient, is the effect of the passions of the mind in abetting disorders of the body. Bramble's complaints, the reader infers, are caused not by any organic obstruction, but by his irascible temper and chronic vexation, which Dr. Lewis is endeavoring to allay through the classic remedy of a long and arduous journey.[2]

The irascibility of Matthew Bramble's temper becomes fully apparent in an incident described in a letter written by his nephew, Jeremy, to his friend at college. Upon the arrival of the Bramble party at their new lodgings at Bath, Bramble's "irritable nerves" suffer the confusion of Aunt Tabitha's unpacking, a dogfight, a concert of street musicians, and dancing lessons given by a half-blind, one-legged dancing master in the rooms above. Bramble has just silenced all these irritants to his peace when two black servants of another lodger begin to practice upon French horns in the stairwell:

You may guess what effect they had upon the irritable nerves of uncle; who, with the most admirable expression of splenetic surprize in his countenance, sent his man to silence those dreadful blasts, and desire the musicians to practise in some other place, as they had no right to stand there and disturb all the lodgers in the house. Those sable performers, far from taking the hint, and withdrawing, treated the messenger with great insolence; bidding him carry his compliments to their master, colonel Rigworm, who would give him a proper answer, and a good drubbing into the bargain; in the mean time they continued their noise, and even endeavoured to make it more disagreeable; laughing between whiles, at the thoughts of being able to torment their betters with impunity. Our 'squire, incensed at the additional insult, immediately dispatched the servant, with his compliments to colonel Rigworm; requesting that he would order his blacks to be quiet, as the noise they made was altogether intolerable – To this message, the Creole colonel replied, that his horns had a right to sound on a common staircase; that there they should play for his diversion; and that those who did not like the noise, might look for lodgings else-where. Mr. Bramble no sooner received this reply, than his eyes began to glisten, his face grew pale, and his teeth chattered. After a moment's pause, he slipt on his shoes, without speaking a word, or seeming to feel any further disturbance from the gout in his toes. Then, snatching his cane, he opened the door and proceeded to the place where the black trumpeters were posted. There, without further hesitation, he began to belabour them both; and exerted himself with such astonishing vigour and agility, that both their heads and horns were broken in a twinkling, and they ran howling down stairs to their master's parlour-door. The 'squire, following them half way, called aloud, that the colonel might hear him, "Go, rascals, and tell your master what I have done; if he thinks himself injured, he knows where to come for satisfaction. As for you, this is but an earnest of what you shall receive, if ever you presume to blow a horn again here, while I stay in the house." (29–30)

Jeremy's description of his uncle's angry outburst, resembling as it does a physician's summary of the presentation of his patient's symptoms, reveals how heavily Smollett was indebted to his experiences as a physician for the materials of his comic art.[3] Like a doctor recording his patient's progress through a fever, Jeremy describes the conditions that provoked his uncle's anger, notes the signs in Bramble's face that indicated the onset of his passion, and observes his uncle's extraordinary ability to overcome his physical disabilities while caught up in his rage. The case history concludes with a direct quotation of Bramble's challenge to the Creole colonel whose incivility provoked the incident, suggesting that his uncle has managed to relieve his constipation by means of an upward, vocal evacuation of his spirits.

Jeremy's diagnosis of his uncle's malady is that he is "a hypochondriac... infected with good-humour" (46). In eighteenth-century medicine, the term "hypochondriac" was used in a somewhat different sense from its modern meaning. According to Ilza Veith, hypochondria emerged early in the seventeenth century when physicians recognized symptoms of hysteria in men, which conflicted with the widely held belief that hysteria was particular to women, having its organic basis in the womb. In order to resolve the discrepancy, the term "hypochondriasis" was introduced to explain emotional disturbances in men that were accompanied by physical swellings, headaches, and nervous excitement, sometimes to the point of convulsion.[4] Thomas Sydenham (1624–89) expanded the definition of the disease to include a variety of ailments that had previously been thought to have only organic, rather than emotional, origins, with the result that he came to consider hypochondria

and hysteria the commonest of all chronic diseases, frequently afflict-
ing persons of sound judgment and superior intelligence (Veith, *Hysteria*,
141–42). Because one of its effects was to stimulate the nervous system,
Sydenham considered it a disease of the imagination, but by no means
an imaginary disease. Sydenham's theory of hysteria and hypochondria
was given wider circulation in the work of Giorgio Baglivi (1668–1706),
who argued that nervous diseases were caused by disturbances of the
passions, and were to be cured only by restoring emotional tranquility,
rather than by physical or chemical remedies. To this end, it was important for the physician to carefully record the emotional conditions
of the patient that brought on the attacks, in order to identify their specific causes. If, as it appears, Bramble's malady is hypochondria, then
Jeremy's (and Smollett's) task is to identify and record the external stimuli
that overly excite his uncle's passions.

By the end of the eighteenth century, it was conventional to distinguish hypochondria from melancholy, as if they were different diseases
with different origins. Thus Benjamin Rush described hypochondria as
a "partial derangement" or an "error in opinion" that the patient held
toward his "person, affairs, or condition," while "melancholia" indicated a derangement arising in "objects external to the patient."[5] This
distinction worked to the disadvantage of the hypochondriac, in that it
dissolved the connection between the disease and the personal or social
conditions over which the patient may have had legitimate grievances. In
Matt Bramble's case, for example, the diagnosis of hypochondria seems
to invalidate his complaints about the vices of his times as so much cant,
brought on by his degenerate physical condition.[6] But Rush's distinction between hypochondria and melancholy was not shared by Thomas
Sydenham and the physicians who named the disease; for them, "melancholy" was merely a descriptive term for symptoms of the disease of
hypochondria, which might well have either emotional or social causes.
In this older sense of the word, Bramble's hypochondria does not invalidate his claim to be a modern-day Jeremiah, the Old Testament
prophet whose "lamentations" warn of a disaster about to befall Israel
because of its taste for luxuries and its unholiness; indeed, Bramble self-
consciously adopts that role when he refers to his letters to Dr. Lewis as
"the lamentations of Matthew Bramble" (31).[7]

Even more to the point, Bramble's one-sided exchanges with Lewis
resemble the virulent social criticism in the genre of poetry named
after Menippus of Gadara, including the satires of Varro and Lucian
of Samosata. According to Northrop Frye, the defining characteristic of

Menippean satire is its sharp attack on "mental attitudes" that underlie some forms of social behavior, including "[p]edants, bigots, cranks, parvenus, virtuosi, enthusiasts, rapacious and incompetent professional men of all kinds" for their "occupational approach to life."[8] Menippean satire "anatomizes" and classifies these attitudes prepatory to seeking a cure for them. For Frye, the classic eighteenth-century Menippean satires are *Gulliver's Travels* and *Tristram Shandy*, but a strong case might be made that *Humphry Clinker*, with its letters and their implied answers substituting for classical dialogues, also belongs in that list.[9]

Matt Bramble's explosions of vitriolic anger are typically directed at certain recurring mental attitudes and their corresponding social behaviors, including incivility, professional pedantry, and the luxury of the modern age. In the incident on the staircase, for example, he is offended by the insolence of the horn-players and the refusal of the Creole colonel to discipline them, in contrast to the civility of Sir Ulic McGillicut, who ceases his dancing lessons upon learning that they are disturbing the peace of the gentleman in the rooms below. Bramble's most Menippean moment, perhaps, occurs during his controversy with Dr. Linden over the healthful effects of the waters at Hot-well. The doctor, a physician in the rationalist tradition, relies on medical theory at the expense of empirical observation; he is oblivious to the affective qualities of stinks, and all of his learning cannot help him cure the syphilitic wart on his own nose (16–18). What most arouses Bramble's anger is the doctor's rigid orthodoxy: "He has read a great deal; but without method or judgment, and digested nothing" (23). Finally, in Bramble's strictures on the city of Bath, he traces the effects of discord and disorder back to England's sudden prosperity: "All these absurdities arise from the general tide of luxury, which hath overspread the nation, and swept away all, even the very dregs of the people" (34). Bramble's verbal eruptions, therefore, are not merely the product of a hypochondriacal temperament, any more than his constipation is caused by a weak constitution; rather, both disorders arise from external causes, and demonstrate the effects of irritation upon the nerves of a man of sensibility.

In one other respect, however, Jery's diagnosis is accurate: his uncle's partial derangement contains its own cure in the form of a counter-infection of "good-humour." This infection of benevolence first appears in the glimpses we get of his secret charities, such as his gift of twenty pounds to a poor widow, witnessed by his nephew Jery through a keyhole (19). Ultimately, Bramble's sensibility to the pain of the unfortunate cures both his own afflictions and those of his company: his offer of employment to the unfortunate farrier, Humphry Clinker, whom he considers guilty only of "sickness, hunger, wretchedness, and want" (76), eventually brings concord out of discord and gives the expedition a unity and purpose that it had very much wanted. Bramble's sensibility enables him to play the same role for the members of his party that is performed by Dr. Lewis for him – that is, the philosopher-physician of the mind. Bramble claims this role for himself in a letter written at the end of the expedition's first month: after describing his sister Tabitha's latest flirtation, his niece Lydia's delicate nerves, and his nephew Jery's jealous vigilance, Bramble asks Lewis ironically to understand "what an agreeable task it must be, to a man of my kidney, to have the cure of such souls as these" (45).

Bramble's phrase "have the cure" suggests the offices both of a physician and of a curate, or curator – one whose task it is to heal, preserve, and protect the souls placed in his charge. Of all the souls that Bramble cures, the most distressed is that of his friend Baynard, whom Bramble frees from the thralldom of a domineering wife and then rescues when Baynard threatens suicide over his wife's death (270, 313). The global irony of the book, of course, is that Bramble's own soul is very much in need of a cure, which occurs near the end of the journey. The cure is effected through (in Northrop Frye's term) a "ritual death" in which Bramble is nearly drowned (but is saved by his own son Humphry), and through Bramble's *cognitio*, in which he recognizes the consequences of the folly of his youth, which (being repressed) had apparently caused his longstanding constipation.[10] The most hopeful sign that the cure may be permanent is Bramble's declaration, in his last letter, that this erstwhile Menippus intends to write no more letters (322).

SWIFT TO ARBUTHNOT: "YOU ARE A PHILOSOPHER AND A PHYSICIAN"

In this final letter to Dr. Lewis, Bramble pays his physician a high compliment by associating him with the famed John Arbuthnot (1667–1735), physician to Queen Anne, John Gay, Jonathan Swift, David Hume, Alexander Pope and other luminaries in the age prior to Smollett's. It was Dr. Lewis's gentle "hints," Bramble says, that have brought him peace of mind: "You are an excellent genius at hints. – Dr. Arbuthnot was but a type of Dr. Lewis in that respect" (*HC*, 321). By invoking Arbuthnot's name as the "type" for Dr. Lewis, Smollett grounds the fictional relation he describes between Bramble and Lewis in terms of a well-established paradigm in eighteenth-century letters. It was the poet John Gay who first identified Dr. Arbuthnot as the modern incarnation of the philosopher-physician:

> *Arbuthnot* there I see in physicks art,
> As *Galen* learn'd or famed *Hippocrate*;
> Whose company drives sorrow from the heart,
> As all disease his med'cines dissipate.[11]

Arbuthnot's ability to cure disease by treating the spirit, rather than merely the body of his patient, is evident from a letter in which Jonathan Swift vented his anger to Arbuthnot during the final weeks of the Tory ministry in 1714:

The fashion of this world passeth away: however, I am angry at those who disperse us sooner than these may need. I have a mind to be very angry, and to let my anger break out in some manner that will not please them at the end of a pen ... Writing to you much would make me stark mad. Judge his condition who has nothing to keep him from being miserable but endeavouring to forget those for whom he has the greatest value, love, and friendship. But you are a Philosopher and a Physician, and can overcome by your wisdom and your faculty those weaknesses which other men are forced to reduce by not thinking on them. Adieu, and love me half so well as I do you.[12]

Similarly, in 1734 a melancholy young student named David Hume wrote a letter to a physician, now presumed to have been Dr. Arbuthnot, complaining of symptoms consistent with "the Disease of the Learned," and asking if there were any possibility of a cure.[13] "All the Physicians I have consulted," wrote Hume, "though very able, cou'd never enter into my Distemper; because not being Persons of great Learning beyond their own Profession, they were unacquainted with these Motions of the Mind." Hume hinted at the hypochondriacal nature of his disease, and at its cure, in observing "you know 'tis a Symptom of this Distemper to delight in complaining & talking of itself." And Alexander Pope praised Arbuthnot's skill at helping patients rid themselves of imaginary diseases, or diseases of the imagination, when Pope wrote of Arbuthnot, "I think him as good a Doctor as any man for one that is ill, and a better Doctor for one that is well."[14] Pope may have been thinking of Arbuthnot's successful treatment ten years earlier of the philosophical idealist, George Berkeley, who as Arbuthnot confided to his fellow Scriblerians, "has now the idea of health, which was very hard to produce in him, for he had an idea of a strange feaver upon him so strong that it was very hard to destroy it by introducing a contrary one."[15]

Pope's greatest tribute to Arbuthnot, however, is a "Bill of Complaint" about the spiritual ills of mankind, the *Epistle from Mr. Pope, to Dr. Arbuthnot.* This satirical poem is at once an attack on particular persons and a general denunciation of mankind's vicious nature, revealing in Pope what David Morris has described as "a capacity for Juvenalian indignation that will surprise his readers" – surprising in view of the fact that Pope placed this poem at the head of his imitations of the gentler satirist, Horace.[16] Unlike Horace, the Juvenalian satirist intends to inflict pain – if not to cure the vices depicted in the satire, then at least to deter others from following the same course – and for this purpose a controlled expression of anger is appropriate. In addition to this indignation, however, the poem has a second purpose – that of purgation – for which Arbuthnot is a particularly appropriate audience. As Rebecca Ferguson puts it, " 'Purging' as a medicinal concept is ... central to the *Epistle to Dr. Arbuthnot.* "[17] As if admitting that his anger may neither cure nor deter a single evil, the poet contents himself with emptying his ill humours into his physician's ear, much as Bramble does with Lewis, in order to lessen the anguish he feels at vice's universal sway. Finally, his anger spent, the poet draws a comparison between Arbuthnot's care for him and his own concern for an aged parent, in doing which he "reenacts the concerned care of Arbuthnot towards himself as a patient."[18] By thus identifying himself with his physician, he at least cures the passion of anger in himself, if he is unable to cure the passion for vice in others. The role played by Arbuthnot in Pope's poetic *Epistle* – that of the sympathetic friend endeavoring to moderate the raging anger of the poet – is virtually identical to that of Dr. Lewis in Smollett's epistolary novel.

It is not always the case, however, that the doctor who restores his patient's disturbed passions to equanimity in eighteenth-century texts is a doctor of medicine. It is equally likely that this doctor has been trained as a metaphysician – that is, as a clergyman or philosopher – rather than as a physician. Thus the learned Dr. Harrison, who orchestrates the resolution of Henry Fielding's *Amelia* (1752), is a member of the clergy; his skills as a doctor derive not from a knowledge of the body, but rather from the fact that, as Amelia puts it, "you understand Human Nature to the Bottom, ... and your Mind is the Treasury of all ancient and modern Learning."[19] Amelia's husband, William Booth, explains the unusual gifts of such a doctor as Harrison:

Of all Mankind the Doctor is the best of Comforters. As his excessive Good-nature makes him take vast Delight in the Office; so his great Penetration into the

human Mind, joined to his great Experience, renders him the most wonderful
Proficient in it; and he so well knows when to sooth, when to reason, and when
to ridicule, that he never applies any of those Arts improperly, which is almost
universally the Case with the Physicians of the Mind, and which it requires very
great judgment and Dexterity to avoid. (104)

Speaking through Booth, Fielding defines in Dr. Harrison the ideal traits
of the physician of the mind. Whether he belongs to the clergy or the
medical profession, this doctor's authority rests in part on the fact that
he is effective outside the normal limits of that profession: that is, he
is a physician who eases the mind of his patient, or a clergyman who
restores the body. He uses sympathy, reason, and ridicule instead of
herbal preparations or sermons in his healing art, though few doctors
are able to use these tools wisely. In some cases, the "doctor" may be a
trusted friend or counselor without any professional qualifications. His
task is to bring about a cure of a disturbance of the spirit so severe that
it has endangered the physical and mental being of his patient, either
through illness or the patient's self-destructive behavior.

   Until the middle of the eighteenth century, the philosopher-physician
is assumed to be male, but the question of gender is explicitly raised
by the presence of a female counselor in Charlotte Lennox's *The Female
Quixote*. Arabella, the heroine of that novel, suffers from an exaggerated
sensibility to her own danger and pain, or (in matters of the heart) her
power to inflict pain on others, a sensibility that she acquired from the
romance novels on which she was brought up. Under the influence of this
passion, she throws herself into the Thames to escape some approaching
horsemen, whom she believes are intent on ravishing her. She is rescued,
"senseless, and to all Appearances dead," and put to bed with a fever so
high that her physicians give her over.[20] A "worthy Divine," however – a
"Pious Learned Doctor" who "had the Cure of Arabella's Mind greatly
at Heart" (368) – comforts Arabella until her fever abates, and then sets
about disabusing her of ideas that he considers dangerous. Using a cure
composed of equal parts of logic and literary criticism, the doctor tactfully
(though modern readers often find his arguments clumsy) leads Arabella
to see the dangers to which she has exposed herself and others in prefer-
ring stories that are marred by "physical or philosophical Absurdities"
to those that describe the ways of the world accurately (378). The danger
of such stories, the doctor insists, is not in their presentation of vice as
such, but in their effect on the passions, such as revenge and love, to
which they "give new Fire," but which "must be suppressed if we hope
to be approved in the Sight of the only Being where Approbation can

make us Happy" (380). In the end, the Doctor's reasoning, coupled with the near glimpse of mortality that Arabella has had, effects the desired cure.

The incident raises the gender question because, as many readers have noted, another person had already begun Arabella's cure. This person is the Countess whom Arabella had encountered at Bath, whose "Sense, Learning, and Judgment," together with her social stature and her knowledge of the language of romance fiction, earned her Arabella's admiration (322). The Countess is resolved to "rescue" Arabella from the ridicule brought upon herself by her romantic notions, and engages her in a dialogue about the "lovely and afflicted" heroines of romance fiction (323–25). Unlike the Doctor, whose rigorous logic is yet to come, the Countess's manner is sympathetic, and she adopts rather than contests the language of her patient. By this means, she makes the point that "one cannot help rejoicing that we live in an Age" in which " 'tis impossible such Adventures should ever happen" (326). Vice and virtue, says the Countess, are defined by the customs of the times in which we live, not by practices in ages past. By the end of the conversation, the Countess's discourse "had rais'd a kind of Tumult in [Arabella's] Thoughts," though the impression she made "came far short of Conviction" (329). Before completing Arabella's cure, however, the Countess is unceremoniously hustled out of the book. One commentator has pointed to Lennox's decision to finish the novel in two volumes, rather than three, for the Countess's hasty exit; yet there was space enough left to create a new character, the "worthy Divine," and accomodate his prolix arguments.[21] Whether the decision was Lennox's or some other person's, it appears that gender, not length, took the cure out of the Countess's hands. For the cure to be credible, it had to be accomplished by a "doctor," and the doctor had to be gendered male.

Despite the failure of *The Female Quixote* to rise above the gender categories that prevailed in its time, the figure of the Countess is significant. It is her sympathetic manner, built on an understanding of her patient's semiotic world, that first makes an "impression" on Arabella and prepares her to receive the doctor's arguments. The use of both the doctor and the countess, in Janet Todd's view, allowed Lennox to make "a firm statement of patriarchal and sentimental doctrine combined."[22] A similar strategy is employed in Fielding's *Amelia*, in which Amelia employs the same "remedies" as those used by Dr. Harrison, though she applies them in a more sympathetic way. When, for example, Booth

becomes alarmed at the unaccountable coldness of his friend Colonel
James toward him,

[Amelia] applied as judicious a Remedy to his disordered Spirits, as either of
those great mental Physicians, *Tully* or *Aristotle*, could have thought of. She used
many Arguments to persuade him that he was in an Error; and had mistaken
Forgetfulness and Carelessness for a design'd Neglect. (IV: v)

Through the use of the female "mental Physician," the mid-century
novelist was able to incorporate what G. J. Barker-Benfield has called
the "culture of reform," based upon a "new ideology of femininity," into
the older and primarily male tradition of the cure of the passions by the
suppression of their effects.[23]

In sum, then, the rage and eventual gentling of Matthew Bramble
and other fictional patients represents a social pathology that the early
novel was uniquely suited to address: the cure of a disturbed sensibility
in a world in which tradition and rationalism, which had once been the
exclusive remedies to the passions, have themselves become aggravating
factors. The cure is generally brought about by a doctor, but the defining
characteristic of the "physician of the mind" is finally not the person's
training, profession, or sex; rather, it is the ability to calm the passions
through a combination of arts that may include the hints of Dr. Lewis,
the gentle reproaches of Dr. Harrison, the reasoned arguments of the
"worthy Divine," or the sympathetic sensibilities of Amelia. For Fielding,
Lennox, and Smollett alike, the title "Physician of the Mind" is an hon-
orific not to be granted to every physician or clergyman, but to be earned
only by those who combine with their learning an essential, unteachable
goodness of heart.

THE STOICS AND THE THERAPY OF DESIRE

The therapy of the passions in eighteenth-century fiction originates in
an ancient tradition in which "ordinary-belief philosophy" was used
to address the problems of everyday life, including the preservation of
health. F. H. Sandbach notes that, in aristocratic Roman homes, the
philosopher-physician was considered the "doctor of the soul"; his function was that of "the 'paedagogus' of the human race, that is the servant
who supervised the behaviour of the growing child."[24] In Hellenistic
Athens, as Martha C. Nussbaum has shown, the therapeutic application
of the critique of desire to solving the real-world problems of troubled
individuals was one of the defining characteristics of the three principal
schools of philosophy – Epicureanism, Skepticism, and Stoicism – which

set them apart from Platonism and Aristotelianism.[25] The analogy between medicine and philosophy appears repeatedly in the teachings of the early Stoics, Zeno, Chrysippus, and Posidonius, in the dialogues and moral essays of the later Stoics, Cicero and Seneca, and in the letters and maxims of Epicurus. While Plato and Aristotle also employed analogies with medicine to show how philosophy could cure the mind's errors, or to show the connection between emotional health and an ethical life, the commitment to action – to healing disturbances of the passions – was not a necessary goal of their teaching. For philosophers whom Nussbaum calls "worthy of the name," the understanding of how human lives are diseased led inevitably to the attempt to cure them.[26] Epicurus emphasized the connection between philosophy and therapy when he said "[e]mpty is that philosopher's argument, by which no passion of a human being is therapeutically treated. For just as there is no use in a medical art that does not cast out the sicknesses of bodies, so there is no use in philosophy, if it does not throw out passion from the soul."[27] The Skeptics sought to remove diseases of reason by opposing healing arguments to dogmatic beliefs, as a doctor seeks to apply remedies appropriate to a patient's symptoms, while the Stoics, who conceived happiness to lie in the absence of desire for anything other than virtue, sought to extirpate the passions through which humans place their affections on unworthy objects.[28]

The Epicurean and Stoic accounts of the passions, according to Nussbaum, are "indispensable starting points for any future work," particularly in the theory of narrative. Lucretius's Epicurean poem, *De Rerum Natura*, contains "culturally narrated scenarios" through which the emotions of love are "enacted" in his readers' lives, leading to a cognition of their dimensions, pace, and structure.[29] The Stoics used *exempla*, brief narratives that engage the reader's imagination and arouse *phantasia* about his or her own case. The reason for arousing the passions is to expose the false and non-neccessary nature of their objects, and thus expose them to the surgeon's knife. The passions must be not merely suppressed, but extirpated root and branch.[30]

The founder of Stoicism, Zeno of Citium (334–262 B.C.), recognized four generic kinds of passion: fear, lust, mental pain, and mental pleasure.[31] The passions, Zeno said, are not material, as are the humours, but are states of the *psyche* with both mental and physical manifestations. Neither are passions identical to emotions, which were regarded by the Stoics as natural and proper. The passions are instead exaggerated responses to objects that are "morally indifferent," things not essential to one's moral nature. These morally indifferent things may be powerfully attractive or repellant, but they are not in themselves either good or evil. Death, for example, is common to all and therefore not an indicator of one's moral being: death comes equally to good and evil persons. We may feel sadness over the death of a loved one, but if we understand death as part of nature's providential plan, we do not fear it. The fear of death results from an error in judgment about the rightness of things; this error gives rise to a passion, a contraction of the psyche that is reflected in physical symptoms: a contraction of the body, shivering, pounding of the heart. The continuation of a passion over an extended period of time may have a permanent effect on a person's well-being, manifested as disease. By clarifying nature's plan and one's place in it, a philosopher may eliminate these errors of judgment and fits of passion in himself, herself, or others, and so, metaphorically speaking, act the part of the physician of the soul.

Just as fear has a contracting effect on the *psyche*, thus affecting one's judgment, so lust, in its various forms, causes a distorting expansion of the *psyche*.[32] Unlike simple desire, which one may feel for an object of moral worth, lusts send us in pursuit of chimerical goals that are indifferent or harmful to our moral well-being. Covetousness, jealousy, envy, and even anger, which is a desire to obtain revenge for an injury done us by another, are the products of such lusts. Similarly, pains and pleasures of a strictly mental nature are passions when they arise from the apprehension of supposed benefits or misfortunes which are, in fact, non-existent or irrelevant to one's moral well-being. Excessive joy and grief are frequently twinned as examples of these mental events: for examples in eighteenth-century literature, one might think of the episode in Defoe's *Colonel Jack* when, as a boy, Jack dropped a sack of stolen booty down a hollow tree. Thinking it was lost forever, he "cry'd, nay, I roar'd out, I was in such a Passion," until, climbing down the tree and finding his money at the base of it, he "run to it, and snatch'd it up, hug'd and kiss'd the dirty Ragg a hundred Times" in the "Transport of my Joy."[33] Or one might think of Fielding's Parson Adams, who is sermonizing Joseph Andrews on the topic, "no Christian ought so to set his Heart on any Person or Thing in this World, but that whenever it shall be required or taken from him in any manner by Divine Providence, he may be able, peaceably, quietly, and contentedly to resign it," when news is brought that his son has drowned. Adams "began to stamp about the Room and deplore his Loss with the bitterest Agony," until a second messenger contradicts the news, at which the "Parson's Joy was now as extravagant as his Grief had been before; he kissed and embraced his Son a thousand times, and danced about the Room like one frantick."[34] In both cases described by Defoe and Fielding, the displays of joy and grief would appear to the Stoic as hasty indulgences that betray a weakness of character in the principals; in the case of Parson Adams, however, we prefer his joy in the recovery of his son to the unfeeling Stoic doctrine he had been teaching just before the incident occurred.

Fielding's caricature of the Stoic doctrine in the form of Parson Adams' denial of human feeling may not be entirely fair. Zeno and the two principal early Stoics, Cleanthes and Chrysippus, held that the philosopher who would treat the diseases of the soul must himself be without strong feelings, including pity; only a philosopher who possessed such internal calm and consistency could be of any help to others. Yet they warned that the philosopher must not eliminate compassion, for it is through sympathy with the sufferer that his or her disturbed passions can be calmed. The proper spirit for the Stoic sage was not complete unfeeling, which in the technical language of the Stoics was called *apatheia*, but rather the replacement of strong feelings by *eupatheia*, a state of benevolence, tranquility, and equanimity.[35] This complex doctrine of sympathy is grounded in the Stoic theory of matter, which held that all things and all beings are connected through a divine essence that they share. The world, as Ludwig Edelstein describes the doctrine, "is made up of parts that hang together, cooperate, and are bound to one another by sympathy."[36] For some Stoics, particularly the Pneumatists, this force took the form of *pneuma*, or a vital air that gave the soul its life, while others described it as a divine element in nature.[37] Whether through a vital air or divine essence, all elements are interrelated and capable of acting upon one another. Consequently, the Stoic sage who sought to return a disturbed mind to reason did so by recognizing the identity between himself and that other person, the shared burden of duty and suffering that characterizes human life.[38]

Of the Stoics in the middle period, the most influential in developing the cure of the passions is Posidonius of Apamea (c. 135-c. 51 B.C.), who was, according to Ludwig Edelstein, "very famous for his medical skill" (*Ancient Medicine*, 219). He wrote an extensive analysis of the passions, though only fragments of it now remain (*Meaning of Stoicism*, 55-56), and much of what we know of his work has been reconstructed through quotations in later writers, notably Galen, Cicero, Seneca, and Strabo.[39] He differed from the early Stoics in some important respects, one of them being his interest in science; from his teacher Panaetius he learned to rely on the observation of nature rather than on speculation for the causes of events.[40] Another major difference lies in his description of the *psyche*: the early Stoics, rejecting Plato's division of the soul into rational, irascible, and concupisible faculties, had insisted that the soul is rational in nature, and that irrationality – including passion – results from errors of judgment. Posidonius returned, at least in part, to the Platonic model by acknowledging that irrationality and passion are part of the soul and contend with reason for control of the will. The passions compete with reason "like riders trying to mount the same horse"; the wise man learns to distinguish them and to follow the rational element in the soul, while the unwise man grants supremacy to his passions and puts them in control of his judgment, leading to errors.[41] The irrational element is a quality that man shares with brute animals, who lack the rational capability that man has; the goal of therapy is not to eradicate this brutal element, which is a fundamental part of the *psyche*, but to tame it, as if it were an animal being trained for service.[42]

There is, therefore, a subtle but significant difference in the metaphors used by the early and middle Stoics to describe the management of the passions. Where the early Stoics spoke of a disease that was to be cured, the middle Stoics figured a brute that was to be tamed; where the first Stoics saw the cure as the return to a natural condition from which the patient had deviated, the later saw it as a permanent reformation. The passions were not to be eradicated in the latter case, but subordinated to man's will. Posidonius taught that poetry, drama, and music are more effective than reason in taming the passions – that a good *daimon*, or divine element in the soul, can be used to draw out the bad. The task of taming the passions is not left to reason, for, in Edelstein's words, it is "only by irrational means that passions can be tamed."[43] These irrational means – music, poetry, drama – appeal to the affections, stimulate the imagination, and arouse the passions so that they can be tamed. It is therefore not contradictory for a satirist such as Pope to passionately denounce mankind's passional nature, since it is the task of the poet – particularly the satirist or dramatist – to raise the passions of the soul, and that of the physician or philosopher to cure them.

GALEN AND THE CURE OF THE PASSIONS: THE NARRATIVE OF THE MAN FROM CRETE

Important as the later Stoics were for transmitting the therapy of desire to the modern age, it was the physician Galen of Pergamon (129-c. 210) who formalized the cure of the passions by reconciling it with elements of both Platonism and Aristotelianism, and by emphasizing certain features – such as the providential design of nature, the sympathy of the parts of the body, and the nourishment of the soul through respiration – that happened to resemble points of doctrine in an emerging Christianity.[44] Galen did not belong to any school of philosophy, but neither was he (as he is sometimes called) an "opponent" of Stoicism; the only Stoic he regularly attacked was Chrysippus, whose atomistic view of the universe was unacceptable to him. Of the several hundred treatises that he wrote on anatomy, physiology, and medicine, many were known in the eighteenth century through translations in Latin or Arabic, and a few were available in French or English.[45]

In one of these treatises, "On the Diagnosis and Cure of the Soul's Passions," Galen responds to a correspondent's question about a work on the passions written by Antonius the Epicurean.[46] Antonius' treatise concerns the necessity of "guarding" the passions, and Galen's correspondent wants to know the meaning of that term. Galen explains (rather contemptuously) that Antonius has fallen into the common mistake of confusing passions with errors of conduct, against which we may guard ourselves by becoming familiar with our passions. Errors, says Galen, are false opinions, while passions, which arise from "an irrational power within us which refuses to obey reason" (28), are states of mind that permit us to commit or to persist in an error. Thus a man who is "angry over little things and bites and kicks his servants" is committing an error of conduct to which he has been predisposed by his anger (29). As a young man, Galen says, he watched a man who was frustrated in his attempt to open a door. "I saw him," says Galen, "bite the key, kick the door, blaspheme, glare wildly like a madman, and all but foam at the mouth like a wild boar" (38). If such a man could be made aware of how his behavior appeared to others, he might be able, over time, to "keep in check the unseemly manifestations of his passion." The objective of Galen's therapy is not to suppress the passion itself, but to control its manifestations, and "to keep it within." It is not possible to deny the passions entirely; as a younger man, Galen had thought that the first step in avoiding error "was for a man to free himself from his passions," but he eventually found that "no one is free from passions and errors" (36). The best way to avoid errors is to examine one's passions on a daily basis, so that one remains perfectly in control of them. Even the worst passions, such as anger, wrath, fear, grief, envy, and violent lust, as well as "excessive vehemence in loving or hating," can be managed by a man who knows himself; and if he can manage his passions, then his errors will be less numerous and more easily corrected.

Galen outlined his therapeutic method in a treatise, now lost, called "On Moral Character." This treatise suggested that one might "cultivate obedience" in the soul, implying that the nature of the soul can be shaped by human agency. "That same treatise," says Galen, "also made it quite clear to you how you might use the irascible power itself to help you fight against the other power, which the philosophers of old called the concupiscible, by which we are carried, without thinking, to the pleasures of the body."[47] For Galen, as for Aristotle and Posidonius, the soul exists in three parts, or powers: the rational, seated in the brain; the irascible, in the heart; and the concupiscible, in the liver.[48] The rational power controls reasoning, sensation, and motion; the irascible governs the passions and directs the vital force; the concupiscible is responsible for nutrition. The passions classified as irascible – anger, wrath, fear, grief, envy, lust, even "excessive vehemence in loving or hating," – are the origin of the soul's errors, while the concupiscible passions, such as erotic desire, gluttony, drunkenness, and luxuriousness in eating, are the source of the body's appetites.[49] The irascible power, unlike the concupiscible, can be disciplined. Galen likens the irascible to horses and dogs, which are wild but can be trained, and the concupiscible to "the wild boar and goat and any of the wild beasts which cannot be domesticated" (47). Though these latter powers cannot be trained, they can be weakened and "chastised" by a person who has strengthened his mind by exercising control over anger. Thus the sequence to be followed in the therary of desire is to discipline the irascible passions, which permits reason to develop in strength and in turn limits the power of the concupiscible passions to do harm.

The working of this therapeutic method is illustrated by a story that Galen tells about a friend of his, a man from Crete who came to him seeking treatment for his "cursed anger" (39–41). Some years earlier, Galen and this man had been returning to Athens from Rome together. It happened that some of the man's luggage was lost en route. When he sent two servants to fetch it and they returned empty-handed, the man "fell into a rage" and struck them several times with a sword. Even though the sword was still in its scabbard, the servants were seriously wounded by the blows, and their master fled to avoid the punishment that he might suffer if one of them died. But after they recovered, the man became penitent for what he had done in the grip of anger, and begged Galen to flog him for it. Galen at first refused, and then relented if he could have a few words with his friend before administering the punishment. He spoke to the man at some length about the necessity "to train the irascible element within us." When he had chastised his friend, Galen told him that he had flogged him in that way, rather than as he had asked. His friend reflected at length on what Galen had told him, and Galen assures us that, after a year had passed, his friend "became a much better man."

This simple narrative, which Galen says he told often as part of his lectures on the management of the passions, may be regarded as a paradigm of all of the case histories – and analogically, the fictional narratives – that are resolved through the intervention of the physician of the mind. The narrative is not original in Galen, nor is he the only one to tell it; it appears in discourses on the passions by Seneca, Descartes, and others.[50] Galen's version, however, is particularly useful in identifying the narrative elements of Stoic therapy. It is important, first, to note that Galen's patient is "an estimable person ... simple, friendly, good, and anything but miserly" (39–40) – in other words, a gentleman, the sort of person Defoe would later describe as being "above the world."[51] The narrative describes a situation in which an essentially healthy and moral person has temporarily – though perhaps chronically – lost control of his passions. The patient's loss of self-control has resulted either in an outburst of violence, as in this case, or in a profound illness affecting his physical or mental well-being. Galen does not undertake to change the nature of his patient's temperament, or to alleviate cases of madness; such cures were rarely even attempted until the mid-eighteenth century.[52] On the other hand, neither is his goal merely to teach his patient how to conceal his anger. For Galen, acquiring self-restraint is not a masquerade, but is part of the process of curing a disease of the soul. "Do you not think that anger is a sickness of the soul?" he asks his correspondent. "Or do you think that men of old were wrong when they spoke of grief, wrath, anger, lust, fear, and all the passions as diseases of the soul?" (43–44).

Besides self-restraint, other narrative elements that are important to the therapy include dialogue, reflection, and delay, which Galen emphasizes repeatedly in his treatise. When angry at a servant, Galen advises his audience, "you must exhort yourself never to strike a slave with your own hands, nor to assign the task to another while you are still angry; put if off until the next day," when the punishment may be decided without wrath (42). Delaying action allows time for reflection: "go over to your soul and see there, too, the nature of insatiate desire; reflect on each thing which is the matter for trouble" (61). Delay also provides an opportunity for dialogue with a "guardian" who has observed one's errors and is willing to reprove them. Such guardians are not necessarily philosophers or doctors; they need only be "men who are old in years but who have given adequate proof throughout their whole lives that they possess the judgment of free men" (68).

In the course of teaching his therapeutic method, Galen advises his auditors that they must "try to cut away something – even if it cannot be a large portion, at least some small part – from the bulk of their passions" (68). The radical "extirpation" of the passions practiced by the early Stoics is not sought in Galen's therapy, but amputation or cutting away an infected body part still forms the underlying metaphor. When this operation has been performed, the cure is ready to begin, but, warns Galen, it will only take hold gradually. Passions and their appetites cannot be mastered at once; only after a lifetime of practice will the patient achieve some control over his or her passions, and even then, mastery will not be perfect. Anger, for example, will occur repeatedly in varying circumstances until the patient learns to exhibit some restraint. The more often the patient restrains his anger, the less strongly will he feel its influence over him, until finally he will feel only "slight" anger over matters of great importance, and none over unimportant ones (38). The patient's progress can be measured only as incremental reductions of anger experienced, or as successively higher tolerances of frustration before anger is manifested.

Because of its emphases on delay, dialogue, reflection, and restraint, the Galenist therapeutic method is a suitable platform on which to structure a narrative. The process of reducing one's anger over a long period of time virtually requires a narrative in which to recall and order these events. It also requires a narrator, whose voice – soothing, yet mildly scolding; sympathetic, yet admonitory – might resemble the self-conscious, paternalistic, and occasionally condescending philosopher who narrates Henry Fielding's novels. In Smollett's *Humphry Clinker*, as we saw at the beginning of this chapter, the narrative takes the form of a dialogue between the patient and his doctor, whose voice is implied but never heard. In Defoe's fictional autobiographies, in which the physician and the patient often are the same person, the narrative voice is reflective, confessional, and exculpatory by turns, but always aware of the need to reform its passions. Robinson Crusoe's voice, full of penitent self-recrimination, is that of the patient whom Galen's therapy was intended to create.

"A TUMULT RISING IN HIS BREAST":
THE NARRATIVE OF MONRO

For a dramatic instance of the survival of Galen's Stoic therapy in the eighteenth century, we may turn to the autobiography of Dr. Alexander Monro, whose career as the first professor of anatomy at the University of Edinburgh will be examined in the next chapter. Writing of himself in the third person, Monro admits that, as a youth, he had been known for his "warm Temper," and that "he had been an impetuous Rogue when a Boy."[53] As a youth, he had frightened himself by the appearance of his own bad temper:

before he became a Man he had seen some striking examples of the bad Effects of yielding to the Passion of Anger, which had made him alwaies afterwards endeavour to guard against it . . . & that when he was sensible of a Tumult rising in his Breast, such as he was affraid he coud not command[,] he ran away from the Cause of Offence.

As he became a man, however, he learned to contol his anger. On one occasion later in life, he was infuriated by the impudence of a servant, much as the master in Galen's narrative had been:

[Monro] had wrote Directions to a Servant for making some Improvements in his House in the Country after a Manner specifyed in the Letter. The Servant caused them to be done in a quite different way on a Plan of his Own by which the Masters Intentions were to be altogether disappointed, who therefor upon going to the Country made the Mechanicks destroy this new Work and execute what was to be done according to his former Directions. When about to mount his Horse to return to Town, he desired the same Servant to cause some new Orders which he had given him to be literally observed without pretending to alter any thing without his Leave. The Servant returned a most saucy impertinent provoking Answer, when the Master without making the least return in words immediately returned into the House to write the following Note. "I am now too angry to reprove properly your last Answer to me, but recommend it to you to consider your Expressions in it, and I insist on this Article of your Service to me, That tho' you may give Reasons against what I propose, or may make to me what Proposals you will, yet what I order, after this, must not be changed at your Pleasure, nor must such an Answer be again given me, unless on the Condition of instantly leaving my service for ever." After sealing and addressing this Note, he returned to his Horse, which he mounted, then delivered the Note to the Servant and rode away. Humble Remonstrances were made for Forgiveness, which was granted on the Conditions just now mentioned in the Note.

Monro's narrative of his struggle with anger resembles and also differs from Galen's narrative of the man from Crete in some interesting ways.

In both narratives, the anger of a wealthy and powerful man is provoked by a servant who has failed to follow instructions. In both, there is an undertone of pride in the philosopher-physicians' accounts of how they effected a "cure" of the passion of anger. Again in both, the narrator is central to the action, but particularly so in Monro's, where the physician is his own patient. In Galen's narrative, the violent outburst of the man from Crete leads him to seek the help of an older and wiser man, who counsels delay and reflection; in Monro's, the physician delays responding to the servant's "most saucy impertinent provoking Answer" while he retires to write out his response in a note, which he hands wordlessly to the servant. The delay prevents an incipient outburst, and also permits the angry physician to sublimate his irascible passion by transforming it into a text. One important difference between the classical and modern narratives, then, is that the eighteenth-century version, while employing elements from the classical tradition, adds to it the act of writing as an instrument with which to discipline the passions.

Another difference is that the meaning of the anger changes in the modern version of the narrative. Galen's philosopher-physician represses the anger in his patient without addressing the issues of class and power that underly it, and may even be said to have given rise to it; there is no change in the social relations that put the master in a position to abuse his servant with impunity. In Monro's narrative, while the physician is still centered as the locus of authority, he is clearly an employer who has a contractual relationship with his worker; he uses his anger, and particularly the text that results from it, as a means of re-signifying the terms of that relationship, which he thinks have begun to slip from his control. In effect, he uses his anger as the signifier that deconstructs a social relation of which he disapproves and reconstructs one that is acceptable to him.

In writing his autobiography, Monro not only describes an incident in which a passion is transformed into a text, but also creates another text about that process. The techniques that he uses in so doing are not essentially different from those employed by Defoe to describe Robinson Crusoe's or Colonel Jack's stuggles to master their passions: Monro's narrative, like that of a novelist, begins with an incident in childhood that recalls the tumult rising in the breast of the boy, and then chronicles the success of the man in keeping his anger within. Monro's autobiography, like Defoe's "spiritual autobiographies," becomes an opportunity to reflect upon and recommend to others the process of reducing irascible passions to the manageable form of texts. The method Monro employs for controlling his anger may imitate a classical model in Cicero or Seneca, but the technique of reducing his passion to a text appears to derive from a more recent model. It would, perhaps, be doing the humble genre of the novel too much honor to credit it with having invented the technique of controlling the passions by making them into texts. But by the 1760s, when Monro wrote his autobiography, the novel had fully demonstrated its utility as an instrument for raising, anatomizing, instructing, and re-signifying the passions.

CHAPTER 2

The heart, the Holy Ghost, and the ghost of Michael Servetus

In the year 1647, Heneage Finch (1621–82), who after the restoration of Charles II would become the first Earl of Nottingham, recorded in his commonplace book some thoughts on the human heart. "The heart of man," he wrote, "is triangular. Now a triangle cannot be comprehended by a circle, therefore a man should not set his heart upon this Earthly globe as being not capacious enough for such a subject as the heart of man. The heart of man being trinar, showeth it is a fit tabernacle for the trinity."[1] Finch's sentiments, erroneous as they may be in anatomical, geometrical, or theological terms, express a set of beliefs about the human heart fervidly held in conservative seventeenth-century circles: that the heart has three chambers, rather than four; that it is the seat of the passions and vital spirits of the body; that it regulates the body much as a king keeps his court and commonwealth; and that it is the "tabernacle" of the Trinity, the dwelling-place of the Holy Ghost.[2] Written just two years before the execution of Charles I, and almost twenty years after the publication of William Harvey's *De Motu Cordis*, the passage now reads like a defiant statement of faith in the face of approaching catastrophe: not only does the earthly globe no longer seem to Finch capacious enough to contain its heart, the King, but the very basis of the heart's (and the King's) spiritual and temporal authority has been undermined. Harvey, who was Finch's friend and personal physician (as well as the King's), had shown in 1628 that the heart has four chambers instead of three; that its function is not to concoct vital spirits but to refresh blood by circulating it through the lungs; and that the blood does not rush to it from the other two points of a triangle, formed by the liver, the heart, and the brain, but rather that it sends the blood in a circle through the rest of the body.[3] At the time that Finch wrote his apothegm, such critics as Jean Riolan and Caspar Hofmann were attacking Harvey's hypothesis about the circulation of the blood on the grounds that it was both irreligious and inconsistent with the ancient teachings of Galen and Aristotle.[4] In

35

describing the heart as "trinar," and in insisting that the triangle is greater than the circle – a transparent allusion to the circular flow of blood in the body – Finch aligned himself with these critics of his own relative, an irony that dramatically illustrates the significance that the seventeenth century attached to the triangular shape of the heart.[5] In this chapter, we will consider some of the effects of the discovery of the anatomy and function of the heart, particularly the emergence of the philosophy of individualism in the person of Michael Servetus, whose writings challenged the dogmas of both the medical and religious establishments.

A HEART LIKE A TRIANGLE

The dogma of the triangular heart is found in many medieval and renaissance anatomical texts, including those of Avicenna, Henri de Mondeville, Mondino di Luzzi, and Hieronymo Manfredi.[6] It also appears as the seat of both spiritual and social order in philosophical works by Samuel Purchas, Sir Thomas Browne, and Baltasar Gracián y Morales. Purchas represented the heart as a triangle in his *Microcosmus, or the Historie of Man* (1619), which constructs an analogy between the anatomy of the human body and the structure of the "greater World."[7] According to Purchas, the heart is like a great prince, lying in his private lodging, the pericardium; its form, a slightly flattened pyramid, is "evidence of his imperfect perfection, which it seemes to seeke and can only find in that Trinitie and Unitie, which this globous Triangle, in a mortall immortall figure represents" (63). From this seat, the princely heart adds "the Royal Assent" to the laws given by the Parliament, or brain, and sends those laws out "by the swift Posts, the Passions, thorow the whole Microcosme" (61). The triangular design of the heart consists of "a fleshie Parenchyma, with two hollow Ventricles"; one of these ventricles receives blood from the vena cava, some of which it supplies to the lungs for their nourishment, the rest being "closely by invisible passages transmitted to the left Ventricle, communicating cooler ayre for the generation of the vitall spirits" (64). The operation of this system – heart, brain, spirits, and passions – is under the direction of the Holy Spirit, "because that third Person from the Father and the Sonne, immediately by himselfe conferreth those Graces," that is, the gifts of regeneration and spiritual well-being enjoyed by mankind (61).

Purchas's description of the heart as the triangular seat of "the swift Posts, the Passions" derives from anatomical and physiological principles found in Aristotle and Galen. Aristotle held that the heart consists of three cavities in animals of "great size," including man; Galen thought there were only two.[8] Aristotle's heart was the *sensorium commune*, the seat of the soul, whose affections and alterations, such as anger or fear, he described as "movements of the heart."[9] Galen correctly identified the brain as the center of sensation in the body, but like Aristotle he regarded the heart as the source of the vital spirits, which animate the body and give it motion.[10] According to Galen, this process begins when blood travels from the right ventricle to the lungs, where is it refined and purified through *anastomosis*, or the communication of the pulmonary vein and artery; it then travels to the heart, where it passes through minute perforations which Galen assumed to exist in the wall between the right and left ventricles (May, *Galen on the Usefulness of the Parts of the Body*, I: 47; 324). In passing through these perforations, the blood is exposed to innate heat and converted into vital spirits. These invisible perforations, or intraventricular pores, are a key element of Galenist physiology, an essential part of the process through which matter becomes spirit. Purchas's account of the "generation of the vitall spirits" by the transmission of blood through "invisible passages" clearly alludes to this point of Galenic physiology.

This mixture of Aristotelian and Galenist physiology is also the basis of Sir Thomas Browne's *Religio Medici* (1643).[11] Browne did not see a contradiction between the practice of medicine and the mysteries of religion; in fact, he saw them as complementary. He professed himself enamored of "those wingy mysteries in Divinity, and aery subtilties in Religion which have unhing'd the brains of better heads"; for him, "there be not impossibilities enough in Religion, for an active faith; the deepest mysteries ours contains, have not onely been illustrated, but maintained by syllogisme, and the rule of reason" (16). Of all the mysteries, the most profound is the Holy Trinity, in which, though two persons are father and son, "we must deny a priority." The paradox reminds him of the Galenic division of the soul into rational, irascible, and concupiscible parts, which yet remain one soul: "for there is in us not three, but a Trinity of Souls, because there is in us, if not three distinct souls, yet differing faculties, that can, and do subsist apart in different subjects, and yet in us are so united as to make but one soul and substance; if one Soul were so perfect as to informe three distinct bodies, that were a petty Trinity: conceive the distinct number of three, not divided nor separated by the intellect, but actually comprehended in its Unity, & that is a perfect Trinity" (22). In this respect, Browne prefers Galen to Aristotle: "in some things there appears to me as much Divinity in *Galen* his Books *De usu partium*, as in

Suarez Metaphysics: Had *Aristotle* been as curious in the enquiery of this cause as he was of the other, he had not left behind him an imperfect piece of Philosophy, but an absolute tract of Divinity" (28).

Since Browne was writing his treatise in the context of the English civil war, he was concerned not only with the unity of the three parts of the soul, but with the reasons for conflict among them. As a doctor, he always "endeavoured to compose those fewds and angry dissentions between Affection, Faith, and Reason: For there is in our soul, a kind of Triumvirate, or triple government of 3 competitors, which distract the peace of this our Common-wealth, not lesse than did that other the State of Rome" (40). This triumvirate is currently at war with itself, but may one day be restored to harmony: "As Reason is a rebel unto Faith, so Passion unto Reason: As the propositions of Faith seem absurd unto Reason, so the Theorems of Reason unto Passion, and both unto Reason; yet a moderate and peaceable discretion may so state and order the matter, that they may be all Kings, and yet make but one Monarchy" (40–41). If his allegory of a three-part kingdom at war with itself sounds vaguely like Purchas's "globous Triangle," the heart, the reason is that he is building on Purchas's analogy between the microcosm of man and the larger world. "There is no man alone," says Browne, "because every man is a *Microcosme*, and carries the whole world about him; *Nunquam minus solus qu'am cum solus*, though it be the Apophthegeme of a wise man, is yet true in the mouth of a fool; for indeed, though in a Wildernesse, a man is never alone, not onely because he is with himself, and his own thoughts, but because he is with the Devil, who ever comforts our solitude, and is that unruly rebell that musters up those disordered motions, which accompany our sequestered imaginations" (160–61).

A final seventeenth-century treatise that employs the dogma of the triangular heart is *El Criticón*, by the Jesuit philosopher Baltasar Gracián y Morales (1601–58).[12] In this work, a shipwrecked mariner who styles himself Critilo engages in a dialogue with a child of nature called Andrenio about, among other things, the anatomy of man. Citing as his authority "*Galen* that retainer of flying Life, and searcher into Nature" (155), Critilo tells Andrenio that the heart is the

principal part of man, the Original of all the rest, the Fountain and Spring of Life, . . . the King of other Members, and therefore [it] is placed in the Centre of his Dominions, greatly and inwardly conserved, and is sometimes in Latin called *Cura*, or *Care*; for that which rules and governs, is always placed in the Centre. It . . . is fixed in the middle, denoting how much our Affections ought to be moderated, and not to exceed the bounds of Reason. Its form is with a point downwards, as if an Indivisibility were enough to touch the Earth, but upwards is of a spacious breadth; enlarging it self to receive the bounty of Heaven, and greedy to suck those dews, which can only content, and satisfie the Soul; ... its coulour is ruddy and sanguine, the Emblem of Charity, and from hence springs the best Bloud, to show that noble Persons should be qualified with best Hearts. (168–69)

Here again we see the heart figured as a triangle, a shape that fits it to receive the "bounty of Heaven" and the "dews" of grace. Like the seat of a king, the heart is the governing center of the body, from which point it can best moderate the affections. The heart's heat and color give it (in healthy persons) its sanguinity, which explains why the best-hearted people are the most noble and charitable. For Gracián, as for Purchas, Browne, Finch, and other adherents of ancient physiology, the triangular form of the heart proves its function, which is to oversee the passions, just as a lord – spiritual or temporal – regulates his unruly people.

From these several treatises roughly contemporaneous with Finch's apothegm, it is easy to see why he resisted the substitution of a circle for the triangle in the figuration of the heart. The basis of both the pyramidic organization of society and the mystery of the Holy Trinity were threatened by that substitution. Also threatened were two central functions of the Galenic heart: the production of the vital spirits and the regulation of the irascible soul, both dependent on the exposure of blood to innate heat through interventricular pores. Harvey's deconstruction of this system broke the link between the passions of man and the organ in which they were thought to be produced and regulated. Had Daniel Defoe, writing from the vantage point of the second decade of the eighteenth century, wanted materials with which to construct in *Robinson Crusoe* an allegory of man's struggle to understand and regulate the warring parts of his soul, he need have looked no further than Purchas, Browne, or Gracián.[13] Indeed, Defoe probably knew all three of these writers, since copies of Purchas's *Microcosmus*, Browne's *Religio Medici*, and Gracián's *The Critick* are listed in the sale catalogue of the libraries of Defoe and Philips Farewell.[14] The question here, however, is not whether the formal aspects of Defoe's fictional method were affected by his reading of Purchas, Browne, and Gracián – that is, not just whether Defoe's narratives describe circles rather than triangles – but whether (and how) the decline of the Galenic orthodoxies contributed to the conditions that gave rise to the novel.[15] When those orthodoxies were thrown into question by the discovery of circulation, so also were the forms of spiritual and temporal regulation of the passions that drew their authority from Galenist systems of anatomy. Since no answers were immediately forthcoming from either medicine or religion, humanists like Defoe turned to such natural historians as Francis Bacon and Robert Boyle for materials through which to finish the work of "remapping" the heart.[16] This project had begun a century before in the revival of the ancient dream of curing the passions of the mind by such Galenist philosopher-physicians as Robert Burton and Tobias Venner.

DEMOCRITUS AND GALEN REDIVIVUS: ROBERT BURTON AND TOBIAS VENNER

The classic study of the pathology of the passions in English literature is Robert Burton's *The Anatomy of Melancholy* (1621). Though not the first to write about diseases of the mind, Burton was the strongest exponent of the view that the cure of the passions is an endeavor equal in importance to any other field of scientific or humanistic investigation. The disease of melancholy, declared Burton in the preface to his book, is so general that "few there are that feel not the smart of it"; "it is a disease so grievous, so common, I know not wherein to do a more general service, and spend my time better, than to prescribe means how to prevent and cure so universal a malady, an epidemical disease, that so often, so much, crucifies the body and mind."[17] Anatomizing the passion of melancholy, Burton continues, "through all the members of this our *microcosmus*, is as great a task as to . . . find out the quadrature of a circle, the creeks and sounds of the north-east or north-west passages, . . . to perfect the motion of Mars and Mercury, which so crucifies our astronomers, or to rectifie the Gregorian kalendar" (I: 23).

Though trained in divinity, Burton did not shy from intruding himself into the preserves of the medical profession. "What have I to do with physick?" he asks rhetorically in the preface to the *Anatomy*. His answer is that the choice was made for him by a crisis in his personal mental history: he could more profitably have written on a subject with which he was more conversant, but "I was fatally driven upon this rock of melancholy, and carried away by this by-stream, which, as a rillet, is deducted away from the main chanel of my studies" (I: 20). The confusion of the secular with the holy was not unusual in early medicine; it was common for physicians to take holy orders in hope of a benefice, or for "poor countrey vicars" to "turn mountebanks, quicksalvers, empiricks" to supplement their incomes – "'tis a common transition" (I: 21). Combining divinity with physic was not only a common practice, but essential to the cure of melancholy: "It is a disease of the soul, on which I am to treat, and as much pertaining to a divine as to a physician . . . . One helps the vices and passions of the soul, anger, lust, desperation, pride, presumption, &c. by applying that spiritual physick, as the other uses proper remedies in bodily diseases" (I: 22).

Though paying homage throughout the *Anatomy* to "those great masters" Aristotle and Galen (I: 18), Burton in his preface adopts the persona of the "laughing philosopher," Democritus of Abdera, who blamed the miserable condition of most of mankind, "ever unquiet, ever impelled on a vain search for happiness, now seizing one thing and now another, without obtaining permanent satisfaction," on the immoderateness of human desires.[18] Burton's reason for adopting the persona of "Democritus Junior" is not to "usurp his [master's] habit," but to complete that early physician's project of curing madness and melancholy by discovering their seats in the body. Like Alexander Monro a century later, Burton dates the history of the anatomy of the passions from the visit that Hippocrates is said to have made to Abdera upon reports that Democritus was mad because he laughed continuously at the follies of mankind.[19] Hippocrates finds Democritus

under a shady bower, with a book on his knees, busie at his study, sometime writing, sometime walking. The subject of his book was melancholy and madness: about him lay the carkasses of many several beasts, newly by him cut up and anatomized; not that he did contemn God's creatures, as he told Hippocrates, but to find out the seat of this *atra bilis*, or melancholy, whence it proceeds, and how it is engendred in mens bodies, to the intent he might better cure it in himself, by his writings and observations teach others how to prevent and avoid it. (I: 6)

The result of Democritus's anatomical investigations, however, is the discovery that madness and melancholy are not organic, but are caused by the follies and passions of men: "some to love dogs, others horses, some to desire to be obeyed in many provinces, and yet themselves will know no obedience – some to love their wives dearly at first, and, after a while, to forsake and hate them – begetting children, with much care and cost for their education, yet, when they grow to mans estate, to despise, neglect, and leave them naked to the world's mercy. Do not these behaviours express their intolerable folly?" (I: 34). Despite the passage of centuries, says Democritus Junior, the disease is as widespread as ever: were Democritus alive today, he would find more folly than one man could laugh at alone; he would "break the rim of his belly with laughing" (I: 39). Melancholy and madness persist in the modern age because there is a general reluctance to cure underlying passions: if we are sick, we send for a physician, "but, for the diseases of the mind, we take no notice of them. Lust harrows us on the one side, envy, anger, ambition on the other. We are torn in pieces by our passions, as so many wild horses, one in disposition, another in habit; one is melancholy, another mad; and which of us all seeks for help, doth acknowledge his error, or knows he is sick?" (I: 56–57). The cure is self-knowledge and self-control: "if men would attempt no more than what they can bear, they should lead contented lives – and, learning to know themselves, would limit their ambition, they would perceive then that nature hath enough, without seeking such superfluities, and unprofitable things, which bring nothing with them but grief and molestation" (I: 35–36). The need for such cures is general: the Stoics taught, says Burton, that all men are fools, and "all fools are mad, though some madder than others" (I: 25). For all these reasons, then – "the generality of the disease, the necessity of the cure, and the commodity or common good that will arise to all men by the knowledge of it" – the proper study of mankind is not divinity exclusively, but also himself, his own madness.

If Burton's cure of the passions derives from Democritus, his system of anatomy resembles Galen's. He divides the human body into three regions, dominated by three organs – the brain, heart, and liver – and gives precedence to the brain, which he says "is the most noble organ under heaven, the dwelling house and seat of the soul, the habitation of wisdom, memory, judgement, reason, and in which man is most like God."[20] The heart, however, is "the seat and fountain of life, of heat, of spirits, of pulse, and respiration: the sun of our body, the king and sole commander of it: the seat and organ of all passions and affections" (I: 25–26). The brain "gives sense and motion to the rest, and is (as it were) a privy counsellour, and chancellour, to the *heart*," which "keeps his court [in the second region], and by his arteries communicates life to the whole body" (I: 23). The heart, which is "of pyramidical form, and not much unlike to a pine-apple," has as its function "to stir and command the humours in the body; as, in sorrow, melancholy; in anger, choler; in joy, to send the blood outwardly; in sorrow, to call it in; moving the humours, as horses do a chariot" (I: 26). It is evident that, for Burton as for Renaissance thinkers generally, the heart is the prince of the body, and the brain its second in command.

While *The Anatomy of Melancholy* did much to establish the cure of the passions as a theme in English literature, its Galenist physiology limited its value as a study of the passions themselves. Published in the same decade as Harvey's *De Motu Cordis*, the *Anatomy* was the high watermark of Galenism in the English popular imagination, after which the tide on which it rode in began to ebb. Burton's view of the passions is, anatomically speaking, backward-looking; it relies more heavily than he would admit on such humouralist treatises as Thomas Wright's *The Passions of the Mind in General* (1601), Timothy Bright's *A Treatise of Melancholie, containing the causes thereof* (1586) and Thomas Rogers's *A Philosophicall Discourse, entitled, The Anatomie of the Minde* (1576), which in turn derived from Aristotle, Cicero, and Augustine.[21] Burton's remedies for melancholia and other disturbances of the passions reflect his materialist and humouralist orientation: his remedies depend on purges, vomits, diet, and herbal preparations such as laurel, white hellebore, and tobacco. As Roy Porter has noted, Burton's treatise does not anticipate the nerve theory of Thomas Willis, later in the same century, which eventually led physicians such as Alexander Monro *primus*, Robert Whytt, and William Cullen to look for the seat of the passions not in the heart, stomach, or liver, but in the nervous system.[22] Nor does it advance a theory of benevolism, despite the emphasis laid by "Democritus Junior" on the association of melancholy with moral behavior. Neither Democritus nor Burton developed a therapeutic method for treating the passions, although the *Anatomy* offers a highly eclectic array of advices on ways to contend with melancholy. Their contribution was not in method, but in setting forth a critique of false desires that established a field of action for philosopher-physicians in their respective ages.

A similarly Galenist anatomy of the heart and the passions was offered by a doctor born in the same year as Burton, Tobias Venner (1577–1660), whose popular guide to health, *Via Recta ad Vitam Longam* (1637), eventually found its way into the sale of Daniel Defoe's library.[23] Venner opens his discussion of "Perturbations, or Passions of the minde" with a good question: given that passions are "inevitable . . . borne with us, and bred up with us," how do they come to be the "morbificall causes" of disease in the body? The answer, which he draws from Cicero, is that passions are "morbifical" only when they "shall exceed and be immoderate" (302). In excess, passions become "perturbations indeed" and, by affecting the natural levels of heat and cold in the body, they "weaken and overthrow the faculties thereof." Immoderate joy, for example, "relaxeth the heat, and causeth such an effusion of the spirit, as that oftentimes ensue sicknesse, great debility of the body, swounings; and . . . death it selfe." Sadness and fear, likewise, deprive the limbs of heat, causing them to tremble as the blood rushes inward, toward the heart. But how could joy, which causes an effusion of spirits, and fear or grief, which draws them in, affect the heart in the same way? Venner argues that in fear and grief, "the imagination, which is earnestly bent and troubled in preventing and withstanding the imminent mischief and perill" to the body, abates the spirits in the heart, so that the heart, thus weakened, is put in danger of being "conglobulated" by "overmuch blood," and the person of being "exanimated" (303).

Venner notes that anger, like joy and fear, has an ambiguous effect on the body. Anger is generally a dangerous passion in that it stirs up heat, breeds choler, and inflames the spirits in most bodies. In "phlegmatick and dull bodies," indeed, it may aid digestion by arousing their sluggish heat, the better to "concoct, discusse, and consume their crude and moyst superfluities," but even phlegmatics must beware that they should not "fall into that most detestable truculent and megereon kind of furie, from whence arise tumults, strifes, homicides, and the like mischiefs." Beware sadness, "embrace moderate joy," and strive to live "soberly, uprightly, and godly in this present world," he counsels his reader (304–05). The only anger of which Venner approves is "that, which by the bridle of Reason is restrained from furie." Unbridled anger is "to all hot, drie, and leane bodyes most hurtfull, because it quickly overheateth them, adusteth their blood, dryeth the substantiall moysture, and resolveth the strengths"; the remedy for it is "Patience," through which we may "bridle all irrational motions of the mind" (304). Persons whose passions are well-bridled are able "to observe a mediocrity in their passion, wherein consisteth the tranquillity both of mind and body, which of this life is the chiefest happinesse." Virtue, then, was for Venner largely equivalent to good horsemanship, and happiness depended upon attaining an Aristotelian mediocrity in the exercise of passion.

The notion that virtue lay in keeping a middle course between extremes of passion was rejected by such seventeenth-century thinkers as Thomas Hobbes, in whose mechanistic philosophy the passions were firmly established as a primary and essential component of human nature. In *The Elements of Law* (1642), Hobbes proposed a "scientific" model of morality in which virtue lies in the cause of an action, rather than in its conformity to an Aristotelian mean. "As for the common opinion," Hobbes declares, "that virtue consisteth in mediocrity, and vice in extremes, I see no ground for it, nor can find any such mediocrity."[24] In *Leviathan* (1651), the passions are said to be by nature neither sinful or pathological; they are the necessary and primary causes of motion in mankind, and thus of life itself: "Life it selfe is but Motion, and can never be without Desire, nor without Feare, no more than without Sense."[25] To have no passion, for Hobbes, is to have no desire, and "to have no Desire, is to be Dead: so to have weak Passions, is Dulness" (57). What makes an action virtuous is not the "Much or Little" of it, but the desire that forms its cause, and the conformity of that desire to the laws of the commonwealth: "In summe all actions and habits are to be esteemed good or evill, by their causes and usefullnesse in reference to the commonwealth, and not by their mediocrity nor by their being commended."[26] Virtue lies not in moderating passions, but in deliberating over the foreseeable consequences of one's actions and their conformity to the law.

This displacement of ancient by modern views of the passions can be readily observed in eighteenth-century novels. Venner's advice of observing "mediocrity" in the passions is consistent with that offered to Robinson Crusoe by his father, who counseled him "that mine was the middle State, or what might be called the upper Station of *Low Life*, which he had found by long Experience was the best State in the World, the most suited to human Happiness."[27] That middle state is usually interpreted economically and socially by readers of the novel, but it appears also to refer to a mediocrity in one's emotional life: Robinson's father tells him that by sticking to that middle state, he may avoid becoming "enrag'd with the Passion of Envy, or secret burning Lust of Ambition for great Things" (5). As we will see in a subsequent chapter, Robinson's departure from home represents the rejection by the early modern age of the ethical system that drew its authority from the discredited (but still current) regimen of the passions associated with Aristotle, Galen, Burton, and Venner.

The displacement of ancient by modern theories of the passions during the seventeenth century is also evident in a shift in the relation between doctor and patient. Though both Burton and Venner recommend therapeutic methods developed by the Stoics and other classical authorities, neither of them quite fits the figure of the "physician of the mind" that we will elaborate in the next chapter – Burton because he is not a physician, and Venner because he does not narrate the cure of any patients. Together these differences from the classical model reveal an important modification in the paradigm. The cure of the passions in the early modern world is no longer centered in the doctor, but in the patient: Burton's anatomy describes the self-cure of his own melancholy, undertaken even though he lacked the professional status of a physician, and Venner's self-help manual reflects the popularity of books on health, hygiene, and diet written for consumption by lay readers. In both cases, the personal relationship between doctor and patient is broken: in Burton's, the absent physician is replaced by a text that is dedicated to an abstract, perhaps mythic doctor; in Venner's, it is the patient that is absent, replaced by a text in which a multitude of patients is implied. In each case, the text mediates the doctor or patient with an abstract or implied other. It is just this mediative role that is played by the English novel when it appears in its modern form at the dawn of the eighteenth century. *Robinson Crusoe,* to once again take the best case, depicts the solitary struggle of a patient over a period of twenty-eight years to distinguish among his passions and to prefer the useful ones to the harmful; he ministers to himself without the aid of a physician, but with the assistance of such texts as his journal and his Bible. When he has (or believes he has) cured his own passions, Robinson begins to instruct the reader, who is his absent but implied patient, through the medium of his memoirs. The absence of a physician in *Robinson Crusoe* is not an anomaly caused by Robinson's isolation on the island, but rather the culmination of a process of individuation in the doctor–patient relationship that began over a hundred and fifty years earlier with the writings of Michael Servetus (1509–53), whose challenges to both religious and medical authority cast a long shadow over the eighteenth century.

THE HOLY GHOST AND THE GHOST OF MICHAEL SERVETUS

In the early 1690s, the members of the whiggish "Athenian Society" (which included an aspiring minor poet, Daniel Defoe) asked William Wotton, the chaplain to Daniel Finch, second Earl of Nottingham, to write a defense of modern learning.[28] In 1694, this young chaplain published his *Reflections upon Ancient and Modern Learning,* a response to some of the more extreme assertions in Sir William Temple's "Essay upon Ancient and Modern Learning."[29] Temple had charged that there had been no advances in such sciences as astronomy, physics, or medicine to match the accomplishments of the ancients, excepting the work of Copernicus, William Harvey, and Bishop Wilkins, and that even these improvements were of no practical value. Wotton's reply was respectful to the ancients, but indicated a preference for the empirical methods of "the Generality of Physicians" practicing in the modern age: "*That the Ancients did very well for their Time; but that Experience, and further Light, has taught them better things.*"[30] He praised Galen as a man of "very piercing Genius" who built his "Argument upon Nature as far as he knew her," but whose defective knowledge of anatomy, particularly of the circulation of the blood, led to grievous errors in understanding the uses of the parts of the body (192, 221). Anatomy in the age of Galen was "a rude, imperfect Thing," based on the dissection of apes and other animals, instead of human corpses, "which sometimes led [Galen] into great mistakes" (298, 191). Further, while the ancients had excellent knowledge of the "*containing* Parts" of the body, which were visible to the naked eye, they made "very few Experiments" on the "Nature and particular Texture of the *contained* Parts" (193), so that in questions having to do with the contents of glands, blood vessels, or nerves, "the Ancients were constantly at a Loss" (232).

Of the many ways in which Wotton believed moderns to have added to the stock of knowledge, perhaps the most important was in understanding the circulation of blood. Hippocrates, Aristotle, and Galen had all made statements about the "Usual and Constant Motion" or the "Recurrent Motion" of the blood, which implied to Wotton that they "did believe it as a *Hypothesis*," but they "did not know what this constant accustomed Motion was" (208, 210, 215–16). Their faulty understanding of circulation led the ancients into numerous errors; in particular, "the manner of the forming of the *Animal Spirit* in the Brain was wholly unknown" (197). The doctrine of the humours, too, depended on a flawed understanding of the circulation of the blood: "The Original of all these Notions was Ignorance of the Anatomy of all these Parts, as also of the constant Motion of the Blood through the Lungs and Heart" (221). The erroneous doctrine of the humours, in turn, obstructed an understanding of the function of the nervous system, which the ancients believed governed only motion, not sensation. Wotton accords William Harvey full credit for describing the circulation of blood in 1628, but, consistent with his aim of showing that knowledge is cumulative, rather than dependent on individual genius, he takes pains to show that the work of others had led Harvey to his conclusions. "The first Step that was made towards [the discovery of circulation] was, the finding that the whole Mass of the Blood passes through the Lungs, by the Pulmonary Artery and Vein," says Wotton, and the first of the moderns "that I could ever find, who had a distinct *Idea* of this Matter, was *Michael Servetus*, a *Spanish* Physician, who was burnt for *Arianism*, at *Geneva*, near 140 Years ago" (211).

Michael Servetus, whose ghost Wotton resurrected as the spirit of modern learning, had been convinced as a youth that the reformation movement then sweeping the Christian faith had not gone far enough, particularly in not challenging the dogma of the Trinity that the Church had adopted in 325 A.D. at the Council of Nicaea. After failing to convince leading reformers that they should no longer maintain that Jesus Christ had the same divine and eternal substance as that of God the Father, and also that they should abandon the practice of infant baptism, Servetus at the age of twenty-two published his views in a book called *De Trinitatis Erroribus, Libri Septem* (1531).[31] The reviewers were not kind; even such reformers as Martin Bucer called for Servetus to "have the guts torn out of his living body."[32] Somewhat chastened, Servetus issued a retraction, although he failed to retract the heresies for which he had been condemned. Defiantly, he initiated a correspondence with John Calvin in which he pushed the Geneva churchman on the question of the Trinity, among other theological matters. He even went so far as to annotate Calvin's book, the *Institutio Religionis Christianae*, detailing its errors in the margins, and he sent the annotated book to Calvin with a request for Calvin's response. After several years of such correspondence, Calvin wrote to Farel that if Servetus should come to Geneva, "I would see to it, in so far as I have authority in this city, that he should not leave it alive" (Zweig, *Right to Heresy*, 263). When he did come to Geneva in 1553, he was captured by the civil authorities and, after a trial of several months' duration, was burned to death along with copies of his books.

During the twenty years that the protest against his religious works prevented him from pursuing a career in the church, Servetus studied medicine in Paris with Andreas Vesalius, who is generally credited with renewing the ancient practice of studying anatomy by dissecting human cadavers. Though his dissections revealed how mistaken some of Galen's teachings were, Vesalius himself refused to challenge the humouralism that is part of the Galenist physiology. In particular, Vesalius did not contest the doctrine of intraventricular pores, or passageways between the heart's ventricles through which blood is conveyed upon returning from the lungs. He therefore left intact the belief that the vital spirits of the blood are created entirely within the heart.[33] For Michael Servetus, however, it was impossible to resist attacking the errors of orthodoxy. In a manuscript written no later than 1546, he argued that God created Christ as his son by breathing the Spirit into the nostrils of Mary, thus making the virgin birth, as G. H. Williams says, "physiologically plausible."[34] In his next manuscript, he demonstrated the plausibility of this argument by describing the lesser pulmonary circulation, through which he showed that the human body is animated by the oxygenation of blood in the lungs.

This manuscript, published in 1553 as *Christianismi Restitutio*, took as its aim the restitution of the church to its original principles – a direct affront to Calvin's *Institutes*. The opening paragraph resumes the thread for which he had been previously chastised: "I have held that one should begin with the Man," wrote Servetus, "for I see that many, having not the foundation of Christ, in their flight of speculation on the Word ascribe little or nothing to the Man, and even give the true Christ completely over to oblivion." While not denying the Trinity, Servetus argued that Christ was the "visible aspect" of God, and that "there is no other *hypostasis* of God but he."[35] On the question of the Incarnation of God in Christ, Servetus held that Christ was born a man, into whom God "breathed" divinity at the time of his birth: "That God breathing, breathed into Christ, as into us, the Holy Spirit coming upon him." The body of Christ was a human body, created by "the celestial dew over-shadowing the virgin, and mingling itself with her semen and blood, transform[ing] the human matter into God." The nature of absolute Deity is unknowable and inaccessible to mankind; the works of Christ and the word of Scripture, which Servetus subjected to a "natural sense" interpretation and rational criticism, are the only assurances of and means to salvation (Allen, *Historical Sketch*, 37, 45).

Had Servetus written only those words, his heresy would have been sufficient to obtain for him the capital punishment that the authorities in Geneva ultimately imposed, but he committed a further offence by advocating adult baptism.[36] Consistent with his usual practice of founding reforms on Scripture alone, he believed that the ceremony of baptism should consist of total immersion of the person no earlier than the age of thirty, the age at which Christ was baptized at Jordan. His opposition to infant baptism was connected to the meaning of the ceremony: for Servetus it was a redemption from sin, of which children can have no awareness, and for which adolescents are not yet prepared. In adolescence, he wrote, the "spirit of divinity is submerged in the storms of youth and that hidden fire [the Spirit] is unable to be felt amidst the flowing saps [humor] of maturing flesh."[37] Baptism signifies a renunciation of the rule of passion and acceptance of the Holy Spirit, which for Servetus is one with Christ. During baptism, Christ enters the heart of man, as during the Lord's Supper the body of Christ is united with man through his "digestive mechanism," which is faith and love (Williams, *Radical Reformation*, 315, 339). For Calvin, however, Servetus's doctrine seemed to suggest that salvation could be bestowed by human, rather than divine, agency, and it also threatened to revive the anabaptist movement that had recently been suppressed.

Whatever Servetus's offenses were, his description of the pulmonary circulation appears to have compounded his crime. Servetus and Calvin had sparred over this question as early as 1534, when Calvin denounced an unnamed adversary, now believed to have been Servetus, who maintained that the soul "is merely a vital power which is derived from arterial spirit on the action of the lungs, and being unable to exist without the body, perishes along with the body, and vanishes away and becomes evanescent till the period when the whole man shall be raised again."[38] The discovery that the intraventricular wall of the heart was impermeable to blood led Servetus to conclude that there were not three kinds of spirits – vital, natural, and animal – in the human body as Galenic orthodoxy maintained, but only two, and that these two were perhaps separate states of a single animating spirit. Servetus argued that the natural spirits are communicated from the arteries to the veins during the passage of blood from the heart to the lungs, where, upon its exposure to "inspired air," the "substantial generation of the vital spirit itself" takes place, after which the blood "flies upward, where it is further refined, especially in the *plexus retiformis*, under the basis of the cerebrum, where the vital spirit begins to be changed into the animal one, drawing nearer to the true nature of a rational soul."[39] Servetus probably intended with this theory to demonstrate the means by which God breathes divinity into all mankind, thereby proving that God dwelt in all persons as he had in Christ. But to Calvin, who held that the soul was immortal, that it was individually created by God in the fetal stage, and that it was wakeful after death pending resurrection, the doctrine of Servetus appeared to suggest that the soul had material origins, that it was subservient to the body and its drives, and that it did not survive the body after death, at least not individually and in a wakeful state, all of which he regarded as capital heresies.[40]

It was this point that particularly struck Wotton when, early in the 1690s, he was shown a passage on circulation by Dr. Charles Bernard, a surgeon at St. Bartholomew's hospital in London. The passage had been copied out of a collection of Servetus's works by the antiquarian Abraham Hill, who gave it to Bernard.[41] Wotton printed the entire passage from the *Restitutio* in the margin of his *Reflections upon Ancient and Modern Learning,* marking the first time that the Latin passage had appeared in an English book. In the second edition of the *Reflections* (1697), he added a postscript in which he discussed the significance of Servetus's discovery, based on his reading of a manuscript copy of the *Restitutio* belonging to Dr. John Moore, Bishop of Norwich. Restoring the passage to its context, Wotton now realized that the significance of the passage is not that it first demonstrates pulmonary circulation, but that it tends to prove "that the *Substance of the Created Spirit of Jesus Christ is Essentially joined to the Substance of the Holy Ghost.* To explain this, he talks much of God's Breathing the Soul into Man, which, by his Manner of Explication, it is plain, he believed to be Material."[42] The critical assertion here – which Wotton emphasizes with italics – is that the joining of the spirit of Christ with that of the Holy Ghost in mankind is similar to anastomosis, or the communication of blood between the arteries and the veins.

This he reasons long upon, to prove, that the Blood is the Soul of Man, and seems to allow no other but what is thus made; first elaborated in the Liver, thence carried by the Veins into the right Ventricle of the Heart, and so into the Lungs; where being mix'd with Air, it becomes Vital; and afterwards being carried by the Arteries into the Brain, it is there further sublimed, till it receives its last Perfection, so as to be fit to perform the noblest Operations of the Animal Life. (Wotton, *Reflections*, xxxii–xxxiii)

In demonstrating that the natural spirits of the blood, created in the liver, are transformed into vital spirits as a result of their exposure to air in the lungs, and then into animal spirits in the brain, Servetus had showed that mankind's spiritual being has a material basis in the respiratory and circulatory operations of the body.

Wotton concludes his postscript on the discovery of circulation with a generous acknowledgement of Servetus' claim, offset however by a firm avowal of Harvey's right to the glory of having presented it to the world:

If we compare now this Notion thus explained by *Servetus*, with Dr. *Harvey's Theory of the Circulation of the Blood*, we shall plainly see that he had imperfect Glimmerings of that Light which afterwards Dr. *Harvey* communicated with so bright a Lustre to the learned World: Which Glimmerings, since they were so true, having nothing in them of a False Fire, I much wonder that he went no further; though at the same time I cannot but heartily congratulate the Felicity of my own Country, which produced the Man that first saw the Importance of these noble Hints which he improved into a Theory, and thereby made them truly useful to Mankind. (Wotton, *Reflections*, xxxiii)

Wotton's final words in this passage are probably directed at Sir William Temple, who had described Harvey's "modern" discovery as being of no practical value. But even Wotton seems to have only glimmerings of the full import of Servetus's theory. The question is not who first discovered circulation, but rather what effects the discovery had on medicine, religion, and literature. In medicine, the discovery of circulation rendered obsolete a rationalist orthodoxy based on the doctrine of distinct humours and spirits, which provoked a new anatomy of the body that in turn necessitated a new theory of the passions. In religion, the discovery provided a material connection between the inspiration of air and the generation of the rational spirit or soul of man, which the growing anti-trinitarian movement used to describe the manner in which God created his Son as a union of human flesh and divine breath. In sum, the discovery of circulation appeared to many to have expelled the Holy Spirit from the human heart, and to have reduced the soul, once believed to be divine and eternal, to no greater duration than a single breath. The heart and the passions – and soon, the idea of the self – were becoming fit subjects for the dissecting room of the anatomist, the meeting-room of the conventicle, and the study of the novelist. As we shall see in the following chapters, Wotton's enthusiastic re-introduction of the name of Michael Servetus into public discourse was not universally well received: even those who benefited from Servetus's radical reforms, such as Dr. Alexander Monro in medicine, the Reverend John Lewis in religion, and Daniel Defoe in letters, regarded Servetus as little better than an unwelcome ghost. When Heneage Finch anxiously re-asserted the dogma of the heart as the tabernacle of the Trinity, it was the heretical doctrine of Michael Servetus, rather than the anatomical theories of his uncle William Harvey, that he most feared. His son Daniel Finch would attempt to re-establish the Trinity in the heart of the state by force of law, but the effort would prove futile in the end.[43]

CHAPTER 3

Alexander Monro and the anatomist's gaze

In the fall of 1766, at the age of twenty-one, Benjamin Rush arrived in Edinburgh for the first of two years of study that were to lead to his degree as a doctor of medicine.[1] Rush was soon acquainted with several members of the faculty at Edinburgh, including his professor of anatomy, Alexander Monro *secundus*. This Dr. Monro, Rush recorded in his journal, was the third son of the famous Alexander Monro *primus* (1697–1767). The senior Dr. Monro had brought his namesake up to succeed him at the University and to carry on his life's work of detailing the anatomy of the human bones, heart, and nerves. This carefully planned succession had been jeopardized at first, it seems, by a disinclination in young Alexander to attend to his books; according to Rush, Alexander Monro *secundus* was

12 Years old before he could be prevailed upon to apply himself to study of any kind; by means of a strategem his Father contrived to throw *Robinson Crusoe* into his Hands which he read with great pleasure, & thus contracted a Taste for History – Travels etc. which his Father in a little time transferred to the more useful studies.[2]

So if Rush's anecdote is correct, we have *Robinson Crusoe* to thank for the continuation of a medical dynasty that trained as many as 17,800 students in anatomy, physiology, and surgery, including, as well as Rush, such physicians as John Hunter and Alexander Crichton and such writers as Tobias Smollett and Oliver Goldsmith.[3] In addition, Monro *primus* and *secundus* published an impressive body of work on anatomy, osteology, neurology and other medical matters.[4] Though they made some original contributions to medical research, their most important accomplishment was probably the establishment of the human body as an object of academic study in Britain and the wide dissemination of questions, if not answers, about the way that the passions of the mind are related to the sensibility of the body. If the rise of the novel in Britain began with the raising of such questions, then the works of the Monros might be the place in

ALEXANDER MONRO SEN.ᴿ M.D.

Professor of Anatomy, Fellow of the Royal College of Physicians at Edinburgh, and F.R.S.

Alexander Monro *primus* (1697–1767), engraved by James Basire (1730–1802) after a portrait by Allan Ramsay (1713–1784), frontispiece of *The Works of Alexander Monro* (1781).

which to make some connections between eighteenth-century medicine and the origins of the English novel.

Such a connection has long been sought in the writings of other physicians, notably George Cheyne, the friend of Samuel Richardson.[5] However, while Cheyne's works on the maladies of the nervous system were widely read, they did little to advance either neurological theory or novelistic practice.[6] Connections have also been sought between the novel and advances in the study of neurology made by Robert Whytt, Albrecht von Haller, Georg Ernst Stahl, William Cullen, Charles Bell and others, generally on the assumption that increases in knowledge of the nervous system must be linked to the formation of a "cult of sensibility," which was then exploited by novelists and their readers interested in delicacy of feeling, the vicarious experience of pain and suffering, and the refinement of sentiment.[7] But as G. S. Rousseau has pointed out, the novel of sentiment had already reached its fullest expression by the late 1740s, before the works of most of these neurologists had been written; the novel, says Rousseau, "ultimately owed nothing to the notorious neurological debates between Haller and Whytt, or even to Richardson's earlier debt to Dr. George Cheyne."[8] The origins of the novel, as we have already seen, are implicit in much older questions concerning the nature of the passions, the errors into which they lead us, and the narrative strategies through which these illnesses of the soul may be cured. The same questions, or very similar ones, had prompted anatomical investigations by Democritus, Aristotle, Galen, Servetus, Vesalius, and Harvey, to name a few, all of whom sought the seat of the passions in order to understand the causes of disease and to restore the body to health. The work of the novelist and the neurologist is similar in that both employ the anatomist's gaze in seeking some vital component of mind that cannot be derived from a strictly mechanistic model of humanity. The connection between neurology and the novel is not simply that one gave rise to or affected the development of the other, but that both sought answers to questions about the nature and function of the passions and the nerves in the "microcosmus" of man.

DR. MONRO AND THE HERESIES OF ANATOMY

The anatomy of the nervous system defined the frontier of knowledge about the human body in 1725, when Alexander Monro *primus* was appointed as Edinburgh University's first professor of anatomy.[9] The circulation of blood had been traced by William Harvey a hundred years earlier, hastening the decline of Galenic medicine, but the functions of the nerves were still unknown. In Galenic anatomy, both sensation and motion were conveyed in *pneuma* between the organs and muscles and the brain, which acted as the *sensorium commune*.[10] Galenism's medieval practitioners translated this theory of *pneuma* into a doctrine of spirits, in which the vital, natural, and animal spirits of the body, seated in the heart, liver, and brain, controlled the body through the vascular system of veins and arteries.[11] Though this doctrine failed to explain either sensation or motion, it permitted physicians to view the body as a system that operated according to the laws of hydrostatics, hydraulics, and mechanics – in Hermann Boerhaave's phrase, a *machina nervosa*, a "moving nervous machine," driven by its passions, appetites, and affections.[12] Because he based his deductions solely on mechanical principles which could readily be observed in the functions of the body, Boerhaave avoided speculations on the nature of the soul and its relation to the body. This empirical and practical approach was useful in the treatment of diseases, but it was less helpful in explaining such mental acts as memory, passions, and imagination, not to mention sensation and motion. The materialist La Mettrie explained all such acts as "a simple disposition of the *sensorium commune*, which is nothing but a purely mechanical arrangement of the parts of the medulla of the brain," while the vitalist Stahl accounted for all physical activity in terms of an immaterial soul, working through the will.[13] Boerhaave's teaching, as Kathleen Wellman has explained, offered either materialist or vitalist explanations for diseases as seemed appropriate for each case.[14] This eclectic, clinical approach was the method he taught to the first five professors in the school of medicine at Edinburgh, including Alexander Monro.[15]

During the year he spent at Leiden, studying under "the incomparable Boerhaave," Monro sent some letters to his former professor, Dr. William Cheselden, commenting from a Boerhaavian perspective on the second edition of Cheselden's *System of Anatomy*. Cheselden published these letters, accidentally making it appear that Monro had plagiarized from Boerhaave. So when Monro published the second edition of his *Anatomy of the Humane Bones* in 1732, he revised these letters into three treatises, one on the nervous system, one on the heart, and one on the lacteal sac and duct, which he appended to the volume. This time he acknowledged his debt to "that great Master" Boerhaave for his deductive method of explaining "the Mechanism of the several Parts . . . all taken from the Life."[16] In the oxymoronic spirit of humble pride that appears frequently in his work, Monro explained that he ventured to write on the nerves, heart, and lacteal sac and duct "because they are not rightly described in the common Books of Anatomy; and in 1719 I imagined my self the only Anatomist who could give a complete Demonstration of them in the humane Body" (iv). It is an intriguing coincidence that Monro should have rather boldly addressed the letters that formed the basis of these treatises to Cheselden in 1719, the year that *Robinson Crusoe* was published; perhaps it was something of himself he saw in the intrepid mariner of York that led Monro, some twelve years later, to put that book into his son's hands.[17]

When he returned to Edinburgh and assumed his duties as professor of anatomy, Monro *primus* lectured in English rather than in Latin. Transcripts of these lectures, written by students and preserved in a number of medical libraries, provide us (to the degree they can be accurately dated) with one means of observing the subtle shift in the early decades of the eighteenth century from a mechanistic or Boerhaavian view of the body to a more vitalistic account, in which sensibility plays a significant role.[18] His annual course of lectures on the history of anatomy began with a description of the legendary meeting between Democritus and Hippocrates, who had been summoned to Abdera to treat the mad philosopher. Hippocrates finds Democritus surrounded by the remains of dissected animals in which he has been searching for the seat of the passions and humours:

[he was] sitting under a shade, staring first at his notes, then at a subject he had before him. After having asked him what he was doing, he answered he was searching for the Seat of the Bile, by which according to his theory, he could discover the cause of many Phenomena and diseases, and for that End he dissected the Body's [sic] of many animals, judging it impossible to account rightly for Phenomena without an exact knowledge of the structure of the Parts.[19]

Monro's account of the meeting between Hippocrates and Democritus resembles that given by Robert Burton in the *Anatomy of Melancholy*, except that Monro diminishes the irony in Burton's telling of the story, through which Burton warns that the anatomist is likely to acquire the reputation of a heretic or a madman among his fellow citizens. Instead, Monro emphasizes the importance of dissection – of revealing the hidden structures beneath the skin, thus inferring the causes of observable phenomena from the relationship of the parts to the whole – that characterizes the anatomist's gaze.

In the course of his lectures on the history of anatomy, Monro discusses the works of Galen, treating him with the mix of veneration and disparagement that reflects the conflict between rationalist and empiricist philosophies of medicine in his day. Galen, says Monro, was "perhaps one of the greatest anatomists that ever lived," but he cautions that some of Galen's followers have carried their "blind esteem" to such a height that "they would rather be in the wrong with Galen than in the right with any other person."[20] Through the middle ages, Galen's authority was unquestionable: "none durst attack him, he almost banished Aristotle out of the schools." Galen's few detractors were equally unreasonable and prejudiced; they have "not stuck to defame what he gives for his Opinion, they likewise attacked him with his never having dissected a Human Body in his life time," a charge which Monro admits has some truth. The dangers of dissection caused Galen to do it seldom, "far less can we expect that he had his Subjects before him, when he wrote down the description of the parts, whence they must be imperfect, as in truth we find many are, besides some great Blunders in giving the description of the parts of Brutes, intermixed with those of the Human Body" (32–33). The tone of Monro's comments on Galen is calculated to encourage respect among his auditors for the rationalist system of medicine, yet also to warn them of the necessity for experiment and observation.

As Monro nears the modern era in his history of anatomy, he traces the decline of Galenist orthodoxy in the mid-sixteenth century, specifically in the first and second editions of the "great system of anatomy" of Andreas Vesalius, *De Humani Corporis Fabrica*, published in two editions of 1543 and 1555.[21] In the first edition of the *Fabrica*, according to Monro, Vesalius "severely attacks Galen" for having based his descriptions of human anatomy on that of animals, and in the second edition "he attacks Galen in a stronger manner than before," particularly on the matter of Galen's description of the vascular system (47). In the edition of 1543, Vesalius had merely expressed wonder at the Galenist doctrine of intraventricular pores, or the invisible passageways by which blood was supposed to pass from the right ventricle of the heart to the left. In the edition of 1555, however, Vesalius doubts that any such passageways exist, though he admits that "not long ago I would not have dared to diverge a hair's breadth from Galen's opinion."[22] Monro does not speculate about what happened to encourage Vesalius to challenge the Galenist orthodoxy between 1543 and 1555, but it was during that period that the lesser pulmonary circulation was first described by the heretical Spanish physician Michael Servetus, who preceded Vesalius in the role of demonstrator for lecturers in anatomy at the University of Paris. In a manuscript written in 1546, Servetus denied the existence of the intraventricular pores and argued that blood travels from the right to the left ventricle by way of the lungs, where the "vital spirit" is created through exposure to "inspired air." While far short of William Harvey's later description of the circulation of the blood through the entire body, Servetus's skepticism of the Galenist model was the opening wedge of a new science of anatomy, based on experiment, dissection, and observation. Servetus's condemnation by John Calvin as a heretic, however, complicated the acceptance of anatomical dissection, which encountered objections on religious as well as philosophical grounds.[23]

Monro was clearly aware of Servetus's contribution to the discovery of circulation, though his references to them include many hedges and reservations. In his lectures on the history of anatomy, Monro acknowledges Servetus's work and mentions the "good luck" by which the Edinburgh University library obtained a manuscript copy of the *Christianismi Restitutio*.[24] Monro usually introduces him as "Michael Servetus, a Spanish physician, who in 1553 wrote a book called *Christianismi Restitutio* wherein he maintained amongst other heretical doctrines that there was no such thing as a trinity . . . "; in some lectures, however, Monro calls him not a "Spanish physician" but a "heretick Fryar" or "heretick Monk." A collation of two sets of notes, in which the base text is a set dated c. 1725 and the other c. 1735, reads as follows:

Another opinion whereby they endeavour to rob Harvey [1735: of his glory] is that of Michael Servetus who in 1553 having wrote a book called *Christianismi Restitutio* wherein he maintained amongst other heretical Doctrines that there was no such thing as a trinity, for which in the same year He was burnt at Geneva by the instigation of Calvin with as many of his Books as could be got whence it comes that there are but few in Europe tho' we by good Luck have one in this Library here [1735: in Edinburgh] comparing [1735: he in this book compares] the Mystery of the Trinity to the three Juices of our body [1735: viz. the blood, Phlegm and Spirit. He then takes notice] He says that the Blood being sent from the Right Ventricle to the Pulmonary Artery passes through the Lungs where it receives considerable changes [1735: alterations] and returning impregnated [1735: with its Œther] to the Left Auricle with its Œther it goes into the Ventricle and thence into the Aorta to the rest of the parts of the Body here we find him leaning too much to [1735: upon] the Ancient Doctrine of the fine Œther neither does he mention how this Blood is returned nor whether in a continued or discontinued [1735: nor how it is propagated into a continued and discontinued] Stream.[25]

Monro's discussion of Harvey's predecessors concludes with some reflections on Realdus Columbus (1510–99), who he acknowledges had read Servetus on the circulation before publishing his own treatise on the subject:

Columbus is another to whom the Honour of the Circulation has been given and indeed he comes so very near the truth that if you'll only [1735: if you had only] read his Chapter *de Pulmonibus* you would swear that he had it plainly laid [1735: set] down; for he has commented on Servetus's opinion and adds something to it [1735: very evidently giving the use of the valves of the Heart, but in his Chapter] but if again you read the Chapter *de Hepate* it is evident he relapses [1735: he appears to be a rank Galenist and relapses] into the old opinions about the Bowel serving thus to let us know that neither he nor Servetus knew anything beyond Conjecture in [1735: of] the Affair, whence we may conclude that he's by no means entitled to the honour of this Important Discovery. (fol. 105)

The hedges in Monro's discussion of Servetus's and Columbus's accounts of pulmonary circulation allow him to discount their significance, thereby reserving the discovery for his countryman Harvey. He describes the attention paid to Servetus as an effort to "rob" (later, "deprive") Harvey of his glory, and characterizes Servetus as a heretic.[26] He alleges that Servetus denied the existence of the Trinity, though Servetus maintained at his trial that he had only questioned the means through which the Son of God had been created. Monro fails to credit Servetus with challenging either the Galenic doctrine of the three "juices" of the body or the existence of intraventricular pores, two points that were important in the discovery of circulation. He suggests that the refinement of the blood in Servetus's system is accomplished by combination with an "Œther," when in fact Servetus had shown that the blood is refined by a change in its quality, not by the addition of an ether. Finally, while he admits that Columbus benefited from Servetus's work, he undercuts that admission by calling Columbus a "rank Galenist," suggesting that the discoveries of the fifteenth century left Galenic anatomy unshaken. In short, while Monro was conscientious enough to note the claims of Servetus and Columbus in his early lectures, national pride and religious orthodoxy prevented him from examining those claims in depth.

In the lectures that date from the 1740s, however, there is a subtle but significant change in Monro's tone toward Servetus. The passage that had formerly begun with the charge that Harvey was "robbed" of the credit for his discovery by persons citing the "heretical" works of Servetus instead commences as follows: "The first of the Moderns that is opposed to Harvey as having any Idea of the Circulation is Michael Servetus, a Spanish physician, who in 1553 wrote a book called *Christianismi Restitutio*."[27] In the ensuing discussion, he explores the nature of Servetus's contribution in greater and more accurate detail than before. Implying that Servetus's religious heresy was grounded in his skepticism of Galenic orthodoxy, Monro says that "[Servetus] in this book [compares?] the Mysteries of the Trinity to the 3 juices of our Body, the Blood, phlegm, and Spirit. And afterwards says that the vital Spirits are not produc'd from Blood passing through the partition betwixt the right and left ventricle, as was at that time commonly believed, but from the Blood being sent from the right Ventricle through the lungs, where it receives considerable changes, and returning impregnated to the left auricle, it thence goes with its Œther into the left Ventricle and so into the Aorta."[28] While still critical of Servetus for his reliance on the "ancient Doctrine" of an "Œther," Monro does correctly identify Servetus's essential breakthrough – that is, that the Galenic doctrine based on intra-ventricular pores was not correct, but that the blood instead traveled to the lungs, where it was impregnated with "ether," and returned to the heart for circulation to the body. This more accurate description may well be due to Monro's having read William Wotton's *Reflections Upon Ancient and Modern Learning* (1697), which introduces Servetus in almost identical language.[29] But the cultural (rather than merely intertextual) significance of Monro's willingness to recognize Servetus's contribution is that it signals a shift in his thinking from the mechanistic model of the circulatory and nervous systems to a more vitalistic theory, one in which the body functions not merely as a hydraulic system, but rather as an organism capable of protecting, governing, and reproducing itself through nervous sensibility.

DR. MONRO AND THE MECHANISTIC PHILOSOPHY

A second means of tracing the process by which Monro *primus* gravitated from a mechanistic towards a vitalistic view of the body is available by comparing the editions of his textbook on anatomy, first published as *The Anatomy of the Humane Bones* in 1726. In the second edition (1732), Monro identifies as one of his themes the way in which "Physicians or Anatomists explain the several Motions in the Fluids or Solids of the Body, which accompany any Passion," which has has led him to in-clude in this edition a treatise on the nerves.[30] The prevailing theory of the structure and function of the nerves is that they are solid cords whose vibrations convey the impulses that govern motion and sensation, but his examination of nerves beneath the microscope reveals "open Orifices" which, "when seen in a Nerve cut transversely, are in hazard of making us believe, that we have discovered the Cavities of the nervous Canals" (2). By injecting the nerve, Monro proves that fluid is conveyed through-out its length. The nerves are packed so tightly together that Monro doubts that they could vibrate individually; for this reason, he says, "I rather incline to believe the Nerves to be Vessels containing a Fluid, which is sent into them from the Brain in an equal constant Stream, in the same Way as is done by other Glands to their Excretories, and can serve to solve all the *Phaenomena* that are commonly remarked in either muscular Motion or Sensations" (4–5). To prove this theory, he cites an experiment in which a live dog was opened and the nerve governing the diaphragm was compressed. The nerve was stripped of "fluid" down to the diaphragm, which responded by contracting, but once only; when the muscle was de-compressed, and the nerve allowed to re-fill with fluid, the process could be repeated. This experiment proved to Monro that the nerves must convey a fluid to the muscle that causes it to respond. To account for the two-way flow of sensation in the nerves, Monro supposes that there are also "venous" nerves that return fluid to the brain (6).

The tubular-nerve theory, according to which the brain functions like "other Glands," might explain how the nerves govern muscular motion, but Monro has difficulty explaining how nerves filled with fluid excreted by the brain could convey motor impulses and sense impressions at the same time. He supposes, along with Boerhaave, that motion is controlled by the arterial nerves, while the venous nerves convey sensation back to the brain. To those critics who object that fluids do not travel as quickly as our senses appear to transmit information, Monro responds that "all Objects of our Senses act by a plain mechanical Impulse or Pressure" (6). The sensations of smell and taste, for example, are responses of the nerves to pressure from particles of matter in the air or on the tongue. When the particles press the sides of the nerves, "their Fluid must be hindred to flow so freely as it did before this Pressure; which Resistance will instantly be felt at the Fountain-head or Origin of the Nerves, and, as Reaction is equal to Action, will have the same Effect as if the Impulse had been made here" (7). Using quasi-Newtonian terms, Monro seeks to prove that sensation could be conveyed not by the movement of fluids, but by the pressure to which they are subjected. A gentle pressure is pleasurable; a violent one, threatening the separation of the nerve, causes pain. Beyond this distinction between pleasure and pain, however, Monro is not able to say how the brain differentiates the nature of the object that caused the sensation.

It is in the third edition of his *Anatomy* in 1741 – which, coincidentally, was approximately the year that he recommended *Robinson Crusoe* to his son – that Monro begins to speculate on the means by which nerves convey sensations that translate into ideas. Significantly, the title of the book becomes *The Anatomy of the Human Bones and Nerves* with this edition, elevating the treatise on the nerves to equal status with that on the bones.[31] The nerves are seen here not as mere ducts for conveying cerebral fluid to the muscles, but as organs capable of initiating motion and sensation. Far from ideas residing in an immaterial soul, sensations are the products of the nervous system: "Whenever the Impulse proper to the Object is regularly applied with due Force to a Nerve rightly disposed to be impressed by it, and is communicated . . . to the *Sensorium*, it gives a true and just Idea of the Object to the Mind" (31). These sensations are not limited to pleasure and pain, but affect a sense of what is beneficial or hurtful to the body. Lacking any English word to denote this capability, Monro calls it the "*Nisus* of the Mind to free the Body of what is in Danger of being very hurtful," and remarks that it "may serve to explain the Phaenomena of a great many Diseases" (34).[32] Monro's use of the Latin word "*Nisus*," which means an impulse directed toward a particular end, suggests a moral sensibility imprinted in the nervous system itself.[33] This *Nisus*, he expects, may explain some phenomena that are not explicable under the Boerhaavian fluid theory – for example, the fact that a muscle can respond to a stimulus, such as a warm breath or pin prick, even after it has been separated from the body (38). By helping Monro overcome the dualism between mind and body that is inherent in mechanistic philosophy, the theory of the "*Nisus* of the Mind" opens the way for a concept of sensibility in which the nervous system directs the body to take the actions necessary to save or reproduce itself.

In the third through sixth editions of his *Anatomy*, published in 1741, 1746, 1750, and 1758, Monro fully develops his theory of the nerves, which he clearly models on the vascular circulation of the blood.[34] By 1758, he no longer sees a need for the "two Sorts of Nerves" theory – arterial and venous – because he now believes that the nervous fluid is not pumped through the body as is the blood, but moves "constantly, equally, and slowly, unless when its Course is altered by the Influence of the Mind, or by the Pressure of some neighbouring active Organ" (6th edn., 352). The nervous fluid consists of a "desecated Water, with a very small Proportion of the other Principles extremely subtilized," which he describes as oily, saline, and terrestrious particles, all substances necessary to the nutrition of the body (351). Thus the nervous fluid not only conveys motion and sensation, but it nourishes the body and is itself refined and purified as it passes through the brain. This flow of nutritional and vitalizing elements can be slowed or hurried by the passions of the mind, in a way still unknown to Monro:

We have not, and perhaps cannot have any Idea of the Manner in which Mind and Body act upon each other; but if we allow that the one is affected by the other, which no Body denies, and that the Fluid of the Nerves (whatever Name People please to give it) is a *Principal* Instrument which the Mind makes Use of to influence the Actions of the Body, or to inform itself of the Impressions made on the Body, we must allow that the Mind can direct this Instrument differently, particularly as to Quantity and Celerity, though we must remain ignorant of the Manner how many Phaenomena depending on this Connexion of Mind and Body are produced. (354)

Though Monro cannot explain how the mind is able to control the movement of fluid in the body, he is certain that it "can direct this Instrument" to produce motion. Nervous sensibility for Monro, then, is not merely the mechanical response of the nerves to irritation, nor simply the faculty by which sensation is conveyed to the brain, but is the means through which the nervous system assists in the formation of desires and directs the body to accomplish them.

Ultimately, Monro's loyalty to Boerhaave did not allow him entirely to give up the fluid theory of the nerves in favor of some of the new explanations then appearing. In particular, he resisted the alternative theory, derived by Bryan Robinson from Newton's *Opticks*, that predicated the existence of a "subtle aether" that circulated through the nerves.[35] In the third edition of 1741, he expressed skepticism about the existence of this aether; in the sixth of 1758 he denied it emphatically, along with the theory of animal electricity: "We are not sufficiently acquainted with the properties of an aether or electrical effluvia pervading every thing, to apply them justly in the animal oeconomy; and it is as difficult to conceive how they should be retained or conducted in a long nervous cord. These are difficulties not to be surmounted."[36] At the same time, Monro's intellectual honesty obliged him to admit that there were many phenomena which the mechanistic system failed to explain. How does the heart know how much fluid to pump, or the brain how much to secrete? How does a frog continue to move purposefully after its heart has been cut out? How does a muscle separated from an animal, and thus from the source of its nervous fluid, continue to move when stimulated? Such questions hang unanswered over the treatises on the nerves and heart, and eventually cause Monro to declare in the preface to the seventh edition of 1763, the last to appear in his lifetime, that Boerhaave's doctrine of the purely mechanical operation of the heart, "though simple and beautiful, not appearing sufficient to account for the Phaenomena of the Motions of the Heart, I have omitted it in this Edition" (original not paginated; 323–24). Though Monro with this admission virtually severed his ties with mechanistic philosophy, his skepticism about the new doctrine of animal electricity prevented him from advancing his theory of sensibility beyond this point.

THE MONROS AND THE PROBLEM OF SENSIBILITY

Monro's *Anatomy of the Bones and Nerves* would remain in print for almost twenty more years, new editions appearing in 1775, 1777, and 1782. The treatise would also occupy a prominent place in the collected edition of *primus*'s works published by Alexander Monro *secundus* in 1781. But within two years of that edition, Monro *secundus* published his own *Observations on the Structure and Functions of the Nervous System*, in which he went far beyond his father's investigations of the nervous system. Monro *secundus* demonstrated conclusively that his father was correct in arguing that nerves do not operate by an elastic impulse as a muscle does, but he also showed that his father's hydraulic theory was equally impossible.[37] In fact, his examination of the ganglia, whose function had mystified his father, revealed that more nerves leave a ganglion than enter into it, thus disproving his father's supposition that all nerve fibres are distinct from their origin to their terminus in the brain, which was essential to the fluid theory of sensation (56–57). He agreed with his father "that the living and feeling principle, which we commonly call the mind of the animal, is seated within the head, and occupies there a *sensorium commune*," but he also noted that, in the case of a member amputated from the body, "effects follow which we cannot account for on mechanical principles" (88). Puncturing the heart of a frog that had been separated from its body, for example, "throws all its fibres into violent motion. Such a cause appears so disproportionate to its effects, that we cannot help conceiving that some living principle has been influenced: Or that there are two kinds of feeling, one with, and another without consciousness" (88–89).

In proposing "some living principle" that resides in the nervous system, and which works through both voluntary and involuntary responses, Monro *secundus* approaches an anatomical definition of the sentient principle in the nerves that his father referred to as the "*Nisus* of the Mind" in the third edition of his *Anatomy* in 1741. "I have long thought and endeavoured to prove," says Monro *secundus*, "that our nerves, independent of the encephalon, possess an energy or principle of life, which they derive from their proper *pia mater* and its vessels" (36). That is to say "that the Nerves do not receive their energy wholly from the Head and Spinal Marrow, but that the texture of every branch of a Nerve is such as to furnish it, or that the structure of each Nerve is similar to that of the Brain."[38] This description of an innate sensiblity in the nervous system provides an alternative to the mechanistic explanations offered by the materialists, who argue that the body responds only to the stimuli of external objects or changes in the state of its fluids, and the metaphysical doctrines of the immaterialists, for whom the body is governed by an in-dwelling spirit. Monro finds an example of this independent sensibility in the case of a parrot whose pupil seems to dilate and contract not in response to the stimulus of a strong light, but at the whim of "the passions of the mind of the animal, independent of the light upon the eye."[39] He concludes that such effects "cannot be accounted for on the yet known principles of mechanism"; that they imply the presence of "some principle of control that recognizes different situations"; that these operations "are the best calculated for the preservation and well-being of the animal," and that they must therefore "be directed and conducted by a wise agent, intimately acquainted with the structure, and with all the effects it is capable of producing" (100–1). If in these experiments Monro *secundus* is searching for that "*Nisus* of the Mind" that his father described as the tendency of the nerves to "free the Body of what is in Danger of being very hurtful," he also seems to be seeking an empirical basis for those secret hints, those "merciful Dispositions of Heaven, in the Dangers we run through in this Life," upon which Robinson Crusoe learned to rely "when Sense, our own Inclination, and perhaps Business has call'd to go the other Way, yet a strange Impression upon the Mind, from we know not what Springs, and by we know not what Power, shall over-rule us to go this way."[40]

Of course, the Monros were not alone in searching for a non-mechanistic theory by which to explain the operation of the muscles and nerves. Studies on the nerves were also being conducted by Monro *primus*'s colleague on the faculty of medicine at Edinburgh, Robert Whytt, who was appointed Professor of the Institutes of Medicine in 1747, and his successor, William Cullen, appointed on Whytt's death in 1766.[41] It was Cullen who coined the term "neurosis" to refer specifically to diseases of the nervous system, and Whytt who, in Roy Porter's terms, "enlarged the map of mind-body relations" by describing a set of involuntary motions that "neither fell directly under conscious will nor yet were automatic like heartbeat" (Porter, *Mind Forg'd Manacles*, 180). As early as 1751, Whytt argued that such reactions as salivating at the sight of food were purposive acts of the mind, "of whose action, however, we are no way conscious."[42] In 1765, Whytt attributed the "increased secretion of tears" occasioned by joy or grief "not [to] any compression of the lachrymal glands or their ducts by the neighboring muscles, as has been commonly imagined," but to the effects of the "passions of the mind" acting on the nerves. In so saying, he, like Alexander Monro *primus* before him, explicitly rejected the mechanistic theory of the nervous system.[43] "Nothing produces more sudden or surprizing changes in the body," said Whytt, "than violent affections of the mind, whether these be excited by external objects, or by the exercise of the internal senses. Thus doleful or moving stories, horrible or unexpected sights, great grief, anger, terror and other passions, frequently occasion the most sudden and violent nervous symptoms . . . nay, excessive fear, grief, joy and shame have been sometimes followed by sudden death" (212–14). The passions are not merely the body's mechanical responses to external or internal objects of perception, but are emotions, or "affections of the mind," that are capable of initiating action by themselves. "Sudden terror, or excessive grief, or other violent passions of the mind," says Whytt, "may affect the brain so as to produce a continued *mania* or melancholy. But in what manner the passions, or the morbid matter of nervous diseases change the state of the brain or *common sensorium*, and occasion such disorders, is entirely unknown" (315).

The concept of sensibility that emerges from the works of Whytt and the Monros is that of a nervous system "animated by a living principle different from matter and of powers superior to it," that is, by some principle other than mechanism.[44] With Cullen, Whytt and the Monros rejected the various mechanistic explanations that were still being offered: that this living principle is the result of "effervescences of nervous and arterial fluid," or that it is "a subtle, aetherial, or electric matter" actuated by the will, or that the nerves themselves are capable of moving the muscles in response to irritation (Schofield, *Mechanism and Materialism*, 204). Similarly, they rejected humouralist theories of the passions, based on the movement of fluids through the body, in favor of a theory of sympathy, through which organs and muscles of the body move toward the same intentional goal, actuated by conscious and unconscious states of feeling. It would be difficult, and probably pointless, to argue that they were drawn to this conclusion by representations of the passions in such early "natural histories of the passions" as Defoe's *Robinson Crusoe* or Fielding's *Tom Jones*. But it is the argument of this chapter, and the ones that follow, that the shift from mechanism to a more complex rendering of the interplay between the passions and the nerves in the works of eighteenth-century neurologists is paralleled by, and must be understood in conjunction with, the development of a complex view of human emotion and moral sensibility in the novels written in that same period.

CHAPTER 4

Defoe and the natural history of the passions

In the preceding chapters, we have seen that the works of Michael Servetus, though known more by reputation than at first hand, haunted the seventeenth and eighteenth centuries in at least two major areas of public discourse. One was the emerging interest in the anatomy of the human body, to which Servetus had made a major contribution in his description of the lesser pulmonary circulation. While sketchy and incomplete, his account correctly identified the true function of the heart and opened a gap in Galenist orthodoxy through which Harvey and others eventually drove. The other area was the Protestant Reformation, which had stopped short of contesting the Athanasian dogma of the Trinity. Servetus's criticisms of the "errors" in that doctrine were incorporated into the ideologies of anti-trinitarian movements such as the Socinians, and his martyrdom by Calvin gave an unintended lift to the radical wing of the Reformation. Socinianism made slow but steady progress among Presbyterians and other nonconformists in England until, in the second decade of the eighteenth century, it broke undeniably into public consciousness in a series of controversies.[1]

One such controversy occurred in the dissenting congregation at Stoke Newington in July, 1718. In that incident, a minister named Martin Tomkins had switched pulpits for a day with a Reverend Asty, who took the occasion to warn Tomkins's congregation about "the Danger of Pernicious Errors and damnable Heresies creeping in among us."[2] The heresies that concerned Asty "particularly referr'd to Errors about the Doctrine of Christ's Deity," which, he made clear, he thought Tomkins had fallen into. Hearing about this sermon the following week from his parishioners, Tomkins preached a sermon on July 13 in his own defense, arguing on the basis of John 20: 21–23 that the terms of salvation belong to Christ to settle, not to man, and that the tendency to denounce as heretical any doctrine that conflicts with one's own beliefs only causes disharmony among the Christian faiths. On the specific question of the deity, Tomkins denied that "the Orthodox Doctrine of the Trinity, in plain words, *That the Son and the Holy-Ghost are the same Substance, the same individual Being with the Father; or in all respects Equal to the Father*" is "a *Fundamental Doctrine of Christianity*" or supported by any passage of scripture (22–23). A man must be a "declared Enemy to Reason, who declares against free Examination in any Matter whatsoever," Tomkins argued, warning that "we are not left at liberty to pronounce every Thing Heresy, that we apprehend to be contrary to the Doctrine of Scripture: Then, for ought I know, might every Man call each other Heretick" (116–17). Notwithstanding this impassioned plea for liberty of thought, the congregation voted to eject Tomkins from his pulpit as a suspected Socinian.

Less than a year later, the much more famous controversy at Salters' Hall erupted. Salters' Hall, which was used as a meeting house by dissenters for religious services and lectures, was the scene of a series of convocations held in February and March, 1719, in an effort to settle a dispute that had erupted at Exeter. In brief, two dissenting ministers in that town – James Peirce and Joseph Hallet – had been excluded from their pulpits because of their heterodox views on the divinity of Christ. Peirce stated openly that he believed "the Son and Holy Ghost to be divine persons, but subordinate to the Father," while Hallet, who kept his views to himself, joined Peirce in certifying for ordination a student who subscribed to the Arian views of the reverend Samuel Clarke.[3] By a vote of 57 to 53, the convocation at Salters' Hall advised the Exeter Assembly that "no human compositions, or interpretations of the doctrine of the Trinity" should be made a test of orthodoxy. But the close vote did not end the controversy, and the convocation split into two groups – one subscribing to a trinitarian declaration, and another refusing to subscribe on the grounds that "the Bible is the only and the perfect Rule of Faith."[4] The separation into subscribers and non-subscribers brought an end to the controversy, but it also made public and permanent a division in the dissenting interest between trinitarians and unitarians, those who accepted the Athanasian creed and those who sought revelation in Scripture alone.[5]

These incidents are relevant to the origins of the novel in that, in both cases, the soon-to-be novelist Daniel Defoe was certainly a close observer, if not participant. He was a resident of Stoke Newington, and no doubt knew the members of Tomkins's meeting. He was also a prominent member of the group that had originally met at Salters' Hall, and he had occasionally preached there.[6] He had been engaged throughout his writing career in efforts to fashion a truce between the dissenters and the political and religious establishments that extended them a grudging toleration, although the exposure of his relationship with Robert Harley, and particularly his authorship of *A Letter to the Dissenters* (1713), had cost him the trust of many dissenters.[7] He well understood that the appearance of Socinianism among the dissenters, however justified in conscience, might give their High Church enemies an opening to renew their attacks. He had personally suffered at the hands of Daniel Finch, the second Earl of Nottingham, who had been principally responsible for his imprisonment in 1703 for libel, as well as for several acts of parliament designed to restrict the civil liberties of the dissenters, and he knew the vindictive measures of which Nottingham was capable.[8] It is probable that what principally annoyed Defoe was not the heresy so much as the political indiscretion of the controversialists, through which the dissenters were exposed to persecution by their enemies. In May of 1719, following the Salters' Hall controversy, he published a second *Letter to the Dissenters*, rebuking them for carrying on in public a scandalous "disagreement in the very first and principal Article of Faith, *viz.* The Union of the Godhead," by which they had "brought the Truths of God declar'd in his Word to be doubtful, inextricable, and past our Understanding."[9] In his monthly news magazine, the *Mercurius Politicus*, which was aimed at a Tory audience, he charged that the denials by the dissenting ministers of a basis in scripture for the doctrine of the trinity were similar to those of "*Arius, Socinius,* and other Antient, or indeed Primitive Hereticks," by which he probably meant Michael Servetus.[10] Years later, in his *History of the Devil* (1726), Defoe named Servetus as the encourager of those nonconformists who had allowed themselves to be ruled by their religious passions – or their devils – rather than by reason and moderation.[11]

As Paula Backscheider and Maximillian Novak have both observed, Defoe was engaged throughout the Salters' Hall controversy in writing the book that became *Robinson Crusoe*, and the debates over individual sovereignty and revelation without dogma are strongly reflected in that novel.[12] Contrary to the position Defoe appeared to take in the Tory journal *Mercurius Politicus*, in the novel he dramatizes the conversion of two persons – Robinson Crusoe and Friday – to Christianity by Scripture alone, without the aid of any creeds, dogmas, or priests. Robinson arrives at a revelation of the providential design of his life through, as we will see below, a joint process of reading Scripture and empirically investigating his relation to the natural world; with that knowledge, he initiates Friday into an understanding of how God dwells in him, and how the devil, who enjoys "a secret access to our Passions," causes us "to run upon our Destruction by our own Choice."[13] As an aside to the reader, Robinson points out that the entire process of revelation was accomplished on the basis of Scripture: "We had here the Word of God to read, and no farther off from his Spirit to instruct, than if we had been in England" (*RC*, 159). Robinson clearly means to say that the process of revelation proceeded more quickly for Friday in the *absence* of dogma and priests: "As to all the Disputes, Wranglings, Strife and Contention, which has happen'd in the World about Religion, whether Niceties in Doctrines, or Schemes of Church Government, they were all perfectly useless to us," as were also "any Teacher, or Instructer (I mean, humane)" (160). Defoe's indirect allusion to the trinitarian controversy suggests that the ghost of Servetus did have, by a curious negative process, a positive effect on the making of the novel. By calling the dogma of the trinity into question, the latter-day followers of Servetus started a controversy that ended in Defoe's rejection of the entire debate, including the terms and rhetorical forms in which that debate was carried on, in favor of a fictional model of the conversion process, conceived as happening at a far distance from the irresolvable disputes of Stoke Newington or Salters' Hall. Through this fictional model – which we now insist on reading as a novel – Defoe proposed a new plan for moderating the religious, civil, and family passions that had so distracted the dissenters from their duties to God and their own interests.[14] His purpose in writing *Robinson Crusoe* was not that of a "novelist," even in the highly ambiguous sense in which that term was used in the early decades of the eighteenth century, but rather that of a historian, one who saw the hand of the Devil in the troubled passions of mankind and projected a cure for them.[15]

DEFOE, HISTORY, AND THE NATURAL HISTORY OF MAN

As Paula Backscheider has shown, Defoe was a historian long before he turned to fiction, and in his best works he reported the origins and progress of historical events from the standpoint of an imaginary or fictionalized observer.[16] Defoe's habit of adopting the persona of an editor of historical memoirs was not merely a way of hiding his authorship of prose fictions, but rather of advancing his ambitions as a historian – that is to say, a commentator on manners, persons, and public events of recent memory. The pretense that the memoirs of a shipwrecked sailor or reformed prostitute were those of real persons endowed them with a public significance that novels or romances could never claim. According to Backscheider, Defoe wrote his fictional memoirs to show his readers how "to bear themselves prudently in the present and providently towards the future."[17] Only if they were taken as works of personal history could Defoe's narratives have the reforming effect on the passions that he sought for them.

As Max Novak, Robert Mayer, and others have long pointed out, Defoe's fictional narratives share many formal qualities with his much larger corpus of histories, satires, and moralistic works.[18] Mayer contends that all of Defoe's narratives, including *The Life and Strange Surprizing Adventures of Robinson Crusoe* and *The Fortunes and Misfortunes of the Famous Moll Flanders*, were read as works of "Baconian historiography" by his contemporaries, and only subsequently were "read into fictional discourse" as novels.[19] Attempting to read all of Defoe's works in the tradition of Baconian historiography, however, creates its own set of problems. While some of them, such as *The Storm*, do appear to fit the Baconian model, and others such as the *History of the Union of Great Britain* show an interest in narrative method, including the practice of tracing historical effects back to their original causes, Defoe's major fictions are very different kinds of histories. As Mayer himself admits, the narratives written by Defoe between 1719 and 1724 are part of a "crucial shift," or, as Michel Foucault put it, a "sudden redistribution" in modes of discourse, after which writers of fiction no longer had to disguise their works as histories.[20] What is new in these works is an interest in the undetermined operation of mind in the individuals who are the subjects of these "histories." It would be both inaccurate and anachronistic to describe this interest as "psychological"; a better term would be "iatrophilosophical," an unlovely but suitable way of describing the effort to evaluate, regulate, and cure the passions of a culture in the early stages of expansive growth. Defoe's "novels" are efforts to develop a theory of mind by writing the histories of particular persons whose stories raise questions of both political and philosophical interest as a result of their struggles with their passions.[21]

In her studies of Defoe's historical practice, Paula Backscheider has observed that Defoe sought to find explanations in natural law behind historical events, an approach that prevented "his consideration of God's actions in history in anything but the most superficial statements."[22] In his *History of the Union*, for example, Defoe attributes the union of England and Scotland ultimately to the workings of Providence, but then restricts his historical narrative to mundane matters, thus blunting the connection between Providential causes and specific effects. As a novelist, Backscheider continues, Defoe often suggests that Providence or the Devil is the hidden agent behind the actions of his characters, but he undercuts the "otherworldliness" of the suggestion by providing characteristics of personality that serve as more proximate causes.[23] In this view, while God may be the final cause of all that happens in nature, man's knowledge and power are limited to second causes, to those observable hints, promptings, and necessities through which man infers the nature of divine will. The challenge faced by Defoe's narrators is to distinguish these manifestations of divine will from their own fears and desires – in short, from their passions. Religion is an aid to virtue, but, like reason, it is ultimately insufficient to keep mankind from error; the only sure path is a rigorous, constant, and life-long self-examination. This need for self-examination of one's own passions may not make Defoe a psychological novelist in the usual sense, but it does suggest a new balance between religious and humanist elements in Defoe's fiction. If Defoe makes use of the conventions of spiritual autobiography, he does so because that medium affords the best opportunity for examining the distinction between the passions and the will of God. The religious elements that are present in Defoe's narratives are there not to reinforce a dying theology, but to assist in the formation of an emerging view of man that is natural, scientific, and humanistic.

As Ilse Vickers has shown, Defoe's background in the "New Sciences" of the seventeenth century led him to think of his literary work not as fact or fiction, but as "a natural history of man and his activities."[24] Defoe was well grounded in both ancient and modern theories of mind, though he favored the latter.[25] He had received the equivalent of a university education at Charles Morton's dissenting academy, including the traditional readings in Aristotelian philosophy – moral, metaphysical, and natural – but in the experimental sciences of Sir Francis Bacon as well.[26] His library, which was sold together with Phillips Farewell's at the time of his death, is described by Helmut Heidenreich as holding "an astonishing number of medical books," including a French translation of Galen's *On the Uses of the Parts of the Body* and standard works by Andreas Vesalius, Thomas Sydenham, Theodore Mayerne, John Freind, George Cheyne, and Daniel LeClerc.[27] The library sale catalogue also lists four works by Thomas Hobbes, including *Leviathan*, and commentaries on Hobbes by the Earl of Clarendon and others; the third and the fifth editions of Locke's *Essay Concerning Humane Understanding*, with a commentary on Locke's life and work by Jean LeClerc; and a copy of Charles LeBrun's study of the passions as subjects for painting and sculpture.[28] If Defoe's natural histories of the mind seem "realistic," it is not only because he acquired his knowledge of human nature through a naive empiricism, by conversing with people in the shops and streets, but also because he opened himself to the new theories of mind appearing in the works of such "natural historians of man" as Robert Boyle, John Locke, Jean LeClerc, and Giorgio Baglivi.

To illustrate what is meant by Vickers' phrase "natural history of man," we may look at the work of Giorgio Baglivi (1668–1706), whose medical manual, *De Praxi Medica* (1696), described a new method for treating illnesses.[29] Following the lead of Thomas Sydenham in England, Baglivi declined to speculate on the general origins of diseases, and instead urged physicians to question their patients about the "occasional cause" of their illnesses, particularly the role that disturbances of the passions may have played. He asked his fellow physicians to help him find answers to three questions: whether passions of the mind influence the body; how they may influence it; and how diseases arising from such influences may be cured. Baglivi's method aimed to do "what had never before been done: to obtain good and clear histories of every passion and care of the mind."[30] He sought to know the symptoms of every disease that arose from emotional sources, as well as their incidence, duration, and transformation into other diseases. His method emphasized the role of the physician in talking the patient through the disease: "I can scarce express what Influence the Physician's Words have upon the Patient's Life, and how much they sway the Fancy; for a Physician that has his Tongue well hung, and is Master of the Art of persuading, fastens, by the mere Force of Words, such a Vertue upon his Remedies, and raises the Faith and Hopes of the Patient to that Pitch, that sometimes he masters difficult Diseases with the silliest Remedies."[31]

Recognizing Defoe's debt to natural historians such as Bacon and Baglivi may help to reconcile the dissatisfaction that readers sometimes feel at the end of those of his works that we now read as novels. Novels, unlike histories, are expected to follow a dramatic pattern, either tragic or comic, that leads toward and eventually reaches a sense of closure. Defoe's histories, whether personal or general, seldom reach closure. On the contrary, they often end expansively, with a view toward improvements to come in either the material or spiritual worlds described in the history: thus the third volume of *Robinson Crusoe*, entitled *Serious Reflections During the Life and Surprising Adventures of Robinson Crusoe, with his Vision of the Angelick World*, endeavors to provide the reader with a map of the world of spirits; the *Tour through the Whole Island of Great Britain* projects a view of England's future prosperity; and the *History of the Devil* promises that, if men and women can learn how the Devil acts on them through their passions, they can enjoy lives of perfect peace and calm. Only the history of *The Fortunate Mistress* ends in a way that readers of novels expect it should – with the barest hint that the narrator will suffer for her crimes – and yet this insufficient sense of closure only disappoints the expectations that the narrative raises by its resemblance to a novel.[32] It is ultimately not as a novelist, but as a historian of the passions, that Defoe must be read.

DEFOE'S NATURAL HISTORY OF PASSION: *THE CONSOLIDATOR*

Defoe's interest in the effect of the passions on history appears as early as 1705, the year in which he published *The Consolidator*.[33] *The Consolidator* is a satire of politics, religion, and science in England, as well as a parody of such purported histories or anatomies of mankind as Samuel Purchas' *Microcosmus*, Gracián's *El Criticón*, and Augustine's *Confessions*. The vehicle of the satire is the purported narrative of a traveler to China, a land with many marvelous inventions besides those already known to the West. These inventions include machines for writing copies at the same time an original is made, machines for remembering, and even machines for writing down a speaker's words as he says them. In the library of the Emperor of China, the traveler discovers the works of an author, born on the Moon, who was persuaded many centuries ago to impart his knowledge to the Chinese, which is how they came to be so advanced.

In the course of surveying these works, the traveler discovers some interesting metaphors used on the Moon to describe the anatomy and function of the mind. For example, among the works of the lunar philosopher is a "Mathematical Description of Nature's strong Box, the Memory, with all its Locks and Keys" (18–19). In the memory, "Nature has placed the Materials of reflecting; and like a *Glass Bee-Hive*, represents to you all the several Cells in which are lodg'd things past, even back to Infancy and Conception." In this "Repository" all knowledge is disposed and catalogued, "Classically, Annually, Numerically, and Alphabetically":

There you may see how, when the perplext Animal, on the loss of a Thought or Word, *scratches his Pole:* Every Attack of his Invading Fingers knocks at Nature's Door, allarms all the Register-keepers, and away they run, unlock all the Classes, search diligently for what he calls for, and immediately deliver it up to the Brain; if it cannot be found, they intreat a *little Patience*, till they step into the *Revolvary*, where they run over little Catalogues of the minutest Passages of Life, and so in time never fail to hand on the thing; if not just when he calls for it, yet at some other time. (18)

This discussion of memory is a comic parody of the well-known passage in Augustine's *Confessions* that describes the memory as a "storehouse" where are kept "the treasures of innumerable images of all kinds of objects," some of which are brought out on demand, while others "require a longer search, and have to be drawn out as it were from more recondite receptacles."[34] Though comical, Defoe's adaptation of Augustine is not frivolous. What is most marvelous in it, at least to modern eyes, is the description of memory as a permanent repository of everything implanted in the mind, "even back to Infancy and Conception." Probing deeper into the mind, the traveller elaborates on the contents of this repository:

Next you have the *Retentive* in the remotest part of the Place, which, like the Records in the Tower, takes Possession of all Matters, as they are removed from the Classes in the Repository, for want of room. These are carefully Lockt, and kept safe, never to be open'd but upon solemn Occasions, and have swinging great Bars and Bolts upon them; so that what is kept here, is seldom lost. Here *Conscience* has one large Ware-house, and the *Devil* another; the first is very seldom open'd, but has a Chink or Till, where all the Follies and Crimes of Life being minuted are dropt in; but as the Man seldom cares to look in, the Locks are very Rusty, and not open'd but with great Difficulty, and on extraordinary occasions, as Sickness, Afflictions, Jails, Casualties, and Death; and then the Bars all give way at once; and being prest from within with a more than ordinary Weight, burst as a Cask of Wine upon the Fret, which for want of Vent, makes all the Hoops fly. (19–20)

The chambers of memory – particularly those two dark warehouses that we never look into – are repositories of guilt and sinful intentions, never acted upon but never forgotten. The second of these, the Devil's warehouse, is guarded by Pride and Conceit, which allow thousands of good deeds to pass by unremarked and unremembered; but within the warehouse, one finds many deeds "not only Deposited, but Planted, Transplanted, Grafted, Inoculated" and otherwise cultivated: "these are the most pleasant, delightful, and agreeable things, call'd Envy, Slander, Revenge, Strife and Malice, with the Additions of Ill-turns, Reproaches, and all manner of Wrong" (21). The passions in the Devil's warehouse are the source of the violent eruptions that manifest themselves as physical and mental illnesses. It is interesting that, for Defoe's lunar philosopher, the passions are not spirits that travel from the liver or spleen to the brain through the blood, nor are they voices, gases, sylphs, or any agents external to the body. Rather, they are non-material faculties of mind that can only be represented by metaphors. They are the treasures of a strongbox, the swarms of a beehive, the secrets of a library, the stores in a warehouse, the poisonous flowers of a garden cultivated by the Devil. It therefore follows that the Devil is also a metaphor, a wholesaler who panders to mankind's selfish nature. Harm comes to man not through the supernatural intervention of the Devil in human affairs, but through the ordinary operation of the passions, which the Devil keeps and cultivates.

Having raised the question of the Devil's work, the lunar philosopher launches into discussions of politics and religious schism, until finally he comes to the nature of the soul. On the moon, there are powerful glasses that allow such things as the soul – normally invisible – to be seen. Some philosophers, by means of these "explicative Glasses," have "pretended to give us the Parts; and we have heard of Chyrurgeons, that could read an Anatomical Lecture on the Parts of the Soul; and these pretend it to be a Creature in form, whether *Camelion* or *Salamandar*, Authors have not determin'd; nor is it compleatly discover'd *when* it comes into the Body, or *how* it goes out, or *where* its Locality or Habitation is, while 'tis a Resident" (92–93).[35] Though its habitation is said to be uncertain, the narrator locates the soul, "like a Prince, in his Seat, in the middle of *his Palace the Brain,* issuing out his incessant Orders to innumberable Troops of *Nerves, Sinews, Muscles, Tendons, Veins, Arteries, Fibres, Capilaris,* and *useful Officers,* call'd *Organici,* who faithfully execute all the Parts of *Sensation, Locomotion, Concoction,* &c" (93). When things go badly, and these orders are not faithfully carried out, "immediately other Expresses are dispatcht to the Tongue, with Orders *to cry out,* that the Neighbours may come in and help, or Friends send for the Chyrurgeon: Upon the *Application* and a Cure, *all is quiet,* and the same Expresses are dispatcht to the Tongue *to be hush,* and say no more of it till farther Orders" (94). This anatomy is written in jest, as a parody of Purchas, Browne, van Helmont, and other physicians who have tried to describe the soul, but it nevertheless re-enacts, as a defining moment in the macrocosmic and microcosmic life of man, a crisis in which the soul is thrown into a panic, the passions are perturbed, a surgeon is called for, and a cure is applied.

In addition to accidents of memory, *The Consolidator* speculates on the causes and cures of other mental pathologies, such as the capacity for "*Wilful Forgetfulness,*" or lying. The lunar philosopher declares that intentional forgetting is contrary to nature, "for that it is impossible for any Man to oblige himself to forget a thing, since he that can remember to forget, and at the same time forget to remember, has an Art above the Devil" (22). Like Gulliver's Houyhnhnm master two decades later, the lunarian finds it difficult to believe that humans have the ability to do something contrary to natural reason, which appears to give them powers superior to those of the Prince of Darkness. On the Moon, such accidents, whether intentional or not, are avoided through the use of a machine called the Cogitator. This machine allows the human subject to be wired directly to the objects of his thoughts, so that he cannot lose his concentration while thinking. The Cogitator would have been particularly useful in preventing some recent unfortunate incidents in history caused by political and religious passions: "This Engine prevents all sorts of *Lunacies, Love-Frenzies,* and *Melancholy-Madness,* for preserving the Thought in right Lines to direct Objects, it is impossible any *Delir-iums, Whimsies,* or *flattering Air* of Ideas, can interrupt the Man, he can never be Mad; for which reason I cannot but recommend it to my Lord S[underland], my Lord N[ottingham], and my Lord H[arley], as abso-lutely necessary to defend them from the State-Madness, which for some Ages has possest their Families, and which runs too much in the Blood" (107). Apart from the outrageous insolence of this passage – coming as it does from a man who had spent half of the year 1703 in Newgate prison at Nottingham's order, and was released only at Harley's – it is noteworthy for its proposal of a mechanical, rather than spiritual, means of regulating the passions. Of course, it is the lunarian speaking, not Defoe; even so, it smacks strongly of that skeptical (his biographer says "pessimistic") frame of mind toward humanity that Defoe showed at this time.[36]

Perhaps it was that skepticism – the fear that neither Galenist medicine, Stoic philosophy, nor Puritan theology could cure the troubled passions of his time – that led to a delay of a decade and a half before Defoe explored these nascent theories of mind in fiction. Another reason for the delay is that from the time of his release from Newgate in 1703 to the death of Queen Anne in 1714, and perhaps as late as 1717, Defoe was deeply engaged in political work for Harley and others, work that prevented his growth as a writer.[37] By the time these obligations had ceased, and he was free to resume the course of his early literary interests, his experience in political life had affirmed his conviction that it is neither angels that prompt man to goodness, nor demons that lead him to do evil, but the diseased condition of man's own willful nature. The cure, as Defoe had learned with the help of "natural historians of man" like Boyle, Baglivi, and LeClerc, is to be found not through the application of political or moral controls, nor through the use of mechanical devices or mechanistic philosophies, but by recording the origin and progress of diseases as they arise in this "revolvary," and untangling the complex interaction of rational will and irrational passion that composes the mind. As we will see in later chapters, the trope of the revolvary recurs in each of the major fictions – as the cave in *Crusoe*, the pit in the *Journal*, Newgate prison in *Moll Flanders*, and the daughter Susan in *The Fortunate Mistress*. Each of these repositories of memory and desire is entered, searched, and sounded, and in each case the narrator endeavors – with or without the assistance of counsellors, and with varying degrees of success – to distinguish the promptings of Providence from those of the Devil. The quality in which these fictional histories approach becoming "novels" in the modern sense is precisely in their probing exploration of that "retentive" dimension of the mind, that "Devil's warehouse" which sooner or later must be opened and its plaguey *pneuma* vented.

PROVIDENCE, THE PASSIONS, AND THE DEVIL

Perhaps the most difficult problem facing the narrators of Defoe's histories is to establish the extent to which their passions have been affected, either for good or for ill, by Providence or by the Devil. In one of the best-known examples, Robinson Crusoe discovers grain to be growing at the entrance to his seaside cave. His first response to the sight is that these stalks are "the pure Productions of Providence for my Support," and the thought brings tears of joy to his eyes and religious thanks to his mind (*RC*, 58). Upon reflection, however, he recalls that he had shaken out a sack of corn on the spot a month before, and his thankfulness begins to abate "upon the Discovering that all this was nothing but what was common." His third and final view on the subject, as he writes the narrative of his life, is that he "ought to have been as thankful for so strange and unforeseen Providence, as if it had been miraculous," because nature had provided for him in its common way, though not for him particularly (58). The question at stake in this incident is not whether he ought to feel joy and give thanks, but whether he ought to thank Providence for intervening in his particular situation, or to be joyful that it operates generally, according to natural law. In the time in which Defoe wrote, Puritan theologians were still attempting to determine whether the function of angels was to intervene, at God's direction, in the particular affairs of men and women in order to show them the way to grace, and the function of devils was to give them the opportunity to fall, in both cases by affecting their passions.[38] If Defoe were a Puritan in the spirit of Milton and Bunyan – or Richard Baxter or Increase Mather – he would have demonstrated unambiguously that those "secret impulses, notices of thought, pressing urgencies of inclination to or from this or that" that influence his characters at critical moments and help to determine their fates are the signs and means of particular providence at work.[39] If, however, his purpose was to offer an alternative to Puritan doctrine, he would have hedged on this question by representing Providence as natural law, which his characters may believe to be particular to themselves, but which is not absolutely affirmed in the text. The incident of the grain would in that case be neither "miraculous," as Robinson (and one of his critics) reads it at first, nor a sign of particular providence, but a proof of the providential design of nature to which man may, given experience and the time to reflect on it, accomodate himself.[40]

Defoe's relation to the debate on particular providence is of crucial importance in determining the function of the passions in his natural histories of man. If angels and devils determine the fortunes of mankind, then the passions are no more than their handmaidens; but if men and women are driven primarily by their passions to determine their own fates, then angels and devils are only metaphors for those passions. Rodney Baine has argued that Defoe did accept a version of particular providence, but he admits that Defoe was "troubled" by the Protestant doctrine of angelology, that his position was "unorthodox," that he was "inconsistent and sometimes vague" about the way angels are supposed to have intervened in human affairs, and finally that he "aligned himself with the philosophers like [Jean] LeClerc . . . against Milton and many other Protestant predecessors" on the question of the corporeality of spirits. Baine allows that, under the mounting attacks of rationalist theology and the advance of science, there was "a shift of opinion during Defoe's lifetime away from the belief in direct, physical intervention" by Providence in the affairs of men and women (23). Though Defoe endorsed the existence of guardian angels and devils early in his writing career, he later conjectured that "there are a certain middle species of spirits in being" who may appear to mankind; that these intermediate spirits may not be acting under God's direction; and that "angels center their ministry upon the mind and soul of men by apparition, voice, dream, and other, even more subtle media."[41] Clearly, if Defoe *did* accept the doctrine of Providence, he did not believe that it functioned as the Puritan fathers had held.

In fact, there is evidence that Defoe had quite another view of Providence. Defoe himself, throughout his essay on angelology in the third volume of *Robinson Crusoe*, speaks of "the notion of spirits, and their intermeddling with the affairs of men, and even of their appearing to men" as a belief appropriate only to biblical times, which "prevailed so universally in those ages of the world, that even God's own people, who were instructed from Himself, believed it," but that such beliefs were no longer maintained except by "vapourish, melancholy people, whose imaginations run this way."[42] Defoe maintained only that "God guides by his providence the whole world" and that "Providence manifests a particular care over and concern in the governing and directing man" as a species, not as individuals.[43] Providence speaks to us not by supernatural events, but through our fears, dreams, and desires, and "our duty is to study these things, to listen to the voice of them and obey their secret dictates" (III, 191). Jean LeClerc, with whom Baine says Defoe "aligned himself," disbelieved in the separate embodiment of spirits – that is, that either angels or the Devil appeared to man in any form – suggesting instead that whatever communications man receives from a spiritual world act upon him through the *pneuma*, an element in all living things that conveys spirits through the body. The implication of this pneumatological doctrine, however, is that Providence speaks to mankind not directly, but through the language of the passions, which the individual must examine for any providential import it may have. Insofar as Defoe aligned himself with LeClerc's theory of mind, then, he moved beyond the pale of Puritanism toward a rationalist, humanist, and psychological view of man.

If Defoe believed that Providence speaks through the passions, it follows that the Devil speaks the same language. His most important statement on the means by which the Devil affects the passions is *The History of the Devil*, which marks the end of his career as a writer of fictional histories.[44] As Baine points out (*Supernatural* 38), Defoe had promised in 1705 that the discovery of the part played by the Devil in human affairs would be one of the themes of his life's work, and in this book he distilled the psychological principles he had worked out in his fictions. Like Providence, the Devil intervenes in human affairs through the secret hints or promptings that Defoe's characters occasionally think they hear. However, just as Defoe doubts that Providence works through guardian angels, so he denies that there is an "attending *evil Angel*" who "is with you in every Action, prompts you to every Mischief, and leaves you to do every Thing that is pernicious to your self" (*HD*, 242). "Some tell us every single Man, every individual has a Devil attending him," writes the narrator, but "as to this Story of good and evil Angels attending every particular Person, 'tis a good Allegory indeed to represent the Struggle in the Mind of Man between good and evil Inclinations; but as to the rest, the best Thing I can say of it is, that I think 'tis a Fib" (*HD*, 242). The Devil never appears as a character in Defoe's histories, nor does any character stand for or represent the Devil, as might happen in allegory; rather, the Devil, or at least his legions, are *in* Robinson Crusoe or Moll Flanders or Roxana in the form of "intermediate spirits," or passions and affections, which appear to them in the form of voices, dreams, and hallucinations – apparitions that are rooted in their own imaginations. Nor is the Devil a single entity: just as the term "Providence" refers not directly to God, but to God's attributes in nature, so "Devil" is to be understood as *"a noun of multitude,"* referring either to Satan alone, or to *"Satan with all his legions* at his heels."[45] The Devil may appear in the form of apparitions, which may include "spirits assuming human Shapes" (*HD*, 358), or through dreams, which he enters by taking advantage of "the Treachery of the Garrison" within the fortress of the mind; once inside, "he opens and locks without a Key . . . in the Dark he gets in and parlees with the Garrison (the Affections and Passions), Debauches their Loyalty, stirring them up to Disloyalty and Rebellion, so they betray their Trust, Revolt, Mutiny, and go over to the Beseiger" (*HD*, 363).

The vulnerability of dreams to the Devil's infiltration is dramatised in a remarkable scene in the *History of the Devil* in which the narrator recounts the case of a friend who was "haunted" by sexual fantasies (360–61). This gentleman, "a Man of a virtuous Life and good Morals," dreamt virtually every night of "naked Women, fine beautiful Ladies in Bed with him, and Ladies of his Acquaintance too, offering their Favours to him." These sexual fantasies began after the man had been "really something freer than ordinary" in "common Conversation" with a beautiful lady of his acquaintance, after which, in his sleep, he "actually went about to debauch her, she not at all resisting; but that he wak'd in the very Moment, to his particular Satisfaction." The afflicted gentleman is convinced that the Devil had the "chief Hand" in his dream, but wants his friend, the narrator, to advise him on several points: whether he is guilty of adultery for willing the act, even in a dream; whether he is responsible for an incident prompted by the Devil; and how he should prevent it from occuring again. The narrator engages his friend in a dialogue through which the dreamer answers his own questions: he admits that he is guilty of adultery because the Devil could have had no reason to tempt him if he had not consented to it; he is therefore

responsible for the fantasies; and he can prevent them in the future by
bringing "his Mind to such a stated Habit of Virtue" as to make himself
invulnerable to "any wicked Motion, even in Sleep." The narrator notes
specifically that not "all my Divinity or his own [could] keep the Devil
from attacking him again" if his mind remained open to these desires; but
if the gentleman tamed his passions, he could cure himself of these nightly
visitations. The narrator does not propose to exorcise the man's disease
by any rituals or paraphernalia appropriate to casting out devils, nor even
by prayer; the disorder is located entirely within his fevered imagination,
and is to be cured, if at all, by dialogue, reflection, moderation, and
self-control.

As the gentleman's dream shows, neither good nor evil desires are
particular to any individual man or woman, but are natural and common
to all. The Devil "knows where the *Common Foible* lies, which is UNIVERSAL
PASSION, what Handle to take hold of every Man by, and how to cultivate
his Interest," warns the narrator of the *History* (236–37). It is "a great
Part of human Wisdom to know when the Devil is acting in us and by
us, and when not; the next and still greatest Part would be to prevent
him" from dominating our passions, "and bring a stronger Power to take
Possession" (*HD*, 401). The first step toward such wisdom is "to look a
little into the Microcosm of the Soul, and see there how the Passions
which are the Blood, and the Affections which are the Spirit, move in
their particular Vessels; how they circulate, and in what Temper the Pulse
beats there." If the "Affections are regular and exalted to vertuous and
sublime Objects, the Spirits cool, and the Mind sedate," the person is
secure from the Devil; but if "the Mind is ruffled, if Vapours rise, Clouds
gather, if Passions swell the Breast, if Anger, Envy, Revenge, Hatred,
Wrath, Strife" and other strong emotions are present, "the Case is easily
resolv'd, the Man is posses'd, the *Devil* is in him" (401–02). There is no
shame in such a discovery, because such disturbances are part of the fabric
of human nature. "[N]othing is more common . . . than for our Passions
and Affections to flow out of the ordinary Channel; the Spirits and Blood
of the Soul to be extravasated, the Passions grow violent and outragious,
the Affections impetuous, corrupt and violently vicious" (402–03).

Whence do such disturbances arise? By what handle does the Devil
take hold of every man and woman? When religious meetings dissolve
into the "Disputes, Wranglings, Strife and Contention" of Salters' Hall,
or when a virtuous gentleman is tortured by sexual dreams, "whose Door
must it lie at? Pride swells the Passions; Avarice moves the Affections; and
what is Pride, and what is Avarice, but the *Devil* in the inside of Man?"

What else can it be, and how comes it to pass that Passion and Revenge so often dispossess the Man of himself, as to lead him to commit Murther, to lay Plots and Snares for the Life of his Enemies, and so to thirst for Blood? How comes this but by the Devil's putting those Spirits of the Soul into so violent a Ferment, into a Fever? that the Circulation is precipitated to that Degree, and that the Man too is precipitated into Mischief, and at last into Ruin; 'tis all the *Devil*, tho' the Man does not know it. (403).

How comes it, indeed? This question – how the Devil, working through the passions, corrupts the natural goodness in every man, woman, and child – was the subject of Defoe's literary work for at least twelve years, from the first edition of *The Family Instructor* in 1715 to the second edition of the *History of the Devil* in 1727. That period includes all of the natural histories of fictional persons that we now refer to as novels, and to which we now turn.

CHAPTER 5

Crusoe in the cave: family passions in Robinson Crusoe

Why does young Robinson Crusoe leave his home? Why should a young man from a financially secure and loving family with good, if not great, expectations risk everything in an adventure sanctified neither by economic necessity nor by a vocation from God? This question, which probably troubles as many parents in our time as it did in the expansive world of Daniel Defoe, provides the readiest "way in" to Defoe's most complex, multivalent work of fiction. A search among critical studies of *Robinson Crusoe* turns up a variety of reasons for Robinson's departure, reasons that both reflect and condition each critic's reading of the entire work. For Ian Watt, Robinson leaves his home and family "for the classic reason of *homo economicus* – that it is necessary to better his economic condition."[1] For George Starr, Robinson's departure is an act of rebellion, an incarnation of man's original sin: "the episode seems to rest on an orthodox Calvinistic conception of man's innate waywardness and obstinacy."[2] For Maximillian Novak, Robinson's reasons are multiple, reflecting his personal characteristics: "his lack of economic prudence, his inability to follow a steady profession, his indifference to a calm bourgeois life, and his love of travel."[3] For Paul Hunter, Robinson's sinful act is the result of his "natural propensity to evil"; his life is "simply a battleground" on which the general struggle between good and evil takes place.[4] For Lincoln Faller, Robinson's flight is a criminal act, a violation of a code of social civility or sovereign power (as these terms are defined by Norbert Elias and Michel Foucault) which must be either punished or repented in the course of the genre of criminal biography.[5] For Leopold Damrosch Jr., Robinson's journey is an empty mockery of the spiritual quest in Bunyan's *Pilgrim's Progress*: the novel "resists any theoretical explanation that sees its meanderings as planned," and, as a consequence, fails "to develop an inner logic at all."[6] Most readings of the novel share the conviction that Robinson's departure is in some way a violation of reason or faith, a rebellion against goodness that must be set right by the end of his travels. In attempting to find a rational explanation for this act – or in faulting Defoe for the absence of one – critics have sometimes lost sight of the most distinctive insight of the novel: after twenty frustrating years of proposing, negotiating, and investing in various schemes, treaties, and projects for the improvement of mankind, Defoe had found that it is not the rational dimension of human life that is most in need of examination and remediation, but the irrational – the sway of passion over opinions, judgments, and characters.

It is true that the need to find a rational explanation for Robinson's departure originates in his own narrative. Robinson himself wants to understand his passion in rational terms, and he finds a means to do so in the language of repentance, through which, at the end of his life, he retrospectively interprets its significance. This "perspective of the end" presents an almost insurmountable problem for readers of the narrative: Robinson's memory of what happened is the subject of frequent re-interpretation in the light of subsequent events, which radically alters the significance of what is remembered.[7] If, in the years following his religious conversion, he describes his departure from home as a manifestation of mankind's "original sin," or as a fatal "Propension of Nature," his reason for doing so may be to locate the causes of his conduct in forces that lie outside his control, though at the time they lay within himself. By re-interpreting his life in Christian terms or in those of natural law, Robinson establishes a rational basis for his conduct and exculpates himself from blame by performing a ritual act of penitence. But we as readers are not bound to accept the terms of Robinson's interpretation, particularly when they are simply laid on at the end of a life, where they may obscure rather than reveal the real causes of the events of that life.

There is, in fact, only one way to account for Robinson's irrational conduct without imposing a rational system of value on it. This way is to read his life as a succession of acts of passion, as a contest between appetites and aversions in which mediocrity is seldom an option. Young Robinson's determination to leave home and see the world is one of those consuming desires in the breast that drives out every other consideration, including the countervailing desires that constituted authority privileges as "reason." Such desires, as we have seen, were regarded as sinful, unethical, or pathological by most thinkers in the long tradition of examining the passions, with the exception of Hobbes, the Epicureans, and some others, so it is not surprising that Robinson himself would express lifelong regret over his "Inclination."[8] The desires that drive him, however, appear to be natural to the Crusoe family, since they affected one or both of his elder brothers and even Robinson's father, who as a young man had emigrated from Bremen to seek his fortune in a foreign land. In struggling against these desires, Robinson is attempting to suppress elements – perhaps the best elements – of his own nature. If he at times seems a "psychotic" subject, he is most nearly so when those desires are in conflict with a system of belief or reason through which he is endeavoring to cure them.[9]

FAMILY PASSIONS AND *THE FAMILY INSTRUCTOR*

Before examining the passions of Robinson Crusoe, let us take another look at the dynamics of the family that produced him. As Maximillian Novak observed many years ago, it was in *The Family Instructor* that Defoe first developed characters who "seem to be overwhelmed by passions which complicate and intensify their relationships with their families and children."[10] The first volume of *The Family Instructor*, consisting of three parts, appeared in 1715 and was immediately popular; a second volume of two parts was published late in 1718. Each of the five parts is in effect a short story, combining narrative and dramatic dialogues to anatomize the structure and causes of a family quarrel. In each part, the quarrel is resolved through talk: one of the participants is taken aside by a friend or another family member and forced, through dialogue, to reflect on his or her conduct. Though many contributing causes of family strife are uncovered – a young girl's infatuation with romance novels, a husband's insistence on his wife's attendance at family prayer, a youth's desire to pursue a more adventuresome career than his father has designed for him, a father's anger at his son's dilatory performance of an errand – the constant factor in all these quarrels is passion. Passion is cited repeatedly as the reason that disagreements escalate to quarrels; it is metaphorized several times as the handle by which the devil takes us, without which he could have no hold. Though passion plays a role in both volumes, it is more significant in the second volume, in which extreme passions and a lack of religious instruction are generally found simultaneously in the family; it is as if, between 1715 and 1718, Defoe had discovered that instruction is useless without regulation of the passions.[11] The opening pages of the second volume, for example, set out in third-person narrative the causes of one family's troubles:

The husband, provoked by some rash words of his wife's, and especially by her speaking slightly of his performing family worship, takes the worst method in the world with himself, flinging away in a passion, without calling his reason, or conscience, or duty to his assistance; and having not called his family together to morning prayer, as was before his constant practice. In this fury he walks out into a field near his house, where he had the advantage of conversing with himself without being heard; and his passion being not much abated, as you may suppose, he fell to reasoning himself out of his duty, instead of into it, and to forming the arguments to justify his laying aside the thoughts of it for the future.[12]

Under the effects of this passion, the husband reasons himself out of performing the "ceremony" of family prayer, an unfortunate decision that leads to further quarrels between himself and his wife and finally to a "lethargy" of spirits in her, a "confirmed melancholy" resembling madness, from which she never fully recovers. When the husband confesses the whole affair to a friend, the friend lays the blame for his wife's illness on the husband's failure to manage his passions:

Your great mistake has been, that you went out into the fields, as you said, and consulted with your enemy; had you looked into your own conscience, or into the word of God, the faithful counsellors of all that sincerely consult with them, you would have found the difference; you consulted your passions, your resentment, and the just cause you had to be angry; and the devil, who watches all advantages, took you by the right handle; so you argued yourself out of your duty, instead of arguing yourself into it. (43)

It is interesting that this "friend" is able to bring the husband to penitence, and to restore the family to at least a semblance of its former order, when neither of two men who are physicians of the mind by virtue of their training is able to help. One of them is the wife's uncle, who is also a Christian minister; he lives with the family for four months, laboring the entire time to reconcile the wife to her husband, and concludes his visit with a sermon, addressed to both parties. The wife, however, rejects her uncle's didactic religious instruction, and some time later falls into a languishing melancholy. Her husband then consults a physician, who "often attempted to speak to her, but found she would not answer a word, or if she did, it was either to desire him not to trouble her, or something remote from what he said, for she was too much stupified by the distemper to talk, and unwilling to discourse when she was otherwise" (69–70). Neither the minister nor the physician is able to engage the passions of the wife, which is where the trouble lies, and so both are ineffective. The wife, in time, makes a partial recovery, but everyone is careful not to remind her of her affliction for fear of a relapse, and the husband has learned a lesson about his own passion, which "has cost me very dear" (72).

There are many such small psychodramas in *The Family Instructor*, but let us clear up one point before moving on: the failure in the preceding dialogue of the appointed physicians of the mind. If, as this book suggests in other chapters, Defoe is the heir of a narrative tradition passed down from the Stoics via Galen, Robert Burton, and others, in which a physician of the mind intervenes in cases of disturbed passions, why does he seem to throw it away in a book on the regulation of conduct? In fact, he does *not* discard the principle, only the establishment of the office in either ministers or physicians. Defoe desacralizes the office by giving it to the husband's friend, a layperson, to emphasize an important point about God's grace: the real physician of record in such a case is Christ, from whom alone salvation may come. That same husband explains Christ's primary role in the healing process in a subsequent dialogue with his rakish brother-in-law, Sir Richard, who is skeptical that grace could be extended to such a sinner as he. The husband tells Sir Richard the gospel story in which Christ is rebuked by the pharisees for not healing them, but tending instead to publicans and prodigals. "*The whole need not a physician*," Christ replies to the pharisees, which, as the husband explains, means that "Christ came as the physician, to heal those who were most dangerously sick; to justify such publicans as durst not go up to the temple to pray; to receive such prodigals as were yet afar off."[3] Christ does not heal pharisees, but rather those most in need of God's grace, the sinners who, like Sir Richard, "have run such a horrid course of all kinds of wickedness." Sir Richard rejoices, with some prophetic imagery: "Methinks I am like one shipwrecked, and that being sunk twice in the water, is taken by the hair of the head by some kind unlooked-for hand, just in the moment as he was sinking the last time, and brought up into a boat and set on shore" (171).

Whether the dialogues in *The Family Instructor* deserve Novak's term "psychological realism" or not may be debated. The operation of the passions in those dialogues may appear stilted and artificial to modern readers. But no one can dispute the emphasis that Defoe puts on psychological elements in the two volumes of that work, particularly the second. Religious instruction is necessary, but it only works on those whose passions have first led them into sin, and whose sense of guilt has been sufficiently aroused to interest them in the possibility of receiving grace. Those who, like the wife in the first dialogue, are unable to believe in grace are likely to sink into despair and irremediable madness. Like Sir Richard, the best case for examining the relation of passion and grace is the prodigal who has gone furthest astray; he is a shipwrecked sailor, castaway yet saved, who must work out his own salvation by first ordering his own disturbed habits of mind. Defoe's growing fascination with the cure of disturbances of the passions, which he appears to have discovered in the course of writing the second volume of *The Family Instructor*, would reach its fullest expression in *The Life and Strange Surprizing Adventures of Robinson Crusoe*.

THE PASSIONS OF THE CRUSOE FAMILY

The troubled family in *The Family Instructor* presents some interesting similarities to the Crusoe family at the beginning of *Robinson Crusoe*. The Crusoe family is ruled by a patriarch who was something of a merchant adventurer in his youth, having emigrated from Bremen, made his fortune, married an English woman of good family, and obliterated his origins by Anglicizing his name.[14] He is now known to his neighbors as a "wise and grave man," but his success as a merchant suggests that in his youth he must have participated in that dialectic between passion and virtue that shaped the emerging European economy, which John Pocock has described as a "mobile, somewhat Hobbesian, universe in which every object was potentially a source of either profit or loss, a subject of both hope and fear."[15] When Robinson approaches his father with his plan to go to sea, the father refuses "very warmly," but "earnestly, and in the most affectionate manner," to approve the scheme.[16] The elder Crusoe offers many rational arguments in favor of "the Blessings attending the middle Station of Life," but the strongest proofs are the tears that "run down his Face very plentifully" when he speaks of Robinson's elder brother who was killed (6). Robinson is unmoved by the arguments, but "sincerely affected" by the tears, which cause him to put off his departure for several weeks. Eventually, however, his desire to leave overcomes his affection for his father, thus setting up a pattern of competing affective states that continues throughout his history. His departure, at the end of a full year of negotiations with his parents, is not a rebellion against his father's authority, but rather a re-enactment of his father's own youthful passions.

In view of the family dynamic revealed in *The Family Instructor*, it is useful to examine what role passion plays in the final rupture of the Crusoe family. Where Robinson's father has been firm in his refusal, he has used no passion (other than grief) in his arguments, but Robinson's mother cannot restrain herself. We get a hint of his mother's temperament when

Robinson tells us that he tried to approach her "at a time when I thought her a little pleasanter than ordinary" with a request that she intervene for him by conveying a compromise proposal to his father. Robinson's proposal, however, "put my Mother into a great Passion," in which she refuses to assist him, rebukes him for making a request of which his father had already disapproved, and in effect withdraws her affection and support (6–7). Though muted in the memory of the mature Robinson as he writes his memoirs, the angry scene in the Crusoe household clearly made an impression on the young man.

Robinson's departure from home is, therefore, less an act of rebellion or disobedience than an expression of that overreaching desire with which romances (and some histories) have traditionally begun, and which sustains such stories until the passion has been gratified, punished, or cured. Robinson's almost objectless desire dominates the contradictory passions to which he is exposed in his early travels, such as the fear induced by the storm he experiences at sea or the dreadful warnings of the master whose ship sinks off Yarmouth; though he hears the master's direful prediction of disasters to come, which is spoken in "a strange kind of Passion," he pays no attention to it at the time (11). Instead, his reason obeys his desires, and like the husband in the *Family Instructor*, he reasons himself out of his duty instead of into it. Faced with a decision between returning home and going again to sea, he chooses to persist only out of fear of being laughed at by his neighbors. From the perspective of the end of his travels, the elder Robinson comments that "I have since often observed, how incongruous and irrational" the temper of youth is "to that Reason which ought to guide them in such Cases" (13), but of course he is incapable of making any such reflection at the time. Instead, his desire for adventure is fed by other passions, such as the acquisitory lust he feels upon the success of his first voyage to Guinea, and he resolves upon "the most unfortunate of all Enterprises," a slaving voyage to Guinea, from which his subsequent misfortunes arise.

His shipwreck some four years later on an island in the Caribbean, which perforce puts an end to his lusts both for wandering and acquiring, provides him with the opportunity to reflect on the connection between passion and error. In the natural setting of the island, he experiences a wider range of human emotions than he had formerly known. After his initial despair, he learns to feel joy at his survival, grief for his missing companions, and wonder that he alone was spared. He is by turns miserable, fearful, hopeful, grateful; through a process that some critics have attacked as an inconsistency of characterization, Defoe takes

Robinson through nearly every passion known to man, even – as we will see – something akin to sex. If Defoe were a proponent of natural law, as Rousseau seems to have wanted him to be, Robinson's education in the passions would have resulted in a natural balance, the result of a growing harmony with his surroundings; if he were a Puritan, "defining nature," in Damrosch's words, "as a fallen realm that cannot be man's true home," he would have had to achieve grace by denying the natural passions in himself.[17] In fact he does neither, but uses both the natural world and his Bible to cure his troubled soul. To describe the events that take place on the island solely as the product of nature or as a religious conversion is to miss the psychological complexity of the experience, the dimension that marks *Robinson Crusoe* as a distinctly modern work.

ROBINSON AND THE INTERPRETATION OF DREAMS

The psychological depth of Robinson's narrative is evident in an illness that occurs during his first year on the island. The illness takes the form of a "strong Distemper," accompanied by a violent fever. The fever brings on delirium, a state in which consciousness is distorted and made strange to itself; in this state, whether induced by fever, art, music, or stimulants, the disturbance of the passions from their usual course allows us a new perspective on ourselves – a moment at first frightening, but later revelatory of new possibilities. Robinson blurts out cries for help that signify the confused state of his passions; in a properly instructed person, these cries might have been prayers, but in him they are only the sounds of fear and distress (66–67). On the third evening, he thinks of remedies for the distemper that he has heard were used by the native Brazilians, indeed the only one: tobacco.[18] In an act that the post-conversion Robinson tells us was "directed by Heaven no doubt," he opens his chest to find his tobacco, where it is packed with his Bible (69). Not knowing how to prepare the tobacco, he is forced to experiment. He first chews a leaf, "which indeed at first almost stupify'd my Brain," then steeps some in rum, and finally inhales the fumes of some leaves burned in a pan. While waiting for the tobacco to steep in the rum, he tries to read the Bible, but finds "my Head was too much disturb'd with the Tobacco to bear reading"; all that he can manage is single verse, *Call on me in the Day of Trouble, and I will deliver, and thou shalt glorify me* (Psalms 50: 15), which made "some Impression" on his thoughts at first, "tho' not so much as they did afterwards" (69). The impression is sufficiently strong to cause him to repeat the passage by his bedside as he retires, which he follows by quaffing the strong brew of rum and tobacco. The vapors of the medicinal dose "flew up in my Head violently," but also "doz'd my Head so much, that I inclin'd to sleep," a deep sleep that lasts until the next afternoon, or perhaps the day after, from which he wakes much refreshed (69–70). For several days thereafter "I renew'd the Medicine all the three Ways," doubling the quantity, and he is soon well, a deliverance for which he thanks God (71). Robinson tells us that he had found in the chest "a Cure, both for Soul and Body" (69). The narrative is deliberately ambiguous, however, on the crucial question of whether it was the tobacco or the Bible that cured him.

Robinson's vagueness on the latter question is a reflection not of artistic looseness, but of one of the finer points of Defoe's narrative technique. The reader, given the interpretive clues that Robinson provides, would ordinarily suppose that he means that the Bible cured his soul, while the tobacco cured his body, but that equation is never drawn. The text leaves open the possibility that it was the tobacco that cured the passions of his soul, or, even more significantly, that Defoe's formulation of the cure rejects the Cartesian dualism of body and soul in favor of a naturalistic and, we might say, unitarian concept of personhood: that is, body and soul being one thing, a single regimen cures both. If this cure, in which both material and immaterial elements abound, were meant to depict a religious conversion, it would be a strangely heretical one. Like many latter-day converts, Robinson exhibits in his journal a zealous attachment to his faith, but the way in which Defoe has structured the incident reveals a profound skepticism of the adequacy of a cure based on faith alone.

It will be helpful to examine in passing what Defoe meant by the word "cure," which he uses twenty times in various forms in the first volume of *Robinson Crusoe*.[9] The word can refer to the relieving of an illness, as when Robinson remarks that the use of tobacco to bring down a fever was an "Application" which was "perfectly new," and was perhaps "what had never cur'd an Ague before" (72); but more often it refers to a process through which something is transformed from a raw to a more refined state. Thus when he first arrives in Brazil, Robinson purchases "as much Land that was uncur'd, as my Money would reach" (27), and when he harvests his first crop of tobacco, he rejoices that it yields fifty rolls that weighed one hundred pounds each, "well cur'd and laid by against the Return of the Fleet from *Lisbon*" (29). The tobacco that he uses to relieve his fever is of two kinds, some "which was quite cur'd, and some also that was green and not quite cur'd" (69). Among his first discoveries on the island are the abundant clusters of grapes, which make him ill in their raw state, but which he found "an excellent Use for," which is "to cure or dry them in the Sun, and keep them as Grapes or Raisins are kept," (73), or eventually make them into wine. Thus, to "cure" for Robinson (and Defoe) means to improve the condition of something that is dangerous or useless in its raw state, but palatable and healthful when refined by human arts. The cure of the passions for Defoe, as we will see, is of this latter sort.

If the cure of Robinson's fit of ague draws on the text of Psalms 50: 15 for its spiritual element, we might ask if it draws on an equivalent text for its medical authority. Though Robinson attributes his tobacco cure to the lore of the Brazilians, the source text could well have been a treatise on tobacco appended to Tobias Venner's *Via Recta ad Vitam Longam* (1637), the book previously cited as a source for father Crusoe's praise of "mediocrity" as a cure for the excesses of passion.[20] This treatise of twenty pages declares tobacco to be "of much antiquitie and reputation among the Indians of America." With respect to its qualities as a drug, "it is hot and drie in the third degree, and hath a deleteriall, or venomnous qualitie, I suppose: for it being any way taken into the body, it tortureth and disturbeth the same with violent ejections both upward and downward, astonisheth the spirits, stupifieth and benummeth the senses and all the members" (345–46). These effects are "best perceived upon the taking of the fume at the mouth: for thereupon followeth a drunken-like lightnesse of the head, and . . . a benumming sleepinesse of the limbs and senses." The Indians inhale the smoke, says Venner, "against all diseases, especially such as are gotten by cold, or that proceed from a cold and moyst cause" – such as, we might note, the rainstorm that precedes Robinson's fever. But the Indians also take it in combination with drink, a practice of which Venner disapproves, since "by this their preposterous and unreasonable mingle-mangle of smoak and drink, farre more crudities and superfluities are bred, than can by vertue of the fume be consumed or excreted" (352). The Indians take tobacco not only to prevent disease, but also for its psychological effects: it produces in them "a drunken-like lightnesse of the head, and thereupon sleep, with sundry phantasmes or visions," from which they awake "greatly eased, and refreshed," and able to presage the future based on the visions they have had (347). Robinson is not able to tell the future, but his experience with tobacco resembles that of the Indians in all other respects, and it assists him in seeing into the meaning of the prophetic passage from Psalms.

If Robinson is ambivalent about whether it was the tobacco or the Bible that cured his illness, he is equally uncertain about the origin and

meaning of dreams. At the beginning of the illness narrative that cul-
minates in his spiritual awakening, Robinson has a dream that contains
a terrible vision. In this dream, he sees the figure of a man "descend
from a great black Cloud, in a bright Flame of Fire, and light upon the
Ground: he was all over as bright as a Flame, so that I could but just
bear to look towards him" (64). The man has a countenance "most in-
expressibly dreadful"; when he steps on the ground, the earth trembles,
and the air is filled with flashes of fire. He moves toward Robinson over
rising ground, carrying "a long Spear of Weapon in his Hand, to kill
me"; he seems to speak, or at least Robinson heard "a Voice so terrible,
that it is impossible to express the Terror of it"; his words are not intel-
ligible, but Robinson assigns to them the meaning ("all that I can say I
understood, was this") that he is to be killed for having failed to repent.
The vision arouses "the Horrors of my Soul" in Robinson, impressions
which remain even after he has awakened and realized that it was only
a dream.

The penitential Robinson, writing his memoirs from the perspective
of the end of his adventures, implies that the dream was divine in origin,
and numerous readers of the narrative have accepted his interpretation
of this "terrible Vision" as an encounter with an angel or messenger
of providence.[21] But such supernatural readings of the incident ignore
the fact that Robinson's experience is entirely natural; the text provides
no evidence that the vision was anything more than a projection of
Robinson's fevered imagination, brought on by his illness, his dehydra-
tion, and his consumption of tobacco.[22] Defoe scrupulously avoids com-
promising the realism of his narrative by having the vision take place,
for example, during Robinson's waking hours. Furthermore, while the
words that Robinson believes he heard sound vaguely scriptural (*"Seeing
all these Things have not brought thee to Repentance, now thou shalt die"*), there is
in fact no such passage in the Bible.[23] It is not Scripture, not God, not
Providence, not an angel, and not Robinson's father that speaks; it can
only be the "Revolvary" of Robinson's unconscious guilt and desire that
produces this terrible vision.

The fact that the vision is not supernatural, however, does not deny its
power or psychological validity: on the contrary, by frightening Robinson
into a thorough examination of his spiritual state, the dream forces him
to integrate his recent experiences into an expanded sense of personality,
and it raises questions for him about himself that he can not ignore. Several important commentators have called Robinson's dream the "turning
point" or "pivot" of the narrative, but they barely acknowledge that this

crisis is reached in Robinson's first year on the island, with twenty-seven years and three quarters of the book yet to go.[24] If Robinson's dream is a turning point, the balance of the book must complete in some sense a process begun, rather than concluded, by the dream. To a degree not generally appreciated, the second and third quarters of the history depict a carefully structured progression through which Robinson first investigates and then rationalizes the passions revealed by his dream.

This structured progression begins well before the dream, with his survival of the shipwreck. Robinson had felt extremes of both joy and grief at his singular escape from the waves; he likens the "Extasies and Transports of the Soul" that he feels to those of a convict reprieved at the foot of the gallows, which could kill him unless a surgeon is called "to let him Blood that very Moment they tell him of it, that the Surprise may not drive the Animal Spirits from the Heart, and overwhelm him" (35). The joy felt by Robinson at his deliverance soon gives way to fear, and it is interesting, in view of Venner's comments on tobacco and melancholy, that he appears to smoke a pipe of tobacco while reflecting on his desperate predicament: "I had nothing about me but a Knife, a Tobacco-pipe, and a little Tobacco in a Box, this was all my Provision, and this threw me into terrible Agonies of Mind, that for a while I run about like a Mad-man" (36). After recovering his spirits overnight, he sets about bringing stores ashore on his raft, a landing which, as one critic has noticed, he describes in explicitly sexual terms: he guides his raft into "the Mouth of a little River, with Land on both Sides, and a strong Current or Tide running up," into which he "could thrust her directly in," taking care not to spill his cargo, "and thus I lay 'till the Water ebb'd away, and left my Raft and all my Cargoe safe on Shore" (38–39).[25] As a realistic description of sexual experience, Robinson's landing leaves something to be desired, but as a metaphorical enactment of the libidinous pleasure felt by a survivor, the passage is interesting indeed. Within his first twenty-four hours on the island, Robinson has experienced the emotions of joy, fear, and sexual release, all soon to be replayed in his dream.

The dream is further conditioned by two threatening incidents, each of which serves to raise his passions after they have been lulled into an illusion of security. Shortly after getting his goods on shore, Robinson is alarmed by "a Storm of Rain falling from a thick dark Cloud, a sudden Flash of Lightning ... and after that a great Clap of Thunder" (45). Robinson fears that the lightning may blow up his gunpowder, taking himself and his goods with it; his fear causes him to make practical improvements in his shelter, but the psychological effects of the incident are not forgotten. The second incident occurs after he has completed digging out his cave: an earthquake threatens to bury him in the cave with all his goods, "the Noise of the falling of the Rock awak'd me as it were, and rousing me from the stupify'd Condition I was in, fill'd me with Horror, and I thought of nothing then but the Hill falling upon my Tent and all my houshold Goods, and burying all at once; and this sunk my very Soul within me a second Time" (59–60). As before, his conscious response is a practical one – moving his shelter into a walled enclosure – but again the impressions are stored up in what Defoe had once called "Nature's strong Box, the Memory, with all its Locks and Keys" (*Consolidator*, 18–19).

When, some months later, Robinson has his visionary dream, we can easily recognize in it these same impressions, transformed into metaphors by both desire and guilt – the desire to survive, and guilt at having done so. Defoe knew very well that dreams originate in visual and auditory experiences during waking hours: one of his "correspondents" in *Mist's Journal* writes that "[i]t is, I think, beyond all doubt that Dreams are generally the Effect of the Day's Thoughts, especially of such Thoughts, as we have fixed deepest in our Minds"; these thoughts, which can include loud noises or strong smells, become "Apparitions" under the influence of "Fear and Imagination," and a "disturbed animal Faculty."[26] As for the specific content of dreams, Defoe's "correspondent" suggests that "the Nature and Difference of Dreams is chiefly to be attributed to the particular Complexion; as Cholerick, Melancholick, &c" – in short, they are dependent on the subjective characteristics of the dreamer, not on divine or supernatural agents. In his dream, Robinson experiences again the dark storm cloud, the blinding flash of lightning, the trembling of the ground caused by the earthquake, and the threat to his life posed by the stores of gunpowder. The unintelligible voice that Robinson hears in the dream may be the thunder, or the wind of the hurricane, or the anticipated noise of the explosion, or it may even be the repressed memory of the dire prediction pronounced by the ship's captain at Yarmouth, who blamed Robinson for the loss of his vessel, and who told him, "with a strange Passion," that he should go back to his father, *"And young Man, . . . depend upon it, if you do not go back, wherever you go, you will meet with nothing but Disasters and Disappointments till your Father's Words are fulfilled upon you"* (13, emphasis in the original).

This interpretation of Robinson's dream helps to explain subsequent events of the narrative, which rises and falls in cycles that replicate the

process of raising the passions, taming or emasculating them, and re-
integrating them into the self in ways consistent with Robinson's unconscious desires. This cyclical pattern of the action has been criticized
by some as episodic, and its form is admittedly more naturalistic than
conventionally dramatic.[27] But if it betrays Defoe's lack of grounding
in dramatic form, it also reflects the interest of natural historians of his
time in finding correspondences between the natural world and the mind,
correspondences which are more likely to be detected through empirical
observation than through rational theory. The point is brought home
to Robinson in an incident that provides a metaphor for understanding
the rhythm of the entire middle section of the book. When Robinson
attempts to escape from the island in his canoe, he is nearly swept out to
sea, and he experiences that sharp sense of loss that signifies the raising of
the passions: "Now I look'd back upon my desolate solitary Island, as the
most pleasant Place in the World, and all the Happiness my Heart could
wish for, was to be but there again. I stretch'd out my Hands to it with
eager Wishes. O Happy Desart, said I . . ." (101–02). When a contrary
current returns him to shore, he thanks God for his deliverance, and
resolves not to make the attempt again. Some readers are moved to cynicism, then, when they find, not many pages later, that Robinson is once
again contemplating a voyage around the end of his island, evidently
having forgotten both his thankfulness and his resolution. If the moral
concerns of the book were limited to Robinson's discovery of his duty to
God, the skepticism of these readers would be justified; as we have said,
however, the work is also about the rising and falling rhythms of the passions, and the process through which Robinson discovers the means for
managing them. In the weeks after the first incident, Robinson's passion
for venturing overpowers both the fear and gratitude he had felt in his
fortunate escape. In his second attempt, however, his passion is tempered
by experience. Approaching the outflowing current with more caution,
Robinson "resolv'd to spend some Time in the observing it, to see if nothing from the Sets of the Tide had occasion'd it" (109–10), and finds that,
by careful timing, he might sail around the point in safety. Though reason
tells him "[t]hat I had nothing to do but to observe the Ebbing and Flowing of the Tide, and I might very easily bring my Boat about the Island
again," nevertheless "a Terror upon my Spirits at the Remembrance
of the Danger I had been in" prevents him from making the attempt
(110). Not the fear of God's punishment, but respect for the memory
of his former terror is the source of Robinson's prudence. In allowing
Robinson to observe the tides and see in them a correspondence with

his own rising and falling passions, Defoe seems to be recalling William Wotton's praise of the physicians who followed Hippocrates' diagnostic method in observing the symptoms of illness. Wotton described them as "scrupulously exact in . . . taking notice of their Times and Accidents, thereby to make a Judgement how far they might be esteemed dangerous, and how far safe."[28] Like a physician learning to read the body of his ailing patient, Robinson learns how to read the island's body, and by analogy to cure the passions of his mind.

ROBINSON, THE GOAT, AND THE CAVE

During the course of some twenty more years on the island, Robinson lulls himself into a sense of security, even sovereignty over his Edenic condition. The only voice that he now hears in his dreams is that of his parrot, whose "bemoaning Language" reminds Robinson of how he had used to speak of himself (104). In this state, in which his passions seem to have ceased to exist, he "had now had enough of rambling to Sea for some time, and had enough to do for many Days to sit still" (104). But the happiness that results from "this Government of my Temper" (104) is finally broken by the discovery of a footprint in the sand, which releases all the frightened imaginings and irascible passions that he thought he had put under control. He is "exceedingly surpriz'd" by the print, he suffers "innumerable fluttering Thoughts, like a Man perfectly confus'd and out of my self," and his affrighted imagination fancies an enemy behind every tree (112). At first he fears that the Devil has visited his island; then he realizes that "it must be some more dangerous Creature," that is, a man (113); finally he rebukes himself for letting his new religious sensibility put him off his guard (114). For two or three days, Robinson suffers the affections of hope, fear, belief, and unbelief; measuring his own foot against the print, he finds it "not so large by a great deal," which "fill'd my Head with new Imaginations, and gave me the Vapours again, to the highest Degree; so that I shook with cold, like one in an Ague" (115). His fear drives him to spend two years improving his security; that done, fear ripens into an extraordinary fit of anger at the "Savages," which brings him to the point of murder. The weary preparations for an attack, however, give him time to reflect on his anger, and he discovers that it has led him into error: he admits that "my Passions were at first fir'd by the Horror I conceiv'd at the unnatural Custom of that People of the Country," (123), and that such passions are not acceptable as reasons for attacking them. Robinson does not, however, abandon his military preparations; as he reflects, he gradually replaces his "Thoughts of Revenge" with a plan to save one of the intended victims of cannibalism, thereby securing for himself a "pilot" who can help him navigate through the currents to the mainland. This plan is perfected in another dream, which seems to have become the mechanism through which Robinson's unconscious desires enter his consciousness. Over the course of several years, then, Robinson has moved from fear, anger, and rage – a state in which he was, as Hobbes said, at war with mankind, and with himself – to reflection, the realization of error, the retrieval of his desires from the "revolvary" through dreaming, and the transformation of anger into ethical action – a process that suggests that his desires have become integrated into his conscious mental life, and are now directing his steps. He has not achieved this mastery of himself, however, through the imposition of either civil or ecclesiastical law, but through the cure of his passions.

Though the cure of Robinson's passions is a gradual and inconstant process, there is an incident that more or less signals its end, in that the incident reverses the images that, some twenty years before, had filled Robinson's survival dream. It is worth noting that the incident happens at a time when Robinson's passions are still aroused by the discovery of the footprint, as they had been earlier by his experience of shipwreck, survival, illness, and tobacco. In a state of mind that Robinson describes as "very Melancholy," he resolves to explore the interior of the island, in search of a safe retreat.[29] Following the "secret Intimations" that "direct us this Way, when we had intended to go that Way," Robinson arrives at the mouth of a hollow at the bottom of a rock, covered by a tangle of underbrush (128). In a scene which, like his arrival on shore with his goods, is rich with unconscious sexual imagery, he discovers "a kind of hollow Place; I was curious to look into it, and getting with Difficulty into the Mouth of it, I found it was pretty large; that is to say, sufficient for me to stand upright in it" (128). He retreats hastily from the cave, however, when he sees the "two broad shining Eyes of some Creature, whether Devil or Man I knew not" looking back at him. He breaks into a cold sweat, his hair stands on end, and he withdraws in a panic. But after calming himself by thinking that "there was nothing in this Cave that was more frightful than my self," Robinson takes up "a great Firebrand, and in I rush'd again, with the Stick flaming in my Hand." He hears a very loud sigh, "like that of a Man in some Pain," followed by "a broken Noise, as if of Words half express'd" and another deep sigh. Like the words in Robinson's dream, the source and meaning of these noises is deliberately ambiguous: they might have come from the goat, or possibly even from Robinson himself, in the echo of his own prayers, or a sudden release from sexual tension. At the end of the cave, by the light of his torch, Robinson finds "a most monstrous frightful old He-goat, just making his Will, as we say, and gasping for Life, and dying indeed of meer old Age" (129).

The hermeneutic possibilities of this scene have tantalized critics of the book for years. The disembodied eyes of the beast that Robinson encounters in the cave seem to evoke some biblical or mythological connection, and Robinson himself thinks at first that it may be Satan.[30] But once he has discovered the natural cause that lay behind his superstitious fears, he seems determined to attach no transcendental significance to the goat.[31] After trying to rouse it to its feet, in the hope that he may be able to use it to frighten off the cannibals, he ignores it while exploring the rest of the cave. Returning to the cave the next day and passing the goat without comment, he creeps through a narrow passageway into a high vaulted room whose ceiling seems to sparkle with a hundred thousand lights reflected from his torch, as if it were covered in diamonds and gold. In the security of this chamber, Robinson fancies himself "one of the ancient Giants, which are said to live in Caves, and Holes, in the Rocks" (130). When he emerges from the cavern, he discovers that the goat has died, and, in a phrase reminiscent of his recollection that he had run away from his father's house "to prevent any of my Father's farther Importunities" (6), he unceremoniously buries the goat "to prevent the Offence to my Nose" (130). If the goat at one point raised Robinson's fear of the devil, it is now just so much rubbish.

Rather than fixing a symbolic meaning on the goat, contrary to the clear spirit of the text, we might better examine the way that the encounter between Robinson and the goat completes the narrative process that began with Robinson's survival dream. If we can for a moment imagine Robinson's entrance into the cave from the goat's perspective, we can see that he must appear to the goat very much as the man of fire had appeared to Robinson many years earlier in the dream. Just as the fiery figure had stood above him on rising ground with a long spear or weapon in his hand, and had spoken to him some unintelligible words that seemed to signify that he had come to kill Robinson, so in the cave Robinson advances toward the dying goat, holding his firebrand in one hand and his gun in the other, mumbling some broken words that might be prayers or exclamations, but which would be unintelligible sounds to the goat.[32] Though Robinson appears not to recognize the

"Robinson Crusoe terrified at the dying goat," engraved by Charles Heath (1785–1848) after a drawing by Thomas Stothard (1755–1834) for *The Life and Adventures of Robinson Crusoe, Embellished with Engravings from the Designs by Thomas Stothard, esq.* (London: T. Cadell, 1820).

resemblance, the scene in the cave is the mirror image of his dream, in which he has become the fiery figure, and the goat has become him. The goat functions for Robinson, as it did for Galen, as a metaphor for those passions which, like "the wild boar and goat and any of the wild beasts . . . cannot be domesticated," and must finally be destroyed.[33] The threatening words in the dream, *Seeing all these Things have not brought thee to Repentence, now thou shalt die*, seem to take on new meaning: it is not an angel or parent speaking to Robinson, or even a distorted memory of the prophetic ship's captain, but Robinson speaking to his own wild and uncured self, the one dominated by its fears and libidinous desires. The reversal of roles that occurs in the cave corrects the distortions of the dream and allows Robinson to discard the primitive self, driven by animal and infantile passions, that he had brought to the island.

In the larger context of Defoe's writing career, Robinson's experience in the cave recalls Defoe's paraphrase in *The Consolidator* of the passage on memory in Augustine's *Confessions*. In that work, Augustine describes memory as a "huge cavern, with its mysterious, secret, and indescribable nooks and crannies," where sensations and images are deposited "to be recalled when needed and reconsidered."[34] In this cavern of memory, "[t]here also I meet myself and recall what I am, what I have done, and when and where and how I was affected when I did it . . . I combine with past events images of various things . . . and on this basis I reason about future actions and events and hopes" (186–87). The cave functions for Robinson as it did for Augustine, a place where images from the past can be not only stored, but recalled and re-examined for significances they may have gained (or lost) in view of subsequent events, and through which a different kind of self may be reconstructed. Ideas and affections that once disturbed the mind can be recalled as images in the memory and re-ordered; it is this process of ordering images, says Augustine, that makes man a thinking being and gives him control over his concupiscent self (189).

In another sense, however, *Robinson Crusoe* is a very different – a much more modern – work from Augustine's *Confessions*. From the moment Robinson emerges from the cave, the signifying power – the ability to determine the meaning of a providential sign – rests entirely with him. Robinson's passions, like Augustine's, are still with him, and still troublesome, but he has acquired the power to re-signify them in a way that Augustine would have considered heretical. When, for example, he dreams of, and then witnesses another visit by the cannibals, he takes the intrusion not as an occasion for anger, but as permission to rescue one of their victims ("I was call'd plainly by Providence to save this poor Creature's Life," 146), and so to effect his escape from the island. This translation of a desire into a providential sign is the first instance of what is to become a dominant pattern in the balance of the first volume, and throughout the continuation, of Robinson's history. That is not to say that Defoe considers Providence irrelevant to human fortunes; in the preface to *Robinson Crusoe*, he counsels the reader to find a "religious Application" in the story, and to "justify and honour the Wisdom of Providence in all the Variety of our Circumstances, let them happen how they will" (3). But there is usually a natural, or, as we might now say, psychological basis for these "secret Intimations" through which Robinson becomes aware of his unconscious desires, with the result that they are always under his control. Rather than an intervening presence in Robinson's world, Providence is an absence, a blank space whose meaning remains to be signified – for good or for ill – by his individual sensibility.

The modernism of *Robinson Crusoe* is reflected in the fact that recent criticism has sought to describe Robinson's regeneration on the island in terms of the Oedipal process, through which the child separates itself from the parents' authority.[35] While the use of modern psychoanalytic terms extends the meaning of the text in interesting ways, it also can be misleading. The possibility that *Robinson Crusoe* contributed to the subsequent formation of theories of the unconscious cannot be ignored, but to find the meaning of the text in these terms is to suggest once again that Defoe's psychological system was insufficient in itself to sustain the narrative. The premise of this chapter is that *Robinson Crusoe* is an important work not because it led to the formation of psychoanalytic theory, but because it offered a way out of two major crises of the late seventeenth century: the collapse of humoural physiology, with its attendant struggles between rationalism and empiricism, and the factionalism among Christians over doctrinal issues such as the nature and function of the Holy Spirit, or the existence of angels, devils, and particular providence. Robinson's dream, which otherwise hangs as an unfulfilled prophecy, is the initial moment in a process through which the passions are explored in turn and found to have a place in the nature of man. Between the dream and the cave, Robinson encounters the master passions – anger, fear, and desire – and masters them in himself. Just as the fiery figure he associates with Providence is a projection of his own fears and guilt, so the sense of indivdual sovereignty that guides him after his emergence from the cave is a product of his developing moral sensibility. If anything, *Robinson Crusoe* looks forward not to psychoanalysis, but to Francis

Hutcheson's notion of a moral sensibility founded on the benevolence of passions that have been cured of disease, and to Adam Smith's vision of a society based on the controlled employment of the passions, directed by individual self-interest.[36]

The great weakness of Robinson's cure – and of Defoe's handling of the passions generally – is this very individualism. There is no friend, no physician, no minister or counselor to require Robinson to distinguish between his desires and his delusions. When in his relations with Friday, Friday's father, and the Spaniard he fails to distinguish between himself and the other ("I was absolute Lord and Lawgiver; they all owed their Lives to me, and were ready to lay down their Lives, *if there had been Occasion of it*, for me," 174); when he makes sharecroppers of his colonists ("I shar'd the Island into Parts with 'em, reserv'd to my self the Property of the whole," 220); and when in his future travels he reverts to anger, vengeance, and violence, however justified, it is all too plain that Robinson's cure is not complete. He neither subjects himself to the regulation of a "guardian," as Galen had counseled his patients to do, nor does he extirpate passion – except, perhaps, fear – from his heart. Instead of completing the cure in this way, he substitutes intermittent recriminations directed as much at the reader as at himself. In view of the imperfect cures presented by the narrators of the histories we will look at in the next chapter, it seems likely that Defoe was aware of this shortcoming in Robinson, and that he understood that the price of individualism is the incurability of passion.

CHAPTER 6

The sinner, the saddler, and the brewer's wife: three case studies in desire

Of all the illness narratives in English literature since Burton's *Anatomy of Melancholy*, perhaps none is so justly famous as Defoe's *A Journal of the Plague Year*. Defoe's interest in the plague, both as a public emergency and as a severe test of the ability of mankind to maintain its rationality and morality in the face of an implacable adversary, began with reports in his *Review* on the progress of the plague in eastern Europe in 1711 and 1712, continued with his frequent warnings in *Mist's* and *Applebee's Journal* of its appearance at Marseilles in 1720 and 1721, and culminated in a treatise, *Due Preparations for the Plague, as Well for Soul as Body*, early in 1722.[1] Many of these journalistic pieces contain vivid representations of the disease, and *Due Preparations*, like the *Family Instructor*, employs narratives and dialogues that are largely the fruits of Defoe's imagination. None of these efforts, however, attained literary distinction until Defoe unified detail, narrative, and dialogue by centering them in an individual consciousness, a technique that he had mastered, if not perfected, in *Robinson Crusoe*. In the *Journal of the Plague Year* Defoe explores the classical division of a single consciousness into rational and irrational souls: one that feels a sense of duty toward the affairs of the world, and another that feels grief, fear, and morbid curiosity in the presence of danger and death.

To a degree not previously appreciated, two other of Defoe's books usually read as "novels" are, like the *Journal of the Plague Year*, illness narratives. In *The Fortunes and Misfortunes of the Famous Moll Flanders*, also published in 1722, Defoe focuses his attention on cupidity, a disease of the concupiscent soul, which is abetted in Moll's case by her lack of a mother. In the story of *Roxana*, or *The Fortunate Mistress* (1724), he writes the history of a case of hysteria, or a paralysing fear brought on by the denial of one's self and one's past, and he evinces a radical skepticism about whether the pathological effects of such passions can be cured. Each of these narrators – the saddler H. F., Moll Flanders, and Roxana – is driven by a desire whose object is unknown, unattainable, and irresistible to its subject. Unlike a story in which the protagonist desires a specific object external to himself or herself, which would provide the basis for an epic or a romance, the history that interested Defoe was one whose protagonist feels a desire for an object which he or she cannot name – except, perhaps, in retrospect – and who struggles, with varying degrees of success, to master or manage the passions aroused by this desire. Such stories – ones in which the apparent irrationality of the absent object of desire brings the narrator close to, or pushes her into illness – interested Defoe because they took him deeper into that warehouse of the mind, that revolvary of memory and dreams that he had uncovered in *The Consolidator* at the beginning of his career as an author. Each of his narrators pursues this desire into a dark repository of memory and fear and, like Robinson Crusoe, finds an elemental passion there, which the modern world knows as the self, but which the ancients knew as the Devil.

"A TERRIBLE PIT IT WAS": CURIOSITY IN *THE PLAGUE YEAR*

If the initiating action of *Robinson Crusoe* is the narrator's desire to leave home, that of the *Journal of the Plague Year* is the desire to stay. The narrator of the *Journal*, a saddler who signs himself "H. F.," is a man both *in* the world and yet *above* it, in Defoe's sense of the term; as a tradesman, he is engaged in the affairs of the world, but his success in those affairs places him above the economic necessity that limits the freedom of some of Defoe's other narrators. When the plague returns to London in the first weeks of the year 1665, H. F. is free to leave the city, as many others of his class did – to shut up his house, entrust his business to his "Family of Servants," and save his life by retiring to the home of his sister in Lincolnshire.[2] H. F. worries that his trade will not be safe in the hands of his servants, but his elder brother counsels him strongly to flee, satisfying even his religious scruples on that point. He resolves several times to leave, and is put off each time by a trifling obstacle, which could easily be overcome: there are no horses (but he could leave the city on foot); his servant leaves him (but he could get another); his sense of duty troubles him (but his brother laughs that away). Each time he resolves to go, as he tells us, "one way or another, I always found that to appoint to go away was always cross'd by some Accident or other" (10). These "accidents" are not without cause: they arise, or assume the significance that they do for the narrator, because they allow him to obey his hidden, almost inadmissible desire to stay. This desire is inadmissible because it is irrational, particularly in the world of business to which the narrator is accustomed; but because it is irrational, a product of his irascible soul, it is more powerful than any of the reasons for going that can be ranged against it. His case is the mirror image of Robinson's: where that young man had every reason to stay, or to turn back once he had left, he found a way to turn every sign into an endorsement of his desire to go; where H. F. has every reason to go, the "strong Impressions which I had on my Mind for staying" and "Intimations which I thought I had from Heaven, that to me signify'd a kind of Direction to venture" his safety in the afflicted city persuade him to make the irrational decision to stay (10). These "Impressions" and "Intimations," it is clear from the text, originate in his desire to witness the full horror of the epidemic; though he attributes them to heaven, they have no source but his own curiosity.

The tension between rational and irrational impulses that marks H. F.'s decision to stay continues to affect him throughout the plague year in London. "Business led me out sometimes" to the end of town that was afflicted with the plague, says H. F., speaking as a man of reason and worldly affairs; yet on one of these trips, "Curiosity led me to observe things more than usually; and indeed I walk'd a great Way where I had no Business" (16–17). Curiosity is the desire to know without object – to know what one has no business or reason to know. Curiosity was frequently included among the passions in the eighteenth century, though, as Alan McKenzie points out, it was "one not found on most classical lists."[3] Curiosity is sometimes cited in *The Spectator* as a cause for investigations of a questionable (yet sympathetic) nature, such as Mr. Spectator's conversation with a young prostitute; later in the century, curiosity would be described by David Hume as a passion contributing to the love of knowledge among the young, and by Samuel Johnson as a passion disposing a contemplative mind to take in new objects.[4] As the admissibility of certain passions rose in the eighteenth century, so did the moral standing of curiosity; in Defoe's day, it was an emotion more appropriate for a tradesman than for a gentleman to feel. The limited form of curiosity to which H. F. admits is circumscribed by a rational skepticism that prevents him from sharing the specious beliefs of the common people, whose curiosity knows no restraint. His skepticism is best illustrated in the well-known incident in which he stands amongst a crowd, looking up as they do at the sky. "I join'd with them to satisfy my Curiosity," he tells us, but where they all see an avenging angel of death, he sees only a white cloud lit by the sun (22–23). The difference between H. F. and the common people is that they "were terrify'd, by the Force of their own Imagination" (23);

they supplied the absent object of their fears and desires by imagining it, which the rational soul of the saddler does not permit him to do.

This inadmissible passion – this curiosity – is repeatedly cited in the text as the cause of his venturing into places where he has no business to go. When at the beginning of September he hears of a great pit dug in Aldgate parish to receive the dead, he makes an exception to his policy of staying within doors, because "a terrible Pit it was, and I could not resist my Curiosity to go and see it" (59).[5] About one week later, H. F. returns for another look: "It was about the 10th of September, that my Curiosity led, or rather drove me to go and see this Pit again, when there had been near 400 People buried in it" (60). His interest is not that of the historian or the surveyor, who might be satisfied merely with recording the place or size of the pit: he must needs see the bodies being thrown in, which he can do only at night. What he wants to measure is the effect of the horrible pit on his mind, and what he finds is a sight that exceeds any measurement: "it was indeed *very, very, very* dreadful, and such as no Tongue can express" (60). Defoe makes it perfectly clear that H. F.'s desire lacks an object in the usual sense: much as Robinson Crusoe had been drawn out of curiosity to the cave, and found in it that he was the source of his own fears, H. F.'s fascination is with himself, his own affective responses to a terror beyond words. The sexton of the churchyard endeavors to dissuade him, telling him that those engaged in burying the dead might hope to be preserved, since it is "their Business and Duty to venture, and to run all Hazards," but that "I had no apparent Call to it, but my own Curiosity," which is not sufficient to protect him (61). Despite this clear warning, H. F. follows his desire to know, rather than his reason not to, and ventures into the churchyard.

What he finds there surpasses even the horrors he had anticipated. It is not the mass of bodies that holds his attention, but the grief of a single man, whom for want of a name we may call the man of sorrows.[6] This man functions in the narrative much as the goat does in Crusoe's cave, and is described in much the same manner. He is muffled up in a brown cloak, so that his human shape is barely discernable; he makes the random, aimless motions and noises of a creature in agony, and the buriers think he is mad: they suppose he is "one of those poor delirious, or desperate Creatures, that used to pretend, as I have said, to bury themselves; he said nothing as he walk'd about, but two or three times groaned very deeply, and loud, and signed as he would break his Heart" (61). His grief is caused by the death of his wife and children, all of whom now lie in the dead cart, which "he followed in an Agony and excess of Sorrow" (63). He is a walking paradigm of pain, which he bears in a stoic manner until his family is tumbled into the pit, upon which he "cry'd out aloud unable to contain himself" (63). He faints, and when he recovers his senses, his family has been covered with earth; there is nothing of them to be seen, despite the candles that ring the pit. The buriers take him to a nearby tavern, where he becomes the object not of pity, but of jeers and taunts from a "dreadful Set of Fellows" who make their sport of mocking mourners (64). Brought face to face with the man of sorrows, the mockers are at first angry at the innkeeper for admitting him; they then "turned their Anger into ridiculing the Man, and his Sorrow for his Wife and Children" (64). The scene is a powerful study of both the stoic acceptance of grief, on the one hand, and the effects of denial on the other: the mockery of the fellows proceeds directly from their refusal to regard death with awe, or to acknowledge their fears of it, leading them instead to vent their passions on the miserable object whose grief is a flat contradiction to their blasphemy.

Even more interesting than the effect of the man of sorrows on the blasphemers is his effect on the narrator. H. F. cannot forget the man's grief after he leaves the graveyard, and, driven by a curiosity that he cannot resist, he follows the man to the tavern. There he witnesses the abuse under which "the Man sat still, mute and disconsolate" (65). H. F. intervenes, "gently" reproving the impudent men, who immediately turn their anger on him. "I kept my Temper," H. F. assures us, and he summarizes the discourse that he used to persuade the men out of their angry passions, but the results were not what he had hoped for. "I cannot call exactly to Mind the hellish abominable Raillery, which was the Return they made to that Talk of mine" says the disappointed saddler (65), but he remembers that it was full of "horrid Oaths, Curses, and vile Expressions," including further blasphemies and "devilish Language" (66). Finding that his rational discourse has had no effect on their unreason, H. F. confesses that "it fill'd me with Horror, and a kind of Rage, and I came away, as I told them, lest the Hand of that Judgment which had visited the whole City should glorify his Vengeance upon them, and all that were near them" (66). Since H. F. elsewhere denies that the plague can be a punishment or judgment upon particular persons, but is rather the hand of God working through Nature upon all persons equally (75, 194), his prophecy of doom upon the blasphemers suggests the degree to which his own judgment has been affected by his anger at them and his sympathy for the man of sorrows. It is evident that he speaks his last words to them in an angry tone, the only time he admits having lost his temper. After a period of reflection, he acknowledges that "I had indeed, been in some Passion, at first, with them, tho' it was really raised, not by any Affront they had offered me personally, but by the Horror their blaspheming Tongues fill'd me with" (69). He feels a "Weight of Grief upon my Mind," caused by his doubt "whether the Resentment I retain'd was not all upon my own private Account," rather than on the purer motives of religion. In the course of praying to God to pardon these men, he puts his heart to a trial, and is satisfied that his angry out-burst was caused by resentment of their insults not to him, but to "God and his servants" (68). To the readers, H. F. recommends this method of delay and self-examination in order that they may "distinguish between their real Zeal for the Honour of God, and the Effects of their private Passions and Resentments" (69).

Defoe's appreciation of the ambiguous relationship between the pas-sions and moral action is underscored by a secondary character in the *Journal*, a philosopher/physician named Dr. Heath.[7] Dr. Heath is described by H. F. as "a very good Friend, a Physician . . . who I fre-quently visited during this dismal Time" (77). Because Heath "was a good Christian, as well as a good Physician," the saddler looks to him for moral counsel as well as advice on methods for preventing infection. Early in August, "Dr. Heath coming to visit me, and finding that I ven-tured so often out in the Streets, earnestly perswaded me to lock my self up and my Family, and not to suffer any of us to go out of Doors" (77). This advice is sound both medically and morally, since it tends to protect H. F.'s family as well as himself, and he endeavors for a time to follow his doctor's counsel. He lays in provisions for brewing and baking "which seem'd enough to serve my House for five or six Weeks," making it un-necessary for him to go out (77). Yet we find that, before the end of the month, "tho' I confin'd my Family, I could not prevail upon my unsat-isfy'd Curiosity to stay entirely within my self; and tho' I generally came frightened and terrified Home, yet I cou'd not restrain; only that indeed, I did not do it so frequently as at first" (80). One of his outings – the visit to look in on his brother's house – has a certain legitimacy, but the other – the visit to the Aldgate churchyard at the beginning of September – has no necessary motive behind it. When he returns on September 10 to see the bodies being dumped at night, it is clear that his curiosity is more powerful than his physician's moral and medical advice.[8]

The saddler's unauthorized visit to the churchyard, much like Robinson Crusoe's discovery of the hidden cave, uncovers in him both a sensibility to suffering and an irrational soul beneath his stoic and rational exterior. In both stories, the narrator enters into a vast area of darkness, a domain of the dead, drawn in by his curiosity and no other reason. He experiences fear, followed by anger or resentment at the object supposed to have caused it; but on reflection he discovers that those passions arise in himself, not in the object, and that discovery becomes a treasure for him. Henceforth the saddler, like Crusoe, if not quite the master of his emotions, is at least able to distinguish between courses of action that arise in legitimate moral reasons, including a sense of duty to God, and those that proceed from superstition, fear, and other pollutants of judgment. He still has his curiosity, and the capacity to be frightened; unlike other people, however, who "began to give themselves up to their Fears" (171), the saddler uses the intervals between his terrifying rambles in the city to write memoranda about proper steps to be taken in the event of future epidemics (76). This moral action redeems, in some measure, his earlier indulgence of curiosity at the expense of morality, and suggests that Defoe believed that our passions may sometimes lead us on courses whose moral ends – to say nothing of their immediate objects – are not visible to us at the time.

Once the course of the narrative has been set by the saddler's visit to the Aldgate churchyard, the journal proceeds – with greater unity of purpose than is usually accorded it – to document the ways in which the plague raises the passions of the afflicted city and the means by which those passions, if not the disease itself, may be cured (using the word as Defoe used it in *Robinson Crusoe*, to mean refined or improved by art). H. F.'s curiosity is stirred not so much by the disease as by the passions that are freed by it, which seem to pose a greater threat to civility in the city than does the plague itself. He sees the irrational greed of men and women released from ordinary moral constraints by these extraordinary times: "the Women were in all this Calamity, the most rash, fearless, and desperate Creatures" (84), a general observation given particularity when the saddler visits his brother's house and finds the women of the neighborhood helping themselves to hats from the warehouse. After considering the consequences of "showing my Resentment," H. F. contents himself with taking down their names and asking them "how they could do such Things as these, in a Time of such general Calamity" (88). Similarly, while on an outing to the Post-House, H. F. observes an impromptu pantomime between fear and avarice over a bag of money lying in the street that no one is willing to touch. The bystanders say they are reluctant to pick it up because "they did not know, but the Person who dropt it, might come back to look for it" (105), but the saddler knows that the reason is their fear that it might be infected. As if to confirm his suspicion, one man goes through an elaborate procedure involving red-hot tongs, gunpowder, and a pail of water to recover the money. And there is also the anecdote of the waterman, whom the saddler discovers when he walks down to the landing at Blackwall, "for I had a great mind to see how things were managed in the River, and among the Ships" (105). The waterman is an exception to the fear that grips the city and makes everyone mindful only of self-interest; he risks his life every day to earn a few shillings for the support of his infected family, an unambiguous act of goodness that bears no trace of self-service or personal gain, and serves as a standing rebuke to all the citizens, watchmen, physicians and clergy who desert their duty to the city during the crisis.[9]

Just as the onset of the worst stages of the disease in H. F.'s parish is marked by the warnings of Dr. Heath to stay indoors, so it is Dr. Heath who forecasts the lifting of the disease at the end of September. "I remember my friend Doctor Heath coming to see me the Week before, told me, he was sure that the Violence of it would asswage in a few Days," says H. F., who doubts the prediction because the bills of mortality are higher than ever before (224). The doctor's prophecy, however – which depends neither on supernatural means of knowledge nor on a belief in providence, but on rational calculations based on the increasing length of time that his patients take to die, and the increasing number who recover – proves correct: "accordingly so it was, for the next Week being, as I said, the last in September, the Bill decreased almost two Thousand." As the plague begins to lift, "the audacious Creatures were so possess'd with the first Joy" (227) that they lose the fear of the disease that had saved many of them before, with the result that the epidemic begins to revive. The saddler's passion for knowledge has been "cured" at the end of his narrative – that is, his curiosity has been gratified and he has drawn some useful conclusions about human nature from the behavior he witnessed during the pestilence – but "the very common People" (247) seem to have reflected little and learned less about themselves from their close encounter with death.

"MY COLOUR CAME AND WENT": CUPIDITY IN *MOLL FLANDERS*

Moll Flanders marks several significant advances in Defoe's natural history of the passions, one of which is his connection of events in childhood to the character that his heroine exhibits as an adult. It is not the only time

Defoe would cut against the grain of early eighteenth-century fiction by paying close attention to childhood: as T. G. A. Nelson shows, Defoe had made a six-year-old boy the "hero" of *The Family Instructor*, and would later develop the lost innocence of childhood as a backdrop for *Colonel Jack*. In both that book and in *Moll Flanders*, however, Nelson thinks that Defoe "still seems diffident about pursuing too relentlessly the still unfashionable subject of childish hopes and fears," with the result that his account of childhood is "rudimentary."[10] Rudimentary or not, we still learn enough about Moll's childhood to understand how her passions as an adult, an obsessive secrecy and a cupidity both for money and for love, are rooted in the formative experiences of her youth.[11]

Born in Newgate prison to a convicted felon and taken as an infant from her mother, Moll becomes the ward of an "old Gentlewoman" and aspires to that station in life herself, rather than to a life in service.[12] She is given small gifts of money by other gentlewomen who find Moll's ambitions amusing, and gradually larger gifts of money by the men who find her attractive. The result of these repeated gifts is an association in her mind between money and love, which represent the attention she receives by giving pleasure and the pleasure she receives by getting attention. Like Robinson, her growth as a person is not linear, but passes through cycles of expansion and contraction: the gifts of money and attention encourage her concupiscible passions, inciting both vanity and lust; the moments of fear, which occur when she is reminded of her tenuous social standing as an orphan and a servant, bring a contraction of her desires, followed by an even greater longing (14–15). By the time she is eighteen years of age, her concupiscence has ripened into cupidity, a state of inordinate lust for love or money, which in Moll's case is the same thing.[13]

Despite Nelson's reservations, it is possible to push even farther the analysis of Moll's "childish hopes and fears." We must ask why Moll feels such intense pleasure at acquiring money, and the text hints at an answer. Moll loses her mother when she is six months old, and she feels very strongly the absence of a maternal figure in her life. We can glimpse her insecurity in the adverbial way she tries to convert her nurse into a mother: "my good Motherly Nurse," she calls her (10), and later "the good Motherly Creature" (11), and finally "my good old Nurse, Mother I ought rather to call her" (14). The terms in which Moll describes this relationship express both her desire for a mother, and her awareness that this nurse, though a good and honest woman, is not her mother. The lost mother becomes an absent object of desire that sparks a passion identical to the wandering impulse that drives Robinson Crusoe to leave, or the curiosity that compels H. F. to stay at home. Since she cannot fill this absence with a mother, Moll substitutes money instead, as indeed she is taught to do by the ladies who visit her at the parish school, and by the women in her foster home who teach her airs above her station (11–14). Money provides a temporary and material satisfaction for Moll, but since it is a substitute for her real need, the hunger always returns. The love of money and the fear of losing it, or the attention it signifies, become a passion for Moll, one she cannot satisfy no matter how much money she acquires. Moll's sense of necessity is always before her, even when her material needs have been satisfied, which suggests that "necessity" for Moll is not economic, but psychological.

This sublimation of love into money explains Moll's relations with the family in Colchester that takes her in when her nurse/mother dies. Her standing in the family is ambiguous: she is nominally a servant, yet their own encouragement of her pretensions to gentility confuses the distinctions of class that govern her identity. She receives the attentions of the elder brother not unwillingly, particularly after he rewards her with five guineas on one occasion, and "almost a Handful of Gold" on another (20–21). The arousal of Moll's passions by money is plainly evident: she is "confounded" by the guineas, "so elevated, that I scarce knew the Ground I stood on." Later, in a ceremony that surrogates for the marriage he cannot give her, the elder brother presents her with a silk purse filled with a hundred guineas, and again Moll reacts with an involuntary physiological response: "My Colour came and went, at the Sight of the Purse, and with the fire of his Proposal together" (24). Her blushes and palings reflect the expansive and contractive movements of her passions as she feels lust, both for the man and the money, and fear of the social and moral taboos she is about to break. In this first affair, replete with the trappings of romance – secret notes passed in the garden, intrigues involving coaches and back lanes – Moll's innocent affections may still be engaged more by love than by money; but before it is over, she learns to be suspicious of love. The learning occurs when the younger brother makes her an honest proposal of marriage, which she cannot refuse without betraying her prior, secret relation with the elder brother. The elder brother advises her to marry the younger, saying that she may by this means "come into a safe Station" in life, to which Moll replies "angrily" that she believed herself already married to him (31). Just as young Robinson found his passion for life blocked by the parental offer of a safe but mediocre station, so Moll finds her passion for the elder brother being brokered into a "maintenance," to which her acceptance of his gifts of money has already committed her.

Moll's passions – which include anger, love, lust of several sorts, and a persistent sense of fear – are wrought to their highest pitch at this moment. She "burst out into such a Passion of crying" that the elder brother, "sensibly mov'd" at her tears, tries "to abate the excess of my Passion," but cannot promise her the main thing, which is marriage (33). Marooned within herself, Moll cannot open her heart to the mother in the family, whom Moll had at first called "my new generous Mistress" (15) but now calls the "old Lady" (37). Like Robinson Crusoe, who suffered an ague soon after arriving on the island, Moll falls ill with a fever that lasts for five weeks, which her physicians are unable to explain in medical terms. They do indeed decide that "my Mind was Oppress'd, that something Troubl'd me, and in short, that I was IN LOVE" (34), but in that diagnosis they guess only a portion of the truth. The reader knows that her illness results from her inability to declare her love for the elder brother, aggravated by her inability to vent her passions to a physician of the mind – in particular, to a mother. In the end, Moll is forced to marry the younger brother, the elder paying for her silence with £500, in exchange for which he asks that her passion for him "may be buried and forgotten" (44). In thus denying her love (much against her desire), Moll completes the process of sublimating passion into money that she had been drawn into as a child, a process which the absence of a mother in her life had materially assisted.

Though Moll has "buried" her passion in the revolvary of her memory, as the elder brother had asked her to do, she has not forgotten it; she lives "very agreeably" with the younger brother, but she commits "Adultery and Incest [with the elder brother] every Day in my desires" (47). As is often remarked, she also feels nothing for the children she has from this loveless marriage, regarding them only as an obstacle to the gratification of the material desires that have taken the place of love in her life. Her new cynicism is evident when, after the death of her first husband and the bankruptcy of her second, Moll picks out for her third husband a Virginia planter who believes her to be wealthy. Though she approves of the goodness of this man's temper, affection forms no part of her choice of him; she values his goodness only because she believes that, unlike "some fiery tempered Wretch," he will not harm her when he discovers that she has deceived him (64). She entraps him through his incautious protestation of love for her as they cap each other's sentiments, a romantic streak in him that she recognizes as a weakness. The elements of her courtship of him are calculation, negotiation, and duplicity – an ironic mirror image of the techniques of seduction used on her by the elder brother. When for example she lets her husband know by degrees that she has deceived him about her fortune, she gloats that "I had hook'd him so fast, and play'd him so long, that I was satisfied he would have had me in my worst Circumstances," and when he knows the worst, "he could not say one word, except that indeed he thought it had been more" (65). Moll's cupidity, which began with a desire to fill the absence of a mother, is deepened and confirmed into a cynical materialism by her first, second, and third marriages, a cynicism that comes to include mothers and motherhood as well as lovers, husbands, and children.

The great irony of Moll Flanders' story, of course, is that she does, by accident or providence, find her lost birth mother. Being convinced by her third husband that they would be richer in Virginia, Moll consents, as she puts it, "to be Transported" (64). Once there, she finds that her new mother-in-law is "too kind a Mother to be parted with," and soon comes to refer to her as "my Mother" (68). Through a sign burned in her mother-in-law's hand that disturbs her world as much as the footprint in the sand disrupted Robinson's, Moll finds that this mother is her mother indeed, and that Moll's husband is her own half-brother. Instead of the joyful reunion that might be expected from her discovery of the long-sought object of her desire, Moll is driven deeper into the isolation and secrecy that cupidity has taught her. Confronted with Moll's inexplicable coldness, the "good humour'd" husband becomes "strangely alter'd, froward, jealous, and unkind"; he threatens to confine her in a mad-house, suspects her of having another husband alive, and accuses her of inventing a quarrel "as the effect of my Passion to put him in a Passion" (74–75). He falls ill when Moll hints that their marriage may not be legal, and when she tells him – after obtaining written guarantees that he will "do nothing in a Passion" – that he is her own brother, he attempts to hang himself (81–82). Her husband's attempted self-destruction mirrors and reverses Moll's fever when she learned of the trick played on her by the elder brother in Colchester, and this time Moll determines not to be, as she formerly had been, the fool of passion. Moll resolves the conflict by exchanging her mother, brother, and children for "a very good cargo" (82) and passage to England, thus continuing the syndrome through which she substitutes money for love.

The cost of Moll's cupidity, however sympathetic we may find her as a narrator, is a diseased, incestuous relationship with all of the men in her life. The "compleat Gentleman" she meets at Bath, for example, has a genuine affection for her; he claims he cannot marry Moll because he has a wife, who is "no Wife" to him because she is mad, but he formalizes his relationship with Moll through a ceremony in which her entire stock of wealth is mingled with a handful of his, a ceremony that replicates the substitution of money for love wrapped in secrecy that began with the elder brother and continued with the Virginia planter. Moll lives with this man for six years and bears him three children, of which one survives; yet they are never close, and Moll studies "to save what I could . . . against a time of scarcity" by laying up money (93). When he throws her off after recovering from an illness, Moll pursues him through letters and disguised visits, much as Roxana's daughter will pursue her, until she finally extorts a settlement from him and sends him back a "general Release" from all claims (99).

There is only one man in her life to whom Moll does not relate through money, though this relationship too begins on that footing. James, her Lancashire husband, courts Moll under the mistaken assumption, given him by his "sister," that Moll is a rich widow. Moll likewise believes that he is a wealthy landowner with an estate in Ireland. After they are married, the mistake is discovered, whereupon James "flew out in the most furious Passion that ever I saw a Man in my Life" (115), directed not at Moll but at the spurious sister. When he confesses to Moll that he also has no money, she is moved to sympathy rather than anger at the "double Fraud" (116). As in her previous marriages, she mingles some of her money with his, though in this case it is not fortune but misfortune that they share. His poverty allows her to reflect on his personal qualities: he is "a truly gallant Spirit," "really a Gentleman" though "unfortunate and low," and "a lovely Person indeed; of generous Principles, good Sense, and of abundance of good Humour" (118). For the first time in her life, with the possible exception of the affair with the elder brother in her adopted family, Moll feels something like love. She has not invited the affection, but been surprised into it by deceit – the only circumstance, we may assume, under which a dominant passion may be supplanted by a gentler one. On waking the next morning, she finds that he has left her a note and some money in her pocket, which causes her to protest that she "would have gone with him thro' the World, if I had beg'd my Bread" (120). Numerous critics, beginning with Ian Watt, have cited this incident as proof of Moll's hypocrisy: Watt regards Moll's protest as "a rhetorical hyperbole," and builds on it his case that Defoe, lacking a sense of irony, was unaware of the "contradictions and incongruities that beset man in this vale of tears" (*Rise of the Novel*, 130–31). But in fact the scene is richly ironic: Moll, having finally been tricked into feeling the passion that has eluded her all her life – a love not mediated by money – has been forced back into materialism by her lover, who substitutes money for his own presence. That which she has done to others all her life has now been done to her, and the pain that she feels is precisely one of cosmic irony.

The matter of whether Moll's irony is accidental or intentional is no longer the compelling question it was once thought to be. What is compelling – what should have *always* mattered – is the crisis represented by the confusion of Moll's passions. Moll is caught between two affections, one for James as her lover, and one for money, in which she has always found comfort. Upon her choice between these two passions depends both her personal salvation and the dramatic resolution – whether comic or tragic – of the story. Her cry to her absent lover, "*O Jemy!* said I, *come back, come back*, I'll give you all I have" (120), contains a glimmer of repentance for having concealed from him the bulk of her small estate. The moment represents an epiphany for Moll, a sudden springing-open of what Defoe had called "Nature's strong Box" in which are lodged "things past, even back to Infancy and Conception."[4] James, of course, returns to Moll; though he was several hours out of her hearing when she discovered her loss, he swears he heard her calling. The significance of the incident depends not on whether some unconscious or supernatural communication has taken place, but on its effect on Moll: for the first time in her life, she is able to express a passion without concealing it from herself or others. Through the pain she felt in the loss of the penniless James, she has been forced to admit to herself that it was the man she needed, not the money.

The final stage in Moll's process of self-discovery comes in Newgate prison, the place where she had originally lost her mother. Much as the cave frightened Robinson with its suggestions of a re-entry into the mother and a re-birth, so the thought of Newgate terrifies Moll: it represents for her "the Place where my Mother suffered so deeply, where I was brought into the World, and from whence I expected no Redemption, but by an infamous Death . . . the Place that had so long expected me, and which with so much Art and Success I had so long avoided" (213–14). Having lost both her husband James and the child she bore him, and suffering from the alienating effects of crime and prostitution, Moll seems farther than ever from regaining the sense of self that had been momentarily wakened in her. Her efforts at penitence are fruitless, and the prison Ordinary has nothing but shopworn and hypocritical abjurations to offer her. In the midst of this spiritual wasteland, something calls Moll back "to that thing call'd Sorrow": the sight of James, her Lancashire husband, being brought into Newgate (218). Moll is "struck Dumb at the Sight" of the only man she has loved brought to this condition, as she believes, by her deceit of him (219); in James, Moll sees, as if for the first time, the consequences of her actions, and she repents the life she has lived: "I was perfectly chang'd," she says, "and become another Body" (220).

Some readers find Moll's reformation unconvincing, and indeed it is a little too convenient to be a genuine spiritual conversion. Moreover, the same readers point out (as did Ian Watt) that her subsequent conduct makes a mockery of the idea of repentance.[15] What Watt and others have missed is that Moll's reformation, while it imitates the language and forms of religion, is essentially secular and psychological. Moll takes a renewed interest in life because a sensibility to suffering, "that thing call'd Sorrow," is awakened in her by the sight of her Lancashire husband, James, brought to judgment as a highwayman. The stirrings of her conscience are encouraged by a sympathetic minister who prays with her. The effect of this minister's "honest friendly way of treating me" is to "unlock all the Sluices of my Passions" and cause her, for the first time in her life, to tell her secrets to a stranger. It is this purgation – this regimen administered by a physician of the mind – that cleanses Moll of her cupidity and leaves her with "only a sincere Regret for, and hatred of those things I had done" (226). Like the figure in Robinson's dream, he uses words that Moll is barely able to understand, and any religious doctrine he may have imparted is lost on her – "I am not able to repeat the excellent Discourses of this extraordinary Man; 'tis all that I am able to do to say, that he reviv'd my Heart" – but his words, whatever their content, revive her animal spirits and relieve her melancholy, whereupon her fortunes also begin to revive. By accepting transportation, and persuading James to accept it as well, Moll works out her own salvation in a most Pelagian way. As her future conduct involving her son Humphry shows, Moll has not eradicated concupiscence from her soul, as indeed Galen had said could never be done; but she has cured herself of that inordinate lust called cupidity, and so earned the title of penitent.

"I LOV'D TO BE FLATTER'D AND COURTED": *THE FORTUNATE MISTRESS*

As readers have freed themselves over the past two decades from the conviction that Defoe's perspective was that of a seventeenth-century

Puritan, they gradually have taken greater interest in the psychological dimensions of Roxana, the heroine of Defoe's ironically titled history, *The Fortunate Mistress*. In his 1979 study, *Defoe's Art of Fiction*, David Blewett denied that *The Fortunate Mistress* "is in any sense a psychological novel," but he did admit that "what makes it so unusual among Defoe's novels is the attention paid to the interior drama of moral deterioration."[16] In the same year, Terry Castle described a "psychosexual pattern" in the novel in which Roxana transfers onto Amy her own traumas and maternal responsibilities, thus performing a "psychological retrenchment" against mortality that is threatened by the re-appearance of her daughter.[17] In 1982, Raymond Stephanson showed that Roxana's symptoms are consistent with the seventeenth-century description of melancholy put forward by Thomas Willis (1621–75), and that the conclusion of the book depicts not a spiritual, but a mental deterioration brought on by the murder of her child.[18] Paula Backscheider has offered another diagnosis of Roxana's psychological condition: Roxana, she says, "lives in a world that is both claustrophobic and paranoid."[19] Backscheider attributes Roxana's claustrophobia to Roxana's having trapped herself into a counterfeit identity from which she cannot escape, and the paranoia to her fear that this counterfeit identity will be penetrated by the daughter she had abandoned. The measure of her paranoia, perhaps, is evident in her fear that this young woman *is* her daughter, despite the many contradictions in her story.[20]

The causes of Roxana's mental disturbance, however, are present early in her life, and the signs of her illness are evident well before she is threatened with exposure by the woman she fears is her daughter. Like Robinson Crusoe and Moll Flanders, Roxana is driven by a passion, which in her case is rooted in a historical injustice: her family originally came from Poitiers, the very cradle of the Protestant church in France, and fled to England during the turmoil surrounding the revocation of the Edict of Nantes. From an early age, she was nurtured on her family's desire to set themselves apart from – and above – the Huguenot refugees who came after them. Her father and mother taught her to suppress every trace of her French identity, except her language, and to indulge a sense that her family were "People of better Fashion" than other Protestant refugees (5). Roxana's mission in life – though unknown to her, or unadmitted – is to reclaim her rightful station in a world that has been denied to her. In some ways, Roxana resembles a tragic protagonist: she is a heroine motivated to right a historical wrong whose passion leads her into the obsessive pursuit of a chimerical goal.

Because of her story's historical circumstances, and because her foolish first husband was chosen for her by her father, Roxana seems at first a sympathetic protagonist. She admits, retrospectively, to having been "blinded by my own Vanity," (161), a failing for which we forgive her because of the sense of self given her by her family. Vanity is thought to be, as Robert Burton says in the *Anatomy of Melancholy*, an "acceptable disease," which those afflicted by it have no desire to cure.[21] But in the classical etiology of the passions, the handmaiden of vanity is ambition, represented in this story by Roxana's maid Amy: Roxana calls Amy "an ambitious Jade, who knew my weakest Part, *namely*, that I lov'd great things, and that I lov'd to be flatter'd and courted" (231). Vanity and ambition together are a dangerous combination, particularly in that they take no counsel; unlike Defoe's other protagonists, who have recourse to a friendly counselor, or at least to a Bible, Roxana refuses to listen to those persons, such as the Dutch merchant, who attempt to warn her of the "Distemper" that "lay much in my head" (239). The only confidante whom Roxana trusts implicitly is Amy, who does not have an independent existence from her mistress. Amy is an extension of Roxana, an expression of her unconscious desires; together she and Roxana are a single mind, dominated by the twin passions of vanity and ambition.

Roxana is able to retain our sympathy through much of her story, and to avoid seeking a cure for her "distemper," by locating her unacknowledged desires not in herself, but in Amy. Whenever she does so – for example, when she allows Amy to talk her into receiving their Landlord as her lover in order to satisfy the rent – she characterises Amy's promptings as the work of the Devil: "But that I know you to be a very honest Girl, *Amy, says I*, you wou'd make me abhor you; why, you argue for the Devil, as if you were one of his Privy-Counsellors" (37). As Defoe was soon to remark in *The History of the Devil* (1727), it was two such "prime Ministers" of the Devil, "Cardinal *Richlieu* and *Lewis* the XIV," who were to blame for "the total Extirpation of the Protestant Churches" from France in the Edict of Nantes.[22] If Amy is such a "privy-counsellor," and is at the same time one of the poles of Roxana's own personality, then the Devil has already infiltrated Roxana's mind. There is no better proof of his presence than the incident in which Roxana forces Amy into bed with their Landlord, whose mistress Roxana has been for a year and a half. Roxana had begun this relationship at Amy's prompting, though it had cost her an agony of guilt at the time: "if I yield, 'tis in vain to mince the Matter, I am a Whore, *Amy*, neither better nor worse, I assure you" (40). After eighteen months, Amy gently taunts Roxana for her failure to conceive a child, which would have bound the Landlord to Roxana: "*Law*, Madam, *says Amy*, what have you been doing? why you have been Marry'd a Year and a Half, I warrant you, Master wou'd have got me with-Child twice in that time" (45), articulating a desire that Roxana would prefer not to recognize in herself. That evening, Roxana, provoked by Amy's rebuke, strips her protesting maid and forces her into bed with the Landlord, saying "Nay, you Whore, *says I*, you said, if I wou'd put you to-Bed, you wou'd with all your Heart" (46). To the reader, Roxana confesses that the cause of her anger lay not with Amy, but in herself: "as I thought myself a Whore, I cannot say but that it was something design'd in my Thoughts, that my Maid should be a Whore too, and should not reproach me with it" (47). If Roxana's ambition has led her into whoredom, her vanity will not let her suffer alone for it.

This first outburst establishes a pattern that is mirrored by other instances of anger in the book. Roxana responds in the same way when Amy describes her interview with Susan, the young girl who suspects that Roxana is her mother. When Amy suggests that it might be necessary to murder the girl, Roxana feels the effect of her words as physical sensations: "all my Blood ran chill in my Veins, and a Fit of trembling seiz'd me, that I cou'd not speak a good-while." At last she turns on Amy in anger:

What is the Devil in you, *Amy, said I?* Nay, nay, *says she*, let it be the Devil, or not the Devil, if I thought she knew one tittle of your History, I wou'd dispatch her if she were my own Daughter a thousand times; and I, *says I in a Rage*, as well as I love you, wou'd be the first that shou'd put the Halter about your Neck, and see you hang'd, with more Satisfaction than ever I saw you in my Life; nay, *says I*, you wou'd not live to be hang'd, *I believe*, I shou'd cut your Throat with my own Hand; I am almost ready to do it, *said I*, as 'tis, for your but naming the thing; with that, I call'd her cursed Devil, and bade her get out of the Room. (270–71)

Overcome by passion, Roxana denounces Amy twice for having the Devil in her, and "in a Rage" sends her out of her sight. Her rage is not a righteous anger that does honor to her, but a murderous tirade that shows how well Roxana recognizes in Amy's words her own unarticulated desires to be rid of her first five children and the past they represent; in a sense, she has already committed that crime in sending them to live with a cruel aunt, in whose hands two have died.

The extraordinary tableau of passion that Defoe presents in these scenes suggests that Roxana's anger is a symptom of an underlying pathology. As we noted in Chapter 4, the key to reading these symptoms is given in *The History of the Devil* (1727), in which Defoe says that there is an easy way to determine whether the Devil and his legions are at work within us: by examining our passions. We have "no more to do but look a little into the Microcosm of the Soul, and see there how the Passions which are the Blood, and the Affections which are the Spirit, move in their particular Vessels; how they circulate, and in what Temper the Pulse beats there, and [we] may easily see who turns the Wheel" (*HD*, 401). A person of serene temper has nothing to fear, but if "the Mind is ruffled, if Vapours rise, Clouds gather, if Passions swell the Breast, if Anger, Envy, Revenge, Hatred, Wrath, Strife" fill the soul, "the Case is easily resolv'd, the *Devil* is in him" (*HD*, 402). Because we cannot see the Devil, but can see only his effects in the disturbance of our passions, we cannot prevent him from entering our souls; we can only temper our passions, to eliminate the handle by which he takes hold of us. In effect, it makes no difference whether the Devil is real, or is a metaphor for some disease that inflames the passions; all that can be done is to treat the symptoms, through the calming effects of prayer, reflection, and counsel with a friend, physician, or clergyman. But unlike the melancholic Robinson, who finds good counsel in his Bible, or Moll Flanders, who examines her conscience with the assistance of a friendly minister in Newgate, Roxana has no physician in whom she can confide; she has only two companions, "*first*, Amy, who knew my Disease, but was able to do nothing as to the Remedy; the *second*, the Merchant, who really brought the Remedy, but knew nothing of the Distemper" (239). Her fears have isolated her, preventing her from seeking counsel and forcing her to condone the zealotry of her servant, who lacks even the limited moral sense that restrains Roxana's passions. Her case points up the dangers of an individual's reliance upon her own moral sensibility, particularly when it is that sensibility that is most in need of a cure.

The disease into which Roxana appears to have slipped is not simply melancholia, or a spiritual lassitude, but a more serious illness, of which melancholy is a symptom. Roxana provides us with a clue to the nature of this disease in a passage in which she struggles to explain her apparently irrational refusal of the Dutch merchant's proposal of marriage. Marriage to the merchant would put Roxana beyond the reach of both economic necessity and her husband the brewer, from whom she was never divorced, but she finds herself unable to take advantage of this safe harbor because her ambition and vanity still lead her to dream of marrying a prince. "The Notion of being *a Princess*," says Roxana, "the Thoughts of being surrounded with Domesticks; honour'd with Titles; be call'd HER HIGHNESS; and live in all the Splendor of a Court...all this, *in a word*, dazzled my Eyes; turn'd my Head; and I was as truly craz'd and distracted for about a Fortnight, as most of the People in *Bedlam*, tho' perhaps, not quite so far gone."[23] In an aside to the reader, she self-diagnoses her malady:

So fast a hold has Pride and Ambition upon our Minds, that when once it gets Admission, nothing is so chimerical, but under this Possession we can form Ideas of, in our Fancy, and realize to our Imagination: Nothing can be so ridiculous as the simple Steps we take in such Cases; a Man or a Woman becomes a meer *Malade Imaginaire*, and I believe, may as easily die with Grief, or run-mad with Joy, (as the Affair in his Fancy appears right or wrong) as if all was real, and actually under the Management of the Person.[24]

Roxana's symptoms of anger and constant anxiety, together with her admission that her mind has been possessed by a chimera and her allusion to Molière's play about hypochondria, clearly resemble seventeenth-century observations of hysteria. Like hypochondria in men, hysteria had long been considered a disease of the imagination, particularly after studies in the 1680s by Thomas Sydenham and Giorgio Baglivi argued that it was a nervous, not an organic, disorder.[25] In the eighteenth century, according to Helen King, hysteria was "increasingly classified as a neurosis" in women, a malady that could be brought on by departures from the "prevailing social and biological notions of womanhood," such as Roxana's apparently irrational rejection of marriage.[26] Roxana's possession by the chimera of royalty, her fury at Amy for articulating desires that Roxana herself has had, her vision of her dead husband the jeweler before he is murdered, her adoption of "a kind of Amazonian Language" (171) or a Turkish dress to conceal her identity – each of these moments represents a deterioration not only of Roxana's moral being, but of what we would now call her mental health. The illness eventually infuses her whole character and renders her vulnerable to specters and fears of all sorts, culminating in her terror at the possibility that Susan the cookmaid may be her lost daughter.

In the climactic moment of the history, one that fully captures the paralyzing emotional state of hysteria, Roxana descends into a dark repository of memory and secrets in order to confront the passions that bedevil her. The scene is the equivalent in this book of Crusoe's descent into the cave, of the saddler's visit to the burial pit at Aldgate cemetary, and of Moll Flanders' epiphany in Newgate. It occurs when Roxana encounters the young woman she believes to be her daughter on board the ship that is to carry them to Holland. Roxana enters the dark cabin and stands with the light behind her, hiding both her face and her emotions from view. She cannot avoid saluting her daughter with a kiss, which gave her "a secret inconceivable Pleasure" (277); it was the first time she had kissed her child "since I took the fatal Farewel of them all, with a Million of Tears, and a Heart almost dead with Grief." The kiss makes a deep impression on her spirits: "I felt something shoot thro' my Blood; my Heart flutter'd; my Head flash'd, and was dizzy, and all within me, *as I thought*, turn'd about, and much ado I had, not to abandon myself to an Excess of Passion at the first Sight of her, much more when my Lips touched her Face" (277). For the next hour or two, Roxana struggles to "conceal my Disorder" and must use "all manner of Violence with myself" to suppress the raging emotion within. She escapes recognition, but the same passions are raised again a few days later, when the young woman and her "sister" visit Roxana at the Quaker's house. Their questions, clearly intended to provoke a response from Roxana that will expose her identity, force Roxana again to violently suppress her emotions: "what my Face might do towards betraying me, I know not, because I cou'd not see myself, but my Heart beat as if it wou'd have jump'd out at my Mouth; and my Passion was so great, that for want of Vent, I thought I shou'd have burst: *In a word*, I was in a kind of a silent Rage" (284).

This violent suppression of emotion, fully consistent with a hysterical attack, is aggravated by the fact that Roxana has no friend, no counselor or physician, in whom she can confide: "I had no Vent; no-body to open myself to, or to make a Complaint to for my Relief" (284). Indeed, as soon as the visit is over, she does confide her fears to Amy: "As soon as they were gone, I run up to Amy, and gave Vent to my Passions, by telling her the whole Story" (291), but with disastrous consequences. Amy, after all, is not a Stoic philosopher or a physician of the mind, but a sort of Hobbesian, or perhaps Mandevillean beast in her mistress's breast, who works to further, rather than restrain, Roxana's passions. Instead of comforting Roxana, Amy begins "giving her Wrath a Vent . . . by calling the poor Girl all the damn'd Jades and Fools, (*and sometimes worse Names*) that she cou'd think of" (291). Roxana forbids Amy to murder the girl, but privately harbors a wish for her death ("had she dropp'd into the Grave by any fair Way . . . I shou'd have shed but very few Tears for her" 302). Eventually, Amy reveals her "fatal and wicked Design" to do away with Susan, at which news, says Roxana, "all my Rage turn'd against Amy" and she banishes her from sight, as she had done twice before (311–12).

The ending of *The Fortunate Mistress*, which has dissatisfied many readers because of its lack of closure, is appropriate to the history of a disease that is incurable, yet not terminal. Roxana lives with the image of "the poor Girl . . . ever before my Eyes; I saw her by-Night, and by-Day; she haunted my Imagination, if she did not haunt the House; my Fancy show'd her me in a hundred Shapes and Postures; sleeping or waking, she was with me . . . And all these Appearances were terrifying to the last Degree" (325). This inconclusive end completes the string of "histories" through which Defoe studied the cases of souls – rational, concupiscible, and irascible – affected by passion, though he had yet to rationalize this study in *The History of the Devil*. Of all the histories, *Roxana* most clearly illuminates the spiritual ills brought on by passion, and it acknowledges a profound skepticism about the prospects for a cure. Roxana shows at the end that she has acquired some humility by providing, through her Quaker friend, for her eldest daughter, about whom she is moved to say that "the Girl was the very Counterpart of myself, only much handsomer" (329), and she has tempered her ambition by finally accepting the Dutch merchant as her husband, a man who, however good he may be in the eyes of the world, will never be a prince. But in the end, these abatements of passion do not provide her any permanent relief. Instead of a precipitate fall proceeding from a tragic error, Roxana's agony is the steady decline of a person with a disease; instead of recognizing a cosmic justice in her fate, she senses only the cruel irony of a prosperity that she cannot enjoy. The natural consequence of a life spent in the pursuit of a chimera is neither a sentence at law, nor a religious penance, either of which would bring to the work a sense of closure, but an affliction of the spirit that has no cure.

CHAPTER 7

"Surprized by his passions": the ghost of Servetus and the Reverend John Lewis

Suppose a young woman named Elizabeth should exhibit the signs of love: in Smollett's symptomatology, "her coulour fades, her appetite fails, and her spirits flag. – She is become moping and melancholy, and is often found in tears."[1] Suppose this woman has been reared as the daughter of a clergyman known for his passionate defense of the Church of England against its dissenting brethren, especially the Baptists and Quakers. Suppose the man with whom this young woman has fallen in love should be a Quaker. Suppose the loving couple, to avoid the father's prohibitions and displeasure, should elope, and then contact him in the hope of obtaining his blessing. The clergyman's answer might be very similar to the following letter, found among the papers of the Reverend John Lewis (1675–1747), vicar of the parish of St. Mary's in the village of Minster-in-Thanet, Kent, and of St. John the Baptist in Margate:

Betty,
 I have writ this Letter to you, with the greatest Concern I ever writ in my life. My Duty as your father &our minister, urges me to advise you, to recollect &consider what you are doing; and whither it will tend; for no less than your eternal salvation depends upon it. In all Affairs of moment, it has ever been looked upon as a piece of the greatest prudence, to consult with Persons proper to give Advice in them. But this you have neglected to do in two of the most important Cases. One in Relation to this World, and then to the Next. I mean your Marriage and your Religion. The first cannot now be retrieved, the other may. Therefore shew your self true to your eternal Interest, and seriously weigh what is here offered to your Consideration.
 First by the Principles of Quakerism, you must not own the Scriptures to be a Rule of Faith; that is, you must not try the Doctrines of Religion, whether they be true or false by the Scriptures, which St. Paul in the 2nd Epistle to Tim: 3 Cap. [14?] & 15v. tells us, are able to make us wise to Salvation. And in the following Verses, those Scriptures are said, to be given by the Inspiration of God, and to be profitable for Doctrine, for Reproof, for Correction, for Instruction

Reverend John Lewis (1675–1747), engraved by George White, frontispiece of John Lewis, *The History and Antiquities, as well as Ecclesiastical as Civil, of the Isle of Tenet, in Kent,* 2nd edn. (London, 1736).

Copy of a letter of remonstrance from a clergyman to his daughter Betty, found among the papers of John Lewis (1675–1747). MS. Rawl. D. 376, fols. 187 recto and verso.

& y Pretender to be deceiv'd, if not a Cheat & Impostor also.   188.

for y y plaie, yu must renounce yr Baptism (although rightly baptized &
rightly confirmed) as a thing of no use, if not a wicked thing: although o^r
Sau^r prop lies in wch he says in y 16 of St Mark & y 6.v. y no man shall be saved
but it. He y believeth & is baptized shall be saved: but he y believeth not shall
be damned.

And now, Betty, I advise you to beware of y cunning Craftiness of men, y lye in
wait to deceive; & intreat you in y words of St Paul in y forementioned Cap to
him: to continue in y things as thou hast learned & hast been assured of, knowing
of whom thou hast learned y; even of thy father, who is sollicitous for thy
salvation.

And God of his infinite Mercy give thee Grace to consider y things y belong
to thy Peace, before they be hid from thine Eyes, for y sake of o^r Sav^r Jesus X^t

     Amen.

(Continued)

in Righteousness, that the Man of God may be perfect, thoroughly instructed in all good Work. Now, Betty, laying aside all prejudice, by whomsoever you have received it: judge with calm & sober Reason; judge impartially without Fear or Affection, and then tell me, whether the Scriptures, which St. Paul says, are given by Inspiration of God, and are useful to so many good Purposes, are to be neglected and laid aside, as no Rule of Faith, and the Fancies of weak and wicked Men, substituted in their Room[,] which is the 2nd thing I have to offer to your consideration. For according to the Rules of Quakerism, you must believe, whatever they say, when the Spirit moves them, (either in Preaching or Praying) is by immediate Inspiration from God, and just then dictated and suggested by the Holy Ghost, as things were suggested to the Apostles. But this, if you will use your Reason, will appear to be a Deceit; for unless they could also speak with Tongues, and Heal the Sick, and cure the Lame, and in a word, do such Miracles as the Apostles did, and give the same proof of their Inspiration which the Apostles did evidently give of theirs; which is a thing that is not done by any of them, and therefore plainly shews the Pretence to Inspiration is vain, and the Pretender to be deceiv'd, if not a Cheat and Imposter also.

In the 3rd place, you must renounce your Baptism, (although rightly baptized and rightly confirmed) as a thing of no use, if not a wicked thing; although the Savior implies in what he says in the 16 [chapter] of St. Mark and the 16.v that no man shall be saved without it. He that believeth and is baptized shall be saved: but he that believeth not shall be damned.

And now, Betty, I advise you to beware of the cunning craftiness of men, that lye in wait to deceive; and intreat you in the words of St. Paul in the forementioned Cap to Tim: to continue in the things which thou hast learned and hast been assured of; knowing of whom thou hast learned them; even of thy father, who is sollicitous for thy Salvation.

And God of his infinite Mercy give thee Grace to consider the things that belong to thy Peace, before they be hid from thine Eyes, for the sake of the Savior Jesus Xt.

Amen.[2]

In this poignant letter, the clergyman's anguish for his daughter, his concern for issues of Church doctrine, and his suspicion of the passions of mankind are inextricably mixed. The daughter, it seems, has twice disappointed her father – first, by marrying without his advice or permission, and now by proposing to abandon her faith. In a state of alarm, he takes up his pen to dissuade her from a course of action that he believes will destroy her hopes for eternal happiness. The man whom Betty has evidently married – perhaps even eloped with – is a member of the very sect against which her father has spent his life waging doctrinal warfare. Should Betty join the Quakers, she must renounce her baptism in the Church of England and accept a religion in which inspiration, not Scripture (much less paternal or clerical authority), is the guide and rule of faith. She has placed her soul in the keeping of men who, in her father's eyes, are at best weak and deceived, or at worst imposters and pretenders who claim they are moved directly by the Holy Ghost, although they can perform no miracles to substantiate that divine inspiration. In an age rife with the winds of doctrine, as St. Paul warned the Ephesians (4: 14), Betty has been seduced by the "cunning craftiness of men, that lye in wait to deceive," into a betrayal of her faith. She has placed her private judgment in a sovereign position over the teachings of Scripture and has followed her affections rather than the pastoral or paternal authority that it was her duty to heed. The clergyman recommends to his daughter a cure for her distempered passions similar in form to that used by Robinson Crusoe on his island – that is, to consult her Bible, and then to reflect, "without Fear or Affection," on what she has learned from her father, relying upon her observations of men to ratify the truth of Scripture. At the same time, the letter presents a case often found in works of fiction in the 1740s, including *Tom Jones* and *Clarissa*: the precipitating action in both of those novels is the choice of a young woman to leave her father's home in an effort to assert a degree of sovereignty over the choice of her husband. The letter thus provides documentary evidence of the historicity of the crisis of the passions that is reflected in novels of the period. While it is not possible to say with certainty that John Lewis was the author of this letter, the doctrinal issues raised in it are the same ones that preoccupied the Reverend Lewis as he endeavored to stem the individualistic passions of his age, both in his parisioners and in himself.[3]

THE PASSIONS OF JOHN LEWIS: A SPIRITUAL AUTOBIOGRAPHY

Though now seldom read, John Lewis was a literary figure of some importance in his time, being the author of thirty-five published works and a large number of unpublished manuscripts.[4] His major works were biographies of English prelates who were persecuted for their views, including John Wycliffe (c. 1320–84); Reynold Pecock (c. 1395–c. 1460), bishop of St. Asaph and Chichester; and John Fisher (c. 1469–1535), bishop of Rochester.[5] He also published some antiquarian and topographical works, a history of the translations of the New Testament into English, and a life of William Caxton, emphasizing the connection between the rise of printing and the Protestant religion in England.[6] Lewis' biographer in the *Dictionary of National Biography* (*DNB*) admits that his works are "tedious compilations," but adds that they "contain the result

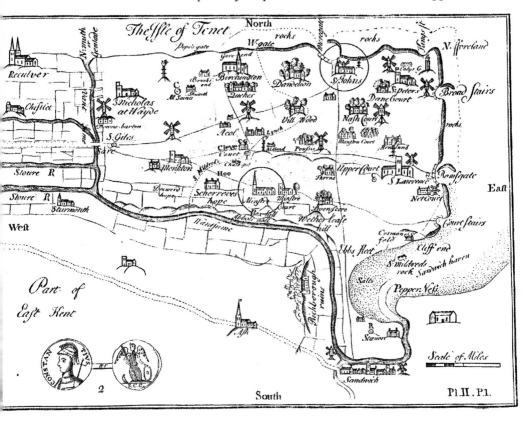

Map of the Isle of Tenet, showing St. John the Baptist Church in Margate and
St. Mary's, Minster, both parishes of John Lewis. Opposite p. vii in John Lewis, *The
History and Antiquities, as well as Ecclesiastical as Civil, of the Isle of Tenet, in Kent,* 2nd edn.
(London, 1736).

of much original research."[7] Thus damned by faint praise, Lewis' zealous
defenses of the English Protestant Reformation have slipped quietly out of
sight; what remains is the remarkable passion with which he defended the
essential elements of the Reformation against the anabaptists, Quakers,
and unitarians who, in his view, threatened to reduce the practice of
religion in England to turmoil and ignorance.

Lewis was not particularly well liked by his brethren in the Church;
the *DNB* confesses that his "whiggish and low church views" often
landed him in controversy, while a recent history of Kent describes
the Reverend Lewis as a tireless reformer, "an energetic parish priest

anxious to promote the highest standards of pastoral care, not just in his own parish, but in those of his neighbours as well."[8] His problems with his fellow prelates began early in his career: as a young man, he published a popular exposition of the Church of England catechism in dialogue form, which was frequently reprinted throughout the eighteenth century.[9] The success of this book, according to Lewis, incurred the animosity of the authors of some earlier catechisms, from which they believed Lewis had borrowed a little too freely, thus beginning a pattern of antagonism between Lewis and his contemporaries that dogged him throughout his career.[10] In 1714, he began an acrimonious and life-long debate with John Johnson, who had nominated him for the vicarage at Margate, over the question of the Eucharist; Lewis took the Wycliffian position that the bread and wine used in that sacrament were not literally the body and blood of Christ, as Johnson and the high church maintained.[11] He also accused another friend and fellow Oxford student, Thomas Hearne, of having papistical tendencies, on which basis Hearne was ultimately deprived of his librarianship in the Bodleian.

While these quarrels blew hot and cold, there were two questions on which Lewis was engaged throughout his life: the Holy Trinity and the baptism of infants. His position on these questions was conservative and dogmatic: that is, he maintained the divinity of Christ as an equal and eternal person of the Trinity, and he stoutly upheld the orthodoxy of infant baptism against the criticisms of the anabaptists, who held that baptism ought to represent the confirmation of faith by adult persons who could understand the significance of the ceremony. Any challenge to these central tenets of his faith aroused in Lewis an ardent passion, which drove him to compose hundreds of pages of closely written manuscript on obscure points of doctrine until he nearly lost his eyesight. This commendable zeal was probably the flaw of character that consigned him for four decades to an arduous ministry on the eastern verge of the Kentish coast serving parishioners who did not always appreciate his scholarship.

A fuller sense of who Lewis was is available from his autobiography, which he left in manuscript at his death in 1747 at the age of 72. The autobiography is an *apologia* for the many quarrels and disputes into which he had entered over matters of ecclesiastical doctrine, church history, and personal business. Speaking of himself in the past tense and in the third person, Lewis says of his penchant for controversy,

he loved free speaking, as far as the world would bear it, and sometimes, perhaps, further, for which he was reproached by his enemies as having an unruly tongue.

But he hated Lying for the Truth, and being a Slave and Bigot to a party, and on that account beating and abusing his fellow Servants [of Christ].[12]

In one remarkable passage from the autobiography, Lewis blames his tendency to embroil himself in controversies on an involuntary passion:

Mr. Lewis however had his faults, the remembrance of which often gave him a very sensible uneasiness. He had a sort of heat or impetus by which he was sometimes hurried to say and do what was both inconsistent with his character and interest. His resentments of supposed wrongs done to him were oftimes too quick and lasting, and he had not always prudence enough and command of himself to conceal them . . . He did not know mankind well enough, nor suspect they were so false and treacherous as they were: and was therefore too frank and open and gave them too much room to wrest his words & entangle him in his talk & compass the designs they had formed of circumventing and betraying him. . . . He was sometimes surprized by his passions when he was put off his guard by Hurries, Indispositions, or such like occasions, yet, he was not alwais angry when he talked louder or quicker than ordinary: but when he really was in a passion which he was not often, even when he had sufficient reason, he was never so angry with any one else, as he would be with himself for having been so: very severly reflecting on and condemning himself: for his being in that passion and for the angry words and expressions which it caused him to use and utter. (fol. 79)

In this revealing piece of self-criticism, Lewis makes passion both his major fault of character and the means of his self-exoneration. He admits that his temperament had at its root "a sort of heat or impetus" that hurried him into actions that he later regretted, not because they were wrong, but because they were inconsistent with the character in which he wanted to appear in the world. Had he more prudence, he would have been able to conceal his resentments better, though he would not have felt them less. In Lewis's estimation, his honest, open, and frank character permitted his passion for the truth to expose him to the "false and treacherous" designs of his enemies, of which there was no shortage in his life. He was often "surprized" by his passions into responses that made him seem angry, and led him to talk "louder or quicker than ordinary," but he eventually turned his anger toward himself for having imprudently betrayed those passions to the world.

An anecdote in the autobiography illustrates both this passion for argument and his position on the key doctrinal question of baptism (fols. 36–37). One day in the market square in Margate, a cooper from Folkestone named Kennet challenged Lewis's well-known views on baptism – in this case, on whether or not total immersion was required.

A crowd drew around them and "became pretty numerous." Kennet, who according to Lewis was "a man very ignorant and not a little conceited," had read in an anabaptist tract that the Greek word for baptism was translated in Latin as "mergo," meaning to dip or plunge into water. Lewis informed him that a sprinkling would accomplish the purpose, and to drive home the point, asked "the good women in the company" if they washed their tables by sprinkling them, or by plunging them into water, which "occasioned the company to treat Kennet with some marks of scorn." Lewis recalls his righteous triumph over the anabaptist Kennet with some pride, but also with a defensive tone that suggests some anxiety over whether his motives proceeded solely from his love of God and religion, or from more personal considerations.

As Lewis explains in his autobiography, the argument with the anabaptist in the town square so affected him that he was moved to write a popular history of the rise and progress of anabaptism in England, which was published in 1738.[13] His objective was to warn the faithful against the false claims of the anabaptists that baptism could safely be deferred until adulthood. Baptism for Lewis was not a ritual through which grace is conferred upon a believer, but the instrument through which heart and soul are cleansed in preparation for the entrance of the Holy Ghost, so that lust and wrath may have no place there.[14] In his catechism, he explained the purpose of baptism by paraphrasing Ephesians 2: 3, in which Paul reminds us that we are "by Nature the children of Wrath" and subject to the rule of passion.[15] The baptism of infants is a ritual curing of the soul *before* it becomes corrupted by passion, without which salvation is not possible. In the early years of the Church, Lewis admits in his *History of Anabaptism*, baptism of adults had been the standard practice; the original baptisms administered by Christ's disciples were of adults, and

for the two first Ages no one received Baptism who was not first instructed in the faith and Doctrine of *Christ*, so as to be able to answer for himself, that he believed, because of those words *He that believeth and is baptized*: but, that afterwards Infant Baptism came in upon the opinion, that Baptism was necessary to Salvation.[16]

The ceremonies of baptism, catechism, and daily prayer were all designed to fortify the human soul against the passions of the body, fortifications which, as the letters of St. Paul and Betty's clergyman warn, must be constantly maintained against the "cunning craftiness of men, that lye in wait to deceive."

Even greater than Lewis's mistrust of anabaptism is his contempt for the Quakers, who shared with the anabaptists the practice of renouncing their Christian baptism, "except that they did not *re-baptize,* as laying aside the Use of *both* the Christian Sacraments."[7] The English Baptists, he says, have relinquished some of their most outrageous practices:

They who now retain the Name [of baptists] have abandoned the greatest part of the Dogmata which the *German* Anabaptists adopted from the Gnostics &c. touching the Incarnation &c. and in lieu of the Fanatic Zeal of the ancient Founders of the Sect have given in to an exemplary simplicity in their Actions, Discipline and Dress &c. not unlike the Quakers.[18]

Their simplicity of dress may be similar to that of the Quakers, but there is one difference. Whereas the dress of the Baptists reflects their beliefs, Lewis says, that of the Quakers is an affectation:

This *Simplicity* here recommended as an example to others, is too well known to be an affected singularity in dress and behaviour; and in many of the Quakers a rude clownishness and inhumanity particularly towards the Clergy of the Church of *England* whom they take all opportunities to defame and oppose ... [unlike the anabaptists of England, who treat the Clergy] as Men and their neighbors, and are ready and willing to do them all good and kind Offices.[19]

Unlike the Baptists, the Quakers, along with the Arians, Socinians and other freethinking sects, intend to subvert the Church of England by casting doubt on its rituals and creeds, which they do by disseminating tracts such as the one owned by cooper Kennet (and perhaps put in the hands of dutiful Betty). In these tracts,

concessions and crude opinions [are] pompously retailed, as if they had never been examined and confuted ... and [it] is a very disingenuous thing to take advantage of other peoples weakness, and put an abuse on plain, honest and well-meaning readers.[20]

Lewis' particular hostility toward the Quakers, then, derives from his belief that their simplicity is a hypocritical mask behind which they hide their true design, which is to undermine the authority of the Church of England and make a mockery of its clergy, its ceremonies, and its creeds. The enemies of the Church could not bring it down by attacking its clergy or the ceremonies of the Lord's Supper and baptism, but they might succeed by discrediting the Athanasian creed, upon which the doctrine of the Trinity depended.

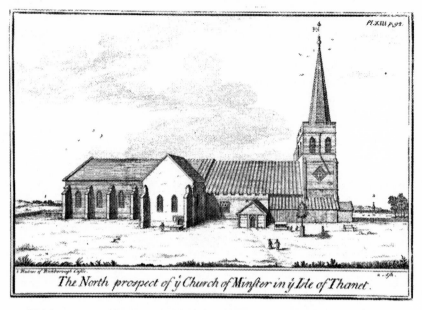

The North prospect of ỹ Church of Minſter in ỹ Iſle of Thanet.

North prospect of St. Mary's, Minster, burial place of the Reverend John Lewis
(1675–1747). Opposite p. 92 in John Lewis, *The History and Antiquities, as well as
Ecclesiastical as Civil, of the Isle of Tenet, in Kent*, 2nd edn. (London, 1736).

DEFENDING THE TRINITY I: LEWIS'S LIFE OF JOHN WALLIS

If the baptism of infants was the cornerstone of the Church of England,
the bedrock upon which that stone rested was the Athanasian creed. It
made little sense to baptize infants "in the Name of the Father, and of the
Son, and of the Holy Ghost" if this blessed trinity of persons were not
believed to exist. As late at 1786, George Horne, dean of Canterbury,
preached a visitation sermon in which he denounced the Socinian challenge to the Trinity, warning his listeners to "[s]ay no more, then, that the
doctrine of the Trinity is a matter of curiosity and amusement only. Our
religion is founded upon it."[21] John Lewis understood the importance
of the Trinity, and labored mightily to expound it throughout his career.
In his first book, the *Catechism*, he taught children that, while the three
persons of the Trinity are the same in their natures, they fulfill a "Diver-
sity of Offices, or Operations. The Father creates. The Son Redeems.
The Holy Ghost Sanctifies" (19). Had he needed any coaching on the
defense of the Trinity, he would have received it from his friend and

correspondent, the Reverend Daniel Waterland, an Oxford don who had singlehandedly smothered the Salters Hall controversy in a flood of ink and paper.[22] But by the 1730s, Lewis seems to have realized that it was not enough merely to insist on scriptural authority to defend the Trinity; he had to show that the doctrine was not inconsistent with the new sciences of mathematics, physics, and anatomy that were being used to buttress the Socinian challenge. In the subject of his next biography, "The Life of the Learned and Reverend John Wallis," Lewis found a champion of the Trinity who belonged to the modern age.

As a student at Cambridge in 1632, John Wallis (1616–1703) had been an adherent of the "new philosophy," including "the speculative part of *physic* or Medicine, and *Anatomy*," and in a "public Disputation [he] maintained the circulation of the blood, which was then a new doctrine."[23] As a professor of geometry at Oxford in 1649, Wallis belonged to a group that discussed "the circulation of the blood, the valves in the veins, the Venæ Lacteæ, the lymphatic vessels" and other subjects, and "brought into fashion and credit these studies which before were despised."[24] In Lewis's words, these new philosophers were known for "setting on foot an impartial examination of the reason of things, and not having an implicit faith on others or using *their* authority for an argument . . . Because *Aristotle* and the Schoolmen were out of request with them, and *ipse dixit* was an argument much out of fashion, therefore they were a bugbear not only to the sour and narrow souls, but to the bigotted zealots of the *Church of England*" (fols. 39r and 38v). The patrons of traditional learning at Oxford tried to isolate and destroy Wallis's group by nicknaming them "Latitude-men or Latitudinarians," choosing the name because they were thought to be "sensual men not having the Spirit, as having wide throats to swallow anything" (fol. 39). In Lewis's view, the Latitudinarians were never a threat to the Church, "which can never be prejudiced by the light of Reason, nor by the improvements of knowledge, nor by the advancement of the works of men's hands, which are the principal parts of this philosophy" (fol. 39). Nevertheless, their opponents resorted to violence in an effort to destroy them, causing Lewis to lament, "To such lengths will men's passions and angry resentments carry them when they can't have their beloved wills" (fol. 42).

The trinitarian controversies of the 1690s put Wallis and other adherents of the new philosophy in a delicate position. Though a respected member of the Royal Society, Wallis was vulnerable to challenges from both right and left about his religious orthodoxy, particularly by those who saw a contradiction between the new rationalism and the mysteries of the Trinity. As Lewis explains,

About 1690 a controversy being raised about the Doctrine of the Trinity by some who stiled themselves *Unitarians*, a friend of the Doctor's was desirous to know his opinion [how] the sacred Trinity of father, son and Holy Ghost are so distinguished each from the other as that the father is not the Son, or Holy Ghost; the Son not the Father, or Holy Ghost; the Holy Ghost not the Father or Son; yet so united, as that they are all one God; [and further] maintained that there is no such Trinity in Unity and Unity in Trinity. (70)

In his response to this "friend," Wallis wrote that "there are three *Somewhats* which are but *one God*, which *Somewhats* we commonly call *persons*."[25] These three persons can be distinguished in their functions, but not in their substance: scripture tells us that "the son is called the express image of the father's person; but if it be asked what these *personalities* are . . . he thought we had little more of it in Scripture than that the father is said to *beget*, the son to be *begotten*, and the Holy Ghost to *proceed*." This quality of personality Wallis believed to be "metaphorical," which he explained by resorting to geometry: in a cubical body or die there are "*Three Dimensions*, Length, Breadth, and Heighth, and yet but *One Cube*." To those "clamorous Socinians" who "importunely suggest the impossibility and inconsistence of these things," the Doctor asked, "because we do not know *how the bones grow in the womb of her that is with child*, shall we therefore say, they do not grow there?"

DEFENDING THE TRINITY II: LEWIS'S LIFE OF SERVETUS

Wallis's uses of the sciences of geometry and anatomy – and, we might add, the new psychology of personality – to explain the mysteries of the Trinity improved somewhat on the aphorisms entered by the Earl of Nottingham in his commonplace book almost fifty years earlier, but they did not end the debate or answer the questions raised by the Socinians and unitarians about the Trinity. On the contrary, the threat to the Trinity gained headway from the rise of those same sciences, in large part due to the claims made for Michael Servetus. As we have seen, William Wotton's *Reflections upon Ancient and Modern Learning* had helped to revive interest in Servetus by showing that his anatomical discoveries appeared to anticipate those of William Harvey, making him a hero of the modern age. Lewis was not the first English clergyman to comprehend the threat posed by a possible revival of the writings of Michael Servetus; his mentor, Archbishop Tenison, had denounced Servetus in his *Of Idolatry*

(1678) as worse than Arius, declaring "that by that which he had seen of his writing, he judged him fitter to be chained up as a *Madman* than burnt as an *Heretic*."[26] And in 1723, Edmund Gibson, Bishop of London, had suppressed an attempt to reprint the *Christianismi Restitutio*, a project supposedly backed by the physician Richard Mead, and had ordered the destruction of the printed sheets.[27] But in the same year, a new biography of Servetus appeared, titled *An Impartial History of Michael Servetus*, which went to a second printing and was widely disseminated in 1724.[28] This book eventually came to the attention of John Lewis, who believed it to have been written by a dissenting minister named Nathanael Hodges. Though he was mistaken about Hodges, he correctly understood the threat posed by the *Impartial History*, which he rightly regarded as an effort to undermine the Holy Trinity by reconstructing Michael Servetus as a Christian martyr. In a manuscript of about eighty closely written folio pages, titled the "History of the Life of Michael Servetus," Lewis replied to the author of the *Impartial History*, arguing that Servetus had willfully brought his martyrdom upon himself, while admitting that some faults lay on Calvin's side also. As the first attempt by an English cleric to write an extensive critique of the life and death of Servetus, Lewis's "History of Servetus" has much to tell us about Lewis himself and the concerns of his age. For Lewis (as for the author of the letter to Betty), the tragedy of Servetus raised two large questions: the sovereignty of private judgment, and the limits of passion in the pursuit of religious freedom.

The sovereignty of private judgment is a defining issue in Protestantism, as old as the Reformation itself. Roland Bainton has noted that Martin Luther was accused of "opening the floodgates of individualism" by questioning the authority of the Roman Church, thus "producing an inundation of all the vagaries of private interpretation" of Holy Scripture.[29] One such private interpretation, as we have seen, was that of Michael Servetus, who argued in *The Errors of the Trinity* (1531) that there was no basis in Scripture for the Athanasian Creed. In his "Life of Servetus," Lewis seems less concerned with defending the Creed than with questioning the right of a young student of theology to attack it: Servetus was, says Lewis, "but a youth, not 21 years old, when he first set out to propagate his own private judgment of the high and most mysterious points of Divinity, and to dispute about them. Experience sufficiently convinces every thinking person, that, at this time of Life, few or none arrive at a maturity of judgment. Childhood and Youth are folly and vanity. Our reason is then weak, and our passions very strong" (fol. 5). Sounding more like an angry father than a historian, Lewis agrees with Calvin that people must be restrained from speaking on subjects on which they are not qualified. Calvin's judgment was based on the conviction "that in the Church there ought not to be a liberty for everyone to act and believe as he pleases, and that it is lawful to compel them to live well, and have a right faith" (fol. 40). No one ought to be put to death for religion, but "it is lawful for the Magistrate to mulct or fine and put to death the obstinate and disobedient" (fols. 40 r and 40v). Even though faith and unbelief are invisible things, "Yet clamor, evil-speaking, behaving unseemly, and breaking the peace and Order of Society are outward, overt acts, and as such to be punished and restrained" (fol. 40v., Lewis paraphrasing Calvin). The lesson of the history of Servetus, Lewis believes, is the danger of privileging individual opinion over established authority; his life is "an instance of the ill use which may be made of asserting the Sovereignty of private judgment" (fol. 5).

At the same time, however, Lewis is aware that Calvin had gone far beyond the limits of what a Christian conscience could accept in his persecution of Servetus. However provoked Calvin may have been by Servetus's letters, "he seems to *me* to have been too far transported with a zeal against Heresie, and a vehement desire to clear and vindicate the Churches of the protestants from the charge and imputation of it" (fols. 6–7). Like a surgeon, Calvin had to amputate the Arian heresy from the young Protestant church: it was necessary "that a limb incurably wounded, when all things had been tried to cure it, was to be cut off, that the sound part of the Body might not be infected by it" (fol. 7). But the cruelty of the execution was a mistake, in that it exposed the Reformation to the same accusations that had been made against the Church of Rome, as the author of the *Impartial History* had pointed out: "However this be, this burning of *Servetus* bears hard on the memory of Mr. *Calvin*, and has been used by the enemies of the Reformed [Church?] to reproach *them*, whom Mr. *Calvin* intended to serve by his thus shewing his abhorrence of Heresie" (fol. 7). The error lay not in the surgery, but in the zeal with which it was performed.

The second question raised by the history of Servetus is the limit of passion in the pursuit of religious truth. Is a belief that is held in good conscience, even though in error, vindicated by the sincerity and passion of the believer? Defenders of Servetus, such as his contemporaries Sebastian Castellio and Matthew Gribaldi, argued that the claims of belief would be strengthened if revelation were assisted by empirical investigation, which requires the freedom to err, or at least to doubt.[30] For them, Servetus's willingness to suffer martyrdom rather than to recant his books was evidence of the sincerity of his passion. But for Calvin's defenders, including Lewis, sincerity in an error is no defense. Answering the question in the more familiar terms of the English Protestant Reformation, Lewis defends the position of Thomas Cranmer, archbishop of Canterbury, who in 1538 ordered that a copy of the Bible in English be set up in every church in England; despite his part in facilitating lay interpretation, Cranmer found it necessary to discourage the reading of Scripture among lay persons who loved "contention, and perverse disputation" (fol. 4). Perhaps recalling his dispute with cooper Kennet in the market square, Lewis details the religious strife of the sixteenth century: "This was then carried to that height, that every Market Place, ale-house, and tavern, every feast-house, in short, every company of men, even assembly of women, was filled with such talk. By these means their angry passions were raised to that degree, that they not only used very bitter and reproachful words, but also *their fists were whetted*, and they came to blows . . . " (fol. 4). "It would have been happy for the Christian Church in general, and every member of it in particular," says Lewis, if both clergy and laypeople had observed Cranmer's rule, which Lewis paraphrases in these terms:

That it is not fit for every man or woman to dispute the *high questions of Divinity*, but for such as are of *exact* and *exquisite judgments*, who have spent their time before in study and contemplation, and have cleansed themselves as well in soul, as body, or, at the least, endeavour'd themselves to be made clean.[31]

If Calvin were guilty of any fault, it was in not having followed Cranmer's rule – that is, not having cleansed himself of his angry passions before performing the surgery that he believed was necessary to save the Reformation. Though Lewis labors to excuse him, it is difficult to avoid the conclusion that Calvin and Servetus were, in this respect, mirror images of each other – that each was guilty of "beating and abusing [his] fellow servant" in the pursuit of religious truth.

It is also possible to find in Lewis's "History of Servetus" an echo of his own self-criticisms in his autobiography: that, like Servetus, he had within himself "a sort of heat or impetus by which he was sometimes hurried to say and do what was both inconsistent with his character and interest," and that like Calvin, his "resentments of supposed wrongs done to him were oftimes too quick and lasting, and he had not always prudence enough and command of himself to conceal them." Lewis's interest in the paradigmatic struggle between Calvin and Servetus may have arisen in his consciousness of the passions of zealotry in his own breast, and his books and manuscripts may reflect his efforts to cleanse himself of those passions.

LEWIS, INDIVIDUAL SOVEREIGNTY, AND THE NOVEL

The relevance of Lewis's "Life of Servetus" – and indeed, of all his histories of the lives of the English Protestant reformers – to the origins of the English novel is that the tensions between church doctrine and individual sovereignty that motivated Lewis to write the history of Servetus are similar to those that Defoe, Fielding, and Richardson addressed in their fictional histories. There is no basis to suppose that those writers were greatly indebted to Lewis's work, though Defoe and Fielding, at least, probably knew some of it.[32] Novels such as *Robinson Crusoe, Tom Jones,* and *Clarissa,* however, can profitably be read as examinations of the sovereignty of private judgment and the extent to which passion legitimizes (or undermines) that individual liberty of conscience. As we have seen, Robinson's history begins with the exercise of an individualistic desire that is opposed by his parents, but which he defends primarily on the grounds of the sincerity of his passion. Robinson is "cleansed" by the shipwreck, the dream, and the reading of his Bible, but it is interesting, in light of the religious context provided by Lewis's views on baptism, that Robinson's re-baptism in the waves and his conversion come in his adult life, as if Defoe were slyly endorsing the Servetian argument that baptism should occur "at a certain time, and that in a man capable of the Doctrine of Christ," rather than in an infant or young person.[33] At the end of his life, Robinson recants what he now regards as the error into which his passion had led him, but he is only able to recant because, in the course of his solitary penitence on the island, he has "cured," in the sense of cultivating or improving, the passions that had once led him astray. In effect, the story enacts a compromise between Cranmer's and Calvin's authoritarianism on the one hand, and the appeal of the nonconforming sects to individual sovereignty in matters of "private judgment" on the other. In these ways, as well as in the depiction of an ecumenically peaceable kingdom that Robinson establishes on his island (*RC* 174), Defoe seems to propose in the history of Robinson Crusoe a way out of the controversy over individual sovereignty that had divided the English Protestant church. That Lewis was still fighting a rear-guard action against such a compromise in the mid-1740s shows that there was still much work for the novel to do in establishing the right of the individual to form private judgments over the conduct of his or her life.

The letter to Betty, too, has its analogues in the world of the novel. The initiating action of both *Tom Jones* and *Clarissa*, as we have said, is the flight of a young woman from her father's house in order to assert a degree of sovereignty over the choice of her husband. The difference between them is that Sophia Western never judges her decision to leave home to be an "error," while Clarissa Harlow acknowledges that "I did a rash, an inexcusable thing, in meeting [Lovelace]" at the garden door, an error from which her tragedy proceeds.[34] For Anna Howe, and for most other readers of Clarissa's letters, her exercise of private judgment can be excused in many ways, but for Clarissa there is no way to redeem this single false step. In the concluding two chapters of this book, we will examine, among other things, Fielding's adoption of the "new philosophy" of such latitudinarian divines as John Wallis, elaborated by the Earl of Shaftesbury and Francis Hutcheson into moral sense philosophy, as the means by which his fictional protagonists distinguish between virtue and error in the performance of their private judgments. In contrast, we will examine the measures taken by the heroines of Richardson and Burney to correct their errors by extirpating from both body and soul the passions that have led them astray.

CHAPTER 8

"Mr. Jones *had Somewhat about him*": *Henry Fielding and the moral sense*

Early in Henry Fielding's novel *The History of Tom Jones*, Tom arrives at a moral crossroads. He has, without intending to do so, engaged the affections of Sophia Western, the heiress of the estate that neighbors his uncle's, while his own affections lie with the gamekeeper's daughter, Molly Seagrim, to whom he is drawn more by lust, mixed with compassion, than by love. Tom's recent success in his extraordinary request of Sophia – that she persuade her father to appoint the poacher "Black George" Seagrim as his gamekeeper – ought to have signaled to Tom that, by following a prudent course of conduct, he could eventually make himself both Sophia's husband and the master of her father's estate. In this situation, strict attention to prudence – the course so strongly recommended to Tom by Squire Allworthy, and still regarded by many readers as the moral center of the book – would direct Tom to abandon the gamekeeper's daughter and pursue his self-interest.[1] Tom, however, who wrongly believes Molly Seagrim's "Happiness or Misery" to be dependent on himself, declines to do so. The narrator chastises Tom for his "Want of Prudence" in failing to pursue this opportunity to secure his future, offering in extenuation only the "Matter of Fact" that Tom's moral choices are governed by a different kind of instrument than prudence: "Mr. *Jones* had Somewhat about him, which, though I think Writers are not thoroughly agreed in its Name, doth certainly inhabit some human Breasts; whose Use is not so properly to distinguish Right from Wrong, as to prompt and incite them to the former, and to restrain and with-hold them from the latter."[2]

A reader interested in establishing the underlying moral values of *Tom Jones* – and particularly what part the cure of the passions might play in securing those values – must pause at this passage to ascertain the nature of the "Somewhat" in Tom's breast that, contrary to prudent self-interest, compels him to remain faithful to his "not very judiciously placed" first love. The vague euphemism "Somewhat" simultaneously hints at and conceals the elusive moral compass that guides Tom through the book. In a footnote, the editors of the Wesleyan edition gloss the "Somewhat" as "of course, the conscience," but because the text specifies that this somewhat "doth certainly inhabit some human Breasts," they add that Fielding must be using the term in a "pre-Lockean" sense (171 n.1). Fielding, however, would certainly have known that John Locke had defined "conscience" as a learned set of moral rules which men derive "from their education, company, and customs of their country," not from anything "written on their hearts," and it is unlikely that he would have carelessly ignored this fundamental point in Locke's philosophy of human nature.[3] Further, even if the narrator has a pre-Lockean notion in view, conscience does not explain Tom's peculiar choice. Conscience, whether defined as a desire to do right or an awareness of having done wrong, is irrelevant in the present case. Tom has, after all, atoned at this point for his only wrongful act – that of causing Black George's dismissal from Squire Allworthy's service – by obtaining a new post for him with Squire Western; there is no reason for his conscience to be troubling him on that score. Nor would he feel guilt for having broken any fundamental moral law where Molly is concerned, first because he (unlike Mrs. Seagrim) is unaware of "the Alteration in the Shape of Molly" (IV. vii), and second because he does not intend to abandon her. Finally, the narrator tells us in this passage that, unlike conscience, the "Somewhat" does not act on Tom's rational will, allowing him to distinguish between right and wrong, but rather affects him involuntarily, prompting and inciting him toward good, and restraining him from ill.

What, then, is the nature of the "Somewhat about him" that prompts Tom to act in a manner contrary to prudence? For orthodox Christian readers, such as the latitudinarian divine John Wallis, the term "Somewhat" was useful in explaining how the Deity could consist of three entities and yet not be tritheistic: the Holy Trinity, said Wallis, consists of "three *Somewhats* which are but *one God*, which *Somewhats* we commonly call *persons*."[4] Richard Baxter, a Puritan divine, charged that the term was used by dissenting sects, such as the Quakers, to deny the divinity of Christ, "and only call Somewhat within themselves by the Name of Christ."[5] For other readers, the term might refer to an innate idea of goodness, a faculty of mind, a learned behavior, a mechanistic response to pleasure or pain, or a spirit or ether in the blood (thus the narrator's reminder that "Writers are not thoroughly agreed in its Name").[6] It might refer to Providence, the indwelling spirit that, according to Defoe, intervenes in our choices in mysterious ways; or to "Fortune" or

"Accident," those neoclassical surrogates for deities to which Fielding frequently ascribes the events that befall his characters; or to the new doctrine of "Sentiments," which was then coming into use to refer to "emotionalized thought."[7] But if Fielding had meant to invoke any of those agents in this passage, as he does at other junctures in the novel, he could have done so without using a euphemism. Instead, the agent that governs Tom's conduct is deliberately left vague, its nature unsubstantiated, defined only through the working out of the story. Fielding employs a euphemism, not because the nature of this agent is unimportant, but because it is too important to identify with a conventional literary or philosophical device. The nature of the "Somewhat about him" is, in short, the problem at the center of this novel: the anatomical investigations of the two centuries preceding *Tom Jones*, having proven that the only function of the heart is to circulate blood through the body, rather than to manufacture vital heat or to regulate the passions, have left a philosophical black hole where the soul had once been seated.[8]

Numerous commentators have noted this black hole in Fielding's work, and some have offered to fill it by describing the moral or philosophical system Fielding relied upon to govern the passions of the characters in his major novels. One of the first commentators was Samuel Johnson, who in the year after the publication of *Tom Jones* lamented the new taste for "the comedy of romance," in which the novelist imitates "those parts of nature . . . so often discoloured by passion, or deformed by wickedness," without correcting them. "To this fatal errour all those will contribute, who confound the colours of right and wrong," said Johnson of Fielding, whose crime was worse in that he was a skillful writer: "instead of helping to settle their boundaries," such authors mix right and wrong "with so much art, that no common mind is able to disunite them."[9] Boswell, who regarded Johnson's opinion of Fielding as arising from an "unreasonable prejudice," ventured to record in his *Life of Johnson* his rather more approving view of Fielding, that "the moral tendency of Fielding's writings, though it does not encourage a strained and rarely possible virtue, is ever favourable to honour and honesty, and cherishes the benevolent and generous affections."[10] Sir John Hawkins famously declared that Fielding's moral system was "that of Lord Shaftesbury vulgarized," – that, in abandoning "moral obligation and a sense of duty," Fielding (as well as Rousseau and Sterne) reduced virtue into goodness of heart, which was worth "little more than the virtue of a horse or a dog."[11]

Modern commentators have differed over the influence of Shaftesbury on Fielding. In a new biography of Fielding, Ronald Paulson argues that

Fielding was a "critical deist" who, following Shaftesbury, "questioned the authority of readings imposed on Scripture by the clergy, the evidence of the Scriptures themselves, and doctrines that flew in the face of reason."[12] Martin C. Battestin, however, rejects Shaftesbury's influence because he finds deism incompatible with the ethos underlying Fielding's art. Relying in part on an essay by R. S. Crane, Battestin argues that Shaftesbury's doctrine of benevolence is compatible with the thought of such latitudinarian divines as Isaac Barrow, John Tillotson, Samuel Clarke, and Benjamin Hoadley, whom he therefore identifies as the source of the moral thought in the novels.[13] Another commentator, Bernard Harrison, also rejects Shaftesbury's influence on Fielding, but on different grounds: he finds that Fielding's morality, unlike Shaftesbury's, is "as intrinsically volitional and ratiocinative as it is natural, appetitive and impulsive."[14] That is to say that Shaftesbury's system, while it depends on reflection and the cultivation of affections, contains no "active principle" that equates knowing the good with doing it. Such a principle, the narrator of *Tom Jones* had specified, was a necessary part of the "Somewhat" that guided Tom: "This Principle therefore prevented him from any Thought of making his Fortune by such Means (for this, as I have said, is an active Principle, and doth not content itself with Knowledge or Belief only)" (*TJ*, IV. vi). This "active Principle" is not, as it was for Shaftesbury, merely an aesthetic appreciation of beauty or virtue, leaving the beholder to will himself or herself to imitate its example; it is rather an irresistible impulse to the good, a passion that arises in the natural temper of the person. Harrison suggests that the work of David Hume may have offered Fielding such an "active principle," but he finally concurs with Battestin that Fielding probably depended upon "a tradition of Christian orthodoxy" represented by "latitudinarian divines like Barrow and Hoadley" (Harrison, *Novelist as Moral Philosopher*, 120).

Harrison's suggestion that Fielding may have based his moral system on David Hume's philosophical writings has not received much support. In his 1970 study of Hume, Fielding, and Gibbon as narrative historians, Leo Braudy noted that "evidence for the direct influence of Hume on Fielding or vice versa is sparse at best," and observed that the two authors differ sharply on the uses of public and private histories.[15] In an apparent riposte to Battestin, Braudy rejected the "currently popular" reading of Fielding as a "moral" novelist, arguing instead that Fielding is interested in "the way we transmute the mixed and complex impressions of the world into personal statements for action" (95, 148–49). In 1974, Battestin affirmed his moral and Christian reading of Fielding, adding that the novelist may have been provoked to write *Amelia* in order to repudiate the "sensationalist psychology" that Hume developed in his *Treatise of Human Nature* (1739) and *Philosophical Essays concerning Human Understanding* (1748).[16] According to Battestin, Fielding regarded Hume's skepticism as a threat to the "latitudinarian Christianity" that he favored, and he designed the resolution of *Amelia*, in which Captain William Booth renounces his errors and his Epicurean philosophy, to demonstrate the victory of "Christian humanism" over sensationalist psychology. Though fascinating, there are some difficulties with this thesis: Battestin admits that the psychology underlying the novel is very close to that used by Hume; that Dr. Harrison, the moral agent in the book, seems to endorse that psychology; and that Hume's *Treatise*, which in Hume's own words fell "dead-born from the press," was not likely to have given Fielding any cause for alarm.[17] In support of his argument, Battestin cites Hume's biographer, E. G. Mossner, who acknowledges that Hume was widely regarded as "the modern *bête noir*" of Christianity, but the year in which Mossner says Hume achieved that notoriety is 1763, not 1749.[18] It seems unlikely that Hume was either the target for Fielding's outrage or the source for the "active principle" that Fielding euphemized as a "Somewhat" about Tom Jones.

FIELDING, MANDEVILLE, AND HUTCHESON

There is, however, a likely source for the "Somewhat" that has been overlooked by Battestin, Braudy, Harrison, and even Paulson, who prefaces his biography of Fielding with the observation that it is "important to account for Fielding's particular moral sense" in any reading of his life or work.[19] This source is the moral philosophy of Francis Hutcheson, whose career was defined by his defense of Shaftesbury's doctrine of benevolence against the corrupting philosophy of selfishness associated with Bernard Mandeville. To establish the connection between Hutcheson and Fielding, we will briefly review the controversy over Mandeville's *Fable of the Bees* that preoccupied London during Fielding's formative years as a writer.

In the late 1720s, while Fielding was dividing his time between London and Leiden, where he had enrolled at the University as a student of letters, Bernard Mandeville's attack on Shaftesbury's doctrine of benevolence was shaping public discourse about the nature of man on both sides of the English Channel.[20] In 1723, Mandeville had published the second edition of *The Fable of the Bees*, a long commentary upon his earlier satirical poem,

The Grumbling Hive: or, Knaves Turn'd Honest. The vision of human society that Mandeville advanced in those works was essentially similar to that articulated by Hobbes in *Leviathan* and popularized on the Continent by Pierre Bayle and La Rochefoucauld, among others. But Mandeville improved upon the idea that man was a machine driven primarily by his passions by suggesting that society benefited from that fact, in effect dissolving the traditional association between passion and disease. Mandeville's famous dictum that private vices could encourage public benefits, in the form of increased consumption, employment, and trade, inverted the traditional order by which reason was privileged over passion. According to Mandeville, the passions are a function of the natural self-interest of man and woman: people "are never, or at least very seldom, reclaimed from their darling Passions, either by Reason or Precept, and that if any thing ever draws 'em from what they are naturally propense to, it must be a Change in their Circumstances or Fortunes." Rather than diseases, passions are the forces that raise people to activity; without the passions, man is a "lumpish Machine," or "a huge Wind-mill without a breath of Air."[21] As John Pocock has observed, Mandeville's realist critique painfully uncovered the fact that the popular ethos of the emerging world of relatively free individuals was not virtue, nor love, but desire – the shameless pursuit of appetites and passions.[22]

Though the young Fielding was not drawn into the controversy immediately, it provided the framework through which he would interpret human nature to the end of his career.[23] Twenty years after Leiden, he recalled the controversy in *Tom Jones*: in the chapter "Of Love," the narrator attacks "that modern Doctrine" which teaches that there is "no such Passion [of love] in the human Breast," a doctrine spread by a set of philosophers "who, some years since, very much alarmed the World, by shewing that there were no such things as Virtue or Goodness really existing in Human Nature, and who deduced our best Actions from Pride," or love of self (VI. i). The doctrine of self-love is made incarnate in the person of Master Blifil, in whom benevolence is absent and reason is the slave of selfish passion. The corrupting effects of self-love are also evident in the Man of the Hill, whose character name rhymes with Mandeville, and who holds a very low opinion of mankind based on the few bad examples of the species he has known, including himself (VIII. xv). In *Amelia*, Billy Booth is an adherent to the doctrine that man is a machine driven by a dominant passion: "the Doctrine of the Passions had been always his favourite Study; [and] he was convinced every Man acted entirely from that Passion which was uppermost" (*Amelia*, III. iv).

When, however, Miss Mathews approves his doctrine, and expresses doubts that anyone can act from motives of virtue or religion, an idea which she has held "ever since I read that charming fellow *Mandevil*," Booth reveals an important difference between himself and Mandeville: that philosopher, he says, has omitted love from his system, which Booth calls "the best Passion which the Mind can possess" (*Amelia*, III. v). Booth's criticism of the doctrine of selfishness preserves the possibility that his heart is sufficiently good to be redeemed by Amelia's love and Dr. Harrison's counsel at the end of the novel. It also suggests that Fielding accepted the premise of Hobbesism – that men are driven by their passions – while rejecting Mandeville's conclusion that the selfish passions will always predominate.

It is interesting, if not particularly surprising, that Sarah Fielding's *The Adventures of David Simple* takes the same anti-Mandevillian position on the passions. David Simple is a good-hearted man who is seldom affected by passion, and then generally of the sympathetic or compassionate kind; when he does feel anger or hatred, it is "one of those abortive Thoughts which are the first Sallies of our Passions, and which immediately vanish on Reflection."[24] His younger brother Daniel, however, is "one of those Wretches, whose only Happiness centers in themselves" (8). As their father lies dying, Daniel steals his will and replaces it with a forgery which leaves almost everything to himself. He then abuses David and allows the servants to insult him, with the intention of driving him from the house. In a moment of "inconsistent Behaviour, which must always be produced in a Mind torn at once by Tenderness and Rage" (13), David leaves the house, perhaps the only error in a spotless life. His adventures consist in hearing the histories of many others who have suffered the effects of passion until, his fortune restored, he secures the love of Camilla, whose friend Cynthia tells the story of a dying atheist, who confessed that

When I was a young Fellow, I took a delight in reading all those sort of Books which best suited my own Inclinations, by endeavouring to prove all *Pleasure* lay in *Vice*, – and that the *wisest thing* a Man could do, was to give a Loose to all his *Passions*, and take hold of the present Moment for Pleasure, without depending on *uncertain Futurity*. (223)

The dying atheist, of course, is Daniel, whose base nature had been further corrupted by exposure to that circle of freethinkers and deists described by Benjamin Franklin in his autobiography as a "Club" of which "Dr Mandevile, Author of the Fable of the Bees" was the

"Soul, being a most facetious entertaining Companion," and which, according to Battestin, included Fielding's friend James Ralph, if not Fielding himself.[25]

Henry Fielding's repudiation of the doctrine he associates with Mandeville in his major novels has been discussed in detail by several Fielding scholars, and there is no need to review their work here.[26] What has gone unnoticed in these accounts, however, is the degree to which that repudiation and its replacement by moral sense philosophy are indebted to Francis Hutcheson. Recent work on Hutcheson, who received scant attention through most of the twentieth century after being embalmed by Sir Leslie Stephen as a "servile disciple of Shaftesbury" and forerunner of utilitarianism, has established him as a key figure in the Scottish Enlightenment, the link between Shaftesbury on the one hand and Hume and Adam Smith on the other.[27] Fielding was in no sense a "Hutchesonian," but he clearly had the advantage of entering the dialogue on the passions after Hutcheson had clarified the way in which Shaftesbury's moral sense is not only an aesthetic faculty, nor merely a sentimental state of feeling, but the means by which the passions move us to moral action.[28]

When the second edition of Mandeville's *Fable of the Bees* was published in 1723, Francis Hutcheson (1674–1746) was the headmaster of a private academy in Dublin. His associates in Dublin included Robert, Viscount Molesworth, an admirer of Shaftesbury; the Reverend Edward Synge, a close friend of the future bishop, George Berkeley; and James Arbuckle, a literary maverick and editor of the *Dublin Journal*.[29] With their encouragement, he published six letters in the *Dublin Journal* in which he sought to refute the motive of self-interest in both Hobbes and Mandeville.[30] The first three of these letters were a response to an essay on laughter published in the *Spectator* (No. 47, April 24, 1711), which takes as its point of departure Hobbes' argument that what provokes laughter is a sense of "imagined superiority." Hutcheson objects in particular to Hobbes' assertion, as quoted in the *Spectator*, that "[t]he passion of laughter is nothing else but sudden glory, arising from some sudden conception of some eminency in our selves, by comparison with the infirmity of others, or with our own formerly" (Price, *Thoughts on Laughter*, 2–3). Using terms similar to those Fielding would later use to introduce the "Somewhat" which, "though I think Writers are not thoroughly agreed in its name, doth certainly inhabit some human Breasts," Hutcheson endeavors to show that there is "some other ground of that sensation, action, passion, or affection, I know not which of them a philosopher would call it" than pride or self-love that causes people to laugh (19).

Rather than a sudden sense of superiority, Hutcheson suggests that laughter is provoked by a discrepancy between two ideas that resemble each other, yet differ in some "contradictory additional ideas." Thus, the accidents that may befall "a person of great gravity," such as "the strange contortions of the body in a fall, the dirtying of a decent dress, the natural functions which we study to conceal from sight," may occasion laughter in that they contradict the assumed dignity of that person (27). In such cases, we do not laugh because we feel superior to the person who has suffered the fall, but because our sense of the ridiculous has been affected. Similarly, the "more violent passions, as fear, anger, sorrow, compassion" may arouse laughter in certain circumstances: if the passions displayed are ones that are "generally look'd upon as something great and solemn," but have been "artfully raised upon a small, or a fictitious occasion," the spectator senses the discrepancy to be ridiculous, and laughs (29–30). Writers of burlesque have long used this technique, says Hutcheson, by appropriating sentences from "any writing [that] has obtained an high character for grandeur, sanctity, inspiration, or sublimity of thoughts, and boldness of images" in order to describe "low, vulgar, or base subjects," with the result that the audience is invariably diverted, and set to laughing (25). A sense of the ridiculous, even in oneself, "may do good in a wise man's hands . . . Men have been laughed out of faults which a sermon could not reform" (49, 51). It is not difficult to recognize in Hutcheson's letters on the sense of the ridiculous the outlines of the theory of comedy that Fielding was to articulate fifteen years later in the preface to *Joseph Andrews*, where he located the "true Ridiculous" in the affectation of false characters, rather than in the supposed superiority of one person to another, and described laughter as a "Physic for the Mind" that is "better to purge away Spleen, Melancholy and ill Affections" than a tragedy or a grave lecture (5).

At about the time that Hutcheson's letters to the *Dublin Journal* were reprinted in London as *Hibernicus's Letters*, Fielding was in mid-career as a journalist and writer of burlesques and satires. In his "Essay on the Knowledge of the Characters of Men," written prior to 1741, he distinguishes the person of "Good-Nature," who possesses "that benevolent and amiable Temper of Mind which disposes us to feel the Misfortunes, and enjoy the Happiness of others," from that of "Good-Humour," which is marked by "that glavering Smile, whose principal ingredient is Malice," and which arises from "the Triumph of the

Mind, when reflecting on its own Happiness" compared with the lesser happiness of others.[31] Citing the same passage from Hobbes to which Hutcheson responded, Fielding admits that even a person of good temper may laugh at the sight of "a Person well dressed [who] should tumble in a dirty Place in the Street," but that the subsequent reflections of "a good and delicate Mind" will change laughter into compassion. The true character of a person, then, is not to be read in such reflexive responses as laughter, but in that person's reflection upon his internal sense of what is properly ridiculous, and what is not. Like Hutcheson, Fielding supposes that a sense of the ridiculous is best employed not in puffing oneself up, but in detecting hypocrisy and affectation wherever it is found. Some years later, he would draw on this distinction in making Amelia the victim of an accident whereby her nose is disfigured, which makes her vulnerable to the "cruel Insults" of her associates, "several of whom, after many Distortions and Grimaces, have turned their Heads aside, unable to support their secret Triumph, and burst into a loud Laugh in her hearing" (*Amelia*, II. i). Booth, however, whose nature is essentially good, is moved to compassion, rather than laughter, by her misfortune.

Another resemblance between Hutcheson's and Fielding's moral thought appears in their rejection of the Mandevillian thesis that all human actions derive from self-love: "by some bad fortune," says Hutcheson, Hobbes (and by implication Mandeville) "has over-look'd every thing which is generous or kind in mankind; and represents men in that light in which a thorow knave or coward beholds them, suspecting all friendship, love, or social affection, of hypocrisy, or selfish design or fear" (Price, *Thoughts on Laughter*, 3–4). In *Tom Jones*, as noted above, the Man of the Hill overlooks these same qualities in mankind when he prefaces his life story by saying that "great Philanthropy chiefly inclines us to avoid and detest Mankind; not on Account so much of their private and selfish Vices, but for those of a relative Kind; such as Envy, Malice, Treachery, Cruelty, with every other Species of Malevolence" (VIII. x). His contempt is hypocritical in that his own vices, and his choice of friends, are the bases of experience on which he makes these observations of mankind. At the conclusion of his tale, he acts the part of a "thorow knave or coward" by standing aside with his gun as a would-be rapist attacks Mrs. Waters, whom Tom saves with his walking-stick (IX. ii). In *Amelia*, as we have seen, Booth uses much the same terms as Hutcheson's to distance himself from Mandeville, who he says "hath left out of his System the best Passion which the Mind can possess, and attempts to derive the Effects or Energies of that Passion, from the base Impulses of Pride or Fear" (III. v). Such textual similarities are not conclusive, but they do establish the likelihood that Fielding had seen Hutcheson's letters to the *Dublin Journal*, probably in James Arbuckle's collections of 1729 or 1734, and that it was from Hutcheson that Fielding drew the conclusion that, while humanity is driven primarily by its passions, there may still be in some uncorrupted instances of human nature a "somewhat" that approves love of one's fellow man as the uppermost passion.

To the extent, then, that Fielding drew his theory of the passions from Hutcheson, the "Somewhat" that inhabited Tom's breast is an internal moral sense that functions in the involuntary way that a sense of the ridiculous forces us to laugh. Hutcheson's most elaborate statement of this moral sense came in his *Essay on the Nature and Conduct of the Passions and Affections. With Illustrations on the Moral Sense*, published in 1728. A resounding answer to Hobbes, Mandeville, and the Epicureans, the *Essay* was to become the cornerstone of the Scottish Enlightenment; its definitions and figures would be echoed repeatedly by David Hume in the *Treatise of Human Nature* (1739/40), by Adam Smith in his *Theory of Moral Sentiments* (1759), and by Tobias Smollett in his novels, who like Smith attended Hutcheson's lectures at Glasgow.[32] The *Essay* describes the passions neither as inherently sinful or pathological, nor as spirits, *pneuma*, or humours in the blood, but rather closer to what we now call emotions: they are "*Modifications, or Actions of the Mind consequent upon the Apprehension of certain Objects or Events, in which the Mind generally conceives Good or Evil.*"[33] The mind is equipped with "some *Sense* or other" capable of discerning pleasure or pain in the objects of perception, which upon subsequent experiences become "Ideas," or "*Perceptions* of an *internal Sense*" (2). These perceptions arouse "*uneasy confused Sensations*" that are painful or pleasurable, depending on the ideas we have formed about the object. These sensations sometimes produce "violent *Motions* in our Bodies," which can make us "unfit for serious Deliberation about the Means of obtaining the Good desired," or they may be calming in their effect, such as the experience of joy attending the perception of general or public good (47). When we form an idea of good or evil in an object, we acquire an affection for it, which when attended by desire (or aversion) becomes a passion. The moral sense "approves" these passions, or approves the restraint of them, and teaches us, through reflection, to prefer the calm passions attending upon benevolence (31). Reason plays little part in this process, other than to assist over time in the development of "affections," or preferences for one set of sensations over another; they arise "from the very *Frame of our Nature*, however we may regulate or moderate them" (47–48). These passions lead directly to "Action, or the Volition of Motion" (59).

An important distinction between Shaftesbury's system and Hutcheson's has to do with the rewards for benevolence. Rewards and punishments, which raise "considerations of interest," are of limited use in encouraging benevolence because they appeal to self-interest, rather than to the moral sense, but Hutcheson does not exclude them; unlike Shaftesbury, he allows that the pleasurable sensations that attend acts of goodness may be a motive for benevolence. In the case of "a temper wholly vitiated," rewards and punishments are "the only, or best means" of bringing about its recovery, though "there still must be much more to form a truly great and good man."[34] In the case of a mind free of corruption but still afflicted by anger, jealousy, or fear, the passions can be corrected only by showing the disturbed mind that "its state may still be happy . . . that its loss is repairable, or that it has still an opportunity of valuable enjoyments in life" (Mautner, *Francis Hutcheson*, 104). Such recoveries can be brought about not through suppressing the passions, but by presenting the subject with "just representations of the objects of our passions," perhaps through drama or literature: "When we form the Idea of a *morally good Action*," says Hutcheson in the *Essay on the Passions*, "or see it represented in the *Drama*, or read it in *Epicks* or *Romance*, we feel a *Desire* arising of doing the like" (69).

Hutcheson's theory of the origin of benevolence in an internal sense of virtue is, of course, a good deal more complex than this summary suggests. Our concern here is simply to show that Fielding's novelistic art in the 1740s is largely consistent with Hutcheson's philosophical efforts between 1725 and 1735 to promote virtue through the cultivation of public affection, and that this movement amounted to more than a simple revival of Shaftesburianism. Unlike Shaftesbury, who regarded the temperament of man as fixed by nature, and who offered little more in the form of a path to virtue than the admonition to study and reflect upon the balance of passions within the self (*Characteristicks* I: 294–95), Hutcheson saw in the cultivation of public affection an opportunity to alter human nature for the better by restoring fallen mankind to the natural goodness instilled in him by his creator.[34] In his inaugural lecture as Professor of Moral Philosophy at the College of Glasgow in 1730, Hutcheson declared that the "original structure of our nature was destined by divine art and design for everything seemly, virtuous, and excellent," and that "clear signs of this design and art are preserved even in the ruins of this structure" (Mautner, *Francis Hutcheson*, 132). He rejected all moral philosophy based on a supposed "state of nature" in which mankind appears as "naked, mute, wretched, solitary, filthy, uncouth, ignorant, repulsive, cowardly, petulant, rapacious, and unsocial" – a "brute which neither loves nor is loved by anyone" – in favor of a "natural state" of man, which he defined as "the most perfect condition that can be attained by means of the powers implanted in human nature" (131–32). These powers were implanted by a wise and benevolent God who created man in his own image, and who – unlike Shaftesbury's deity, whose characteristics are largely Stoic and deistic – seeks a close and reciprocal relationship with his creation, like a parent or physician.[36] There is no better evocation of man in his "natural state" than Fielding's Squire Allworthy, stepping forth onto his terrace in the morning sun, "a human Being replete with Benevolence, meditating in what manner he might render himself most acceptable to his Creator, by doing most good to his Creatures" (*TJ*, I: iv). Squire Allworthy may be, as numerous commentators have noted, a poor judge of character and an imprudent magistrate, but he is uncorrupted in his natural goodness.[37]

The world that Tom Jones inhabits, on the other hand, more closely resembles the state of nature that Hobbes described. Like the journey taken by Joseph Andrews through much the same territory, Tom's progress from Glastonbury to London exposes him to a world in which selfishness distorts and demeans human nature. Beginning with his brother Blifil, almost all of Tom's acquaintances prove to be driven by private, rather than public, affections: Black George conceals the bankbill Allworthy gave to Tom; Partridge offers Tom his service in hopes of restoring himself to Allworthy's favor; lawyer Dowling hides what he knows of Tom's history to improve his interest with one whom he thinks may someday inherit Allworthy's estate, and so on. Sophia's cousin, Mrs. Fitzpatrick, eventually reveals herself to be, as the narrator declares, one of those "fine Women ... with whom Self is so predominant, that they never detach it from any Subject" (XVI: ix). In the course of embroiling Tom in a scheme by which she hopes to revenge herself on both her cousin and her aunt, Mrs. Fitzpatrick accidentally falls in love with him herself: she "now began to feel a Somewhat for Mr. *Jones*, the Symptoms of which she much sooner understood than poor *Sophia* had formerly done" (XVI: ix). This "Somewhat" is an affection, but it differs from the "Somewhat" that Tom feels: the difference is that, where Tom's affections are public and benevolent by nature, Mrs. Fitzpatrick's are diminished by a love of self to the point that they more nearly resemble appetites than affections.

Even Tom's temperament, which is described by the narrator as "naturally sanguine," a "Disposition of Mind . . . which puts us, in a Manner, out of the Reach of Fortune, and makes us happy without her Assistance" (XIII: vi), is not immune to attacks of passion. A dramatic instance of Tom's irascibility occurs after Tom and Partridge have left the inn at Upton, where Partridge's indiscretion had perhaps cost Tom the love of Sophia. In the grip of despair, Tom blames Sophia's cruelty, then himself, and then fastens on Partridge as the cause of his misery. "'Damnation seize thee, Fool, Blockhead!'" he cries, "'thou hast undone me, and I will tear thy Soul from thy Body' – At which Words he laid violent Hands on the Collar of poor Partridge, and shook him more heartily than an Ague Fit, or his own Fears had ever done before" (XII: iii). After "staring wildly" at the pathetic Partridge for a moment, Tom releases him and "discharged a Rage on himself, that had it fallen on the other, would certainly have put an End to his Being." But by degrees, after having "played the part of a Madman for many Minutes," Tom regains control of himself and begs Partridge's pardon "for the Attack he had made on him in the Violence of his Passion." As in Galen's narrative of the man from Crete, Tom's re-direction of his anger at himself is proof of his natural goodness, but Partridge remains apprehensive that his next word will throw his master back "into another Passion."

Besides his displeasure with Partridge after the incident at Upton, Tom displays his anger several more times: after intervening on Molly's behalf in the battle of the churchyard, Tom "raved like a Madman, beat his Breast, tore his Hair, stamped on the Ground, and vowed the utmost Vengeance on all who had been concerned" (IV: viii), and after he has been expelled from Allworthy's estate, he throws himself down by a little brook and falls into "the most violent Agonies, tearing his Hair from his Head, and using most other Actions which generally accompany Fits of Madness, Rage, and Despair" (VI: xii). When, however, he intervenes in the quarrel between Nightingale and his footman, which in a sense mirrors Tom's earlier quarrel with his own servant, he acts the part of peacemaker: after winning the combat with the footman, and receiving Nightingale's explanation that he had struck his servant because the latter had cast reflections on the name of a certain young lady, Tom admits sympathetically that "I should, on the last mentioned Provocation, have done the same Thing" (XIII: v). The incident reveals the difference between Tom Jones and the Hobbesian world he inhabits: he too is driven by his passions, but his moral sense prompts him to act not only in his own interest but also in the interests of others, an "active principle" in the pursuit of good.

TOM AND NIGHTINGALE, "SITTING MELANCHOLY BY THE FIRE"

Readers who, like Samuel Johnson, are disappointed by the moral implications of *Tom Jones* often note that Tom never attempts to redeem himself in Sophia's eyes for his misdemeanors of conduct with Mrs. Waters and Lady Bellaston, nor does his character undergo any significant reformation. Tom's redemption, however, could not depend on Sophia, because the moral worth of any action that he might take to improve his standing in her eyes would be compromised by self-interest. The moral action of the novel has very little to do with Sophia's consent to marry Tom; she agrees to marry him in obedience to her father's wishes, which she had promised always to respect, and it is only a happy coincidence that her own prior inclinations accord with the commands of her father once he has learned that Tom is Allworthy's rightful heir. The values of affection and duty to parental authority are affirmed by the match, but no moral action is required to bring it about. Tom offers no defense of his conduct with Mrs. Waters and Lady Bellaston other than to say that he has renounced his "Life of . . . Wickedness" (XVII: v), and that a woman as pure as Sophia cannot conceive how little "one Sort of Amour has to do with the Heart" (XVIII: xii). Nor does he offer any guarantees of future fidelity, except to show Sophia her own face in the mirror – an empirical proof, powerful in the age of sensibility, but not one based in either moral principle or his own character history. The moral action of the novel does not depend on Tom's redemption in Sophia's eyes, but on quite another person: his friend Nightingale, whose affection for Nancy Miller has ended in her pregnancy.

When Tom first encounters Nightingale after learning of the pregnancy, he finds him "sitting melancholy by the Fire" (*TJ*, XIV. vii), the very picture of despair. Rather than marry poor Nancy, Nightingale has resolved to betray her and, in obedience to his father's desires, marry an heiress instead. If Allworthy represents a near approach to Hutcheson's "natural state" of man, Nightingale represents the antithesis – a man corrupted and vitiated by the indulgence of selfish pleasures. He is the sort of person Hutcheson had described in a letter to the *London Journal* as the product of Epicurean philosophy: one in whom self-love and the pursuit of sensation have eroded almost all sense of humanity; one for whom the only means of recovering "a temper wholly vitiated, and of altering a corrupted taste of life" lies in an appeal to self-interest, since he is dead to reason or public affection.[38] Tom's stern rebukes to Nightingale for his heartless conduct toward Nancy produce changes of color in the malefactor's face, along with "violent Emotions" and "a deep Sigh," but no resolution to change his conduct. It is not until Tom mentions "the warm, rapturous Sensations, which we feel from the Consciousness of an honest, noble, generous, benevolent Action" and describes the palpable rewards of domestic bliss that Nightingale confesses his love for Nancy and his readiness to honor his promises to her, provided that his father's opposition can be overcome. The "warm, rapturous sensations" that Tom refers to are the physical rewards of benevolence, which Hutcheson had allowed may be a basis for moral action, provided that they arise from a public affection, rather than a private one.[39] Tom holds up the "objects" of affection before Nightingale for his calculus: on the one hand, the consequences of ill or private affection, including the possible death of Nancy, her mother's madness, and the ruin of the family; on the other, the effects of public affection, including Nancy's joy, her mother's exultations, and the family's happiness. Perhaps Tom unfairly weights the scale by adding "the Consideration that it is your Duty" to undo the wrong that he has done, but, as Nightingale says, he does not need this reminder to do right by Nancy. Tom's appeal to the physical rewards of benevolence and the Hutchesonian calculus of happiness are sufficient to show Nightingale that, as Hutcheson says in the *Essay on the Passions,* "the Vice and Misery in the World are smaller than we sometimes in our melancholy Hours imagine" (183).

Unlike the species of melancholy anatomized by Robert Burton, Nightingale's illness originates neither in excessive passion nor in his temperament, which is essentially sound and healthy; rather, his melancholy arises from two sources external to himself: the corruption of the town, which has taught him to pursue his interest at the expense of virtue, and the overbearing authority of his father, who has considered nothing but monetary interests in his choice of a wife for his son (XIV: viii). When Tom shares a bottle with Nightingale after the affair of the footman, he finds that he has "much good Sense, though a little too much tainted with Town Foppery; but what recommended him most to *Jones* were some Sentiments of great Generosity and Humanity" regarding love (XII: v). Subsequent events show these sentiments to be a little disingenuous, but even when the worst is known, the narrator assures us that Nightingale's nature was not one of those "so entirely diabolical, as to be capable of doing Injuries, without paying themselves some Pangs, for the Ruin which they bring on their Fellow-Creatures" (XIV: vii). When Tom asks Nightingale if he has any commitments that compete with his affection for Nancy, Nightingale affirms that "Passion leads me only to her," using a phrase that might equally describe Tom's feelings for Sophia. In both Tom's case and Nightingale's, passion is not the cause, but rather the *cure* of illnesses of the spirit; once the obstacles to mankind's natural benevolence are removed, the "Somewhat" of an affection for public good, working through indirect causes such as Mrs. Miller's gratitude to Tom, is free to find its own resolution.

It is significant that there is no personification of the "Physician of the Mind" in *Tom Jones* other than, perhaps, Tom himself. Parson Adams endeavors to perform that role in *Joseph Andrews*, despite the predominance of his own passions, and the eponymous Friendly assuages the grief of his condemned master Heartfree by promising to protect his wife and children in *Jonathan Wild*, but there is no clergyman, doctor, or friend to comfort Tom Jones. The only reference to a "physician of the mind" in the novel is made by the Man of the Hill, who in recounting his grief upon the death of his father, observes that "Time, however, the best Physician of the Mind, at length brought me Relief" (VII: xiii). By this point in the Man of the Hill's narrative, Tom is already suspicious of the hermit's Stoicism as a rationalization for his alienation from mankind, and the fact that he finds his solace not in a human advisor but in an abstraction only points up the value that Tom – and the novel – places on affection and benevolence, which he so sorely misses after his expulsion from Allworthy's home. Instead of receiving good counsel from an advisor, Tom must instead provide it for others, particularly in the Nightingale episode. The absence of a counselor for Tom emphasizes the internality of the moral sense, the fact that it cannot be taught or otherwise acquired if not already present in human nature. As Booth's story in *Amelia* makes clear, it can be lost through corruption or false beliefs, in which case a physician of the mind like Dr. Harrison is essential for its restoration, but Tom is never in that predicament. He is tempted by his appetites, and indeed succumbs to them, but for Fielding, such weaknesses are not the test of morality. The greatest error is to prefer, in defiance of the natural love of virtue imparted to man by the deity, selfish interests over public benefits.

MELANCHOLY BILLY: "A DULL LIFELESS LUMP OF CLAY"

Fielding's campaign against the error of self-love and his representation of the cure of that passion also inform the design of his last novel, *Amelia* (1751). Martin Battestin, the editor of the Wesleyan edition, seems mystified by Fielding's choice of the year 1733 in which to set the action of the novel, but there is a simple explanation: it was the year that Bernard Mandeville died.[40] Mandeville's theories were then at the height of fashion, and a recent attack on him by Hutcheson's associate, the Reverend George Berkeley, had re-ignited the controversy.[41] Battestin acknowledges that, in the early 1730s, Fielding himself came under the sway of the "little circle of philosophical rakes" that included James Ralph and Thomas Cooke, and that in this period Fielding had a "flirtation with the deistical principles of his clever friends."[42] It is plausible that Fielding memorialized his own recovery from the infection of Mandevillism by setting the story of young Billy Booth, whom the narrator describes as "naturally of a sanguine Temper," in the year of the death of his nemesis.

Though sanguine by nature, Billy Booth is prey to melancholy, in which state he resembles "a dull lifeless Lump of Clay" (IV: iii). The resemblance between Booth and *Tom Jones*'s Nightingale is not accidental: in both cases, a good-natured man is corrupted by the values of the town and by his own philosophical errors, which lead him to betray an innocent woman whose love he undervalues. Both men are able to reverse their declines when their errors are shown to them by a friend, who "well knows when to sooth, when to reason, and when to ridicule," arts that are often improperly used by "Physicians of the Mind" (*Amelia*, III: ii). By making the Nightingale/Booth character the central figure of the novel, rather than a peripheral one, Fielding sought to emphasize the moral nature of the work, which readers such as Samuel Johnson had missed in *Tom Jones*.

The moral action of *Amelia* is also tied more tightly to the resolution of the novel than it is in *Tom Jones*. The resolution of that book depends upon the demonstration of Tom's goodness of heart in the fable of Nightingale and Nancy, which is connected to the story only through Mrs. Miller's testimony; in *Amelia*, Booth's putative "conversion" provides the basis of the resolution. It is, however, a very problematical conversion.

Carla Mulford sees Booth's illness as a "philosophical confusion" which
he cures by means of "self-examination"; when Booth reads Barrow's
sermons, says Mulford, he "bursts forth in praise of the Christian theology espoused by Amelia and Dr. Harrison."[43] Battestin also believes
that Booth undergoes a radical philosophical change amounting to a
religious conversion, brought about "by reading Barrow's eloquent exposition of the Creed."[44] The text of the novel, however, suggests that
Booth's revelation is something less than a conversion. In the crucial
scene, Booth denies that he ever was a "rash Disbeliever" in religion,
admitting only that he had doubts, the chief one being "that as Men
appeared to me to act entirely from their Passions, their Actions could
have neither Merit nor Demerit" (XII: v). This doubt, in turn, led to
scepticism about the prospect of reward or punishment in an afterlife.
His reading of Barrow's sermons convinces him not that his doctrine
of passions is wrong, but that it is not inconsistent with a belief in God
and a distinction between the moral worth of actions. Nothing is said
between Booth and Dr. Harrison that suggests that Booth no longer believes that men are ruled by their passions; what Dr. Harrison does say is
that "that Religion [is] true which applies immediately to the strongest of
these Passions, Hope and Fear, chusing rather to rely on its Rewards and
Punishments, than on that native Beauty of Virtue which some of the
antient Philosophers thought proper to recommend to their Disciples"
(XII. v). In other words, by making use of the passions of hope (for
salvation) and fear (of punishment in an afterlife), Christianity (unlike
Stoicism) proves its validity through its conformity to human nature.
Booth's reading of Barrow has not taught him to repudiate the passions,
but rather that the love of virtue and the hope of eternal reward may
lead a believer into morally just actions. This view is also consistent with
Hutcheson's *Essay on the Passions*, in which he argues that all the "present
Disorders" of life may "be rectified by the *directing Providence* in a future
Part of our Existence," and that the "Belief of a DEITY, a PROVIDENCE, and
a *future State*, are the only sure Supports to a good Mind."[45] Fielding certainly admired Barrow's sermons, and may have found in them a way to
cloak his moral philosophy with orthodoxy and to emphasize its compat-
ibility with religion, but the philosophy itself is firmly grounded in human
nature, not in transcendent values or eternal verities. The "Somewhat"
in human nature (and therefore in the breasts of Heartfree, Tom Jones,
Sophia Western, Nightingale, Billy Booth, Amelia, Dr. Harrison, and
other uncorrupted or redeemed persons) is a passion for those actions
that arise from public affection, that reward us with the warm, rapturous

sensations of having been beneficial to ourselves and to mankind, and that allow us to hope that present disorders will sometime be rectified.

The identification of the "Somewhat" in the breasts of Fielding's protagonists as a Hutchesonian affection for the public good helps to answer some of the larger questions about Fielding's novels. The question of Fielding's deism, which has preoccupied critics in recent years, becomes less puzzling when it is understood that his use of moral sense philosophy betokens neither an attachment to Shaftesburian freethinking, which Paulson argues was the basis for Fielding's lifelong habit of critical reading, nor a pietistic regard for latitudinarian Christianity, but rather is the product of his engagement in a secular campaign against the corrupting philosophy of selfishness.[46] The question of the moral basis of Fielding's art, too, is answered in part by the recognition that his novels depict the cure of the error of an affection for the self through the restoration to a natural state of goodness of a protagonist who has been corrupted by the passions of the town and the evil influence of his "clever friends." The cure requires all of the arts of the physician of the mind, "when to sooth, when to reason, and when to ridicule," arts that are seldom employed with the "very great Judgment and Dexterity" they require (*Amelia*, III. ii). What we do not find in Fielding is the violent suppression or extirpation of the passions through the imposition of a code of manners or the amputation of the affected organ. This latter kind of cure is more likely to be found in Richardson and Burney, to which we now turn.

CHAPTER 9

Burney, Richardson, and the "extirpation" of passion

One of the most compelling descriptions of a medical procedure in the early modern period is the twelve-page letter written between March and June 1812 by Frances Burney to her sister Esther, describing the mastectomy she had undergone in September 1811 to remove a suspected cancer in her left breast. Burney bore the operation like a Stoic, "with all the courage I could exert, & never moved, nor stopt [the surgeons], nor resisted, nor remonstrated, nor spoke," except to express sympathy for their pain in having to inflict suffering upon her.[1] The letter, which is now a standard selection for anthologies of eighteenth-century literature, has received the attention of several literary critics, particularly Julia Epstein, who describes it as an "oddly paraliterary document" that is "part medico-surgical treatise and part sentimental fiction." According to Epstein, Burney employed the codes of both the novel and the medical case history to simultaneously expose and distance herself from the pain and horror that she felt while undergoing the violence of this twenty-minute procedure, which was performed without anaesthesia.[2]

Burney's biographers have interpreted the letter as a key to her life and work. Joyce Hemlow's account is generally literal, emphasizing the letter's emotional content while avoiding its metaphorical implications. Nevertheless, she does describe the seven black-robed surgeons who attended the operation as "ghoulish," and Hemlow's conclusion, "when they carried her away, her head rolled and dropped and her arms hung down like lifeless things, there being no force, almost no life within," paraphrases Burney's suggestion that she had undergone an execution of sorts, perhaps by guillotine.[3] Margaret Anne Doody adopts this metaphor, describing Burney as "the central figure at a species of execution, a macabre sort of theatre," and finds a literary analogue for it in the attempted self-murder in *The Wanderer* of Elinor Joddrel, who plunges a knife into her breast while surrounded by a crowd of men who appear "rather as spectators of some public execution, than as actors in a scene of humanity."[4] Doody sees the central action of the mastectomy as a struggle between "male and professional authority against female autonomy" (Doody, *Frances Burney* 344), relying in part on Julia Epstein's prior interpretation of the operation as "a dynamic of male-female power relations" (Epstein, "Writing the Unspeakable" 146).

Epstein's analysis of the narrative benefits from her long study of the structure of medical case histories and anatomies. Though Epstein recognizes the resemblances between Burney's operation and an execution, she is more interested in what often follows execution, that is, the public anatomization of the body of the convicted felon. She reads the narrative as an imaginative reenactment of "the anatomization of the author's body, a private body violated and made public through the experience of surgery" (131). According to Epstein, the narrative is similar to Burney's novels in that all of these literary works re-present "her analyses of female fear and the forced loss of control that constantly lurks beneath society's polite forms and coerces women into self-suppression" (132). That is, Burney wrote this and other narratives to defuse "the framework of dominance and submission that she found as oppressive as the physical pain" of the operation. Writing is a form of therapy through which Burney converts her pain into a text: "she reopens, relives, and recloses her wound by representing it in writing" (150). It is relevant to Epstein's thesis that the purpose of the operation is the removal of the female breast, "the visible sign of femininity" (155). Heightening the oppressive quality of the incident is the fact that, in the opinion of some modern physicians, the tumor was probably not malignant, in which case the operation would not have been necessary.[5]

While this interpretation of the narrative is strongly persuasive, it is not without its problems. Underlying the interpretations by both Epstein and Doody is the suggestion that Burney was the victim of a patriarchal medical system that sought to enact a form of female castration on her. It is true that it was Burney's husband, Alexandre d'Arblay, who first suggested to her that she should consult a surgeon about the pain in her breast, but it was a letter from Mme. Destutt de Tracy that frightened her into agreeing to the operation; Burney notes that Mme. de Tracy's "long experience of disease, & the most miserable existence by art" lent "urgency" to her "representations" about the danger of breast cancer (*JL*, VI: 599). Burney's personal physician, M. Dubois, whom she calls "the most celebrated surgeon of France," declined at first to operate, prescribing instead a course of medication and rest; in his apparent failure to treat her pain aggressively, Burney reads a dreadful message: "I had not, therefore, much difficulty in telling myself what he endeavoured not to tell me – that a small operation would be necessary to avert evil consequences!" (VI: 600). In response to the physician's perceived indifference – or resignation – Burney's subjective perception of her pain is magnified: "Direful, however, was the effect of this interview; the pains became quicker & more violent, & the hardness of the spot affected encreased" (*ibid.*). Burney insists on another opinion, and through her husband obtains an interview with an army surgeon, Dominique-Jean Larrey, who will not see her until she has written a letter to M. Dubois "to state my affright at the delay" of the operation any longer. Even then, Larrey's first recourse is to prescriptions, not surgery, and the treatment seems to be working until Burney simultaneously learns of the deaths of the Princess Amelia and William Locke Sr., and the illness of George III (*ibid.*). These three "calamities" precipitate a deterioration in her condition such that M. Larrey, "when he came to see me next after the last of these trials, was quite thrown into a consternation, so changed he found all for the worse," and he consents to perform the operation.[6] It is not at all clear that the changes in Burney's condition were physiological in origin; in fact, she remarks that her breast is "no where discoloured, & not much larger than its healthy neighbor." Rather, the necessity for the operation appears to arise in her conviction that there is an "evil" in her breast that she must remove, even at the cost of her life: "I felt the evil to be deep, so deep, that I often thought if it could not be dissolved, it could only with life be extirpated" (VI: 603). In the face of this sequence of events and statements, it is difficult not to see Burney's deterioration as a hysterical response to the fears of breast cancer generated by her husband and her friend Mme. de Tracy, and to the news of the deaths and illnesses of friends she had left behind in her native land.

While no one would suggest that Burney *desired* to have this operation, the language of Burney's representation, taken with the metaphorical meanings of cancer identified by Susan Sontag, suggests that the "evil" that she sought to extirpate from her breast may have been something other than a tumor.[7] Close analysis of this language suggests that the mastectomy may have been a means for Burney to come to terms with the "writing mania" that had driven her for most of her life. In her *Memoirs of Dr. Burney*, published in 1832 when she was almost eighty, she describes her early struggles to suppress her passion for writing, using the third person: "From the time, however, that she attained her fifteenth year, she considered it her duty to combat this writing passion as illaudable, because fruitless" – that is, the fruit that it produced was forbidden by her father.[8] She burned all of her early works in a bonfire, built "with the sincere intention to extinguish for ever in their ashes her scribbling propensity," but this "grand feat . . . extirpated neither the invention nor the inclination that had given them birth." Instead, as we know very well, the passion for writing dominated her waking hours, leading her to compose four major novels, seven complete plays, and thousands of letters, diaries, and journal entries. It may be mere coincidence that Burney chose the same verb – "extirpated" – to describe the removal of the cancer in her breast that she would later use to describe the ceremonial burning of her early literary works through which she sought to suppress her passion for writing. I suggest, however, that her choice of the verb "extirpate" is deliberate, and that she uses it in the radical sense that it carried in Stoic therapies of desire – which, in Martha C. Nussbaum's paraphrase of Cicero, intended to "not only cut out the external manifestation but also tear out the roots of the passion that go deep into the soul."[9]

According to this interpretation of her narrative, Burney associated the pain she felt from the tumor in her breast with her passion for writing, which her father and others had led her to believe was an "evil" quality, but which she knew to be an intrinsic part of her nature whose extirpation she feared she could not survive. The situation was perhaps exacerbated by her inability to finish her final novel, which she had begun in the mid–1790s, some fifteen years earlier. It is possible that, by projecting the guilt and anxiety she felt over her passion for writing onto the tumor in her breast, and then having the tumor removed, she relieved herself of the sense that her writing was evil.[10] Within three years of the mastectomy, this novel – *The Wanderer, or Female Difficulties* – was completed and published.[11] Her renewed interest in the book and her ability to finish it may be causally related to the fact that she had survived an operation to remove what she had feared "could only with life be extirpated."

It is well known that Burney's inhibitions about writing had their proximate cause in the censorious views on female authorship held by her father, Dr. Charles Burney, and her other literary and personal advisors, including Samuel Crisp and William Locke Sr. But the connection between writing and her perception of the tumor in her breast may ultimately be the legacy of the medico-philosophical tradition that has been examined in the previous chapters of this book. As we have seen, this tradition held that illness may result from disturbances of the humours of the body, which in turn are consequences of an excessive or long-continued arousal of the passions. These illnesses could take the form of tumors: one Stoic philosopher warned that "Sickness is an appetitive opinion which has flowed into a tenor and hardened."[12] By the end of the seventeenth century, many physicians doubted the humoural theory of disease, arguing instead that disease was nothing more than a disturbance of the mechanical motion of corpuscles in the body; yet even Robert Boyle, the leading exponent of this view, allowed that the passions of the mind could produce such disturbances, and thus that diseases could arise in emotional states or acts of imagination.[13]

The literary tradition that Burney inherited was also one in which passion, illness, and error are fundamentally connected. In the year prior to her birth, Henry Fielding's *Amelia* described a virtuous woman whose husband, misled by an Epicurean pursuit of the passions of the town, betrays and neglects her, and is redeemed only through the intervention of Dr. Harrison. In 1752, the year that Burney was born, Charlotte Lennox's *The Female Quixote* told the story of a young woman whose passionate attachment to a romantic belief system disposes her to errors that nearly end in her death by drowning, from which she is rescued by a "good Divine, who had the Cure of Arabella's Mind greatly at heart" (368). In 1753–54, Samuel Richardson's *Sir Charles Grandison* presented a hero who, in the words of one of Richardson's correspondents, had "but one fault . . . and that is, he has no fault, no passions"; Grandison is one in whom breeding, education, and the guidance of his "monitor," Dr. Ambrose Bartlett, have made the extirpation of ill passions unnecessary.[14] In the final paragraphs of *The Wanderer*, Burney describes her heroine, Juliet Granville, as "a being who had been cast upon herself; a female Robinson Crusoe"; like that archetypal adventurer, whose passions consigned him to an individualistic existence of loneliness and danger, Juliet (and all of Burney's other female protagonists) is "as unaided and unprotected, though in the midst of the world, as that imaginary hero in his uninhabited island; and reduced either to sink, through inanition, to nonentity, or to be rescued from famine and death by such resources as she could find, independently, in herself."[15] With such precedents as these weighing on her, it is not surprising that Burney saw passion as, if not a disease, at least a fatal flaw in human nature that required extirpation.

PAMELA, EVELINA, AND THE TRIALS OF PASSION

The necessity to extirpate passion from the human breast is nowhere better described than in the novels of Samuel Richardson, whose works were well known to Burney.[16] Unlike Fielding, who believed that even irascible passions could be incorporated into a framework of affection in persons of sound and sanguine temper, Richardson mistrusted the passions. As Morris Golden put it, "Richardson sees at the base [of man's nature] a chaos of passions. Conventionally in his time, he calls these passions bad, and demonstrates that they are so," though paradoxically he regards strong passions as a sign of "admirably strong character."[17] Pamela Andrews, the heroine of his first novel, is caught up in a maelstrom of passion: her fervent defense of her virtue, mixed with unacknowledged desire, leads her to the brink of self-murder, which she narrowly averts by delay, reflection, and revelation; her struggles with passion then work by sympathy on the affections of Squire B. and effect his reformation. Clarissa Harlowe, whose virtue is tested in Richardson's second and greatest novel, is a steady point at the center of the storm of passion that rages around her: her victory over her family's jealousy and greed, on the one hand, and Lovelace's predatory violence on the other, extricates her from this chaos, while her death shames mankind into an examination of its motives. Sir Charles Grandison, the hero of Richardson's final novel, protests to his "monitor," Dr. Bartlett, that he is, contrary to appearances, a man of feeling:

Good heaven! thought I – Do they believe me absolutely divested of human passions? – I have been at continual war, as you know, Dr. Bartlett, with the most ungovernable of mine; but without wishing to overcome the tender susceptibilities, which, properly directed, are the glory of the human nature.[18]

Grandison pays tribute to his "monitor" in a letter in which he takes his leave of the passionate Olivia with a word of reproof:

To what purpose live we, if not to grow wiser, and to subdue our *passions*? Dear lady! Illustrious woman! How often have you been subdued by the violence of *yours* . . . I am the rather entitled to advise, as I have made it my endeavour (and, I bless God, have not been always unsuccessful) to curb my passions. They are naturally violent. What do I owe to the advice of an excellent man, whom I early set up as *my* monitor? Let me, in this letter, be *yours*.[19]

In all of Richardson's novels, the triumph over passion occurs by the extirpation of resentment, desire, and pride from the breasts of their protagonists, and the substitution of a refined sensibility in their place.

That Pamela is a young woman animated by passion can hardly be denied, though it is necessary to suppose (if the book is to be read on its own terms) that she is not aware of the concupiscible origins of her behavior. Her passion for writing signals a persona ambitious to define itself, rather than to be defined by the world; her proclivity to faint when under attack suggests neither weakness nor guile, but a nervous sensibility associated with sexual anxiety; her pride in her appearance ("I took my straw hat in my hand, with its two green strings, and looked about me in the glass, as proud as any thing"), if not self-conscious, is sufficiently strong to arouse the gusts of her employer's passion.[20] When Mr. B. accosts her in the summer-house, she neither faints nor succumbs, but angrily reprimands her master for his violation of manners: "Well may I forget that I am your servant, when you forget what belongs to a master" (55).[21] This incident is followed by a series of verbal exchanges, confrontations, and physical assaults in which Mr. B., who assumes that Pamela's virtue conceals a natural passion like his own, finds himself frustrated, yet challenged by her passive resistance. Her appearance in her new suit of clothes, which she describes as "a good holiday and Sunday suit" and claims to put on only for Mrs. Jervis's viewing, inflames the passions of the adventitious Mr. B., who pretends to kiss her on the assumption that she has put on this masquerade to attract him. Pamela upbraids him, reminding him that "my good lady did not desire your kindness to extend to the *summer-house* and her *dressing-room*," which she admits to the reader was "a little saucy" of her, and which causes Mr. B. to fly "into *such* a passion, that I was forced to run for it" (92). Such incidents establish a pattern of passive resistance and aggressive reproof in the novel through which Pamela, without having admitted her desires to herself, works on the affections of the Squire.[22] By both raising and frustrating his passions, Pamela undesignedly eroticizes her virtue. In a moment of reflection, when the dialectic of wills has nearly run its course, Mr. B. acknowledges the effect of Pamela's resistence on his passions: "I see you on all occasions so watchful for your virtue, that though I hoped to find it otherwise, I cannot but confess, my passion for you is increased by it" (251).

Pamela's passion, considered not only as an element of her psychological being but as a trial to which her virtue is put, takes on many forms in the novel, from the bull in the pasture to the "naughty articles" Mr. B. proposes as terms for Pamela's submission. None, however, presents a greater threat to Pamela than her trial by the pond. Pamela arrives there in the course of an attempted escape, during which her head, hip, and shoulder are bloodied and bruised by a fall. As she lies beside the pond, a "sad thought" comes into her head – "to throw myself into the pond, and so put a period to all my terrors in this world!" (211). Had Pamela surrendered her virtue either to a physical assault or to Mr. B.'s material bribes, the resulting blemish on her honor could be removed by God's grace, of which Pamela is certainly a justified recipient. But had she succumbed to her "sad thought," the sin would have been irretrievable. Her self-destructive impulse is the product of despair, prompted by fear and pain; according to Bishop Butler, the desire to escape from such pain is the highest form of self-love and the goal of Epicurean philosophy.[23] In effect, suicide would be for Pamela a gratification of concupiscible desires, which helps to explain the sinful nature of the self-murder she contemplates. By virtue of her bruises, rather than any philosophical consideration, Pamela is forced to delay her suicidal impulse, which "gave time for a little reflection, for a ray of grace to dart in upon my benighted mind" (211). In the course of these reflections, she wrestles with temptations provided by the Devil, who endeavors to play upon her concupiscence by conjuring up visions of her dead corpse surrounded by mourners, including "my angry master" (212). Addressing herself in the third person, as if speaking the part of a Providential physician of the mind, Pamela conducts both ends of a dialogue: "Hitherto, Pamela, thought I, thou art the innocent, the suffering Pamela; and wilt thou, to avoid thy sufferings, be the guilty aggressor?" (213). A little reflection reminds Pamela that passivity, even when coupled with resistance, is a virtue, while aggression, including that directed against her own being, will always be an act of passion, and thus a grave error. In this long dark night, which Pamela finishes in the wood-shed, she extirpates any traces of passion or concupiscence from her being, an operation that entails a convalescence of three days. She arises on Saturday, "my feverishness seeming to be gone," and on Sunday discovers in her heart that she is "not like other people"; she no longer feels resentment toward Mr. B., but "for my late good lady's sake" determines to reform him, "and O what an angel would he be in my eyes" then (217).

Only very slowly, and with great reluctance, does Pamela acknowledge that her actions have for some time been governed by an affection for Mr. B. Seeking him in the garden on a Wednesday night thirteen days after her temptation, Pamela reflects that it was "by the side of this pond, and not far from the place where I had that dreadful conflict, that my present hopes, if I am not to be betrayed by them, began to dawn" (250). The following Sunday, Mr. B. walks Pamela back to the pond and speaks elliptically of making amends to her for the hardships she has suffered. Pamela can "hardly suppress" her "joyful emotions" at his words, but her joy is mixed with fear, which "will ever mingle with one's hopes, where a great and unexpected, yet uncertain good opens to one's view" (277).

The good is only "unexpected" in that it would be presumptuous of her to think, even to herself, that the Squire could love or propose marriage to her, until he says so himself; yet it is clear that she has had "hopes" of such an outcome for at least the last seventeen days, and perhaps unacknowledged desires before that. When the fears mingled with these hopes cause her to doubt the sincerity of his intentions, and he angrily withdraws his proposal, Pamela is forced to acknowledge that she is in love with him, and does not even know for how long: "love, I imagine, is not a voluntary thing – *Love*, did I say! But come, I hope not: at least it is not, I hope, gone so far, as to make me *very* uneasy: for I know not *how* it came, nor *when* it began; but it has crept, crept, like a thief, upon me; and before I knew what was the matter, it looked *like* love" (283).

Pamela's subjugation of her passions follows the traditional pattern of a Galenist therapy, Christianized by the language of Protestantism, in which delay and reflection allow time for a dialogue between herself and the physician of Scripture.[24] Mr. B.'s passions are also in need of a cure, though he (unlike Lovelace) can argue in his own behalf that he has "hitherto been guilty of no *very* enormous actions," and that "[h]ad I been utterly given up to my passions, I should before now have gratified them" (251). The comic resolution of the novel is perhaps forecast when Mr. B. falls ill after angrily sending Pamela away for her suspicions of his intentions; upon his change of heart, Pamela returns to find him recuperating, which he attributes to her presence. "'I can't be ill,' said he, 'while you are with me. I am well already ... You need not, Mrs. Jewkes,' added he, 'send for Dr. Harpur from Stamford; for this lovely creature is my doctor, as her absence was my disease'" (291). His physical recovery is matched by a spiritual healing a week later; on the day of their wedding, Mr. B. declares himself cured of his wanton habits, and tells Pamela that, "after having been long tossed about by the boisterous winds of culpable passion, I am not now so much the admirer of your beauty, all charming as you are, as of your virtue" (372). Mr. B. is cured neither by medication nor reason, but by a counterinfection of virtue.

Burney's debt to Richardson for the form and language of sentimental fiction is frequently acknowledged, but the structural similarities between *Pamela* and *Evelina* are often overlooked.[25] In both novels, the female protagonist is a "nobody" in terms of the social order into which she eventually rises; Evelina's origins are unknown, except to a few, and Pamela's parents are poor, "*though once*, as you know, *it was better with us*" (45). Like Pamela, Evelina corresponds with a distant guardian who functions as her conscience, a reminder of her duty to herself, and a refuge to which she can return in time of trouble. Like Pamela, Evelina is an acute observer of the details of ordinary life, quick to grasp the social as well as spiritual significance of a harsh word, or an overly kind one. Like Pamela, Evelina cherishes a sense of worth in herself that the world, valuing her virtue much lower, attributes to foolishness, affectation, and guile. Both women avoid the sexual snares that are laid for them, Pamela by her refusal of Mr. B.'s "naughty articles" and Evelina by her repudiation of offers of assistance, such as those from Sir Clement Willoughby, that would place her under an obligation. Both women reject suicide as a means of avoiding the trials of passion, though in *Evelina* the temptation to self-murder is projected into her half-brother, the Scotch poet Macartney, who subsequently thanks her in terms similar to those Pamela addressed to Providence: "you have taught me to curb those passions which bereft me of [my senses]."[26] After the intrinsic worth of both women is recognized by a proposal of marriage from a man of independent means, each must still deflect the violent passions of prejudice, represented by Lady Davers in the one case and Sir John Belmont in the other. Each also makes a complete and voluntary submission to her husband's authority upon marriage, though only after the domestication of Mr. B. and Lord Orville is sufficiently demonstrated to ensure a marriage based on mutual respect.[27] There are, of couse, significant differences in the structure of the novels – *Pamela*, for example, fails to sustain the interest of its second volume through the development of the subplot of Sally Godfrey, while the second and third volumes of *Evelina* connect Macartney's recovery of his senses to Evelina's recovery of her identity and inheritance – but these embellishments of plot do not alter the fact that both novels tell the same tale, one in which passion is finally subdued, if not entirely extirpated, in the breasts of the protagonists, and characters incapable of self-control are threatened with expulsion from the story. "Your violent passions are the only *intruders!*" declares Mr. B. in an ultimatum to his sister, "Lay them aside, and never sister was dearer to a brother than you to me" (445), while Evelina dismisses Sir Clement Willoughby with a similar reflection: "To what alternate *meanness* and *rashness* do the passions lead, when reason and self-denial do not oppose them!" (451).

Pamela and Evelina differ initially in class and character – Evelina is not a servant, and Pamela is not a deprived heiress – but the precipitating circumstance in both books is a change of condition through which a young woman innocent of the consciousness of passion enters a new situation in which she is surrounded by temptation and desire. She avoids error through the violent suppression of her desires, in Pamela's case by imagining a return to her parents' home (which, when it begins to become a reality, she foregoes), and in Evelina's, by stifling her joy at life in town in order that her letters may pass under the censorious eye of the Reverend Mr. Villars without objection. As time passes, however, each young woman makes cautious admission to herself of what Evelina calls "the most sacred secret of my heart" (390) – that she has transferred her affections from her father or guardian to another man. An alliance with this man would, in each case, make it possible for the heroine to redeem her "hopes," or desires – for Pamela, to live a life of Christian charity and compassion; for Evelina, to receive her inheritance, and to extirpate from her own breast the angry seeds of passion that have engulfed her father, mother, grandmother, and brother. Where the novels significantly differ is in the degree of moral action allowed to the female protagonists, and in this respect *Evelina* resembles *Tom Jones* more than *Pamela*.[28] As she approaches the end of her story, Evelina, like Tom, must recover the patrimony that has been taken from her in order for her to marry. Her sense of self is still severely circumscribed, so much so that the mannish Mrs. Selwyn must intervene to assert Evelina's right to an interview with her father, a scene in which Evelina is unable to utter a word in her own behalf. Toward the melancholy Mr. Macartney, however, in whose affairs she cannot have a personal interest – in fact, his mysterious presence at her garden gate jeopardizes her reputation – she acts the very part of benevolence. After intervening to prevent his suicide, which she accomplishes not by force but by fainting, she reflects on the limited forms of accomplishing good that are open to her: "I wish it were in my power to discover the nature of the malady which thus maddens him, and to offer or to procure alleviation to his sufferings!" (206). In seeking to "procure alleviation" for his "malady," Evelina employs the terms of illness to describe his condition, and then casts herself as a physician who would treat it, if she could. Like Tom Jones, whose disinterested intervention in Nightingale's melancholia produces a moral effect that (through Mrs. Miller's testimony) redeems some of his other weaknesses, Evelina's "fortitude and firmness" on this occasion, as Mr. Villars calls it (242), testify that she can be "dauntless in the cause of distress," whatever errors of conduct she may commit in society. Evelina's intervention in Macartney's case, which continues beyond her prevention of his suicide to include forms of financial and emotional support, lifts the story out of the sentimental sphere and into the realm of public and moral action.

THE STEADINESS OF CLARISSA HARLOWE

The connection between Burney's fiction and Richardson's second novel, *Clarissa, or, the History of a Young Lady*, is less easy to draw. Even the redoutable Margaret Anne Doody finds it easier to connect Burney's works with *Sir Charles Grandison*, or with a model shared by the two authors, than with *Clarissa*.[29] But Clarissa Harlowe represents an indispensable link in the derivation of Burney's heroines, who bear their long suffering with so much steadiness.[30] Unlike her irascible sister Bella, who "cannot either like or dislike with temper," Clarissa is known for the evenness of her temper and the steadiness of her mind. "Steadiness of mind," she tells Anna, "is a quality, my good Dr. Lewin was wont to say, that brings great credit to the possessor of it," and raises such persons above the machinations of their enemies.[31] It was Dr. Lewin, Clarissa's clergyman and spiritual physician, who "used therefore to inculcate upon me this steadiness upon laudable convictions." Steadiness of mind and evenness of temper are the signs of emotional health, as hurry and variousness are symptoms of disease. Steadiness is the quality that Lovelace most admires in Clarissa, and most lacks in himself; his own "natural temper," which is "quick and hasty" (46), seeks to possess, and if not possess to destroy, its antithesis in hers. At his first meeting with her Aunt Hervey, he acknowledges his passion for Clarissa, which is "accompanied with an awe that he had never known before" (47); Anna Howe connects this awe to his admiration of Clarissa's steadiness, and warns Clarissa that "Love takes the deepest root in the steadiest minds," a sentiment that Anna attributes to Lovelace (71). Clarissa's steadfast resistance to his hasty passion only spurs it on: "How came the dear soul... by all its steadiness?" he asks, marvelling at her victory over "her brother's rage, her sister's upbraidings, her father's anger, her mother's still more affecting sorrowings" (851–52).

Clarissa's one moment of unsteadiness is that in which she steps outside the garden door with Lovelace. The scene has the same function in her story that Pamela's attempted escape has in hers, except that, where Pamela pauses to reflect, Clarissa momentarily (and irretrievably) allows passion to direct her steps. The scene is preceded by an interior dialogue, much as Pamela has with herself, in which the merits of fleeing with Lovelace from her impending marriage to Solmes are weighed against the more distant, but equally serious consequences of putting herself in Lovelace's power. Clarissa resolves against going, yet allows herself to meet Lovelace to tell him so. The physical symptoms of passion dominate her description of the events that follow: her heart flutters at the first signal, and she is "convulsed" at the sight of him (374); Lovelace's declared intent to defend her against her family makes her "gasp almost with terror" (377); she trembles as she attempts to put the key in the lock to return into the garden (379). At his warning that her pursuers are on the other side of the door, Clarissa's self-control disappears completely: "Now behind me, now before me, now on this side, now on that, I turned my affrighted face in the same moment . . . I ran as fast as he, yet knew not that I ran; my fears at the same time that they took all power of thinking from me adding wings to my feet . . . my voice, however, contradicting my action; crying, No, no, no, all the while . . ." (380). Clarissa is tricked into stepping outside the garden by Lovelace, to be sure, but it is her passion, and not he, that makes her run.

The incident by the garden door has the intensity and some of the signs of a sexual initiation; it may be said that the rape of Clarissa begins here, and is only consummated in those understated terms, "[t]he affair is over" (883), in which Lovelace admits the failure of his "trial" of her passions.[32] Between the escape from the garden and the end of the trial, Clarissa's mental condition undergoes an alteration: once a sign of her unshakable self-control, Clarissa's steadiness becomes a determination to regain the control over herself that she has lost. No longer free by temperament from passion, she rails against it in almost every letter: "My heart struggled violently between resentment and shame to be thus teased by one who seemed to have all *his* passions at command, at a time when I had so little over *mine*" (489). Her own emotions become various, if not hasty, and she despairs of governing passion during her mortal existence: "How lately did I think I hated him! – But hatred and anger, I see, are but temporary passions with me . . . I hope my reason will gather strength enough from his imperfections . . . to enable me to keep my passions under – What can we do more than govern ourselves by the temporary lights lent us?" (679). Through the middle third of the novel, Clarissa is in fact destabilized; her struggle is not so much against Lovelace as against the passions that he is able to arouse in her, which she regards as signs of spiritual illness.

The strategy by which Lovelace endeavors to reduce her to his will is by raising and affecting her passions through his ruses and liberties. An example, one taken from among many, is his theft of one of her letters, innocently dropped on the floor: under cover of a "fervent kiss," Lovelace secures the letter beneath his foot (572). Clarissa, "in a passion at the liberty I took," struggles with him for control of the letter, which, as numerous commentators have pointed out, represents fundamental definitions of identity and self-determination in the novel. "Traitor! Judas!" she screams, "her eyes flashing lightning, and a perturbation in her eager countenance," which Lovelace finds "charming." Clarissa's passion is at the same time affecting – "gasping," she was "ready to faint with passion and affright" – and empowering – "pushing me rudely from the door, as if I had been nothing . . . she gaining that force through passion, which I had lost through fear." "[I]n a passion still," Clarissa double-locks herself in her room and refuses to come out (573). Yet she admits in her next letter to Anna that, while the passion was a reflex, her continuation of it was deliberate, a ruse to hold him off while an appeal to her Uncle Harlowe goes forward (576). Her continuation of a passion, even as a ruse, suggests the degree to which Lovelace has succeeded in affecting her steadiness.

Like Pamela, Clarissa rejects suicide, but she accepts her impending death, which she attributes to her emotional deterioration: her sense of guilt, her loss of reputation, her disappointment, her friends' resentments, and Lovelace's "barbarous usage" have "seized upon my heart" (1118). When she has finally resolved to die, rather than to accept Lovelace as a husband, she explains her reasons to Anna Howe "in hopes that having once disburdened my mind upon paper, and to my Anna Howe, of those corroding uneasy passions, I shall prevent them from ever returning to my heart" (1115). In her letter, Clarissa enacts both the classical and modern forms of therapy, venting her passions to a sympathetic friend, and reducing them to a text. Forming this resolution gives her "a courage I never knew before," and "such a command of my passions" as she has not felt since leaving her father's house (1117). From this position of relative serenity, she offers some advice to Anna, who admits of herself "I am of a high and haughty temper . . . and very violent in my passions":

Learn, my dear, I beseech you learn, to subdue your own passions. Be the motives what they will, excess is excess. Those passions in our sex, which we take no pains to subdue, may have one and the same source with those infinitely blacker passions which we used so often to condemn in the violent and headstrong of the other sex; and which may be heightened in them only by custom, and their freer education. Let us both, my dear, ponder well this thought; look into ourselves, and fear.[33]

Passions are to be feared and subdued, in women no less than in men; though custom and education breed "infinitely blacker" passions in men, the difference is in the height to which the passions are carried, not in their nature. Because passions are intrinsic to human nature, the attempt to eradicate them entirely would be quixotic; thus Clarissa speaks of "subduing" the passions, rather than of extirpating them. Even so, her method for subduing the strongest passions is to replace them with weaker ones: in another letter to Anna Howe, in which she reflects on the "resentments" she feels toward Lovelace, she expresses the hope that, having "once disburdened my mind upon paper . . . of those corroding uneasy passions, I shall prevent them for ever from returning to my heart, and to have their place supplied by better, milder, and more agreeable ones" (1115). In the phrase "for ever," Clarissa makes it clear that the "corroding uneasy" passions of anger and hate cannot be tamed or held at bay, but must be eliminated entirely from the mind that would be at spiritual peace.

CLARISSA, CECILIA, AND MADNESS

If in Richardson's second novel the passions are acknowledged to have a larger share in his heroine's consciousness than in his first, the same is true in Burney's second novel, *Cecilia, or, Memoirs of an Heiress* (1782). Cecilia shares Clarissa's steadiness of temper through her trials, which include not sexual rape but the rapine of her paternal fortune by one of her guardians, Mr. Harrel, with the consequent reduction of her status from heiress to social nobody. Also like Clarissa, Cecilia is driven into temporary madness by a series of missteps and betrayals. The loss of her father's fortune is aggravated by the discovery that her trusted adviser, Mr. Monckton, has arranged the disruption of her marriage ceremony to Mortimer Delvile and has slandered her to Delvile's father, all in order to obtain what remains of her fortune – her uncle's legacy – for himself. This second legacy is lost when she marries Delvile secretly, giving up her family name and thus violating the terms of the bequest. Expelled from her home, fearful that Delvile has fatally wounded Monckton, surprised by the jealous Delvile in the company of Mr. Belfield to whom she had gone for advice, Cecilia is buffeted by errors, each the product of a hasty passion on her part or some other's. The errors and betrayals culminate in a panic that distantly recalls Clarissa's agony when she discovers that Lovelace, in whose protection she has again placed herself, has tricked her into returning to Mrs. Sinclair's house where the rape – the final assault in the trial that began when she stepped out of her father's garden – is to be staged. This moment, for Cecilia,

teemed with calamity; she was wholly overpowered; terror for Delvile, horror for herself, hurry, confusion, heat and fatigue, all assailing her at once, while all means of repelling them were denied her, the attack was too strong for her fears, feelings, and faculties, and her reason suddenly, yet totally failing her, she madly called out, "He will be gone! he will be gone! and I must follow him to Nice!"[34]

Cecilia's madness differs from Clarissa's in that it is based in a sense of loss, reflected in her fear that Delvile has either been killed or left for France without her, rather than in the revulsion that Clarissa feels for Lovelace; yet feelings of betrayal are common to both heroines, and both blame themselves for the moment of unsteadiness that led to the calamity: "I am married," cries Cecilia, "and no one will listen to me! ill were the auspices under which I gave my hand! Oh it was a work of darkness, unacceptable and offensive! it has been sealed, therefore, with blood, and to-morrow it will be signed with murder!" (903). When Delvile discovers her whereabouts through a notice in the newspapers about a "crazy young lady," Cecilia does not recognize him, but distantly recalls his name: "Tis a name ... I well remember to have heard, and once I loved it, and three times I called upon it in the dead of night. And when I was cold and wretched, I cherished it; and when I was abandoned and left alone, I repeated it and sung to it" (907).

Terry Castle has described the mad scene in *Cecilia* as "garish and hysterical," the product of "sheer paranoid fantasy."[35] Castle finds the ending of the novel disappointing in view of the optimism with which it began – Cecilia's bold vision to become "mistress of her own time" and to live an extraordinary life of taste and charity – from which her descent into madness seems, in retrospect, a punishment. In the early chapters of the novel, Cecilia is surrounded at a masquerade by suitors whose "collective economic fixation" on her, says Castle, makes Cecilia momentarily the center of a carnivalesque fantasy of "female narcissism." But this "initial vision of female authority" begins almost immediately to collapse with the suicide of her discredited guardian, Mr. Harrel, and becomes an "ideological retreat" through which the "masquerade world, with its feminocentric values, is negated" (*Masquerade and Civilization*, 275–76). In this reading, Cecilia's madness is a "parody" of her earlier triumph, a "scene of perverse specularity," and her eventual recovery comes at the cost of "the rebellious, intractable reign of the Heiress" (282). Because of this "severe recoil," says Castle, the "pattern of her narrative contrasts

profoundly with that of previous eighteenth-century masquerade novels"
(289).

While the pattern may be at odds with earlier masquerade novels,
it is consistent with (and, in some ways, it improves upon) the literary
tradition through which dangerous passions are cured – or extirpated –
and replaced by what Richardson's Clarissa called "better, milder, and
more agreeable ones." In a sequence of scenes that strongly recalls the
cure of Arabella by the Countess and the "Pious and Learned Doctor"
in *The Female Quixote* (*FQ* 366), or Dr. Harrison's sharp words to Amelia
and Booth in *Amelia* (XII: iii and XII: v), *Cecilia*'s Dr. Lyster assumes total
control of the narrative action of the novel. Displacing several London
physicians whose training is more narrowly medical, this country doctor,
who is "equally desirous to do good out of his profession as in it" (928),
treats not only Cecilia's symptoms, but also the underlying conditions
that have contributed to her madness – the senior Mr. Delvile's angry
resentments, Mortimer Delvile's impetuous ravings, Henrietta Belfield's
excited lamentations. The "humane physician" shows "the author of this
scene of woe," the elder Mr. Delvile, the consequences of his inflexible
prejudice in the form of Cecilia's comatose body, which sight causes
"rising pangs" and awakens "all the father . . . in his bosom" (*Cecilia* 912–
13). The doctor frightens Henrietta into a more orderly and useful state of
mind, and walks out with Mortimer to prevent his unsteady temper and
excessive sensibility from making Cecilia's condition worse. As Cecilia
recovers, Dr. Lyster helps her obtain a letter from Mr. Monckton that
clears her of any wrongdoing, and carries it to the elder Delvile, where
the "sagacious and friendly" doctor works upon the passions of the proud
but remorseful patriarch to achieve a final reconciliation. In the end, it
is not Cecilia's passions, but those of the Delvile family that are shown
to have been at fault, and it is not patriarchy, but the authority of the
physician/philosopher to which all the parties finally submit. Rather than
an ideological retreat, the novel represents a subtle shift of the paradigm
through which those passions in need of correction are shown to lie not in
the breast of a female quixote, but in the heart of the patriarchal family.

THE WANDERER: A CODA

In Burney's last novel, *The Wanderer*, much of which was written after her
recovery from the mastectomy, the female protagonist at the center of the
action is, in a sense, divided into two persons – Juliet Granville, known
only as Ellis in the first half of the book, and Elinor Joddrel. Though they

are both complex characters, their difference with respect to the question of passion is fairly evident: Juliet is a female Grandison, a woman of taste, education, and accomplishments, an observer of punctilio and propriety, though at the same time a person of profound sensibility. Elinor is a believer in the new revolutionary systems convulsing France at the time the novel is set, a rationalist and materialist, an impulsive woman capable of generosity and courage, but also of jealousy, sexual aggression, and suicide. She has fallen in love with Albert Harleigh, the older brother of the man to whom she had been engaged; Harleigh, however, has cast himself as protector and prospective lover of Juliet. In a confidential moment, Harleigh tells Juliet his objections to Elinor's character:

Unawed by religion, of which she is ignorant; unmoved by appearances, to which she is indifferent; she utters all that occurs to an imagination inflamed by passion, disordered by disappointment, and fearless because hopeless, with a courage from which she has banished every species of restraint: and with a spirit of ridicule, that so largely pervades her whole character, as to burst forth through all her sufferings, to mix derision with all her sorrows, and to preponderate even over her passions! (565)

Elinor's attempted suicide occurs in an assembly room just as Ellis is about to begin a performance on the harp. After Elinor stabs herself in an effort to steal Harleigh's attention away from Ellis ("Turn, Harleigh, turn! and see thy willing martyr! – Behold, perfidious Ellis! behold thy victim!"), Harleigh and a surgeon, Mr. Naird, attempt to stop her bleeding, over Elinor's objections (338–39). As we noted at the outset of this chapter, Doody connects the scene to Burney's mastectomy, reading the dynamics of it as a conflict between "male and professional authority against female autonomy" (Doody, *Frances Burney*, 344), but such a reading seems to value Elinor's action too highly. In context, her act is a desperate and selfish gesture, one that ignores the interests of the other woman in the scene, Ellis, whose debut as a harpist was to have been an important step in her progress toward independence. Elinor's objective is not to extend the rights of woman or female autonomy, but to manipulate the emotions of the entire assembly in a self-serving way; her act lacks even the forgiving grace of spontaneity, because it is clearly premeditated. Burney demonstrates in the scene the theatricality and moral bankruptcy of Elinor's revolutionary passion, and characterizes it as evil.

The conclusion of Elinor's role in *The Wanderer* forms an interesting coda to the question of passion in Burney's work, and in the eighteenth-century English novel as a whole. In response to Elinor's first attempt at suicide, described above, Harleigh denied her any pity, on the grounds that for "all those with whom the love of fame is the ruling passion, Effect, public Effect" is the only guide to conduct (344). Elinor could not bear the outrage of being offered his pity, he tells Ellis, who cries with "involuntary" vivacity, "Give it her, then . . . the sooner to cure her!" (345), implying that pity would have the same effect on her as an emetic. Harleigh declines to provide this remedy, but after Elinor's second attempt at suicide – with a pistol, in the church, between the altar and the tomb – he relents and agrees to speak to her.

When they meet, several weeks later, Elinor asks not for Harleigh's pity, but for his thoughts on death and immortality, of which she is skeptical. The spiritual disease from which Elinor suffers, it seems, is a lack of faith in the immortality of the soul, an evil that underlies all the forms of unsteadiness to which she is given. She has refused the ministrations of both physicians and the "black robed tribe" of clerics for her illness, but she is convinced, through the interventions by which he twice prevented her suicide, that Harleigh is concerned for her soul, and she is thus disposed to accept him in the role of physician of the mind. In a dialogue that recalls many previous struggles between a "doctor" and his patient's passions, Harleigh converts her, if not to religion, at least to a skepticism of the finality of death. Awakening as if from a long reverie, Elinor cries out "Pardon, Albert, my strangeness, – queerness, – oddity, – what will you call it? I am not the less, – O no! O no! penetrated by your impressive reasoning – Albert! –" (762). With his "impressive reasoning," Albert Harleigh has penetrated Elinor more deeply than she was able to do with her own knife, and, like a surgeon, extirpated the passions that had given so much unrest to her soul. It is a contrite and newly charitable Elinor who climbs into her carriage and orders the groom to "Drive to the end of the world!" (764). Perhaps Burney, in bidding farewell to the fictional Elinor, hoped at last to expel the "corroding uneasy passions" from her heart, as her surgeons had extirpated the cancer from her breast.

Epilogue: Belinda *and the end of the origins*

If the question of the passions – that is, the most effectual way of curing, regulating, or extirpating them – was not resolved by the end of
the eighteenth century, it was at least modulated into terms that permitted the novel a greater range of possibilities. At the beginning of that
century, as we have seen, the passions were conceived as fixed and im-
mutable, the material products of humours in the blood and *pneuma* in
the nerves. Through the work of such anatomists and physiologists as
the Monros, Robert Whytt, and William Cullen, mechanistic theories
of the passions gradually gave way to the more malleable psychology of
the emotions, which do not depend on particular organs or humours of
the body, do not travel in the bloodstream or through tubular nerves,
and are more responsive to changes in circumstance or will. Certainly
novelists continued to depend on the passions to explain idiosyncrasies
of character: thus Sir Walter Scott attributes the "romantic tone and
colouring" of young Edward Waverley's sensibility, as well as the "aber-
ration from sound judgement" that provides the dramatic action of his
story, to "the influence of the awakening passions."[1] Jane Austen, too,
depicts the aberrations of passion and the curing of their pathological
effects in her novels: Marianne Dashwood's near-fatal illness is brought
on by Willoughby's betrayal of her violent attachment to him, and her
recovery (assisted by the sympathetic ministrations of her sister Elinor) allows her to avoid "falling a sacrifice to an irresistible passion, as once she
had fondly flattered herself with expecting."[2] But Marianne's quixotic indulgence of her passions only emphasizes how unstable and outmoded
Austen considers attachments based in passion alone, rather than the
deeper emotions of "strong esteem and lively friendship," to be.[3] The
replacement of the passions by the emotions as the primary subject of
fiction in the new century effectively ends the "origins" phase of the
genre of the novel. We will mark that ending by examining one of the
last great cures of the passions in their own time, Maria Edgeworth's

Belinda, which draws together many of the threads of the preceding discussion.

Edgeworth's Belinda Portman is a young woman endowed with a natural sensibility but little fortune. Her aunt, Mrs. Stanhope, places her with the fashionable Lady Delacour to introduce her into society. She soon learns Lady Delacour's secret, which is that she is dying of a cancer in her breast. The cancer, Lady Delacour reveals, is the physical counterpart of her corrupt moral being: "my mind is eaten away like my body by incurable disease – inveterate remorse – remorse for a life of folly – of folly which has brought on me all the punishments of guilt."[4] Though shocked, Belinda is not without feeling: she pledges her sympathy and loyalty to Lady Delacour through the "tortures of mind and body" that are to come. When, however, Belinda finds that Lady Delacour has used her name to trick her husband into paying for some horses she has bought, Belinda is "inspired by anger with unwonted courage" to call Lady Delacour to account – an early instance of the "civil courage" that will eventually distinguish Belinda as a heroine, and also an early signal that passion may for Edgeworth sometimes be a virtue (69).

As the time for Lady Delacour's "horrid operation" approaches, the usefulness of Belinda's self-control becomes apparent. Belinda works to achieve a reconciliation between the dissipated Lady Delacour and all of her estranged loved ones – her daughter Helena, her husband's aunt, Mrs. Delacour, and her husband Lord Delacour. For her pains, Belinda is repaid with anger, jealousy, and suspicion by Lady Delacour, who fears that Belinda is plotting to supplant her. At the same time, Belinda is called upon to intervene in the case of a black servant, Juba, who has been terrified by visions of an old woman all in flames who appears before him every night. Employing sympathy in the first case and rational deduction in the second, Belinda dispels the predominating passions of both the dissipated lady and the superstitious servant. Juba expresses his gratitude to Belinda, "who was the immediate cause of his cure," and Lady Delacour in her madness calls for Belinda, who, as her servant Marriott tells Lord Delacour, is "the best physician, my lord, she could send for" (202, 238).

Notwithstanding Belinda's skill in treating perturbations of the mind, there is in the novel a physician known as Dr. X –, who is "well aware that the passions have a powerful influence over the body," and who therefore "thought it full as necessary, in some cases, to attend to the mind as to the pulse" (288). The good doctor, a perceptive judge of character, recognizes both Belinda's merit and Lady Delacour's "perpetual fever, either of mind or body – I cannot tell which" (101). Belinda persuades Lady Delacour not to entrust her cancerous breast to a quack, and finally that there is no cancer at all – only a bruise, the result of a botched duel with her rival, made worse by hysterical fears and bad medicines. It is Belinda, not Dr. X –, who explains to Lady Delacour the deceptions that have been practiced on her, and who persuades her to give up her laudanum and her hallucinations. Thus, while Dr. X – is the acknowledged physician, Marriott correctly declares that "we may thank Miss Portman for this, for 'twas she made every thing to right" (286).

Dr. X – also recognizes that the kindly and intelligent, but rakish, Clarence Hervey is wasting his talents in Lady Delacour's drawing room, and the doctor sets him on a path toward more noble ends. Fired with the hope of accomplishing an act of benevolence, Hervey sets about to create the perfect wife for himself by protecting – and concealing from the world – a child of nature he discovers in a cottage in the forest. This Rousseauan experiment in education ends badly, as it must, both because "Virginia" is never properly socialized, and because his "benevolent" impulse has a self-serving end. Once again it is Belinda's self-control that prevents her from being deceived by the false reports about Hervey and Virginia, and which also prevents her "esteem" for Mr. Vincent, a rich Jamaica planter, from ripening precipitously into love.

The contrast in character between Hervey and Vincent is particularly instructive. Hervey is a Fieldingesque good-hearted man whose passions are "naturally impetuous," though he has "by persevering efforts brought them under the subjection of his reason" (379). His extended sojourn in France prior to the revolution has endowed him with a love of reason and virtue that causes him to mistrust and ignore the promptings of his heart. As a result, Hervey persists in his initial resolve to marry Virginia even after he discovers that he loves Belinda instead. Vincent, meanwhile, is a Richardsonian man of feeling, a Charles Grandison in all respects save one: he has an inveterate passion for gambling. Vincent believes "that the *feelings* of a man of honour were to be his guide in the first and last appeal," and that while "he was under the domination of one strong passion, he thought he could never be under the dominion of another" (385–86). Thus his love for Belinda will, he believes, be proof against his weakness for the gaming table. In Belinda's absence, however, the old passion returns, he is cheated of his entire fortune, and in a reprise of the near-suicide scene from *Evelina*, he is saved from self-destruction only by Hervey's timely intervention. Hervey is rewarded for saving his rival with sensations "more delightful even than those of the man he had relieved from the depths of despair" (395). The resolution of the novel, in which all is set right, depends in large part on the calmness of mind, the "civil courage" (409), and above all the well-regulated passions of Belinda Portman, whose visit to the disgraced Virginia allows the facts of her mysterious history to be known.

As G. J. Barker-Benfield notes in his useful commentary on the novel, Virginia and Belinda are the equivalents of *Sense and Sensibility's* Marianne and Elinor, the Belinda/Elinor character exhibiting "the superior attractions of a female sensibility tempered by a woman's reasoning power."[5] The same character types appear in Burney's *The Wanderer*, in which Elinor Joddrel is dominated by her revolutionary passions and Juliet Granville is the woman of genuine feeling. All three of these novels may be read as commentaries on Wollstonecraft's *Rights of Woman*, which Edgeworth elsewhere associated with the "shameless phrenzy of passion."[6] All three concur that the new heroine of the novel, and of the coming age, is characterized neither by an "Amazonian" stridency nor by a dependency on the sufferance of others, but by the possession of sovereignty over herself, her sensibility, and her passions. And all three novels answer, each in its own way, the question of the passions raised in such pre-novelistic texts as Defoe's *Robinson Crusoe*, Alexander Monro's autobiography, and the clergyman's letter to Betty.

Appendix 1 : Who was "Betty"?

The letter which salutes its intended recipient as "Betty" is in a letterbook that once belonged to the Reverend John Lewis, now in the Bodleian Library. The document is not in Lewis's hand, nor is it signed or addressed on the verso, suggesting that it is probably a copy of the original letter. It was at one time folded in quarters, as if enclosed in another cover. The internal evidence for Lewis's authorship of the letter rests on the similarity of its style and its doctrinal concerns to those in manuscripts that Lewis composed during the late 1730s, particularly his *History of Anabaptistism in England*. There is no external evidence that Lewis had a daughter named Betty or Elizabeth, but the parish records of St. Mary's in Minster do show that an Elizabeth Lewis married a William Johnson, "both of Minster," on October 27, 1744. Since there were no other Lewises in the parish, and since the *DNB* states that Lewis's wife, Mary Knowler Lewis, died "leaving no issue," the parentage of this Elizabeth Lewis is mysterious.[1]

The parish records show that Reverend John Lewis christened a child Elizabeth (no last name) on September 29, 1717. In one set of records, she is listed as the daughter of Mary Wager, but no father's name is given; in a folio volume with parallel records, she is described as "Daughter of Mary Wager by Thomas Parker, base born."[2] It is possible that Lewis and his wife adopted or protected this base-born child, who would likely have been a ward of the parish anyway, and that Lewis looked upon her as a daughter. Lewis's autobiography is silent as to an adopted child, but he does say of himself that he was "always liberal to the poor," that he laid out part of his salary in reading materials for poor boys, "and often clothed them, besides putting poor girls to school and clothing them . . . He put several poor children to school."[3]

This Elizabeth – a name often shortened to "Betty" – would have been about twenty years of age at the time that Lewis wrote his angry denunciations of anabaptists and Quakers in the late 1730s. If the elopement to which the letter refers also occurred at about this time, the passion with which Lewis attacks those nonconforming sects in his books would be easier to understand. The eventual marriage of Elizabeth Lewis to William Johnson in 1744, then, might suggest that the clergyman's intervention had been successful, and that the daughter had left her Quaker husband and returned home. With William, Elizabeth Johnson had eight children between 1745 and 1766, of whom four died in infancy (perhaps a ninth by another man, if "Mary, Bastard daughter of Elizabeth Johnson," n. d. but mid-1758, is hers). She was buried at Minster on 22 December 1805; the parish register gives her age – perhaps erroneously – as 86, placing her birth within about two years of that of the "base born" daughter of Mary Wager.

It can therefore be said with certainty that there was an Elizabeth Lewis, but not that she was the "Betty" of the letter, or that John Lewis was its author. What remains certain is that the letter reflects the views of clergymen such as Lewis, who saw the rise of nonconforming sects, particularly those that permitted the growth of passion and individualism in the soul by delaying baptism until adulthood, as a threat to paternal and pastoral authority. If John Lewis did not write the letter, it was certainly consistent with his most passionately held beliefs.[4]

Appendix 2: Who was "Sir Benjamin Hodges"?

In an article published in 1993, I argued that the traditional ascription of the *Impartial History of Michael Servetus, Burnt Alive at Geneva for Heresie* to a Sir Benjamin Hodges was incorrect.[1] My reasons were, first, that despite an extensive search, I had been unable to establish the existence of such a person, and second, that the ascription appeared to rest on hearsay evidence. Subsequent research has now enabled me to say more about how the erroneous ascription came to be made, though not to say with certainty who the author really was.

The ascription of the *Impartial History* to Sir Benjamin Hodges first appears in an appendix to the copy of the Reverend John Lewis's autobiography that was made after his death for Sir Peter Thompson. The appendix is a sale catalogue of Lewis's books and manuscripts, drawn up either by Thompson or someone at his direction. Manuscript No. 43 is described as "The Live [sic] of Servetus in answer to Sir Benj. Hodges Life of Servetus printed 1724 ... 0.18.0." This ascription of the 1724 life of Servetus (i.e. the *Impartial History*) to "Sir Benj. Hodges" appears to be an error, either by Thompson or the copyist, perhaps resulting from a misreading of the preface or the appendix to Lewis's "History of the Life of Servetus," which gives the name as "Nathanael Hodges." The ascription was repeated in the Gough catalogue of 1810, in the sale catalogue of the papers of Sir Peter Thompson in 1815, and in the *DNB* article on John Lewis, from whence it became the standard attribution.[2]

In the preface to his manuscript life of Servetus, Lewis says that he wrote it after having read the *Impartial History*. "The author of [that book], I'm informed, was Nathanael Hodges" (fol. 2). A brief biography of Hodges appears twice in the manuscript, once in the preface and once in the first appendix. The appendix has been cancelled with a heavy "X" drawn through it, as if to tell a printer not to set it, but all of the information is incorporated into the preface. It appears that the appendix was written first, copied into the preface, and then cancelled.

Since the information in the appendix is a little more complete, I will quote it rather than the preface:

A Life of Servetus was written & published by one Nathanael Hodges, who was a man of Estate and afterwards Knighted. He was bred at a Dissenting Academy, and became an Anabaptist Teacher and continued so 5 or 6 Years of the general persuasion. Being an Arrian he wrote this Life which he collected from Michael de la Roche's Memoirs of Literature in English, and his Account of Servetus in French. Like Morgan he fell into the commission of the grossest Immoralities and left an infamous Character behind him. On this his people cast him out, and [he] was supported by his Uncle who left him his Estate at his death. He was then made a Colonel of the Militia, and waiting on K. Geo: I with an Address was Knighted by Him: and died about 1730, about six years after his publishing this Life.[3]

Lewis apparently refers to Sir Nathanael Hodges (d. 1727), the author of at least three published sermons, who was knighted on February 24, 1726/7.[4] Lewis does not indicate anywhere in the manuscript why he believes Sir Nathanael Hodges was the author of the *Impartial History*, other than the statement in the preface that he was "informed" that Hodges wrote it, nor does he seem to have personally known Hodges, whose date of death he misstates by three years. Further, the remark in Thompson's letter to Lewis of February 16, 1745 (see Appendix 3, p. 197) that he had made a "mistake . . . regarding Mr. Hodges who I find was a dissenting minister many years" suggests that, first, he may have been the one who informed Lewis of the author's identity, and second, he may have had some other Hodges in mind than the one Lewis identified as the author. Thompson's mistake could well have persisted when he, or his copyist, annotated the sale catalog of Lewis's manuscripts and recorded the author of the *Impartial History* as "Sir Benjamin Hodges."

Appendix 3: The history of the "History of the Life of Servetus," told in letters

We can catch a glimpse of John Lewis's struggle to defend his faith against what he saw as the transient passions of his age by looking at the history of his last manuscript, the "History of the Life of Servetus." As the first critical study by an English cleric of the controversial Spanish heretic, it might be supposed that the "History" would be of great interest to the public. The manuscript was suppressed, however, by one of his literary executors, Sir Peter Thompson, who (as their correspondence suggests) endeavored to moderate the passions of his zealous friend and to protect his literary reputation.

John Lewis completed the life of Servetus on January 31, 1743/4, according to his own annotation on the manuscript, and sent it to Sir Peter Thompson for a critical reading. A Member of Parliament from Bermondsey and a Fellow of the Society of Antiquarians, Thompson was a man opposite in character to John Lewis in almost every respect – he was urbane, successful in worldly affairs, and liberal in religion. Evidently he kept the manuscript by him for almost a year, because on January 10, 1744/5 Lewis sent Thompson the following query:

I'm of the same opinion with a worthy friend of mine, that my friends are welcome to the use of my books, but not to placing them on their shelves. You don't tell me what you have done with Servetus's Life. I hope you han't condemned it to the same execution which the Dr. was sentenced to. I think he had hard measure, and so had Mr. Calvin. There are other ways of persecution: besides burning, as making men gazing stocks by reproaches, bitter contumelies of the Tongue and pen. Servetus had not the Spirit of a Christian Martyr, but rather of an Heathen Rabshakeh. He did all he could, to use A[rch] B[isho]p Land's words, most desperately to abuse and wound Calvin in the minds of the Genevians [sic], & put him to open Shame. [A]nd, as that Prelate observed, it is not every Man's Spirit to hold up against the Venom which Libellers spit, and find out how to swallow and put off those bitter contumelies of the Tongue and pen. I think you too severe on Calvin in representing him as *willfully mistaking our Saviour's doctrine*. Is not this ill nature for matters of speculation? which yet you say you are against. Could you read Le Blancs theses you would there see enough said for predestination to mislead an honest man. For my own part, I dare not judge any fellow servant as being in a wilful mistake.[1]

On January 25 Thompson returned the "History" with a long note, not quite an apology, written in a curiously Shandean style:

I am of the same opinion with you – that no one has a right to place my books on their shelves & let them Sleep there as their own. You'd permit me to assure you that I make it a part of my Religion to return with thanks what books I borrow – as to your life of Servetus it was never shelved in my house – but lockt in my Escritoire – to entertain a thot that I had sent it into flaming atoms – as Calvin did Servetus – would savor something of that Barbarous principle with which Calvin was full fraught – to Burn or destroy a book – looks like burning the Author in Effigie – & that were the poor Author in the burner's power – he would meet no better treatment I assure you. I abhor & detest all manner of prosecution – & am no [accessory?] to controversial disputes – for I think life too short to be spent in ill natured wrangling [over] Speculative points. – I think I long since told [you] I never read controversy nor high flown Sermons – I like to read Christianity in its primitive dress – & am very thankfull we are blest with it in our mother tongue – I know there are many ways of persecution – as despoiling of goods for conscience sake for opposing the popular System of Christianity – Imprisonment, hard names – stigmatized & set up for gazing stocks & reproaches of the Ignorant Vulgar – all this is but flea biting in comparison of roasting alive, – I say notwithstanding I look on Calvin to have been a great Imposter & deceiver & one who wilfully mistook the design of Christianity – In Short of no religion at all – not possessed with the common bowells of compassion used and practised by Heathens – I say – notwithstanding this difference in our Opinions – was Calvin now – alive in Prison, in want of the common necessarys of Life – quite eat up with vermin – I can honestly & truly say my Religion dictates to administer to the sufferings of a prosecuted fellow being without considering whether the prosecutor be right or wrong. Calvin's burning Servetus alive – & calling him Spanish Dog – plainly shows Calvin was no Gentleman, but brim full of revenge & pride – & though he set up against the pope – he would exercise papal authority which came from the wicked one – if this Man did not mistake & that wilfully too – our Savior's words – when He said love your enemies do good to them [that?] Hate you and despitefully use you – & c. & c. to same purpose – He knew those were commands and rules laid down by Christ himself – to be observed I hope, & I hope I shall be excused in saying that those who don't observe them are no Christians – but political Tyrants – from which Good Lord deliver us –[2]

It appears from the exchange of letters that Thompson had not kept the *History* locked in his escritoire out of indolence, but rather because he disagreed with Lewis's tilt toward Calvin. He seems to have feared that his clergyman friend would harm his reputation by publishing a book that was critical of Servetus – an indication that a major change in public opinion had occurred since the time of the Salters Hall controversy in 1718–19. On February 14, Lewis sent the following acknowledgement to Thompson for returning the manuscript:

I think I ought to give my thanks for your kind letter, and sending my MS by so safe a hand. I'm sorry to see you so much set against Mr. Calvin. You seem to have forgot, that Mr. C – was not the author of the predestinarian Scheme, & was not singular in asserting, that the Civil Magistrate has the power of the Sword & is the Keeper of both Tables of the Law, & ought to punish Blasphemy, profaneness, and contempt of God's Holy word & Commandmt as well as theft and murder. La Roche and his Translator are plainly partial to Servetus; witness their attributing to him the first discovery of the circulation of the blood. Quite ignorant! But I am so ill, that I can't enlarge. I most heartily wish you well thro your high and honorable office to your own pleasure & your friends satisfaction & am good Sir your obliged & faithful friend & servant J Lewis.[3]

As was his custom, Lewis gave no ground in his disagreement with his friend over the relative merits of Servetus and Calvin, and instead attacked Michael de la Roche and his "translator," the author of the *Impartial History*, who had indeed lifted much of the book from de la Roche's *Bibliothèque Angloise*. Nevertheless, Thompson seems to have made his point, because nothing more is said on either side about publishing the book. On February 16, Thompson sent the following reply to Lewis:

I am extream sorry to hear you say you are indisposed. I keep no copies of letters I write you knowing if I make a slip youl silently pass it by, not proclaim it on the House tops – one mistake occurs to me regarding Mr. Hodges who I find was a dissenting minister many years. I know Calvin was not the author of ye predestinarian Scheme – nor singular in murdering his fellow beings who did not think his preachments authorized by Jesus Christ and his Apostles – the Pope believed nay practised those cruelties then and continues to do the same still. You know Calvin's cruelties did not die with him for the papistical murdering principle – did not cease at his death for Gentile[4] was murdered if my memory fails me not after Calvin's death – tis true Calvin opposed the Pope's authority and set up another,^ to the peace of society an altogether as absurd^ I think equally as poisonous many learned men opposed Calvin's authority – & because they would not bond they must fly away or stay and be burned to Death. Tis Calvin's justifying so unchristian a principle has set me against him. You know very well that the authority established by Ed. VI & after that by Q. Eliz. would not do – many opposed Law – established and suffered cruel Deaths for so doing – was this right – I am sure youl say no. and agree that the prosecuting the Enthusiasts of those times made the separation from the Church encrease – sufferings for Religion raises pity & proselytes be their tenets never so Absurd. people must be reason'd not forced – you know the great Opposition to

Authority at length produced the Parliament to grant a Toleration to scrupulous consciences, this is a blessing I am very thankfull for. & God of his mercy I hope will ever continue it – I know tis a favorite Law with you – and I dare say tis so to 7/8ths of the nation – you know I am a foolish westcountry man and I am so unhappy as to speak or write my real thots free from all disguise – tis unfashionable so to do but that I am not carefull about all I hope my friends will make proper allowances and pass the most favorable constructions especially as I take the Humane side of the question[.][5]

Despite the incoherent and perhaps unfinished state of the draft letter, it is clear that Thompson endeavored to dissuade his friend from publishing the "History of the Life of Servetus" on the grounds that religious tolera- tion was now the law of the land. Probably his motives were mixed: some concern for freedom of thought, and some concern for Lewis, whom he saw as plunging (as Lewis was prone to do) into an unpopular, hasty, and embarrassing position by aligning himself with Calvin's "papistical mur- dering principle." Lewis, after all, idolized Wycliffe as a Christian martyr at the hands of the Roman church, but would not see how the same prin- ciples applied to Servetus in the Protestant movement, a contradiction of which Thompson seems sharply aware.

John Lewis died two years later, on January 16, 1746/7. His papers and manuscripts were sold at Covent Garden in December 1749, the purchasers being Sir Peter Thompson, Dr. Richard Rawlinson, Joseph Ames, and a Mr. Lovel. Thompson became Lewis' literary executor, an office he endeavored faithfully to carry out, as appears from a letter from him to John Ward, the Master of Gresham College, dated April 23, 1752:

I have put Mr. Lewis's *Life of Dr. Hickes* into the Hands of my Neighbor the Rev. Mr. Stepman [Shipman?] – with a view if it should be thot worthy of public notice, that it may be printed. Dr. Hickes was as much distinguished for his great learning – a life of such a person well wrote would meet with readers – and pay for paper and print. – Mr. Lewis just before his Death had prepared for the press a 2nd. Edition of Wicliff's Life with many alterations and large Additions – which I have agreed with a Bookseller to print in Quarto.[6]

What is remarkable about this letter is not what it says about Thompson's efforts on behalf of his friend's literary reputation, but what it does *not* say. In addition to the manuscript lives of Hickes and Wycliffe, Thompson was at this time again in possession of Lewis's "History of the Life of Servetus," which he had purchased at the sale of Lewis's books and manuscripts.[7] His letter to John Ward makes no mention of this manuscript, though we know from the correspondence between Lewis and Thompson that Lewis never retracted his desire to have it published.

Thompson had a copy of Lewis's autobiography made for himself, and in his own hand he annotated the appended sale catalog as follows:

A Life of Servetus – was submitted to my consideration – I prevented its being printed, as some contracted notions – appeared in defence of John Calvins cruelty to Dr. Servetus. – I don't take nor did not take into my consideration whether the Principles of one or the other was right – I ever did & I hope I ever shall, abhor all cruel prosecuting principles for Notions meerly speculative.

It is an ironic close to the career of the Reverend John Lewis, who admitted in his autobiography that he was prone to being surprised by his passions into making indiscrete statements that he later regretted, that his most passionate statement in defense of the Holy Trinity and against the Arian heresy of Michael Servetus should be suppressed by his good friend Sir Peter Thompson, who thought he knew better than his zealous friend what the world wanted to hear. In Thompson's defense, however, it must be said that, if he did not publish the manuscript, neither did he destroy it; the "History of the Life of Servetus" was sold with the rest of his collection in 1815, and eventually passed through the hands of a Bristol bookseller named Gutch into those of the Clarendon Press, which in 1820 was engaged in bringing out new editions of some of Lewis's works.[8] The Clarendon Press donated the manuscript to the Bodleian library, where, with the correspondence, it now testifies to the efforts of Sir Peter Thompson to cure the passions in the breast of the Reverend John Lewis.

Notes

INTRODUCTION: THE PASSIONS AND THE ENGLISH NOVEL

1. J. Paul Hunter, *Before Novels: the Cultural Context of Eighteenth-Century English Fiction* (New York, 1990), 86. See also Hunter's "Fielding and the Modern Reader: the Problem of Temporal Translation," in J. Paul Hunter and Martin Battestin, *Fielding in His Time and Ours* (Los Angeles, 1987), 1–28.

2. Isaac Watts, *The Doctrine of the Passions, Explain'd and Improv'd: or, a brief and comprehensive scheme of the natural affections of mankind . . . to which are subjoined, moral and divine rules for the regulation and government of them* (1732; 3rd edn. 1739), iii–iv.

3. The figure for 1700–39 is in *Four before Richardson: Selected English Novels, 1720–1727*, ed. W. H. McBurney (Lincoln, 1963), vii; that for 1740–49 in Jerry Beasley, *Novels of the 1740s* (Athens, 1982), xii. In the term "novelistic," Beasley refers to a "heterogeneous class of admittedly fictitious narratives" with stories that synthesize "conventions from many modes of popular narrative" (xiv). J. Alan Downie, reviewing McBurney's figures in "Mary Davy's 'Probable Feign'd Stories' and Critical Shibboleths about 'The Rise of the Novel,' " *ECF* 12 (2000), 309–26, argues that the "rise" implied by such figures is misleading; there were "fluctuations in popularity" for novels that peaked in the later decades of the seventeenth century and in the third decade of the eighteenth (312–13).

4. McBurney, *Novels*, xii. For studies of the novelists named, see, in addition to Beasley's *Novels of the 1740s*, John J. Richetti, *Popular Fiction before Richardson: Narrative Patterns 1700–1739* (Oxford, 1969); Jane Spencer, *The Rise of the Woman Novelist from Aphra Behn to Jane Austen* (Oxford, 1986); Janet Todd, *The Sign of Angellica: Women, Writing, and Fiction, 1660–1800* (New York, 1989); John Richetti, *The English Novel in History, 1700–1780* (London, 1999).

5. The contributions of Behn, Manley, and the early Haywood to the genre of the novel are the subject of continuing debate, centering on whether their works were sufficiently "realistic" to distinguish them from romances. See Jane Spencer, "Women Writers and the Eighteenth-Century Novel," in *The Cambridge Companion to the Eighteenth-Century Novel*, ed. John J. Richetti (Cambridge, 1996), 212–35 (but esp. 214–15); Janet Todd, *The Sign of*

Angellica, 49–51 and 78–98; and Roger D. Lund, "The Modern Reader and the 'Truly Feminine Novel' 1660–1815," in *Fetter'd or Free?*, eds. Mary Anne Schofield and Cecilia Macheski (Athens, 1986), 398–425.

6. Davys, *The Accomplished Rake, or Modern Fine Gentleman* (London, 1727), in *Four before Richardson: Selected English Novels, 1720–1727*, ed. W. H. Burney (Lincoln, 1963), 236.

7. Margaret Doody, *A Natural Passion: a Study of the Novels of Samuel Richardson* (Oxford, 1974), 24.

8. Doody, *A Natural Passion*, 12.

9. Ian Watt, *The Rise of the Novel: Studies in Defoe, Richardson and Fielding* (London, 1957; rep. Penguin, 1963). Watt of course does not present the thesis so baldly, but commentators conventionally do so for purposes of discussion; see, for example, J. A. Downie, "The Making of the English Novel," *Eighteenth Century Fiction* 9 (1997), 249–66. The two colloquia referred to are *Reconsidering the Rise of the Novel*, ed. David Blewett, issued as *Eighteenth Century Fiction* 12: 2–3 (January-April 2000), and *Critical History: the Career of Ian Watt*, issued as *Stanford Humanities Review* 8: 1 (Spring 2000).

10. The studies referred to, in addition to Hunter's *Before Novels*, are Nancy Armstrong, *Desire and Domestic Fiction: a Political History of the Novel* (New York, 1987); G. J. Barker-Benfield, *The Culture of Sensibility: Sex and Society in Eighteenth-Century Britain* (Chicago, 1992); John Bender, *Imagining the Penitentiary: Fiction and the Architecture of Mind in Eighteenth-Century England* (Chicago, 1987); Terry Castle, *Masquerade and Civilization: the Carnivalesque in Eighteenth-Century English Culture and Fiction* (Stanford, 1986); Robert A. Erickson, *Mother Midnight: Birth, Sex, and Fate in Eighteenth-Century Fiction* (New York, 1986); Jean H. Hagstrum, *Sex and Sensibility: Ideal and Erotic Love from Milton to Mozart* (Chicago, 1980); John J. Richetti, ed., *The Cambridge Companion to the Eighteenth-Century Novel* (Cambridge, 1996).

11. G. S. Rousseau, "Nerves, spirits, and fibres: towards an anthropology of sensibility," in *Enlightenment Crossings: pre- and post-modern discourses: anthropological* (Manchester, 1991), 131–34.

12. Ian Watt, *Myths of Modern Individualism: Faust, Don Quixote, Don Juan, Robinson Crusoe* (Cambridge, 1996), 122.

13. Roland H. Bainton, *The Reformation of the Sixteenth Century* (Boston, 1952), 15–16.

14. J. G. A. Pocock, *The Machiavellian Moment: Florentine Political Thought and the Atlantic Republican Tradition* (Princeton, 1975), 65.

15. Owsei Temkin, *Galenism: Rise and Decline of a Medical Philosophy* (Ithaca, 1973), 15–16.

16. *Ibid.*, 164–68.

17. Lester S. King, *The Philosophy of Medicine: the Early Eighteenth Century* (Cambridge, 1978), 64–65; 82–85; 241–44; 250–55.

18. Bainton, *Reformation*, 16.

19. Alistair M. Duckworth, "Michael McKeon and Some Recent Studies of Eighteenth-Century Fiction," *ECF* 1 (1988), 59.

20. Michael McKeon, *Origins of the English Novel, 1600–1740* (Baltimore, 1987), 20–21. See also McKeon, "Generic Transformation and Social Change: Rethinking the Rise of the Novel," *Cultural Critique* 1 (1985), 159–81, rep. *Modern Essays on Eighteenth-Century Literature*, ed. Leopold Damrosch Jr. (New York, 1988), 159–80.
21. Robert Burton, *The Anatomy of Melancholy* (1621), 11th edn., 2 vols. (London, 1813), I: 111; Thomas Hobbes, *Leviathan* (Oxford, 1909), 39.
22. Downie "Making of the English Novel," 256–57.

1 THE PHYSICIAN OF THE MIND FROM ZENO TO ARBUTHNOT

1. Tobias Smollett, *The Expedition of Humphry Clinker*, ed. James L. Thorson (New York, 1983), 31. Subsequent references to this edition appear in the text as *HC*.
2. Such remedies were prescribed by, among others, Thomas Sydenham (1624–89), who is said to have sent a hypochondriacal patient on a journey from London to Inverness to consult a fictional Dr. Robertson, solely to enforce a regimen of fresh air, exercise, and dietary moderation; see Kenneth Dewhurst, *Dr. Thomas Sydenham* (Berkeley, 1966), 53–54.
3. The debt Smollett's novels owe to his medical training is discussed in G. S. Rousseau, "Pineapples, Pregnancy, Pica, and *Peregrine Pickle*," in G. S. Rousseau and P.-G. Boucé, eds., *Tobias Smollett: Bicentennial Esssays Presented to Lewis M. Knapp* (New York, 1971), 81, 108–09.
4. Ilza Veith, *Hysteria: The History of a Disease* (Chicago, 1965), 140–44. In fact, Galen described hypochondriasis as a disease of which melancholy, headaches, cloudiness of vision and mind, and "bestial raving" were symptoms; see Rudolph E. Siegel, *Galen on Psychology, Psychopathology, and Function and Diseases of the Nervous System* (Basel, 1973), 189–99.
5. Benjamin Rush, *Medical Inquiries and Observations, upon the Diseases of the Mind* (Philadelphia, 1812), 74.
6. One such reading is that of Eric Rothstein in *Systems of Order and Inquiry in Later Eighteenth-Century Fiction* (Berkeley, 1975), who says that in Bramble, "Smollett shows us that the bad temper of the satirist comes from a sick body and mind, not necessarily from the disorders of society" (111). Rothstein also denies that the satire contributes to a sense of redemption or a cure (119).
7. Italics in the original.
8. Northrop Frye, *Anatomy of Criticism* (Princeton, 1957), 309–12. See also Percy G. Adams, *Travel Literature and the Evolution of the Novel* (Lexington, 1983), 205–06.
9. In his study, *Ancient Menippean Satire* (Baltimore, 1993), Joel C. Relihan notes that the genre of Menippean satire has recently been expanded "beyond what many would consider its reasonable bounds" (3). Nevertheless, his definition of the essential characteristics of the genre – "a continuous narrative, subsuming a number of parodies of other literary forms

along the way, of a fantastic voyage to a source of truth that is itself highly questionable . . . related by an unreliable narrator in a form that abuses all the proprieties of literature and authorship" (10) – could well describe *The Expedition of Humphry Clinker.*

10. Frye, *Anatomy of Criticism,* 179; *HC,* 288, 292.

11. John Gay, "Mr. Pope's Welcome from Greece," lines 121–24, in *John Gay: Poetry and Prose,* ed. Vincent A. Dearing. 2 vols. (Oxford, 1974), I: 258.

12. Swift to Arbuthnot, June 16, 1714. Appendix to Samuel Johnson, "The Life of Swift," in *Lives of the English Poets.* 3 vols., ed. Peter Cunningham (London, 1854), III: 204.

13. J. Y. T. Greig, *The Letters of David Hume* (Oxford, 1932), I: 12–18. Greig surmised that the unaddressed letter was sent to Dr. George Cheyne; E. C. Mossner, however, argues that Arbuthnot is "the only candidate perfectly fulfilling all the qualifications laid down and implied in the letter." Mossner supposes that, if Hume never sent the letter, it was because the "very act of putting his symptoms into writing may in itself have provoked a psychological catharsis." See Mossner, *The Life of David Hume* (Austin, 1954), 84, 86.

14. Pope to Robert Digbly, September 1, 1724, *The Correspondence of Alexander Pope,* ed. George Sherburn (Oxford, 1956), II: 253.

15. Arbuthnot to Swift, October 19, 1714, *The Correspondence of Jonathan Swift,* ed. Sir Harold Williams, 5 vols. (Oxford, 1963–65), II: 137.

16. David B. Morris, *Alexander Pope: the Genius of Sense* (Cambridge, 1984), 235. I am indebted to Morris, esp. pp. 216–36, for the discussion of Juvenalian indignation that follows.

17. Rebecca Ferguson, *The Unbalanced Mind: Pope and the Rule of Passion* (Philadelphia, 1986), 140.

18. *Ibid.,* 150.

19. Henry Fielding, *Amelia,* ed. Martin C. Battestin (Middletown, 1983), 375.

20. Charlotte Lennox, *The Female Quixote,* ed. Margaret Dalziel (Oxford, 1989), 363–66.

21. See the appendix by Duncan Isles to Lennox, *Female Quixote,* 420–26.

22. Janet Todd, *The Sign of Angellica: Women, Writing, and Fiction, 1660–1800* (New York, 1989), 153.

23. G. J. Barker-Benfield, *The Culture of Sensibility: Sex and Society in Eighteenth-Century Britain* (Chicago, 1992), 215.

24. F. H. Sandbach, *The Stoics* (New York, 1975), 17. See also John Scarborough, *Roman Medicine* (Ithaca, 1969), 120–21.

25. Martha C. Nussbaum, *Therapy of Desire: Theory and Practice in Hellenistic Ethics* (Princeton, 1994), 13–14; 40–43.

26. *Ibid.,* 33.

27. Nussbaum uses her own translation of this passage from the *Epicurea* of H. Usener (Leipzig, 1887) to open her essay, "Therapeutic Arguments: Epicurus and Aristotle," in *The Norms of Nature,* eds. Malcolm Schofield and Gisela Striker (Cambridge, 1986), 31–74, and Chapter 1, "Therapeutic Arguments," in her *Therapy of Desire,* 13–47.

28. Nussbaum devotes a chapter in *Therapy of Desire* to the medical analogy in each of these schools: "Skeptic Purgatives: Disturbance and the Life without Belief," 280–315, and "The Stoics on the Extirpation of the Passions," 359–401.

29. Nussbaum, *Therapy of Desire* 507–08; 279.

30. *Ibid.*, 339–40, 389.

31. Sandbach, *Stoics*, 61–63, upon which the following summary of the Stoic doctrine of the passions primarily relies; see also A. A. Long and D. N. Sedley, *The Hellenistic Philosophers*, vol. 1 (Cambridge, 1987), 2–7. Among the important primary texts, see Cicero, *Tusculan Disputations*, Book III, vi–xiii, and Seneca, *Moral Essays*, "On Anger."

32. Sandbach notes that the Stoic term for this passion, *epithymia*, is often translated as "desire," which he believes is inadequate to express the sense of "yearning after a thing" that the word implies (61).

33. Daniel Defoe, *The History and Remarkable Life of the truly honourable Col. Jacque*, ed. Samuel Holt Monk (London, 1965), 25–26.

34. Henry Fielding, *Joseph Andrews*, ed. Martin C. Battestin (Middletown, 1967), 309–10.

35. Ludwig Edelstein, *The Meaning of Stoicism* (Cambridge, 1966), 2–4; see also Sandbach 63–67.

36. Edelstein, *Meaning of Stoicism*, 24.

37. Ludwig Edelstein, *Ancient Medicine*, eds. Owsei Temkin and C. Lilian Temkin (Baltimore, 1967), 214. See also C. D. Phillips, *Greek Medicine* (London, 1973), 168–69. For the suggestion that Seneca's *spiritus* refers to the Stoic *pneuma*, see Harry M. Hine, *An Edition with Commentary of Seneca, Natural Questions, Book Two* (Salem NH, 1981), 138–39.

38. Edelstein, *Meaning of Stoicism*, 41–43.

39. These reconstructions were edited by Ludwig Edelstein and I. G. Kidd, *Posidonius: the Fragments* (Cambridge, 1972). See also I. G. Kidd, ed., *Posidonius: the Commentary*, 2 vols. (Cambridge, 1988). Seneca, like Galen, derived most if not all of his theory of the passions from Posidonius (Edelstein, *Meaning of Stoicism*, 61, 67; Riese, introduction to *Galen on the Passions and Errors of the Soul*, trans. Paul W. Harkins (Columbus, 1963) 120 n. 11).

40. Edelstein, *Meaning of Stoicism*, 49–50; Sandbach, *The Stoics*, 129–32. These reconstructions were published as *Posidonius: the Commentary*, ed. I. G. Kidd (Cambridge, 1972) and *Posidonius: the Fragments*, eds. Ludwig Edelstein and I. G. Kidd (Combridge, 1972).

41. Edelstein, *Meaning of Stoicism*, 56; Sandbach, *The Stoics*, 136; Kidd, *Posidonius: the Commentary* II: 430.

42. Edelstein, *Meaning of Stoicism*, 56; Sandbach, *The Stoics*, 136–37; Kidd II: 163–64 and 677–78. Kidd and Sandbach appear to reject Edelstein's use of the word *daimon* to mean either "good" or "evil" presences in the psyche, instead restricting it to mean only a rational faculty.

43. Edelstein, *Meaning of Stoicism*, 56. The following sentences rely on Edelstein, *Meaning of Stoicism*, 56–59. See also McKenzie, *Certain, Lively Episodes: the Articulation of Passion in Eighteenth-Century Prose* (Athens, 1990), 38–42,

although he makes no distinction between the early and middle Stoics.

44. R. J. Hankinson, ed., *Galen on the Therapeutic Method* (Oxford, 1991), xix–xxv. The dates given for Galen's birth and death are Hankinson's, which update the traditional ones, 130–200 A. D., cited by Temkin and others. For discussions of Galen in the context of Hippocratic medicine and Hellenistic philosophy, see Phillips, *Greek Medicine*; Siegel, *Galen's System of Physiology and Medicine, an analysis of his doctrines on bloodflow, respiration, humors, and internal diseases*; and C. R. S. Harris, *The Heart and the Vascular System in Ancient Greek Medicine, from Alcmaeon to Galen* (Oxford, 1973).

45. Walther Riese, "Introduction" to *Galen on the Passions*, 3–4. For studies of the textual history of some of these treatises, see Paul W. Harkins, "Translator's Preface" to *Galen on the Passions and Errors of the Soul*, 23–24; Margaret Tallmadge May, "Introduction" to *Galen on the Usefulness of the Parts of the Body (De Usu Partium)* (Ithaca, 1968), 5–8; David J. Furley and J. S. Wilkie, "Preface" to *Galen on Respiration and the Arteries* (Princeton, 1984), v–vi; George Sarton, *The Appreciation of Ancient and Medieval Science during the Renaissance* (Philadelphia, 1955), 17–22, as well as Sarton's "Appendix III: Galenic Texts Available in English Translation," in *Galen of Pergamon* (Lawrence, 1954), 101–07; and B. Ebels-Hoving and E. J. Ebels, "Erasmus and Galen," in *Erasmus of Rotterdam: the Man and the Scholar*, eds. J. Sperna Weiland and W. Th. M. Frijhoff (Leiden, 1988), 132–42.

46. "The Diagnosis and Cure of the Soul's Passions," in *Galen on the Passions* (1963), hereafter cited as "Passions." For Sarton's comment, see *Galen of Pergamon*, 72.

47. Galen, "Passions," 46. In *De Placitis Hippocratis et Platonis* (Leipzig, 1874) 405, 14; 658, 11, Galen makes it clear that this reference to "philosophers of old" is to Plato (*Republic*, 440a), although the distinction between irascible and concupiscible passions is also common to Aristotle and the early Stoics. On Galen's stoicism, see Oswei Temkin, *Galenism: Rise and Decline of a Medical Philosophy* (Ithaca, 1973), 39 and n. 91.

48. Temkin, *Galenism*, 83; May, *Galen on the Usefulness of Parts of the Body*, 45.

49. Galen, "Passions," 32, 46–48.

50. In his commentary on Galen's "Passions" (127–28), Walter Riese observes that Descartes advises delaying a response to the impulses of violent passions to give the blood time to abate its commotion in *Passions of the Soul* (Article 46), for which he may have been indebted to Galen, and that the same advice appears prior to Galen in Seneca's moral essay *On Anger* (I: xviii). In that essay, Seneca relates a story in which Plato delays a blow which is about to give to a servant, and as punishment to himself for submitting to passion he holds himself in the posture of an angry man (III: xii). See also McKenzie's chapter on "Classical Analyses of the Passions," in *Certain, Lively Episodes*, 24–54.

51. In *The Family Instructor*, Part II (Oxford, 1841), Defoe describes the cure of a derangement of passion in a man who "was a substantial trading man, above the world, as we say" (II: 177).

52. On the reluctance of physicians to treat cases of serious mental illness, see Roger French, "Sickness and the Soul: Stahl, Hoffmann and Sauvages on Pathology," in *The Medical Enlightenment of the Eighteenth Century*, eds., Andrew Cunningham and Roger French (Cambridge, 1990), 88–110; Dora B. Weiner, "Mind and Body in the Clinic: Philippe Pinel, Alexander Crichton, Dominique Esquirol, and the Birth of Psychiatry," in *The Languages of Psyche: Mind and Body in Enlightenment Thought*, ed., G. S. Rousseau (Berkeley, 1990), 332–402; Roy Porter, *Mind-Forg'd Manacles: a History of Madness in England from the Restoration to the Regency* (Cambridge, 1987), xii and 169–228; but see also Gregory Zilboorg, *A History of Medical Psychology* (New York, 1967), 177–80, who examines the beginnings of "the first psychiatric revolution" in the sixteenth century. By the mid-eighteenth century, "heroic therapeutics" were employed on the mental patients regarded as curable – treatments such as purgatives, emetics, bleedings, and counter-irritants – at a number of asylums; on this point, see Anne Digby, *Madness, Morality and Medicine: a Study of the York Retreat, 1796–1914* (Cambridge, 1985), 3–5.

53. H. D. Erlam, "Alexander Monro, *primus*," *University of Edinburgh Journal* (1954), 95.

2 THE HEART, THE HOLY GHOST, AND THE GHOST OF MICHAEL SERVETUS

1. Commonplace book of Heneage Finch (c. 1647), College of Physicians of Philadelphia, 10c/18, folio 468. The description of the heart in Finch's apothegm is consistent with a treatise possibly written by a surgeon named Sam Sambrooke, which states in part that "[t]here are in the heart three cells or ventricles, the one in the right side the other in the left and the third in the midst . . . In the pitt of the middell ventricle [the blood] is digestid and purified. Then is itt sent unto the left ventricle where of the bloud is a spiritt engendred that is more pure and subtle then any bodye made of the foure elements" (quoted in Gweneth Whitteridge, *William Harvey and the Circulation of the Blood* [London, 1971], 174 n. 27). Sambrooke, who served as apothecary to Harvey, would have been known to Finch, whose commonplace book includes prescriptions written for him by Harvey.

2. These beliefs about the heart are discussed extensively by Robert A. Erickson in *The Language of the Heart, 1600–1750* (Philadelphia, 1997), 55–56, 63–66, 82–83. See also Scott Manning Stevens, "Sacred Heart and Secular Brain," in *The Body in Parts: Fantasies of Corporeality in Early Modern Europe*, eds. David Hillman and Carla Mazzio (New York, 1997), 263–82.

3. On the symbolism of the circle for Harvey, see Walter Pagel, *William Harvey's Biological Ideas: Selected Aspects and Historical Backgrounds* (Basel, 1967), 82–83. Pagel suggests that Harvey was influenced by a Rosicrucian friend, Robert Fludd, whose mystical anatomy included circular symbolism and an analogy between the macrocosm of the universe and the microcosm of man (113–19).

4. For Hofmann's objections to Harvey's thesis, see his correspondence with Harvey of 1636, in which he denounced circulation as a "monstrous fiction" which contradicted "the one truth whose author and founder is God" (Whitteridge, *William Harvey*, 239).

5. For Harvey's relation to the Finch family, see Geoffrey Keynes, *The Life of William Harvey* (Oxford, 1966), 392. Though Harvey was the uncle of Finch's wife, Finch referred to Harvey as "my loving Cosin" in his will (Keynes, *Life of William Harvey*, 462).

6. Charles Singer, "A Study in Early Renaissance Anatomy," in *Studies in the History and Method of Science*, ed. Charles Singer (London, 1955), 126–30.

7. Samuel Purchas, *Microcosmus, or The Historie of Man* (London: 1619; rep. 1969), 25.

8. *Galen On the Usefulness of the Parts of the Body*, trans. by Margaret Tallmadge May (Ithaca, 1968), I: 295 and n.34. May cites Aristotle's *De Partibus Animalium*, vol. V in *The Works of Aristotle*, 11 volumes (Oxford, 1908–31), III: 4, 666b 23–35; see also Aristotle, *Historia Animalium*, Book I: 17, and Thomas Huxley, "On Certain Errors Respecting the Structure of the Heart Attributed to Aristotle," *Nature* 21: 523 (November 6, 1879), 1–5. Galen described the shape of the heart as "very like a cone" (May, *Galen on the Usefulness of the Parts of the Body*, I: 291), rather than as triangular. See also Pagel, *Harvey's Biological Ideas*, 227, and Charles Coulston Gillispie, ed., *Dictionary of Scientific Biography* (New York, 1970), I: 266–67.

9. Aristotle, *De Anima* (New Haven, 1951), Book I: 4, 408b 7–12. See also C. R. S. Harris, *The Heart and the Vascular System in Ancient Greek Medicine* (Oxford, 1973), 118–23.

10. Galen, *De Usu Partium* (1968), 391; May, *Galen on the Usefulness of the Parts of the Body*, I: 16, 21, 45, 323–24. See also Galen, *On Hippocrates' and Plato's doctrines*, 3.1.25, quoted in A. A. Long and D. N. Sedley, *The Hellenistic Philosophers* (Cambridge, 1987), I, 65.

11. [Sir Thomas Browne], *Religio Medici*, 5th edn., corrected and amended, with annotations by Sir Kenelm Digby (London, 1659).

12. Baltasar Gracián y Morales, *El Criticón* (1653), published in English as *The Critick. Written originally in Spanish; by Lorenzo Gracián, one of the Best Wits of Spain. And translated into English, by Paul Rycaut, Esq.*, London: by T. N. for Henry Brome, 1681.

13. David Fausett makes a similar observation in *The Strange Surprizing Sources of "Robinson Crusoe"* (Amsterdam, 1994), 44–51, though he claims that Defoe's immediate model was Hendrik Smeeks's *The Mighty Kingdom of Krinke Kesmes* (1708), which I regard as unproven.

14. The sale catalogue includes a copy of the 1619 edition Purchas's *Microcosmus* (Heidenreich No. 1018); the fourth edition (1656) of Browne's *Religio Medici* (Heidenreich No. 1186); and the 1681 translation of Gracián's *The Critick*, as well as Gracián's *The Hero* and *The Art of Prudence* (Heidenreich No. 1064, No. 453, No. 1187).

15. Of course, as many commentators have shown, Defoe *did* employ metaphors based on the vascular system to describe the circulation of trade, with

London as the system's heart; see Pat Rogers, *The Text of Great Britain: Theme and Design in Defoe's "Tour"* (Newark, 1998), 45–46, 200. Erickson sees Harvey's discovery of circulation as a motif in narratives of voyage and return in Defoe and others; see *Language of the Heart*, 84–88.

16. Erickson, *Language of the Heart* 70; for Boyle, see Barbara Beigun Kaplan, *"Divulging of Useful Truths in Physick": the Medical Agenda of Robert Boyle* (Baltimore, 1993), 78–79.

17. Robert Burton, *The Anatomy of Melancholy* (1621), 11th edn., 2 vols. (London, 1813), I: 111.

18. Theodore Gomperz, *Greek Thinkers: a History of Ancient Philosophy*, 4 vols. (London, 1901), I: 368. See also Martha C. Nussbaum, *The Therapy of Desire: Theory and Practice in Hellenistic Ethics* (Princeton, 1994), who says that it was Democritus "who first really developed the analogy [between medicine and philosophy] at length in a clearly philosophical context" (51).

19. For the background of this legend, see Gomperz, *Greek Thinkers*, I: 316.

20. Burton, *The Anatomy of Melancholy* I: 26–27.

21. For a discussion of Burton's debt to his English predecessors, see Thomas Wright, *The Passions of the Mind in General*, ed. William Webster Newbold (New York, 1986), 17–23. Burton's value to the eighteenth century as a "refresher course" in the humoural theory of the passions is discussed in Alan T. McKenzie, *Certain, Lively Episodes: the Articulation of Passion in Eighteenth-Century Prose* (Athens, 1990), 64–66.

22. Roy Porter, *"Barely Touching*: a Social Perspective on Mind and Body," in *The Languages of Psyche: Mind and Body in Enlightenment Thought*, ed. G. S. Rousseau (Berkeley, 1990), 58–59.

23. Tobias Venner, *Via Recta ad Vitam Longam, or, A Plain Philosophicall Demonstration of the Nature, Faculties, and Effects of all such things as by way of nourishments make for the preservation of health* (London, 1637). The book was originally published in two parts in 1620 and 1623; an essay, "A Brief and Accurate Treatise, concerning, the taking of the Fume of Tobacco," was published in 1621 and incorporated into the *Via Recta ad Vitam Longam* in 1637. That edition, used as the citation text here, is listed in the catalog of the Defoe/Farewell library sale (Heidenreich No. 1402). The similarities between Venner's treatise on tobacco and Crusoe's tobacco cure suggest that Defoe knew and used the book (see below, ch. 5).

24. Thomas Hobbes, *Elementorum Philosophiae sectio tertia de Cive*, discussed by Quentin Skinner in *Reason and Rhetoric in the Philosophy of Hobbes* (Cambridge, 1996), 323–26. The translation is Skinner's.

25. Thomas Hobbes, *Leviathan* (Oxford, 1909), 48 (Part I: ch. 6). Except as noted, the citations below are to *Leviathan*. There was a copy of the 1651 edition of *Leviathan* in the Defoe/Farewell library sale (Heidenreich No. 126), as well as *De Cive* (originally published in Paris, 1642; this edition in Amsterdam, 1669; Heidenreich No. 861) and Hobbes's English translation of that work, *Philosophical Rudiments Concerning Government and Society* (London, 1651; Heidenreich No. 1141); Hobbes's *Of Libertie and Necessitie*

(London, 1654; Heidenreich No. 1203); and several responses to Hobbes by the Earl of Clarendon, John Eachard, and others.

26. Skinner, *Reason and Rhetoric*, 343.

27. Daniel Defoe, *Robinson Crusoe*, ed. Michael Shinagel, 2nd edn. (New York, 1994), 5.

28. Joseph M. Levine, *The Battle of the Books: History and Literature in the Augustan Age* (Ithaca, 1991), 29–31; Paula R. Backscheider, *Daniel Defoe, His Life* (Baltimore, 1989), 55; Bastian, *Defoe's Early Life*, 157–58.

29. For Temple's essay, see his *Works*, 4 vols. (London, 1814), III: 468.

30. William Wotton, *Reflections Upon Ancient and Modern Learning* (London, 1694), 296. The italics appear in the original.

31. Michael Servetus, *The Two Treatises of Servetus on the Trinity*, trans. Earl Morse Wilbur (Cambridge, 1932).

32. Stefan Zweig, *The Right to Heresy*, trans. Eden and Cedar Paul (London, 1979), 258–63; R. Willis, *Servetus and Calvin* (London, 1877), I: 535–39; Anon., *An Impartial History of Michael Servetus, Burnt Alive at Geneva for Heresie* (London, 1724).

33. The replacement of the intraventricular pores by the lesser pulmonary circulation is discussed extensively in Whitteridge, *William Harvey*, 44–48. Whitteridge notes that Servetus wrote about the pulmonary circulation before either Realdus Columbus or his student Juan Valverde da Hamusco, but doubts that either of these men knew Servetus's *Christianismi Restitutio*.

34. George Huntston Williams, *The Radical Reformation* (Philadelphia, 1962), 336–37; John F. Fulton, "Michael Servetus and the Lesser Circulation of the Blood through the Lungs," in *Autour de Michel Servet et de Sebastien Castellion*, ed. B. Becker (Haarlem, 1953), 68; L. L. Mackall, "A Manuscript of the *Christianismi Restitutio* of Servetus," *Proceedings of the Royal Society of Medicine* 17 (1924), 35–38.

35. Joseph Henry Allen, *An Historical Sketch of the Unitarian Movement since the Reformation* (New York, 1894), 32–33. See also Williams, *Radical Reformation*, 319–23, who says that Servetus objected more to the Nicene Creed than to the concept of the Trinity itself.

36. For Servetus's violations of the code of Justinian on the Trinity, see Williams, *Radical Reformation*, 319–23; on adult baptism, 311–17.

37. *Ibid.*, 313, quoting from Servetus's *Restitutio*, 372/II. 90. The interpolations in brackets are Williams's.

38. John Calvin, *Psychopannychia*, quoted in Williams, *Radical Reformation*, 584–86; see also 612. It is Williams who identified Calvin's "unnamed adversary" as Servetus.

39. Anon., *Impartial History*, 68–69.

40. Williams, *Radical Reformation*, 581–82; see also his discussion of psychopannychism and Averroism, 21–26.

41. The survival of Servetus's book in printed and manuscript copies is traced in John F. Fulton, *Michael Servetus, Humanist and Martyr* (New York, 1953), 85,

and in L. L. Mackall, "Servetus Notes," in his *Contributions to Medical and Biological Research, dedicated to Sir William Osler*, 2 vols. (New York, 1919), II: 767–77.

42. William Wotton, *Reflections upon Ancient and Modern Learning*, 2nd edn. (London: 1697), xxv–xxviii (italics in the original). The manner in which Wotton obtained the passage is described in the postscript, xxv. A copy of the 1697 edition was in the Defoe-Farewell library sale (Heidenreich No. 948).

43. Daniel Finch, 2nd Earl of Nottingham, was a prime mover of the Act for the more effectual suppressing of Blasphemy and Prophaneness (9 & 10 William III c. 32) in 1698, which established penalties for those who denied the Trinity. But as Michael R. Watts observes in *The Dissenters* (Oxford, 1978), "Such measures . . . failed to halt the growth of heresy" (372). See also John H. Overton and Frederick Relton, *The English Church from the Accession of George I to the End of the Eighteenth Century* (London, 1906), 27–28.

3 ALEXANDER MONRO AND THE ANATOMIST'S GAZE

1. For Rush's career in Edinburgh, see George W. Corner, M.D., "Benjamin Rush's Days in Edinburgh and What Came of Them," *University of Edinburgh Journal* 15 (1949–51), 126–35.

2. Benjamin Rush, "Journal, commencing Aug. 31, 1766," fols. 69–70. The original manuscript is at Indiana University Library; a microfilm copy is at Edinburgh University Library (mic. 28). The same passage appears in Rex E. Wright-St. Clair, *Doctors Monro: a Medical Saga* (London, 1964), 69. Wright-St. Clair scoffs that it is "obviously completely false," since the younger Monro began his University studies at 12, the age at which Rush says the incident occurred. But at most this discrepancy suggests that the incident occurred earlier than Rush says it did. Since Monro *secundus* was born in 1733, the incident could have occurred no later than 1745, and possibly as early as 1740 or 1741.

3. E. Ashworth Underwood, *Boerhaave's Men: at Leyden and After* (Edinburgh, 1977), 105; Wright-St. Clair, *Doctors Monro*, 77. Underwood puts the total for Monro *primus* between 4,431 and 4,464 (204, n.126), and Wright-St. Clair accepts the estimate of 13,404 for Monro *secundus* (77). The names of Monro's students are recorded in the "Student Roll Book of Alexander Monro I, 1720–1749," Edinburgh University Library, shelf mark Dc. 5.95. For a letter by Oliver Goldsmith praising Monro written in 1753, see Wright-St. Clair, *Doctors Monro*, 43. See also John Alexander Inglis, *The Monros of Auchinbowie and Cognate Families* (Edinburgh, 1911), 67–68; Dora B. Weiner, "Mind and Body in the Clinic: Philippe Pinel, Alexander Chrichton, Dominique Esquirol, and the Birth of Psychiatry," in *The Languages of Psyche: Mind and Body in Enlightenment Thought*, ed. G. S. Rousseau (Berkeley, 1990), 367; Lewis Mansfield Knapp, *Tobias Smollett: Doctor of Men and Manners* (Princeton, 1949), 143; G. S. Rousseau, "Pineapples, Pregnancy,

Pica, and *Peregrine Pickle*," in *Tobias Smollett: Bicentennial Essays Presented to Lewis M. Knapp*, eds. G. S. Rousseau and P.-G. Boucé (New York, 1971), 91. Smollett mentions Monro favorably in his *Continuation to the History of England* (1761; IV: 120–32), even though he took William Hunter's side in the latter's dispute with Monro.

4. A selective list of the published works of Alexander Monro *primus* includes *The Anatomy of the Human Bones* (1726), to which was added *An Anatomical Treatise of the Nerves, Lacteal Sac and Duct* in the second edition (1732), becoming *The Anatomy of the Human Bones and Nerves* in the third (1741); editor, *Medical Essays and Observations*, 6 vols. (1732–47); *An Expostulatory Epistle to William Hunter* (1762); *An Account of the Inoculation of Small-pox in Scotland* (1765); *The Works of Alexander Monro*, ed. Alexander Monro *secundus* (1781); *A Treatise on Comparative Anatomy*, ed. Alexander Monro *secundus* (1783). The works of Alexander Monro *secundus* include *Observations on the Structure and Functions of the Nervous System* (1783); *The Structure and Physiology of Fishes Explained, and compared with those of man and other animals* (1785); *Experiments on the Nervous System . . . with the view of determining the Nature and Effects of Animal Electricity* (1793); *Observations on the Muscles* (1794); *Three Treatises on the Brain, the Eye, and the Ear* (1797).

5. See Anita Guerrini, "Case History as Spiritual Autobiography: George Cheyne's 'Case of the Author,'" *Eighteenth-Century Life* 19 (1995), 18–27; Guerrini, "The Hungry Soul: George Cheyne and the Construction of Femininity," *Eighteenth-Century Studies* 32 (1999), 279–91.

6. Robert E. Schofield, *Mechanism and Materialism: British Natural Philosophy in an Age of Reason* (Princeton, 1970), 57–62.

7. The question of the contribution of nerve theory to the novel as a study of sensibility is discussed extensively in Chapter I, "Sensibility and the Nervous System," in G. J. Barker-Benfield, *The Culture of Sensibility: Sex and Society in Eighteenth-Century Britain* (Chicago, 1992), and in Ann Jessie Van Sant, *Eighteenth-Century Sensibility and the Novel: the Senses in Social Context* (Cambridge, 1993). For a discussion of advances in nerve theory in the period, see Schofield, *Mechanism and Materialism*, 200–08.

8. G. S. Rousseau, *Enlightenment Crossings: Pre- and Post-modern Discourses* (Manchester, 1991), 133–34.

9. Monro was appointed in 1720 and began teaching immediately, but the chair of anatomy was not incorporated into the University of Edinburgh until 1725. See Wright St-Clair, *Doctors Monro*, 32, 37.

10. Rudolph E. Siegel, M.D., *Galen on Psychology, Psychopathology, and Function and Diseases of the Nervous System* (Basel, 1973), 94.

11. Owsei Temkin, *Galenism: Rise and Decline of a Medical Philosophy* (Ithaca, 1973), 107, 142–43. For the persistence of the physiology of animal spirits in the eighteenth century, see John W. Yolton, *Thinking Matter: Materialism in Eighteenth-Century Britain* (Minneapolis, 1983), 131, 163–72.

12. For Boerhaave's complex relation to mechanistic philosophy, see G. A. Lindeboom, *Herman Boerhaave: the Man and his Work* (London, 1968), 66–67; Lester S. King, *The Medical World of the Eighteenth Century* (Chicago,

1958), 105–21; Lester S. King, *The Philosophy of Medicine: the Early Eighteenth Century* (Cambridge, 1978), 121–24; Kathleen Wellman, *La Mettrie: Medicine, Philosophy, and Enlightenment* (Durham, 1992), 60–71; and Schofield, *Mechanism and Materialism*, 146–56.

13. Wellman, *La Mettrie*, 159, quoting from La Mettrie's *Traité de l'âme*, I: 113; Wellman, *La Mettrie*, 194. For the background of the debate between materialists and immaterialists, see Yolton, *Thinking Matter*, 29–45.

14. Wellman, *La Mettrie*, 83.

15. Underwood, *Boerhaave's Men*, 115–19; Christopher Lawrence, "Joseph Black: The Natural Philosophical Background," *Joseph Black, 1728–1799: a Commemorative Symposium*, ed. A. D. C. Simpson (Edinburgh, 1982), 1–5; Lisa Rosner, *Medical Education in the Age of Improvement: Edinburgh Students and Apprentices, 1760–1826* (Edinburgh, 1991), 3.

16. Alexander Munro *primus*, *The Anatomy of the Humane Bones. To which are added, An Anatomical Treatise of the Nerves; An Account of the Reciprocal Motions of the Heart; and, a Description of the Humane Lacteal Sac and Duct.* 2nd edn. (Edinburgh, 1732), v.

17. It is possible, though not certain, that Monro and Defoe had met. Monro's father, John Monro, was a member of the "Edinburgh literati" that supported the Treaty of Union between England and Scotland in 1707, which was negotiated in large part by Defoe. The Monros were thus part of that circle that included Defoe in "evening after evening of punch and good talk" (Paula R. Backscheider, *Daniel Defoe, His Life* [Baltimore, 1989], 219). Defoe championed the University of Edinburgh against its rival, the University of Glasgow, and enrolled his own son at Edinburgh. He last visited Scotland in 1712, the year Monro ended his schooling and began a medical apprenticeship with his father (Backscheider, *Daniel Defoe*, 308–12; Wright St.-Clair, *Doctors Monro*, 27).

18. For studies of the lectures of the Monros, see D. W. Taylor, "The Manuscript Lecture-Notes of Alexander Monro *secundus* (1733–1817)," *Medical History* 22 (1978), 174–86; "The Manuscript Lecture-Notes of Alexander Monro *primus* (1697–1767)," *Medical History* 30 (1986), 444–67; and "'Discourses on the Human Physiology' by Alexander Monro *primus* (1697–1767)," *Medical History* 32 (1988), 65–81. Taylor, "Lecture-Notes of Monro *primus*," describes and (in some cases) dates twenty-nine sets of notes to lectures by *primus* at eleven locations. I am indebted to Dr. Michael Barfoot of the Medical Archive Centre at the University of Edinburgh for calling these articles to my attention.

19. This quotation is from a transcript of Monro's lectures on anatomy written about 1732, now at the College of Physicians of Philadelphia (Shelfmark 10d/148), fol. 13. This copy was collated with another at the same library (Shelfmark 10a/137) made by John Redman from a transcript by B. Duffield in 1746, and with a transcript in the British Library Manuscripts Department (Add. Mss. 4376, fols. 81–136b), which that library's catalog dates c. 1725. The dates on the transcripts are not reliable, because they may reflect when the copy was made or owned, rather than when the lecture

was given. For a complete listing of these transcripts, see the Bibliography/Manuscripts at the end of this book.

20. Monro, "The History of Anatomy" (Coll. Phys. Phila. 1od/148), fols. 29–30.

21. "History of Anatomy" (Coll. Phys. Phila. 1od/148), fols. 46–48. Monro incorrectly gives the date of the first edition of the *Fabrica* as 1545.

22. Charles Singer, *A Short History of Anatomy from the Greeks to Harvey* (New York, 1957), 89–90. For a different translation of the two passages from the *Fabrica*, see John F. Fulton, *Michael Servetus, Humanist and Martyr* (New York, 1953), 24.

23. For a discussion of these objections, see Barbara Beigun Kaplan, "*Divulging of Useful Truths in Physick": The Medical Agenda of Robert Boyle* (Baltimore, 1993), 77–82.

24. For an explanation of the "good luck" by which one of the three surviving printed copies of Servetus's *Christianismi Restitutio* was given to the Edinburgh University Library by the Duke of Queensbury in 1695, see David Cuthbertson, *A Tragedy of the Reformation. Being the Authentic Narrative of the History and Burning of the "Christianismi Restitutio," 1553* (Edinburgh, 1912), 29.

25. Alexander Monro, "The History of Anatomy," c. 1725 (British Library Manuscript Collection, Add. Mss. 4376) fols. 104–05. The references to [1735] show variant readings that appear in Gen. 578D at the University of Edinburgh Library, dated c. 1735. All dates, however, should be considered unreliable, and are given primarily for purposes of identification of the various transcripts.

26. Monro does not say who was trying to "rob" Harvey of the honor of discovering circulation in this passage, but elsewhere, in a discussion of Nemesius, Bishop of Emissa, he says that "were it not on account of a passage quoted by Douglas to rob Harvey for the honour of the Circulation I should not trouble you with the mention of this Author" (Edinburgh University Library Mic 1134, p. 42). Since Dr. James Douglas in his *Bibliographiae Anatomicae Specimen* (1715) advanced Servetus's claim, as well as that of Nemesius, it seems likely that Monro holds Douglas responsible for the attention paid to Servetus at Harvey's expense.

27. Alexander Monro, "The History of Anatomy." Taylor dates this copy c. 1746 based on internal evidence (Taylor, "Lecture-Notes of Monro *primus*," 463).

28. Edinburgh University Library, Gen. 577D, fol. 54. The word "Œther" appears as "Other" in some transcripts, but "Œther" is almost certainly intended. The word in brackets is conjectural.

29. See above, p. 47. It is interesting that, for the first time in the lecture dated by Taylor c. 1746, Monro quotes a passage from his former teacher, Hermann Boerhaave, which appears to praise Servetus:

We may set down here the words of Boerhaave in *Oratione* XIII. "Mirabilitas hujus Legis, Michaeli Serveto primum conspecta, ab Andrea Caesalpino memorata, Realdo Columbo utcunque descripta, tandem magnifico Guilielmo Harves absolute demonstrata, per Antonium denique Lewenhoekuim oculio subjecta fidelibus." "The wonder of this law, first understood by Michael Servetus, mentioned by Andrea Caesalpino, described in some form by Realdus Columbus, then demonstrated absolutely by William Harvey, and finally presented to the believing eyes of Levenhoek," trans. Robert M. Ryan. The Latin passage is on p. 56 of Edinburgh University Library Gen. 577 D.

30. *Treatise of the Nerves*, appended to the second edition of *The Anatomy of the Humane Bones* (1732). The three treatises on the nerves, the heart, and the lacteal sac and duct in the second edition are separately paginated, and begin after page 344 of the *Anatomy*. The citations in the text refer to the *Treatise*.

31. *The Anatomy of the Human Bones and Nerves: with an Account of the reciprocal Motions of the Heart, and a Description of the Human Lacteal Sac and Duct*, 3rd edn. (Edinburgh, 1741). Despite the integration of the two treatises into a single title, they are still separately paginated in this edition. The page references are to the second treatise.

32. The Oxford English Dictionary cites Monro's *Anatomy* (1741) as the first use of the word "Nisus" in an English text.

33. The question of whether this "*Nisus* of the Mind" is related to the moral sense philosophy of Monro's Scottish contemporary, Francis Hutcheson, is beyond the scope of this chapter. For a fuller discussion of the moral sense, see Chapter 8 below.

34. After the first "Treatise on the Nerves" in the second edition of the *Anatomy* in 1732, the major revisions to nerve theory are made in the 3rd (1741) and 6th (1758). The pagination of the book becomes continuous in 1746, but the length of the section on the nerves remains at about seventy-nine pages.

35. It is doubtful that Monro knew of Robinson's work in 1741, since Robinson's *Dissertation on the Aether of Sir Isaac Newton* was not published until 1743. It is possible, however, that Monro's close friend, the mathematician Colin Maclaurin, knew either Robinson's work or that of his immediate predecessors, such as the anonymous *Examination of the Newtonian Argument for the Emptiness of Space and of the Resistance of subtile Fluids* (1740), and that Maclaurin discussed the aether theory with Monro (see Schofield, *Mechanism and Materialism*, 106–07). Monro delivered Maclaurin's funeral elegy and used it as the basis for his introduction to Maclaurin's *An Account of Sir Isaac Newton's Philosophical Discoveries* (1748), which, as Yolton says, "summarizes the main points" of the materialist/immaterialist debate (Yolton, *Thinking Matter*, 124).

36. Alexander Monro *primus*, *The Anatomy of the Human Bones, Nerves, and Heart*, 6th edn. (Edinburgh, 1758), 349.

37. Alexander Monro *secundus*, *Observations on the Structure and Functions of the Nervous System* (Edinburgh, 1783), 74–76.

38. Alexander Monro *secundus*, *Experiments on the Nervous System, with opium and metalline substances; made chiefly with the view of determining the Nature and Effects of*

Animal Electricity (Edinburgh, 1793), 13. A footnote refers the reader to the *Observations on the Nervous System*, Chapters 10 and 11, emphasizing Monro's belief that he had reached this conclusion ten years earlier. Whytt had articulated the concept of a "living principle" in the nerves in his *Essay on the Vital and other Involuntary Motions of Animals* in 1751.

39. Monro *secundus*, *Observations*, 96. Monro elaborates on the parrot's pupil in "Miscellaneous Observations on the Structure and Function of the Eyes" in his *Three Treatises on the Brain, the Eye, and the Ear* (Edinburgh, 1797), where he notes that he "many years ago, observed in the Parrot, that the Pupil is, alternately, greatly contracted and dilated, whilst the Eye is exposed to the same degree of faint Light; which is quite inconsistent with the idea, that the action of the Iris is produced by the sole and direct affect of Stimuli applied to it" (115). In a footnote, Monro cites "Dr. Porterfield's Book on the Eyes, Vol. II, Chap. v, p. 151," a reference to William Porterfield's two-volume *Treatise on the Eye* (1759). For Porterfield, see Underwood, *Boerhaave's Men*, 107–13; Yolton, *Thinking Matter*, 171–72, 187–82 n. 21. Porterfield's theory first appeared in "An Essay concerning the Motions of the Eyes," in *Medical Essays and Observations of the Philosophical Society of Edinburgh*, ed. Alexander Monro *primus* 2nd edn. (1737–38).

40. Daniel Defoe, *Robinson Crusoe*, ed. Michael Shinagel, 2nd edn. (New York, 1994), 127.

41. Underwood, *Boerhaave's Men*, 122. See also Roy Porter, *Mind-Forg'd Manacles: a History of Madness in England from the Restoration to the Regency* (Cambridge, 1987), 178–80, and Schofield, *Mechanism and Materialism*, 202 n. 12 and 204 n. 14.

42. Robert Whytt, *An Essay on the Vital and Other Involuntary Motions of Animals* (Edinburgh, 1751), 300–01. See Porter, *Mind-Forg'd Manacles*, 328 n. 54.

43. *Observations on the Nature, Causes, and Cure of those Disorders which have been commonly called Nervous, Hypochondriac, or Hysteric, to which are prefixed some remarks on the sympathy of the Nerves* (Edinburgh, 1765), vi–vii. The French translation of this book, published in 1767, included Monro *primus*'s "Une exposition anatomique des Nerfs" as an appendix.

44. Whytt, *Essay on the Vital and other Involuntary Motions*, 200, quoted in Schofield, *Mechanism and Materialism* 204.

4 DEFOE AND THE NATURAL HISTORY OF THE PASSIONS

1. For the rise and spread of Socinianism, see George Huntston Williams, *The Radical Reformation* (Philadelphia, 1962), 567–70, 630–31, 749–56, and Henry W. Clark, *History of English Nonconformity* (New York, 1965), II: 156–58; 191–97.

2. Martin Tomkins, *The Case of Mr. Martin Tomkins. Being an account of the Proceedings of the Dissenting Congregation at Stoke-Newington, upon Occasion of a Sermon preach'd by him July 13, 1718* (London, 1719), 12.

3. Michael R. Watts, *The Dissenters* (Oxford, 1978), I: 374.

4. Anon., *An Authentick Account of Several Things Done and Agreed upon by the Dissenting Ministers lately Assembled at Salters' Hall* (London, 1719), 5, 18.

5. Watts, *Dissenters*, I: 377. It should be noted that not all non-subscribers were unitarians; the division was not over that point, but on whether or not scripture alone was an adequate test of faith.

6. Paula R. Backscheider, *Daniel Defoe: His Life* (Baltimore, 1989), 85.

7. *Ibid.*, 343, 350.

8. *Ibid.*, 101–08; 339–40.

9. Daniel Defoe, *A Letter to the Dissenters* (1719), qtd. in Backscheider, *Daniel Defoe*, 402. This treatise, which is sometimes confused with another of the same name published in 1713, is regarded as Defoe's by John Robert Moore, Maximillian Novak, and Paula Backscheider, but P. N. Furbank and W. R. Owens express doubts about it in their *Defoe De-Attributions* (London, 1994), 119.

10. Defoe, *Mercurius Politicus* (Feb. 1719), 80, qtd. in Backscheider, *Daniel Defoe*, 402.

11. In The *History of the Devil* (London, 1727), Defoe blames religious division on the modern followers of Michael Servetus, who do the Devil's work for him:

> [There are] some eminent Men of Quality among us, whose upper Rooms are not extraordinar[il]y well furnished in other Cases, yet are so very witty in their Wickedness, that they gather Admirers by hundreds and thousands; who, however heavy, lumpish, slow, and backward, even by Nature, and in force of Constitution in better things, yet, in their Race Devil-wards, they are of a sudden grown nimble, light of Foot, and outrun all their Neighbours; Fellows that are as empty of Sense as Beggars are of Honesty, and as far from Brains as a Whore is of Modesty; on a sudden you shall find them dip into Polemics, study Michael Servetus, Socinus, and the most learned of their Disciples; they shall reason against all Religion, as strongly as a Philosopher; blaspheme with such a Keenness of Wit, and satyrize God and Eternity, with such a Brightness of Fancy, as if the Soul of a Rochester or a Hobbs was transmigrated into them; in a little length of Time they banter Heaven, burlesque the Trinity, and jest with every sacred thing, and all so sharp, so ready, and so terribly witty, as if they were born Buffoons, and were singled out by Nature to be Champions for the Devil" (336–37).

Baine supposes that Defoe had the neo-Arians William Whiston and Thomas Emlyn in mind in drawing this character (Rodney M. Baine, *Daniel Defoe and the Supernatural* [Athens, 1968], 61), though the terms of Defoe's denunciation resemble those in which he attacked the "hellish society" of atheists at Oxford University in "A Vision of the Angelic World" (*Serious Reflections of Robinson Crusoe*, ed. G. H. Maynadier [New York, 1903], 307–09).

12. Backscheider, *Daniel Defoe*, 417–18; Max Novak, "Defoe as an Innovator of Fictional Form," in *The Cambridge Companion to the Eighteenth-Century Novel*, ed. John J. Richetti (Cambridge, 1996), 48.

13. *Robinson Crusoe*, ed. Michael Shinagel. 2nd edn. (New York, 1994), 157; hereafter cited as *RC*.

14. As I argue in Chapter 5 below, Defoe had previously explored this same theme in the two volumes of *The Family Instructor*.

15. For the ambiguous definition of the genre "novel," see John J. Richetti, "Introduction," *The Cambridge Companion to the Eighteenth-Century Novel* (Cambridge, 1996), 1–8; for Defoe's relation to the form, see Maximillian Novak, "Defoe as an Innovator of Fictional Form," 41–71 in the same volume.

16. Paula R. Backscheider devotes the fourth chapter of *Daniel Defoe: Ambition and Innovation* (Lexington, 1986) to Defoe's historical works, where she observes that "his histories provide valuable insights into his fictional career" (72), but that not until "he was free to assume an identity or to concentrate on a single personality did he begin to explore the larger themes and profounder insights of great histories" (89).

17. Backscheider, *Ambition & Innovation*, 120.

18. Maximillian Novak, "Fiction and society in the early eighteenth century," in *England in the Restoration and Early Eighteenth Century*, ed. H. T. Swedenberg, Jr. (Los Angeles, 1972), 51–70; Novak, "Defoe as an innovator of fictional form," 41–71.

19. Robert Mayer, *History and the Early English Novel: Matters of Fact from Bacon to Defoe* (Cambridge, 1997), 192.

20. Mayer, *History and the Early English Novel*, 229. Many critics disagree, however, that the shift was "sudden," or that the "novel" was established as a fictional discourse much before the 1770s.

21. Defoe's model for a history of the effect of the passions on human and state affairs of the passions was probably Jean LeClerc's *Life of the Famous Cardinal, Duke de Richlieu*, trans. T. Brown (London, 1695). In *Daniel Defoe*, Backscheider notes that Defoe was an "avid reader" of this book (160). Frequent references to Richelieu in the *Review* and in Defoe's correspondence in May and June of 1704 show that it was in this period – shortly before publishing *The Consolidator* – that he read Leclerc's biography of Richelieu. Defoe discusses Richelieu in a letter to Harley written in mid-1704 and mentions Richelieu in the *Review* on July 1, as well as in May and June (Healey, *Letters of Daniel Defoe* 34). (I am grateful to Paula Backscheider for providing me with this method for dating Defoe's reading of LeClerc). The political lesson that Defoe extracted from LeClerc's history of Richelieu is that monarchy may easily become tyranny when it is not checked by another political body, such as the nobility or a popular assembly, and when the passions of the monarch himself are not subject to restraint; in a digression upon the origins of despotism, LeClerc asks rhetorically "if it be adva[n]tageous to persons brought up in pleasure, infinitely full of violent Passions, and drunk with perpetual Flatteries, to see nothing to contradict their Desires?" ([Jean LeClerc], *Life of Cardinal de Richlieu*, I: 203). The way that Defoe applied LeClerc's *History* is apparent in Defoe's *History of the Devil* (1727), in which he refers to "Satan's most exquisite Management under the Agency of his two prime Ministers Cardinal Richelieu and Lewis the

XIV, whom he entirely posses'd" (230). The Devil extended his influence over mankind, says the narrator, by laying "the Foundations of Eternal Feud . . . not in the Humours and Passions of Men only, but in the Interests of Nations" (232).

22. Backscheider, *Ambition and Innovation*, 83–84.
23. *Ibid.*, 177–80.
24. Ilse Vickers, *Defoe and the New Sciences* (Cambridge, 1996), 3–5.
25. *Ibid.*, 74–75.
26. Backscheider, *Daniel Defoe*, 15.
27. Helmut Heidenreich, ed., *Libraries of Daniel Defoe and Phillips Farewell: Olive Payne's Sales Catalogue* (Berlin, 1970), xxiii. The works referred to include Vesalius's *Anatomia* (1604); Sydenham's *Observationes Medicae circa Morborum Acutorum . . . Curationem* (1676) and *Tractatus de Podagra et Hydrope* (1683); de Mayerne's *Opera Medica*, ed. Jos. Browne (1701); Freind's *Praelectiones Chymicae* (1709); Cheyne's *Fluxionum Methodus Inversa* (1703), *Tractatus de Infirmorum Sanitate Tuenda – De Natura Fibrae* (1726), *An Essay of the True Nature and Due Method of Treating the Gout – An Account of . . . Bath-waters* (1724), and *A New Theory of Acute and Slow Continued Fevers* (1722); Daniel LeClerc's *La Chirurgie Complette* (1708).
28. Among other works by these authors in the Heidenreich catalogue we find Boyle's *A Free Inquiry into the Vulgarly Receiv'd Notion of Nature* (1685–86); Locke's *An Essay Concerning Humane Understanding* (1695), another edition (1706), *Some Thoughts Concerning Education* (1705), and *The Works*, ed. Jean LeClerc, with an account of the life and writings of J. Locke (1714); and LeClerc's edition of Livy's *Historiarum quod Exstat* (1710). For Defoe's interest in Locke, see Maximillian Novak, *Realism, Myth, and History in Defoe's Fiction* (Lincoln, 1983), 7–13.
29. The Defoe/Farewell library included a copy of Baglivi's *Opera Omini* (1719) in two volumes (Heidenreich No. 1380). Baglivi's *De Praxi Medica* (1696) was translated into English as *The Practice of Physic* in 1704, of which a second edition appeared in 1723. According to Ilza Veith, the original Latin edition was "widely quoted by subsequent writers in other countries," *Hysteria: the History of a Disease* (Chicago, 1965), 146.
30. Veith, *Hysteria*, 147–51.
31. *Ibid.*, 151.
32. Roxana herself pointedly reminds us that her narrative follows the discursive pattern of history, rather than fiction:

> The opposite Circumstances of a Wife and a Whore, are such, and so many, and I have since seen the Difference with such Eyes, as I cou'd dwell upon the Subject a great-while; but my Business is History; I had a long Scene of Folly yet to run over; perhaps the Moral of all my Story may bring me back again to this Part, and if it does, I shall speak of it fully. (*The Fortunate Mistress*, 133)

33. Daniel Defoe, *The Consolidator: Or, Memoirs of Sundry Transactions from the World in the Moon*, translated from the Lunar Language, by the author of The

True-Born English Man (London, 1705). In his contribution to *Reconsidering the Rise of the Novel*, ed. David Blewett (*ECF* 12: 2–3), "The Man Who Came to Dinner: Ian Watt and the Theory of Formal Realism," Michael Seidel refers to the passage in *The Consolidator* that I discuss below (211–12), though in rather different terms.

34. Augustine, *Confessions*, trans. Henry Chadwick (Oxford, 1991), 185 (x: viii.12).

35. The identity of these "Chyrurgeons" is unclear. The reference to "salamandars" suggests the Rosicrucian and mystic Jean Baptiste van Helmont (1577–1644) of Brussels, a follower of Paracelsus and founder of iatrochemistry. Van Helmont taught that a life force, or "archaeus," directed all bodily processes by sending organic elements through the veins, arteries, and nerves. See R. O. Moon, "Van Helmont, Chemist, Physician, Philosopher, and Mystic," *Proceedings of the Royal Society of Medicine* 25 (1932), 23; C. G. Cumston, *An Introduction to the History of Medicine, From the time of the Pharoahs* (New York, 1926), 279. The chemist Hermann Boerhaave cited van Helmont favorably, but criticized him for going beyond observed data into speculation about the nature of the soul; see G. A. Lindeboom, *Herman Boerhaave: the man and his work* (London, 1968), 325–26, and Kathleen Wellman, *La Mettrie: Medicine, Philosophy, and Enlightenment* (Durham, 1992), 81, 115.

36. Backscheider, *Daniel Defoe*, 46.

37. Maximillian Novak mentions the suspension of Defoe's career as an imaginative writer after *The Consolidator* and his return to that genre in *Robinson Crusoe* in his essay, "Defoe as an Innovator of Fictional Form," 43. The relation between Defoe's political activities as a propagandist for the Harley administration and his emerging vocation as a novelist is discussed in Chapter 5 of my book, *Defoe and the Idea of Fiction, 1713–1719* (Newark, 1983).

38. Robert H. West, *Milton and the Angels* (Athens, 1955), 56–58, 131. I am grateful to my colleague Diane McColley for clarifying the doctrine of particular providence.

39. Baine, *Defoe and the Supernatural*, 22, quoting a passage from *The Consolidator* as found in *The Earlier Life and the Chief Earlier Works of Daniel Defoe*, ed. Henry Morley (London: Routledge, 1889), 317–18.

40. The critic who sees the sprouting of the grain as "miraculous" is Leopold Damrosch Jr., in *God's Plot and Man's Stories: Studies in the Fictional Imagination from Milton to Fielding* (Chicago, 1985), 190. The leading advocate of the opposing view, Maximillian Novak, holds that, if Defoe was a Puritan, "his Puritanism was that of a contemporary of Locke and Thomas Burnet," not of Bunyan and Milton. Defoe's Providence, says Novak, "works entirely through nature and is often indistinguishable from nature" (*Defoe and the Nature of Man* 13, 1, 6).

41. All of the above quotations are from Baine, *Defoe and the Supernatural*, 16–24.

42. *RC*, III, "The Angelic World," 250, 257.

43. *RC*, III, "On Listening to the Voice of Providence," 186.

44. Daniel Defoe, *The Political History of the Devil, As Well Ancient as Modern* (London: T. Warner, 1726), shortened to *The History of the Devil, as Well Ancient as Modern* for the second edition (1727). The second edition is cited in the text, as *HD*.

45. At both the beginning and the end of the *History*, the narrator recalls the story of the encounter in scripture between Jesus and the possessed man from the tombs, who answers Jesus's question "What is thy name?" both in the singular and the plural, "My name is Legion, for we are many" (*HD*, 19, 406). The paradox expresses the confused identity of the demoniac, who remains at once both himself, and all those demons who possess him. The demons demand of Jesus, "*What have we to do with thee* and *art thou come to torment us before the time?*" which Jesus answers by casting them into a herd of swine, who rush down a steep bank into a lake and drown. Through this miracle, the power of Jesus to cast out devils is demonstrated, which establishes his reputation as a physician of the soul; it also establishes the relation between demons and disturbed passions. Defoe's version is consistent with Luke 8: 27–33, in which there is only one demoniac, while in Matthew 8: 28–32 there are two, making the reference to "we" ambiguous.

5 CRUSOE IN THE CAVE: FAMILY PASSIONS IN *ROBINSON CRUSOE*

1. Ian Watt, *The Rise of the Novel: Studies in Defoe, Richardson and Fielding* (Harmondsworth, 1963), 67.

2. George Starr, *Defoe and Spiritual Autobiography* (Princeton, 1965), 76–78.

3. Maximillian Novak, *Economics and the Fiction of Daniel Defoe* (Berkeley, 1962), 32.

4. Paul Hunter, *The Reluctant Pilgrim: Defoe's Emblematic Method and Quest for Form in "Robinson Crusoe"* (Baltimore, 1966), 129–30.

5. Lincoln Faller, *Crime and Defoe: A New Kind of Writing* (Cambridge, 1993), 33–34.

6. Leopold Damrosch Jr., *God's Plot and Man's Stories: Studies in the Fictional Imagination from Milton to Fielding* (Chicago, 1985), 211.

7. Paul Alkon, *Defoe and Fictional Time* (Athens, 1979), 89, 96–98.

8. Bernard Mandeville, who otherwise might be included in this list, did not arouse critical notice until the second edition of his *Fable of the Bees* in 1723, four years after *Robinson Crusoe*. See Irwin Primer, "Bernard Mandeville," in *Dictionary of Literary Biography: British Prose Writers, 1660–1800*, CI, ed. Donald T. Siebert (Detroit, 1991), 231.

9. Jeffrey Rodman, "Defoe and the Psychotic Subject," in *Ethics and the Subject*, ed. Karl Simms (Amsterdam, 1997), 245–51.

10. Maximillian Novak, *Defoe and the Nature of Man* (Oxford, 1963), 130. Paula R. Backscheider, who published an edition of the first volume of *The Family Instructor* (Scholars' Facsimiles and Reprints, 1989), gives several pages to *The Family Instructor* in *Daniel Defoe: His Life* (Baltimore, 1989), observing that its "psychological insights . . . seem strikingly acute" (364). Nevertheless, the two volumes received little attention until Novak returned to *The Family*

Instructor as a source for Defoe's fictional method in "Defoe as an Innovator of Fictional Form," in *The Cambridge Companion to the Eighteenth-Century Novel*, ed. John R. Richetti (Cambridge, 1996), 43–45.

11. Backscheider also notes this change, and attributes it to events occurring in Defoe's own family in the year 1715, which showed him "the significance of personality," for which reason *The Family Instructor* "is partly a deliberate study of the consequences of 'Temper and Constitution'" (*Daniel Defoe*, 364).

12. Daniel Defoe, *The Family Instructor* (Oxford, 1841), II: 1.

13. *Family Instructor*, II: 162; emphasis in the original. The husband's reference is to Matthew 9: 12, Mark 2: 17, and Luke 5: 31.

14. Defoe's choice of Bremen is appropriate as a spawning place for a family with a passion for adventure. Bremen has a long history as a major maritime center, though it lies forty-six miles from the North Sea on the river Weser. The city is surrounded by the province of Hanover, whose Elector had recently succeeded to the English throne. In 1720, George I acquired the archbishopric of Bremen and named it a free city. Defoe's choice of Bremen may allude to its enterprising spirit, its protestantism, its mercantilist system of government, and its possibilities as a model for such English seaports as Hull.

15. John Pocock, *The Machiavellian Moment: Florentine Political Thought and the Atlantic Republican Tradition* (Princeton, 1975), 457.

16. *Robinson Crusoe*, ed. Michael Shinagel, 2nd edn. (New York, 1994), 4–5. Subsequent references appear as *RC*.

17. Damrosch, *God's Plot and Man's Stories*, 16.

18. Tobacco is used to this day by the native Brazilian people to cure illnesses, stimulate dreams, and induce visions; see Mark J. Plotkin, *Tales of a Shaman's Apprentice* (New York, 1993), 230–34.

19. I am indebted to I. J. Spackman, W. R. Owens, and P. N. Furbank, eds., *A Kwic Concordance to Daniel Defoe's "Robinson Crusoe"* (New York, 1987), for the citations of "cure."

20. See above, Ch. 1. The treatise on tobacco is on pp. 345–64 of Tobias Venner's *Via Recta ad Vitam Longam* (London, 1637). I have previously suggested that the source for Crusoe's tobacco cure may have been the works of Baron Theodore Turquet du Mayerne (1573–1655), a copy of which was included in the sale of Defoe's library (Heidenreich No. 256), but Venner's treatise, which was also in the sale (Heidenreich No. 1402), may have been a source for both du Mayerne and Defoe. See Geoffrey Sill, "A Source for Crusoe's Tobacco Cure," *English Language Notes* 32: 4 (June 1995), 46–48.

21. Rodney Baine describes the dream as "obviously angelic" in *Daniel Defoe and the Supernatural* (Athens, 1968), 28; J. Paul Hunter speaks of it as a "divine manifestation" and a "direct revelation" of God's will in *The Reluctant Pilgrim*, 155–57. Nancy Armstrong and Leonard Tennenhouse in "A Brief Genealogy of Dreams," *Eighteenth-Century Studies* 23 (1990), 458–78, discuss Crusoe's dream as the product of "the irrational rather than the rational mind," and note that the dream allows Crusoe to "regain unprecedented

tranquillity" in much the way the tobacco cures his fever, but they still see the figure in the dream as "the Christian god" (473). In *The True Story of the Novel* (New Brunswick, 1996), Margaret Doody notes that dreams were thought to originate in black bile, the melancholy humour, "according to a medical theory that became widely known through the works of the second-century physician Galen of Pergamum" (419).

22. Defoe's doubts about the usefulness of dreams as warnings of things to come are evident in a series of letters to *Mist's Journal*, Jan.–Feb. 1720, in which various personnae, "White Witch," "E.S.," and "T.E.," debate whether the family in a recent house fire should have been saved by presages in their dreams. For these essays, see William Lee, *Daniel Defoe: his Life, and Recently Discovered Writings* (London, 1869), II: 2; II: 182–84; II: 193–99.

23. The passage is not identified in *The Reluctant Pilgrim*, though Hunter provides analogous passages from Ezekiel, Job, and I Kings (154–55, 160–63). Hunter explains the absence of an exact parallel by noting that in the Bible, God speaks to Elijah through wind, earthquake, and fire, whereas "Crusoe . . . fails to perceive the message, so that God, to effect his purpose, has to speak directly" (155). There are, however, many passages in the Bible in which God speaks directly, any of which Defoe could have used had he wanted to suggest that the figure in the dream represents God's voice.

24. Starr, *Spiritual Autobiography*, 111; Baine, *Defoe and the Supernatural*, 29; Hunter, *Reluctant Pilgrim*, 163.

25. For the suggestion that Crusoe's arrival is described in sexual terms, I am indebted to an unpublished manuscript, "'One Universal Act of Solitude'? Figuring the Female in *Robinson Crusoe*," by Susan Glover.

26. Lee, *Recently Discovered Writings*, II: 194. Defoe's "correspondent" was, of course, probably himself.

27. In *Defoe's Fiction* (London, 1985), Ian Bell described the "central enterprise" of *Robinson Crusoe* as "a tension between mobility and stability, between jeopardy and security"; the novel's "oscillation between adventure and prudence" reflects Defoe's own career (112).

28. William Wotton, *Reflections Upon Ancient and Modern Learning* (London: 1694), 293–94.

29. The meanings of melancholia are examined by Raymond Klibansky, Erwin Panofsky, and Fritz Saxl in *Saturn and Melancholy: Studies in the History of Natural Philosophy, Religion and Art* (London, 1964), and are said to indicate strong passions, including sexual cravings and hallucinations (34–36). Robert A. Erickson has previously noted the similarity of Defoe's language to that of Robert Burton's *Anatomy of Melancholy* in his essay, "Starting over with *Robinson Crusoe*," *Studies in the Literary Imagination* 15 (1982), 51–63.

30. Carol Houlihan Flynn, in *The Body in Swift and Defoe* (Cambridge, 1990), 153, has suggested that the goat signifies Crusoe's "solitary, self-enclosed frailty," while Homer O. Brown, in "The Displaced Self in the Novels of Daniel Defoe," *ELH* 38 (1971), 572–73, numbers the goat among the many "versions of himself" that Crusoe encounters. John J. Richetti, in *Defoe's*

Narratives: Situations and Structures (Oxford, 1975), 50, does not comment specifically on the dying goat, but sees Crusoe's victory over the wild animals on the island as a "re-enactment" of the taming of his own "unruly nature" by God. Similarly, David Blewett in *Defoe's Art of Fiction* (Toronto, 1979), 51, notes that Defoe uses animal imagery to suggest the "brutal side of man's dual nature," specifically his "base passions." Margaret Doody mythologizes the goat in *True Story of the Novel*, calling it "a Dionysiac emblem and sacrifice, that makes the place uncanny" (343). Aaron Santesso notes some differences between the goat and the Devil in "A Note on Goats: Defoe on Crusoe's 'Devil'," *The Scriblerian* 30: 2 (Spring, 1998), 48–49.

31. Defoe debunks the traditional association between goats and devils in *The History of the Devil* (London, 1727). Satan, he scoffs, "knows how much of a Cheat it is" to "bubble the weak Part of the World" by dressing the Devil up in "many frightful Shapes and Figures," including the cloven-footed goat (265). But the goat is not an appropriate representation of the Devil: though "he is counted a fierce Creature indeed of his Kind," and "though he is emblematically used to represent a lustful Temper," still "we do not rank the Goats among the subtle or cunning Part of the Brutes," and therefore the goat "does not fully serve to describe the Devil" (266). In consequence, "good People miss the Devil many times where they look for him" (267), particularly if they hope to identify him by a cloven foot.

32. It is not quite clear whether the "long spear or weapon" in the dream is present in the cave. Crusoe does not specifically say that he carries his gun with him into the cave, but he has said that he always took a gun with him on these expeditions into the interior of the island. Alternatively, the "Stick flaming in my Hand" may correspond to the weapon in the dream.

33. Galen, *On the Passions and Errors of the Soul*, trans. Paul W. Harkins (Columbus, 1963), 47.

34. Saint Augustine, *Confessions*, trans. Henry Chadwick (Oxford, 1991), 186 (x.viii.13).

35. Dianne Armstrong, "The Myth of Cronos: Cannibal and Sign in *Robinson Crusoe*," *Eighteenth-Century Fiction* 4 (1992), 207; James O. Foster, "*Robinson Crusoe* and the Uses of the Imagination," *Journal of English and Germanic Philology* 91 (1992), 186; Geoffrey Sill, "Crusoe in the Cave: Defoe and the Semiotics of Desire," *Eighteenth-Century Fiction* 6 (1994), 225.

36. John Dwyer, *The Age of the Passions* (East Linton, 1998), 17–18.

6 THE SINNER, THE SADDLER, AND THE BREWER'S WIFE

1. F. Bastian, "Defoe's *Journal of the Plague Year* Reconsidered," *Review of English Studies* 16 (1965), 166–67.

2. *A Journal of the Plague Year*, ed. Louis Landa, intro. by David Roberts (Oxford, 1990), 8.

3. Alan McKenzie, *Certain, Lively Episodes: the Articulation of Passion in Eighteenth-Century Prose* (Athens, 1990), 92.

4. McKenzie, *Certain Lively Episodes*, 137, on avarice in Hume; 186, on curiosity in Johnson; and 243 n. 5, on curiosity in *The Spectator*. See also *The Spectator* No. 156, in which Mr. Spectator admits that curiosity is his "prevailing Passion" (111); No. 228, in which curiosity is said to "lay up in the Imagination a Magazine of Circumstances" to be produced later (388); and No. 266, in which he indulges his curiosity "in having some Chat" with a young prostitute (534).

5. In "Defoe's *Journal of the Plague Year* Reconsidered," Bastian supposes that Defoe's fascination with the pit at Aldgate sprang from a "particularly powerful impression" made on him by "a vivid story told him by his uncle," Henry Foe, who survived the plague (171). Perhaps so, but if, as I argue here, there are similarities between the cave scene in *Robinson Crusoe*, the pit scene in the *Journal*, and the Newgate scene in *Moll Flanders*, Defoe had more than autobiographical reasons to explore the scene in depth.

6. Defoe may have had in mind Isaiah 53: 3, "He was despised and rejected of men; a man of sorrows, and acquainted with grief: and we hid as it were our faces from him; he was despised, and we esteemed him not."

7. In his edition of the *Journal of the Plague Year* (1835), E. W. Brayley suggested that Dr. Heath was modeled on Nathaniel Hodges, M.D. (1629–88), largely on the grounds that Hodges remained in London during the plague year and that Defoe used an English translation of Hodges's medical treatise, *Loimologia* (1672), as a source for the *Journal*. Brayley's identification of Heath with Hodges is disputed by Bastian, who believes that the original might have been a surgeon named Jeaffrie (or Geoffrey) Heath ("Defoe's *Journal of the Plague Year* Reconsidered," 157; Bastian, *Defoe's Early Life*, 27). A surgeon, however, was not a "Physician," as H.F. clearly labels him, and probably would not have had the interest in the causes and prevention of disease that a man trained in medicine would have had. "Dr. Heath" thus appears to be a fictional construct based in the tradition of the physician-philosopher.

8. Bastian ("Defoe's *Journal of the Plague Year* Reconsidered," 171–72) argues cogently that Defoe's precision in dating H.F.'s second visit to the pit testifies to his concern for historical accuracy, since the pit was closed on September 20, 1665, and Defoe had to allow time for the blasphemers to fall ill, die, and be buried in the pit before it closed. But an equally strong argument may be made that Defoe wished to emphasize the sequence of events that began with Dr. Heath's warning to stay indoors early in August, proceeded with H.F.'s increasingly flagrant disregard of that prohibition, and concluded on September 10 with the second visit to the graveyard.

9. H.F.'s sympathetic comportment toward the urban poor, particularly the waterman and his family, is discussed by Maximillian Novak in his essay, "Defoe and the Disordered City," *PMLA* 92 (1977), 241–52.

10. T. G. A. Nelson, *Children, Parents, and the Rise of the Novel* (Newark, 1995), 202.

11. As is customary, I will refer to Defoe's heroine as "Moll Flanders," although that is not her real name. She never reveals this "grand Secret" to anyone,

not even to her favorite Lancashire husband. Her secrecy on this point is an essential element in Defoe's portrait of cupidity.

12. *The Fortunes and Misfortunes of the Famous Moll Flanders,* ed. Edward Kelly (New York, 1973), 10.

13. "Concupiscence" and "cupidity" share the same root in Latin, "cupere," to desire (*OED*).

14. Defoe, *The Consolidator: Or, Memoirs of Sundry Transactions from the World in the Moon.* Translated from the Lunar Language, by the author of The True-Born English Man (London, 1705), 18.

15. Ian Watt, *Rise of the Novel: Studies in Defoe, Richardson and Fielding* (Harmondsworth, 1963), 130–31.

16. David Blewett, *Defoe's Art of Fiction* (Toronto, 1979), 130–33. Blewett borrows the phrase "moral deterioration" from Maximillian Novak's "Crime and Punishment in Defoe's *Roxana*," *Journal of English and Germanic Philology* 65 (1966), 446.

17. Terry Castle, "'Amy, Who Knew My Disease' a Psychosexual Pattern in Defoe's *Roxana*," *ELH* 46 (1979), 81–96.

18. Raymond Stephanson, "Defoe's Malade Imaginaire': The Historical Foundation of Mental Illness in *Roxana*." *Huntington Library Quarterly* 45 (1982), 99–118.

19. Paula R. Backscheider, *Daniel Defoe: Ambition and Innovation* (Lexington, 1986), 192.

20. I have elsewhere expressed doubts that the text offers any proofs (but rather complicates the likelihood) that Susan is Roxana's daughter; see "*Roxana*'s Susan: Whose Daughter Is She Anyway?" *Studies in Eighteenth-Century Culture* 29 (1999), 261–72.

21. Robert Burton, *The Anatomy of Melancholy* (London, 1813), I: 177.

22. Daniel Defoe, *The History of the Devil, as well Ancient as Modern* (London, 1727), 230.

23. Daniel Defoe, *The Fortunate Mistress, or, a History of the Life . . . of the Lady Roxana,* ed. John Mullan (Oxford, 1996), 234.

24. *Roxana*, 238–39. In his previously cited article, "Defoe's 'Malade Imaginaire,'" Raymond Stephanson quotes this passage in support of his argument that Roxana suffers from "melancholic obsession and delusion" (109).

25. For Sydenham and Baglivi on hysteria, see Ilza Veith, *Hysteria: the History of a Disease* (Chicago, 1965), 144, 150. Veith also discusses the work of Edward Jorden, *A Briefe Discourse of a Disease Called the Suffocation of the Mother* (1631), in which hysteria was first traced to emotional tensions (120–24). The Defoe/Farewell library includes copies of works by all three authors; see Helmut Heidenreich, ed., *The Libraries of Daniel Defoe and Phillips Farewell: Olive Payne's Sale Catalogue* (Berlin, 1970), items 1374, 138, and 1225. George Rousseau traces the long history of hysteria from its association with witchcraft in the medieval period to its "medicalization" at the turn of the seventeenth century and its coming of age "in the sunlight of the Newtonian Enlightenment" in his essay "'A Strange Pathology': Hysteria

in the Early Modern World, 1500–1800," in *Hysteria Beyond Freud*, eds. Sander L. Gilman, Helen King, Roy Porter, G. S. Rousseau, and Elaine Showalter (Berkeley, 1993), 91–221. The term is now seldom used, but was considered a valid diagnosis at the time that Defoe wrote *Roxana*.

26. Helen King, "Once upon a Text: Hysteria from Hippocrates," in *Hysteria Beyond Freud*, 13. King's phrase connecting hysteria with "notions of womanhood" is quoted from G. B. Risse, "Hysteria at the Edinburgh Infirmary: The Construction and Treatment of a Disease, 1770–1800," *Medical History* 32 (1988), 16.

7 "SURPRIZED BY HIS PASSIONS": THE GHOST OF SERVETUS AND THE REVEREND JOHN LEWIS

1. Tobias Smollett, *The Expedition of Humphry Clinker* (Norton, 1983), 218.

2. Anon., Bodleian Library, Rawlinson MSS, D. 376, fol. 187. The catalogue to the Rawlinson Collection, V, D: 206, describes it as a "Copy of a letter of earnest remonstrance written by a clergyman to his daughter Betty, who, having married without his consent, was now proposing to join the Quakers."

3. For the circumstances under which it is possible that Lewis was the author of the letter, see Appendix I.

4. These works are listed in an appendix to his autobiography (see n. 10 below). A partial list of his works appears in the entry on Lewis in the *Dictionary of National Biography* (*DNB*).

5. John Lewis, *The History of the Life and Sufferings of the Reverend and learned John Wicliffe* (London, 1720, reissued with cancel t.p. and additional material, 1723, new edition with corrections by the author published by Clarendon Press, 1820); *The Life of the learned and Right Reverend Reynold Pecock, Bishop of St. Asaph and Chichester, in the reign of King Henry VI . . . being a sequel of the History of the Life of Dr. John Wiclif* (written 1732, printed in London by John Moore for the author, 1744, reprinted Clarendon Press, 1820); *The Life of Dr. John Fisher, Bishop of Rochester* (written 1730/31, printed 1855).

6. *The History and Antiquities, ecclesiastical and civil, of the Isle of Tenet in Kent* (London, 1723; second edition, printed for the author, and for Joseph Ames and Peter Thompson, 1736); *The History and Antiquities of the Abbey and church of Favresham in Kent* (London, 1727); *A Complete History of the several Translations of the Holy Bible, and New Testament, into English* (London, 1739); *The Life of mayster Wyllyam Caxton, of the Weald of Kent, the first Printer in England* (London, 1738), and others.

7. *DNB*, XI, 1065–67. Some of Lewis's works continue to be cited as important studies. His *Life of Wiclif* is cited in Henry W. Clark, *The History of English Nonconformity* (New York, 1965), I: 36–73 passim, and his *Brief History of the Rise and Progress of Anabaptism* is discussed favorably by Champlin Burrage in *The Early English Dissenters* (New York, 1912), I: 4–5. See also the bibliographies for Wycliffe and Pecock in *The New Cambridge Bibliography of English Literature*, which cite Lewis.

8. Nigel Yates, Robert Hume, and Paul Hastings, *Religion and Society in Kent, 1640–1914* (Kent County Council, 1994), 19. For Lewis's career, see Edward Hasted, *The History and Topographical Survey of the County of Kent*, 4 vols. (Canterbury: Simmons and Kirkby, 1778–1799), III: 348, 410, 435; IV: 332, 359; *DNB*, XI: 1065–67; *British Biography*, V: 2927; and Lewis's manuscript autobiography, British Library, Add. MSS. 28651 (discussed below).

9. *The Church Catechism explain'd by way of Question and Answer, and confirm'd by Scripture Proofs.* Collected by John Lewis (London, 1700). A second edition appeared in 1702; a fourth, with Irish translation, in 1712; the 37th, London and New York, in 1800.

10. John Lewis, "Some Account of the Life of the reverend Mr. John Lewis," British Library, Add. MSS. 28651, fols. 32–33. Lewis explains that he wrote a preface to the catechism, in which he acknowledged having derived the method and some of the matter from similar catechisms by Bishop Williams and Dr. Isham, but that the preface was omitted in the printed text. The proprietors of the Williams and Isham catechisms were "very much alarm'd" at the cheap price of Lewis's catechism and its success in the charity schools.

11. John Lewis, *The Bread and Wine in the Holy Eucharist not a proper Material Propitiatory Sacrifice* (London, 1714), written in response to Johnson's *The Unbloody Sacrifice, & Altar, unvail'd and supported* (1714); see also Lewis's *A Vindication of the right reverend the Ld. Bishop of Norwich, from the undeserved reflections of . . . Mr. John Johnson, in his book . . . "The unbloody sacrifice and altar unvailed and supported . . . by a Christian"* (London, 1714), and continuing letters and manuscripts on the topic in the Clarendon Manuscripts at the Bodleian, items 38046, 38047, and 38049 in *Summary Catalogue of Post-Medieval Western Manuscripts* (Oxford, 1991).

12. John Lewis, "Some Account of the Life of the reverend Mr. John Lewis," fol. 80.

13. *A Brief History of the Rise and Progress of Anabaptism in England. To which is prefixed, some account of the learned Dr. Wiclif, and a defence of him from the false charge of his, and his followers, denying infant baptism* (London, 1738). In his autobiography, Lewis admits his history of anabaptism was written "in a little too much hast" (fol. 68). The *History* was answered by Thomas Crosby, an "ignorant, conceited and abusive man" (fol. 69). Though he felt contempt for the reply, Lewis drew from it "a very good and wise observation, That out of the Anger of others we may fetch this good use; to gather carefully the wholsome warnings or reflections which an angry adversary will give us: For he will be sure to tell us all the Evil which he and his companions see in us, which, perhaps, we our selves see not, or overlook" (69).

14. The anabaptist argument that belief must *precede* baptism is specious, Lewis noted in a memo to himself, because it rests on the assumption that the minister performing the ceremony confers grace on the believer, "as was actually done after Baptism by the Apostles, but which no other persons since have the power of doing," memo of his reply to "One of the late

Answerers of *Christianity not founded on Argument*," Bodleian Library, Clarendon MSS c. 19, fol. 374.

15. Lewis, *Church Catechism Explain'd, by way of Question and Answer*, 5th edn.
(London, 1710), 2. The emendation in brackets is in the original. In the
second part of his catechism, Lewis admonishes children to renew their
vigilance against the passions by praying, morning and evening, "And give
me Grace to resist the several Temptations of the Devil, the World, and my
own corrupt Nature. Possess me with a hatred of all my former breaches
of this sacred Obligation, and to take care to walk more cautiously for the
time to come. Purifie my Heart from all vain Thoughts and Desires; Keep
my Tongue from evil Speaking, Lying, and Slandering, and my Body in
Temperance, Soberness, and Chastity" (79–80).

16. Bodleian Library, Rawlinson MS. 410, fol. 4. Emphasis in original. This
passage is notable for two reasons: first, it acknowledges that adult baptism
was practiced by Christ's disciples and had scriptural authority; second, the
scripture that Lewis cites is the same passage from Mark (16: 16) that the
clergyman recommends in his letter to Betty.

17. John Lewis, *A Brief History of the English Anabaptists*, 2nd edn. (London, 1741),
93. The copy consulted was Rawlinson MS. C409, with manuscript corrections by Lewis for a third edition.

18. Rawlinson MS. 410, "History of Anabaptism in England," fol. 28.9, glossary.
The quoted passage is from a section called the "Kuklopaideia," note M.

19. *Ibid.*, fol. 28.9, note N.

20. *Ibid.*, fol. 3.

21. Yates *et al.*, *Religion and Society in Kent*, 41.

22. Lewis describes his friendship with Waterland in his autobiography, "Some
Account of the Life of the reverend Mr. John Lewis," fol. 66. The corre-
spondence began in 1724, when Waterland had already published his *The
Importance of the Doctrine of the Trinity Asserted, in Reply to some late Pamphlets*
(London, 1719); *A Vindication of the Orthodox Faith and Doctrine of the Church of
England, against the Arian and Socinian Heresies, as they are now Reviv'd (and Taught)
among the Whiggs and Dissenters* (London, 1719 [date given in pencil in the
copy in Dr. Williams's Library]); and *A Critical History of the Athanasian Creed,
Representing the Opinions of the Ancients and Moderns Concerning it* (Cambridge:
Cambridge University Press, 1724).

23. John Lewis, "The Life of the learned and reverend John Wallis, professor
of geometry at Oxford" (dated November 24, 1735). Bodleian Library,
Rawlinson MSS c. 978, fol. 8.

24. *Ibid.*, fols. 20–21. For recent discussions of John Wallis and the Oxford
circle, see Robert G. Frank Jr., *Harvey and the Oxford Physiologists* (Berkeley,
1980), 23–24, and Frank's "Thomas Willis and his Circle: Brain and Mind
in Seventeenth-Century Medicine," in *The Languages of Psyche: Mind and Body
in Enlightenment Thought*, ed. G. S. Rousseau (Berkeley, 1990), 119–26.

25. "Life of John Wallis," fols. 70–73. Lewis is paraphrasing Wallis's *The Doctrine
of the Blessed Trinity Briefly Explain'd* (London, 1690), which was extended by

a series of eight published "Letters" on the Trinity through 1692. The "friend" may have been Stephen Nye (1648?–1719), author of *An Answer to Dr. Wallis's Three Letters concerning the Doctrine of the Trinity* (1691).

26. Lewis, "The History of the Life of Michael Servetus M.D. of Vienne in France, who was burnt at Geneva for Blasphemy, Heresy and Defamation," MS. dated Jan. 31, 1743/4, Bodleian Library, Clarendon MSS. c. 21, fol. 70v. Lewis here paraphrases Thomas Tenison, who had appointed him as vicar of Margate and Minster in 1705 and 1709.

27. R. Willis, *Servetus and Calvin* (London, 1877), 535; John F. Fulton, *Michael Servetus, Humanist and Martyr* (New York, 1953), 88.

28. Anon., *An Impartial History of Michael Servetus, Burnt Alive at Geneva for Heresie* (London, 1724). For a discussion of the authorship of this anonymous work, see my "The Authorship of *An Impartial History of Michael Servetus*," *PBSA* 87 (1993), 303–18, and Appendix 2 below.

29. Roland H. Bainton, *The Reformation of the Sixteenth Century* (Boston, 1952), 44.

30. Bainton, *Reformation of the Sixteenth Century*, 215–17; George Huntston Williams, *The Radical Reformation* (Philadelphia, 1962), 622–30.

31. Lewis, "History of the Life of Servetus," fol. 5. Lewis quotes from the prologue to Cranmer's 1540 edition of the Bible, published in 1689 as *The Judgement of Archbishop Cranmer concerning the Peoples' Right to, and Discrete Use of the Holy Scriptures.*

32. A copy of Lewis's *Catechism* (1712; incorrectly identified as *The Book of Common Prayer*) appears in the Defoe/Farewell sales catalogue (Heidenreich No. 680), and a copy of Lewis's *Life of Wicliffe* is listed in the sale catalogue of Henry Fielding's library, appended to E. M. Thornbury, *Henry Fielding's Theory of the Comic Prose Epic* (New York, 1966), No. 190. In his "History of Servetus" Lewis refers to "one Sam. Richardson" in England who "affirmed, that Dr. Heath's words, 'that Christ is the only Son of God in respect of his eternal Generation as He is the Second Person in the Trinity, and, that the Holy Spirit proceedeth from the father originally, and hath dependence from both father and Son,' contain in them the nature of Blasphemy" (fol. 70r., fol. 69v.).

33. The quotation is from Lewis's "History of Servetus," Clarendon MSS. c. 21, fol. 30, in which he paraphrases Servetus's doctrine on baptism.

34. Samuel Richardson, *Clarissa, or the History of a Young Lady* (Harmondsworth, 1985), 370.

8 "MR. *JONES* HAD SOMEWHAT ABOUT HIM": HENRY FIELDING
AND THE MORAL SENSE

1. The argument that prudence is the basis of the moral doctrine of *Tom Jones*, as providence is its theological basis, is most fully worked out by Martin Battestin in "Fielding's Definition of Wisdom: Some Functions of Ambiguity and Emblem in *Tom Jones*," *ELH* 35 (1968), 188–217, rpt. in *The Providence of Wit: Aspects of Form in Augustan Literature in the Arts* (Oxford, 1974),

164–92. The argument is restated by Eric Rothstein in "Virtues of Authority in *Tom Jones*," *Critical Essays on Henry Fielding*, ed. Albert J. Rivero (New York, 1998), 141–163. Battestin, however, admits that Sophia is the only one of the "good" characters in the book who exhibits prudence (*Providence*, 167), and Rothstein demolishes the notion that either Allworthy or Sophia represent prudence ("Virtues," 152–53).

2. Henry Fielding, *The History of Tom Jones, a Foundling*, ed. Fredson Bowers, with introduction and commentary by Martin C. Battestin (Middletown, 1975), IV: vi. Subsequent citations will refer to book and chapter in this edition.

3. *An Essay Concerning Human Understanding*, ed. A. C. Fraser (New York, 1959), I: 71.

4. This passage from Wallis's *The Doctrine of the Blessed Trinity Briefly Explain'd* (1690) is discussed in the previous chapter.

5. Baxter, *The Quakers Catechism* (1655), quoted in Geoffrey F. Nuttall, *The Holy Spirit in Puritan Faith and Experience* (Chicago, 1992), 162.

6. Fielding's diffidence about the exact mechanism of the passions bears some interesting resemblances to the passage from Watts's *Doctrine of the Passions*, quoted above in my introduction, which concludes "But whether these be some refined spiritous Liquids, or Vapour drawn off from the Blood, or whether they be nothing else but the elastick or springy Parts of the Air drawn in by Respiration, and mingled with the Blood and other Animal Juices, is not yet entirely agreed by Philosophers" (10).

7. Jean H. Hagstrum, *Sex and Sensibility: Ideal and Erotic Love from Milton to Mozart* (Chicago, 1980), 6.

8. On the heart as the seat of the vital heat and emotions, and the effect of the discovery of circulation on this function attributed to it, see Gweneth Whitteridge, *William Harvey and the Circulation of the Blood* (London, 1971), 126–43, 215–21. On the heart as the seat of consciousness or the soul, see C. R. S. Harris, *The Heart and the Vascular System in Ancient Greek Medicine, from Alcmaeon to Galen* (Oxford, 1973), 7, 28, 94–95.

9. *Rambler* No. 4 (31 March 1749/50), 23, 25. Martin Battestin discusses Johnson's comments on *Tom Jones* in *Henry Fielding, a Life* (London, 1989), 504–05.

10. James Boswell, *The Life of Samuel Johnson, LL. D*, ed. G. B. Hill (Oxford, 1887), II: 49.

11. Hawkins, *Life of Samuel Johnson, LL. D.* (London: 1787), qtd. in Morris Golden, *Fielding's Moral Psychology* (Amherst, 1966), 167 n. 3.

12. Ronald Paulson, *The Life of Henry Fielding, a Critical Biography* (Oxford, 2000), 74.

13. Martin Battestin, *The Moral Basis of Fielding's Art* (Middletown, 1959), 14–25; R. S. Crane, "Suggestions toward a Genealogy of the 'Man of Feeling,'" *ELH* 1 (1934), 205–30. Battestin affirms his rejection of deism as the moral basis of Fielding's art in a review essay, "Fielding and the Deists," *Eighteenth Century Fiction* 13: 1 (October 2000), 67–76.

14. Bernard Harrison, *Henry Fielding's Tom Jones: the Novelist as Moral Philosopher* (London, 1975), 119.

15. Leo Braudy, *Narrative Form in History and Fiction: Hume, Fielding and Gibbon* (Princeton, 1970), 5 n.6, 91–93.

16. Martin C. Battestin, "The Problem of *Amelia*: Hume, Barrow, and the Conversion of Captain Booth," *ELH* 41 (1974), 617.

17. Battestin, "Problem of *Amelia*," 633, 635, 643–44; see also Ernest Campbell Mossner, *The Life of David Hume* (Austin, 1954), 116. Fielding did own a copy of Hume's *Philosophical Essays*, but that work, published in 1748, appeared well after Fielding's philosophical outlook was established.

18. Battestin, "Problem of *Amelia*," 635; Mossner, *Life of David Hume*, 223.

19. Paulson, *Life of Henry Fielding*, xii.

20. For Fielding's career as a student, see Battestin, *Henry Fielding*, 62–65; Donald Thomas, *Henry Fielding* (New York, 1990), 49–53. In Holland, he was exposed to the dialogue among continental humanists about the role of the passions in human psychology that was conducted in part through periodical abstracts of recent books. One such periodical, Jean LeClerc's *Bibliothèque Ancienne et Moderne*, included extensive abstracts and critical reviews of Francis Hutcheson's *An Inquiry into the Original of our Ideas of Beauty and Virtue* (London, 1725). According to LeClerc, Hutcheson had emerged with this book as the leading defender of the Earl of Shaftesbury against his detractors, notably Bernard Mandeville. See LeClerc, *Bibliothèque Ancienne et Moderne* 24: 2 (1725), 421–37; 26: 1 (1727), 102–115. For LeClerc's views of Hutcheson, see James Moore, "The Two Systems of Francis Hutcheson: on the Origins of the Scottish Enlightenment," *Studies in the Philosophy of the Scottish Enlightenment*, ed. M. A. Stewart (Oxford, 1990), 37–59.

21. Bernard Mandeville, *The Fable of the Bees: or, Private Vices, Publick Benefits*, ed. F. B. Kaye (Oxford, 1924), I: 182–84. See also Mandeville, *A Treatise of the Hypochondriack and Hysterick Diseases* (1730), ed. Stephen H. Good (Delmar, 1976), 159–60. Mandeville's thesis – whether sincere or satiric – was repeated through some fifteen books, some of which went to third editions, that continued to appear until just before his death in 1733. For a bibliography and brief critical account of Mandeville, see Irwin Primer, "Bernard Mandeville," *Dictionary of Literary Biography: British Prose Writers, 1660–1800*, ed. Donald T. Siebert, CI (Detroit, 1991), 220–39.

22. J. G. A. Pocock, *The Machiavellian Moment: Florentine Political Thought and the Atlantic Republican Tradition* (Princeton, 1975), 465–66.

23. Several of Fielding's essays in *The Champion* and volume one of the *Miscellanies*, which Henry Knight Miller believes were written about 1739–40, take the controversy over *The Fable of the Bees* as their point of departure. See Miller, ed., *Miscellanies by Henry Fielding, Esq;* (Oxford, 1972), I: xlii–xlv, and Paulson, *Life of Henry Fielding*, 218 and 356 n. 34.

24. Sarah Fielding, *The Adventures of David Simple*, ed. Peter Sabor (Lexington, 1998), 219.

25. Benjamin Franklin, *Writings* (New York, 1987), 1346; Battestin, *Henry Fielding, A Life*, 151–57.

26. Battestin, *Moral Basis of Fielding's Art*, 55–56, and *Providence of Wit*, 160; LeRoy W. Smith, "Fielding and Mandeville: The 'War against Virtue,'" *Criticism* 3 (1961), 7–15; Samuel A. Golden, *Fielding's Moral Psychology*, 4, 21–26; William Robert Irwin, *The Making of "Jonathan Wild": a Study in the Literary Method of Henry Fielding* (Hamden, 1966), 59–64.

27. Stephen, *History of English Thought in the Eighteenth Century*, 2 vols. (New York, 1876), II: 57. Recent work on Hutcheson includes James Moore, "Hume and Hutcheson," in *Hume and Hume's Connexions*, eds. M. A. Stewart and John P. Wright (Edinburgh, 1994), 23–57; Stephen Darwall, "Hume and the Invention of Utilitarianism" in the same collection, 58–82; Moore, "Two Systems of Francis Hutcheson," 37–59; and Susan M. Purviance, "Intersubjectivity and Sociable Relations in the Philosophy of Francis Hutcheson," *Sociability and Society in Eighteenth-Century Scotland*, eds. John Dwyer and Richard B. Sher, *Eighteenth Century Life* 15, n.s. Nos. 1 and 2, 23–38.

28. Henry Knight Miller, in his *Essays on Fielding's "Miscellanies": A Commentary on Volume One* (Princeton, 1961), states that "Fielding agrees (strictly) in almost no important regard with the approach of Hutcheson, whose ethics of feeling is very nearly as rigorous and rationalistic as the scheme of Clarke and his followers" (69). As Miller says elsewhere, Fielding was not a systematic thinker and did not write novels to demonstrate the working of any rationalistic scheme. That does not mean, however, that Fielding could not have discovered the "active Principle" that connects passion to action in Hutcheson's thought.

29. William Robert Scott, in *Francis Hutcheson: his Life, Teaching and Position in the History of Philosophy* (1900; rep. New York, 1966), 27–34, describes "a group of earnest young thinkers" adhering to Shaftesbury's thought in Dublin in the early 1720s, including Molesworth, Synge, Arbuckle, and Hutcheson. John Price, however, does not confirm that Arbuckle edited the *Dublin Journal* or was an "intimate" of Hutcheson.

30. Hutcheson's letters on laughter and on the *Fable* were published as a single volume by James Arbuckle in *A Collection of Letters and Essays lately Published in the Dublin Journal* (London, 1729). They were also included in Arbuckle's *Hibernicus's Letters: or, a Philosophical Miscellany* (London, 1734); Fielding could have seen them in either place. A later edition (1758) has been reprinted under the title *Thoughts on Laughter, and Observations on 'The Fable of the Bees' in Six Letters*, ed. John Price (Bristol, 1989). The citations in the text are to Price.

31. Henry Fielding, "An Essay on the Knowledge of the Characters of Men," in *Miscellanies by Henry Fielding, Esq.*, ed. Henry Knight Miller, I: 158. According to Miller, the essay "must date after 1735," possibly as late as 1739–40.

32. Lewis Manfield Knapp, *Tobias Smollett: Doctor of Men and Manners* (Princeton, 1949), 17; Lewis Melville, *The Life and Letters of Tobias Smollett* (London, 1926), 10.

33. Hutcheson, *An Essay on the Nature and Conduct of the Passions and Affections* (London, 1728), 1 (emphasis in the original).

34. Thomas Mautner, ed., *Francis Hutcheson: Two Texts on Human Nature* (Cambridge, 1993), 103–04. Mautner includes a useful bibliography of Hutcheson and appendices on Hutcheson's relations with his contemporaries.
35. As Susan M. Purviance has noted, Hutcheson sees the moral sense as "central to the regulation of the affections, the balance of the passions" in marriage and other social relations. The "providential arrangement of sentiment is evidence of a fundamentally sympathetic nature" in human beings ("Intersubjectivity and Sociable Relations in the Philosophy of Francis Hutcheson," 24, 28).
36. Robert Voitle, *The Third Earl of Shaftesbury* (Baton Rouge, 1984), 140–48; Hutcheson, *Essay on the Passions* 186–87.
37. On Allworthy's errors, see John Preston, "*Tom Jones*: Irony and Judgment," *Modern Essays on Eighteenth-Century Literature*, ed. Leopold Damrosch Jr. (New York, 1988), 302–06. See also Rothstein, "Virtues of Authority in *Tom Jones*," 143–47.
38. "Reflections on the Common System of Morality," *The London Journal* (1724), rep. in Mautner, *Frances Hutcheson*, 96–106 (the cited passage is on 103–04). The letter led to a series of six letters between Gilbert Burnet and Hutcheson in the *London Journal* from April to December of 1725, rep. in an appendix to Hutcheson's *Illustrations on the Moral Sense*, ed. Bernard Peach (Cambridge, 1971).
39. The degree to which the feelings of benevolence may be compatible with the "spurs" of private affection is a critical element of Hutcheson's calculation of morality. In the *Inquiry* he seems to criticize the view that a desire of the happiness of others is necessary "to procure some *pleasant Sensations* which we expect to feel upon seeing others happy" (145–46), and that such desires diminish the benevolence of any action based on them; in the same essay, however, he admits that benevolence "is founded on our being conscious of *disinterested Love* to *others*, as the *Spring* of our Actions." Self-interest may be a "*Motive* in studying to raise these kind Affections, and to continue in this *agreeable State*; tho' it cannot be the *sole* or *principal Motive*" of virtue (197; italics in original). The key distinction is between actions that arise *only* in self-interest, and those in which a natural benevolence is assisted by considerations of self. See also the *Essay on Passions*, 48–50.
40. *Amelia*, Appendix 1. Battestin offers "partly personal and partly political" reasons for Fielding's choice of 1733, neither being Mandeville's death (536).
41. Primer, "Bernard Mandeville," 238. Berkeley's attack was *Alciphron; or, the Minute Philosopher* (1732); Mandeville's response, *A Letter to Dion* (1732).
42. *Henry Fielding*, 156–57.
43. Carla Mumford, "Booth's Progress and the Resolution of *Amelia*," *Studies in the Novel* 16 (1984), 28–29.
44. Battestin, *Providence of Wit*, 633.
45. Hutcheson, *Essay*, 187.

46. Paulson, *Life of Henry Fielding*, 74; Battestin, "Fielding and the Deists," *Eighteenth Century Fiction* 13: 1 (October 2000), 72.

9 BURNEY, RICHARDSON, AND THE "EXTIRPATION" OF PASSION

1. Frances Burney, *The Journals and Letters of Fanny Burney*, eds. Joyce Hemlow *et al* (Oxford, 1975), VI: 613, hereafter cited as *JL*.
2. Julia L. Epstein, "Writing the Unspeakable: Fanny Burney's Mastectomy and the Fictive Body," *Representations* 16 (1986), 131. This essay also appeared in Epstein's *The Iron Pen: Frances Burney and the Politics of Women's Writing* (Madison, 1989).
3. Joyce Hemlow, *The History of Fanny Burney* (Oxford, 1958), 324.
4. Margaret Doody, *Frances Burney: the Life in the Works* (New Brunswick, 1988), 343–44.
5. Epstein, "Writing the Unspeakable," 142. I am grateful to Linda Merians for the information that a hard and painful tumor, such as Burney's, is likely to be benign, while a soft and insensible one is probably malignant.
6. *LJ*, VI: 602; for another description of the effect of this news on Burney's emotional state, see Letter 631 (*LJ*, VI: 706).
7. In *Illness as Metaphor* (New York, 1978), Sontag notes that cancer, like tuberculosis, has been "celebrated as a disease of passion," the major difference between them being that, while TB represents a body consumed by ardor, cancer indicates a repression or a "balking" of "vital energies" (21). Where tuberculosis once invited a moralistic judgment of its victims – that they brought the disease on themselves through their excessive passions – cancer prompted the reverse conclusion: it was thought to result from an inability to express emotions, which have turned inward, "striking and blighting the deepest cellular recesses" (46).
8. Frances Burney (Madame D'Arblay), *The Memoirs of Dr. Burney*, 3 vols. (London, 1832), II: 125–26.
9. Martha C. Nussbaum, *The Therapy of Desire: Theory and Practice in Hellenistic Ethics* (Princeton, 1994), 389.
10. Epstein traces the association between pain, writing, and guilt in the corpus of Burney's work, taking as her central metaphor the dream in *Camilla* in which the heroine, forced to write painfully with a "pen of iron," inscribes "guilty characters" on a page that suddenly becomes blank; see *Iron Pen*, 134–35.
11. Margaret Doody notes that *The Wanderer* was "begun in the 1790s" and that there is evidence that she was "well advanced in the first draft" in 1806 (Doody, *Frances Burney*, 318, 316). It is not clear, however, that Burney was still making progress late in 1810.
12. A. A. Long and D. N. Sedley, *The Hellenistic Philosophers* (Cambridge, 1987), I: 412. The quotation is from Stobaeus, a Greek anthologist of the fifth century A.D.
13. Barbara Beigun Kaplan, *"Divulging of Useful Truths in Physick": the Medical Agenda of Robert Boyle* (Baltimore, 1993), 104.

14. Anne Donnellen to Samuel Richardson, *Correspondence* IV: 76, quoted in Gerard A. Barker, *Grandison's Heirs: the Paragon's Progress in the Late Eighteenth-Century English Novel* (Newark, 1985), 23.

15. *The Wanderer, or Female Difficulties* (London, 1988), 836. For a discussion of Burney's use of *Robinson Crusoe* in creating a "female Crusoe" in Juliet Granville, see Barbara Zonitch, *Familiar Violence: Gender and Social Upheaval in the Novels of Frances Burney* (Newark, 1997), 123.

16. In the Preface to *Evelina*, Burney named Richardson, Rousseau, Johnson, Marivaux, Fielding, and Smollett as her literary models, praising Richardson in particular for his "pathetic powers" (8). Janet Todd describes Richardson as "the most influential male novelist of women's sentimental fiction" in *The Sign of Angellica: Women, Writing, and Fiction, 1660–1800* (New York, 1989), 141–45.

17. Maurice Golden, *Richardson's Characters* (Ann Arbor, 1963), 192.

18. *The History of Sir Charles Grandison* (London, 1810), V: 257.

19. *Grandison*, V: 270.

20. This "Richardsonian moment" is discussed at length by Mark Kinkead-Weekes, who argues that Pamela is aware of the effect that her beauty has on Mr. B. See *Samuel Richardson, Dramatic Novelist* (Ithaca, 1973), 12–13.

21. Samuel Richardson, *Pamela; or, Virtue Rewarded*, ed. Peter Sabor (London, 1980), 55.

22. Richardson's use of letters to enact "the perfect passive-aggressive technique for manipulating how ostensibly more powerful males see and define female identity," and the re-appearance of that technique in Burney's *Evelina*, is noted by Kristina Straub in *Divided Fictions: Fanny Burney and Feminine Strategy* (Lexington, 1987), 156. My view is that passive-aggressive behavior informs not only Pamela's letter-writing technique, but every part of her relations with Mr. B.

23. Joseph Butler, Bishop of Durham, *Five Sermons Preached at the Rolls Chapel* (Indianapolis, 1960), 14.

24. The associations between medicine and Richardson's depiction of the passions have been explored by several writers, among them David E. Shuttleton, "'Pamela's Library': Samuel Richardson and Dr. Cheyne's 'Universal Cure,'" *Eighteenth-Century Life* 23 (1999), 59–79, and Anita Guerrini, "The Hungry Soul: George Cheyne and the Construction of Femininity," *Eighteenth-Century Studies* 32 (1999), 279–91.

25. Many critics have noted Burney's debt to Richardson for the epistolary form of *Evelina*, but few see the similarities in plot or character. In *A Natural Passion: a Study of the Novels of Samuel Richardson* (Oxford, 1974), 372–73, Margaret Doody states that the "most noticeable and direct influence of Richardson on major English literature was to come through *Grandison* rather than his earlier novels." She cites several points of comparison and difference between Richardson and Burney in *Frances Burney*, but she again observes that the character study of Evelina "is influenced by the Richardson of *Sir Charles Grandison*" (42). Mark Kinkead-Weekes (*Samuel Richardson*) likens Harriet Byron's story to Evelina's, suggesting that "[t]he girl from the

country on her first visit to Town was a formula in which Fanny Burney and Jane Austen were to see sprightly possibilities" (295). Patricia Meyer Spacks, in "The Dangerous Age," *Eighteenth-Century Studies* 11 (1978), 433, observes that "Richardson's Pamela and Fanny Burney's Evelina confront their difficulties by 'feminine' strategies."

26. Frances Burney, *Evelina*, ed. Margaret Anne Doody (London, 1994), 258.
27. Elizabeth Bergen Brophy, *Women's Lives and the Eighteenth-Century English Novel* (Tampa, 1991), 151–52; 257–62.
28. It has long been assumed that Burney's fictional method combines Richardsonian characters with Fieldingesque plots; see, for example, Lord David Cecil, "Fanny Burney's Novels," in *Essays on the Eighteenth Century, Presented to David Nichol Smith* (New York, 1963), 212–24. Recent editorial work on Burney's plays, however, suggests that her plots may derive from dramatists such as Molière; see the appendix to *The Witlings* and *The Woman-Hater*, forthcoming from Broadview Press.
29. Margaret Anne Doody, "Heliodorus Rewritten: Samuel Richardson's *Clarissa* and Frances Burney's *Wanderer*," *The Search for the Ancient Novel*, ed. James Tatum (Baltimore, 1994), 117–31, Doody argues that the two novels had a common ancestor in Heliodorus's *Aethiopica*.
30. Patricia Meyer Spacks notes Clarissa's control over her passions during her "steadfast course" in "The Dangerous Age," 425, and also in *Desire and Truth: Functions of Plot in Eighteenth-Century Novels* (Chicago, 1990), 66–67. An alternative reading of "steadiness" as the effect of Clarissa's faith in providence is provided by James Louis Fortuna Jr., in *"The Unsearchable Wisdom of God": a Study of Providence in Richardson's "Pamela"* (Gainesville, 1980), 24.
31. Samuel Richardson, *Clarissa, or the History of a Young Lady* (Harmondsworth, 1985), 104–05.
32. The critical possibilities of the phrase "The affair is over" are explored by Sue Warrick Doederlein in "Clarissa in the Hands of the Critics," *Eighteenth-Century Studies* 16 (1983), 401–14.
33. *Clarissa*, 550. Anna's admission appears in her last letter, 1472.
34. Frances Burney, *Cecilia, or, Memoirs of an Heiress*, eds. Peter Sabor and Margaret Anne Doody (Oxford, 1988), 896.
35. Terry Castle, *Masquerade and Civilization: the Carnivalesque in Eighteenth-Century English Culture and Fiction* (Stanford, 1986), 281.

EPILOGUE: *BELINDA* AND THE END OF THE ORIGINS

1. Sir Walter Scott, *Waverley*, ed. Andrew Hook (Harmondsworth, 1972), 55.
2. Jane Austen, *Sense and Sensibility* (Oxford, 1990), 333.
3. Austen, *Sense and Sensibility*, 333. Austen's disinterest in the passions was noted by Charlotte Bronte, who said, somewhat unjustly, "The passions are perfectly unknown to her; she rejects even a speaking acquaintance with that stormy sisterhood." David Lodge, ed., *Jane Austen's "Emma"* (Nashville, 1969), 50.

4. Maria Edgeworth, *Belinda*, ed. Eva Figes (London, 1986), 24.
5. J. G. Barker-Benfield, *The Culture of Sensibility: Sex and Society in Eighteenth-Century Britain* (Chicago, 1992), 389–90.
6. Barker-Benfield *Culture of Sensibility*, 393, quoting from Edgeworth's *Leonora* (1806).

APPENDIX 1 : WHO WAS "BETTY"?

1. J. M. Cowper, ed., *Canterbury Marriage Licences*, Fifth Series, 1701–1725 (Canterbury, 1906), 298. This source shows Mary Knowler to be "of S. George, Cant. At S. G. or S. M. Bredin, Cant., or Hackington." According to the *DNB* article for Lewis, he married "the youngest daughter of Robert Knowles of Herne, Kent. She died in 1720, leaving no issue." Her name was clearly Knowler, not Knowles, but she may have been related to the Knowlers of Herne, in the county of Kent, since the Knowler family had branches in both Herne and Canterbury.
2. The first set of records are on microfilm, the parallel set is U3/164/1/2 in the Canterbury Cathedral Archives. The phrase "both of Minster" to describe William and Elizabeth, and the baptismal date of William Johnson (September 7, 1718), are also from this manuscript register.
3. "Some Account of the Life of the Reverend Mr. John Lewis," Add. MSS. 28651, fols. 75–76.
4. I wish to express my thanks to Heather Bosence and Yvonne Noble for their assistance in ascertaining certain facts about John Lewis and St. Mary's, Minster.

APPENDIX 2 : WHO WAS "SIR BENJAMIN HODGES"?

1. "The Authorship of *An Impartial History of Michael Servetus*," *PBSA* 87 : 3 (1993), 303–18.
2. The Gough catalogue is *A Catalogue of the Entire and Valuable Library . . . of that eminent Antiquary, Richard Gough, Esq., Deceased, which will be sold at auction by Leigh and Sotheby . . . on Thursday, April 5, 1810, and Nineteen following days*, in which "Sir Benjamin Hodges' History of Michael Servetus, 1724" appears in lot #2131. For Sir Peter's library, see *A Catalogue of the Library of Sir Peter Thompson, Kent, F.R.S.and F.R.A. Sold by Auction . . . by R. Evans*, 1815.
3. Appendix to Lewis's "Life of Servetus," Clarendon MSS. C. 21, fol. 83.
4. Hodges's sermons include *A Sermon preach'd December 31, 1706, being the day of solemn thanksgiving appointed by her Majesty for the late glorious successes . . . during the last campaign* (London, 1707); *A Sermon preach'd Novemb. 29, 1709, in Whitestreet, Southwark, upon occasion of a fast observ'd by several congregations in and about London* (London, 1710); and *The Christian's gain by Death. A funeral sermon occasion'd by the death of the Reverend Mr. Joseph Stennett . . . preach'd August the 22nd, 1713* (London, 1713). None of these sermons would have been given before George I, and nothing in them qualifies Hodges as an Arian, except perhaps

his disagreement in the last sermon with Calvin's translation of Hebrews 2: 15–22 as "Christ is gain to me in living and in dying," which Hodges says is not "agreeable both to the Sense of the Apostle, and the literal Construction of the Original," which tended "to magnify his Saviour in his body, whether by Life or by Death" (10). Hodges's service as "Colonel of the 2nd Regiment of the Tower Hamlets" and the date of his knighthood are recorded in William A. Shaw, *The Knights of England*, 2 vols. (London: Sherratt & Hughes, 1906), II: 283. This Nathanael Hodges is not to be confused with Nathaniel Hodges, M.D. (1629–88), the author of *Loimologia: or, an historical account of the plague in London* (London, 1720).

APPENDIX 3 : THE HISTORY OF THE "HISTORY OF THE LIFE
OF SERVETUS," TOLD IN LETTERS

1. Letter from J. Lewis to "Peter Thompson Esq., at St. Saviour's Dock in Redriff," January 10, 1745. Add. MSS. 18988, fols. 17–18, quoted only in relevant part.

2. Letter from Thompson to Lewis, Add. MSS. 18988, fols. 19–20, dated "25 Jan., 10 at Night." Laurence Sterne's *The Life and Opinions of Tristram Shandy*, of course, was not to appear for another 15 years.

3. Lewis to Thompson, dated "Feb. 14 '45" [1744/5]. Add. MSS. 18988, fol. 21.

4. John Valentine Gentile, called the "second Servetus," was executed in 1566 at Gex after refusing to renounce his criticisms of the Trinity and the Calvinist Reformed Church. See George Huntston Williams, *The Radical Reformation* (Philadelphia, 1962), 635–38 and 745.

5. Thompson to Lewis, dated "Feb. 16, 1744" [1744/5]. Add. Mss. 18988, fol. 22. As Thompson says, this is not a fair copy of the letter, but a first draft, indicated by the roughness of the style, the deletions and insertions (marked here with carats), and the lack of punctuation. Though the fair copy may have differed in some respects, this draft establishes some interesting points: it appears that Thompson may have first suggested that the *Impartial History* was written by a "Mr. Hodges," and Thompson admits having made a mistake about that person's identity or occupation.

6. Thompson to Ward, April 23, 1752. Add. MSS. 6211, fol. 159.

7. Sale catalogue appended to Lewis's autobiography, Add. MSS. 28615, n. p. Item 43 is "The Live [sic] of Servetus in answer to Sir Benj. Hodges Life of Servetus printed 1724. . . . 0.18.0," sold to Mr. P. Thompson.

8. H. S. Thompson, "Sir Peter Thompson's Library," reprinted from "Notes and Queries for Somerset and Dorset," March 1925 (British Library, 11902. c. 53), item 574, "Life of Servetus, manuscript." The reference to Gutch is in a letter to this author from S. R. Tomlinson, Assistant Librarian, Bodleian Library, who assisted me in locating the "History of the Life of Servetus" in the Clarendon Press manuscripts.

Bibliography

MANUSCRIPTS

Anon. "Letter to Betty." Bodleian Library, Rawlinson MSS, D. 376 fol. 187.

Finch, Heneage, Earl of Nottingham. "Commonplace Book," ca. 1647. College of Physicians of Philadelphia, 10c/18.

Lewis, John. *A Brief History of the English Anabaptists*, 2nd. edn. London, 1741, with manuscript corrections by Lewis for a third edition. Bodleian Library, Rawlinson MSS. C 409.

"History of Anabaptism in England." MS. dated Oct. 27, 1738. Bodleian Library, Rawlinson MSS. 410.

"The History of the Life of Michael Servetus M. D. of Vienne in France, who was burnt at Geneva for Blasphemy, Heresy and Defamation." MS. dated Jan. 31, 1743/4. Bodleian Library, Clarendon MSS. C. 21.

John Lewis to Peter Thompson, January 10, 1745. British Library Add. MSS. 18988.

John Lewis to Peter Thompson, February 14, 1745. British Library Add. MSS. 18988.

"The Life of the learned and reverend John Wallis, professor of geometry at Oxford." MS. dated November 24, 1735. Bodleian Library, Rawlinson MSS. c. 978.

Memo of his reply to "One of the late Answerers of *Christianity not founded on Argument*." Bodleian Library, Clarendon MSS. c. 19, fol. 374.

"Some Account of the Life of the reverend Mr. John Lewis, Rector of the desolate Church of East-bridge in Romney-Marsh, Vicar of Minster and Minister of Margate in the Isle of Thanet and Master of East-bridge Hospital in Canterbury. Written in the year 1738." British Library Manuscripts Dept., Add. MSS. 28651.

Thompson, Peter, to John Lewis, January 25, 1745. British Library Add. MSS. 18988.

Peter Thompson to John Lewis, February 16, 1745. British Library Add. MSS. 18988.

Peter Thompson to John Ward, April 23, 1752. British Library Add. MSS. 6211.

Monro, Alexander *primus*. "The History of Anatomy." Transcripts by various hands of notes to lectures on the history of anatomy, c. 1725-c. 1750. The dates, which come from library catalogs or from Taylor 1986, are given for identification only.

[1725] British Library, Add. MSS. 4376 fols. 81–136b.

[1731] College of Surgeons of Edinburgh, Book Store 06.

[1732] College of Physicians of Philadelphia, 10d/148.

[1735] Edinburgh University Library, Gen. 578D. Part I: The History of Anatomy. Part II: Lectures on Physiology.

[1741] Edinburgh University Library, Gen. 577D.

[1746] College of Physicians of Philadelphia, 10a/137.

[1744?] Edinburgh University Library, Dk. 5.1. (title page signed "Jacob Wickham 1760")

[1746] Edinburgh University Library, Mic. 1134, microfilm of copy at National Library of Medicine, Bethesda, MD. Signed on title page by John Redman, "taken from him [Alexander Monro] during his course of Lectures," 1746.

[1747] Edinburgh University Library, Medical Archive Centre, LhB 1/125/10

[1750] Edinburgh University Library, MS. 2670.

[1752–55] Edinburgh University Library, Gen. 73.

[date unknown] Microfilm of Otago MS. 166, at Edinburgh University Library, Mic. 506.

[date unknown] Fragment, fols. 1–52, Bk. 1, chs. 1–4. Edinburgh University Library, LaII 410.

"Student Roll Book of Monro I, 1720–1749." Edinburgh University Library, shelf mark Dc. 5.95.

Rush, Benjamin. "Journal, commencing Aug. 31, 1766." Edinburgh University Library, Mic. 28.

BOOKS AND JOURNAL ARTICLES

Adams, Percy G. *Travel Literature and the Evolution of the Novel*. Lexington: University Press of Kentucky, 1983.

Addison, Joseph, and Richard Steele. *The Spectator*, ed. Donald F. Bond. 5 vols. Oxford: Clarendon Press, 1965.

Alkon, Paul. *Defoe and Fictional Time*. Athens: University of Georgia Press, 1979.

Allen, Joseph Henry. *An Historical Sketch of the Unitarian Movement since the Reformation*. New York: The Christian Literature Co., 1894.

Anonymous. *An Authentick Account of Several Things Done and Agreed upon by the Dissenting Ministers lately Assembled at Salters' Hall*. London, 1719.

An Impartial History of Michael Servetus, Burnt Alive at Geneva for Heresie. London: Aaron Ward, 1724.

Aristotle. *The Works of Aristotle*, eds. J. A. Smith and W. D. Ross. 11 vols. Oxford: Clarendon Press, 1908–31.

On the Soul, trans. W. S. Hett. Cambridge: Harvard University Press, 1936.

De Anima, trans. Kenelm Foster and Silvester Humphries, introduction by Ivo Thomas. New Haven: Yale University Press, 1951.

Armstrong, Dianne. "The Myth of Cronos: Cannibal and Sign in *Robinson Crusoe*." *Eighteenth-Century Fiction* 4 (1992), 207–20.

Armstrong, Nancy. *Desire and Domestic Fiction: a Political History of the Novel*. New York: Oxford University Press, 1987.

Armstrong, Nancy, and Leonard Tennenhouse. "A Brief Genealogy of Dreams." *Eighteenth-Century Studies* 23 (1990), 458–78.

Augustine. *Confessions*, trans. Henry Chadwick. Oxford: Oxford University Press, 1991.

Austen, Jane. *Sense and Sensibility*, ed. James Kinsley, with a new introduction by Margaret Anne Doody (Oxford: Oxford University Press, 1990).

Babb, Lawrence. *The Elizabethan Malady: a Study of Melancholia in English Literature from 1580 to 1642*. East Lansing: Michigan State University Press, 1951.

Backscheider, Paula R. *Daniel Defoe: Ambition and Innovation*. Lexington: University Press of Kentucky, 1986.

Daniel Defoe: His Life. Baltimore: Johns Hopkins University Press, 1989.

Baine, Rodney M. *Daniel Defoe and the Supernatural*. Athens: University of Georgia Press, 1968.

Bainton, Roland H. *The Reformation of the Sixteenth Century*. Boston: Beacon Press, 1952.

Baker, Herschel. *The Dignity of Man: Studies in the Persistence of an Idea*. Cambridge: Harvard University Press, 1947.

Barker, Gerard A. *Grandison's Heirs: the Paragon's Progress in the Late Eighteenth-Century English Novel*. Newark: University of Delaware Press, 1985.

Barker-Benfield, G. J. *The Culture of Sensibility: Sex and Society in Eighteenth-Century Britain*. Chicago: University of Chicago Press, 1992.

Bastian, F. "Defoe's *Journal of the Plague Year* Reconsidered." *Review of English Studies* 16 (1965), 151–73.

Defoe's Early Life. Totowa: Barnes and Noble, 1981.

Battestin, Martin C., with Ruthe R. Battestin. *The Moral Basis of Fielding's Art*. Middletown: Wesleyan University Press, 1959.

"The Problem of *Amelia*: Hume, Barrow, and the Conversion of Captain Booth." *ELH* 41 (1974), 613–48.

The Providence of Wit: Aspects of Form in Augustan Literature and the Arts. Oxford: Clarendon Press, 1974.

"Fielding and the Deists," *Eighteenth Century Fiction* 13:1 (October 2000), 67–76.

Henry Fielding, a Life. London: Routledge, 1989.

Beasley, Jerry. *Novels of the 1740s*. Athens: University of Georgia Press, 1982.

Bell, Ian A. *Defoe's Fiction*. London: Croom Helm, 1985.

Bender, John. *Imagining the Penitentiary: Fiction and the Architecture of Mind in Eighteenth-Century England*. Chicago: University of Chicago Press, 1987.

Bennett, G. V. *The Tory Crisis in Church and State, 1688–1730.* Oxford: Clarendon Press, 1975.

Blewett, David. *Defoe's Art of Fiction.* Toronto: University of Toronto Press, 1979.

(ed.). *Reconsidering the Rise of the Novel. Eighteenth Century Fiction.* 12: 2–3 (January–April 2000).

Bobbio, Norberto. *Thomas Hobbes and the Natural Law Tradition,* trans. Daniela Gobetti. Chicago: University of Chicago Press, 1989.

Bonno, Gabriel, ed. *Lettres Inédites de LeClerc à Locke.* Berkeley: University of California Publications in Modern Philology. LII, 1959.

Boswell, James. *The Life of Samuel Johnson, LL.D,* ed. G. B. Hill, 6 vols. Oxford: Clarendon Press, 1887.

Braudy, Leo. *Narrative Form in History and Fiction: Hume, Fielding, and Gibbon.* Princeton: Princeton University Press, 1970.

Bright, Timothy. *A Treatise of Melancholie, Containing the causes there of.* London, 1586.

Brophy, Elizabeth Bergen. *Women's Lives and the Eighteenth-Century English Novel.* Tampa: University of South Florida Press, 1991.

Brown, Homer O. "The Displaced Self in the Novels of Daniel Defoe." *ELH* 38 (1971), 562–90.

[Browne, Sir Thomas]. *Religio Medici,* 5th edn., corrected and amended, with annotations by Sir Kenelm Digby. London: 1659.

Burke, Edmund. *A Philosophical Enquiry into the Origin of our Ideas of the Sublime and Beautiful.* London: Routledge and Kegan Paul, 1958.

Burney, Frances. (Madame D'Arblay). *The Memoirs of Dr. Burney.* 3 vols. London: Edward Moxon, 1832.

The Journals and Letters of Fanny Burney 1791–1840, eds. Joyce Hemlow *et al.* 12 vols. Oxford: Clarendon Press, 1972–84.

Cecilia, or, Memoirs of an Heiress, eds. Peter Sabor and Margaret Anne Doody. Oxford: Oxford University Press, 1988.

The Wanderer, or Female Difficulties. London: Pandora Press, 1988.

Evelina, ed. Margaret Anne Doody. London: Penguin, 1994.

Burton, Robert. *The Anatomy of Melancholy,* 11th edn. 2 vols. London, 1813.

Burrage, Champlin. *The Early English Dissenters.* New York: Russell and Russell, 1912.

Butler, Joseph, Bishop of Durham. *Five Sermons Preached at the Rolls Chapel.* Indianapolis: The Library of Liberal Arts, 1960.

Castle, Terry. "'Amy, Who Knew My Disease' a Psychosexual Pattern in Defoe's *Roxana.*" *ELH* 46 (1979), 81–96.

Masquerade and Civilization: the Carnivalesque in Eighteenth-Century English Culture and Fiction. Stanford: Stanford University Press, 1986.

Cecil, Lord David. "Fanny Burney's Novels." *Essays on the Eighteenth Century, Presented to David Nichol Smith.* New York: Russell and Russell, 1963, 212–24.

Cheyne, George. *An Essay of Health and Long Life.* London: George Strahan, 1724.

Cicero. *Tusculan Disputations*, trans. J. E. King. London: William Heinemann, 1927.

Clark, Henry W. *History of English Nonconformity*. New York: Russell and Russell, 1965.

Cooper, Anthony Ashley, third Earl of Shaftesbury. *Characteristicks of Men, Manners, Opinions, Times*, 5th edn. 3 vols. London, 1732.

Corner, George W. "Benjamin Rush's Days in Edinburgh and What Came of Them." *University of Edinburgh Journal* 15 (1949–51), 126–35.

Cowper, J. M., ed. *Canterbury Marriage Licences*, Fifth Series, 1701–1725. Canterbury, 1906.

Crane, R. S. "Suggestions toward a Genealogy of the 'Man of Feeling.'" *ELH* 1 (1934), 205–30.

Cumston, C. G. *An Introduction to the History of Medicine, from the time of the Pharoahs*. New York: Knopf, 1926.

Cuthbertson, David. *A Tragedy of the Reformation. Being the Authentic Narrative of the History and Burning of the "Christianismi Restitutio," 1553*. Edinburgh, 1912.

Damrosch, Leopold Jr. *God's Plot and Man's Stories: Studies in the Fictional Imagination from Milton to Fielding*. Chicago: University of Chicago Press, 1985.

Darwall, Stephen. "Hume and the Invention of Utilitarianism." *Hume and Hume's Connexions*, eds. M. A. Stewart and John P. Wright. Edinburgh: Edinburgh University Press, 1994, 58–82.

Defoe, Daniel. *The Consolidator: Or, Memoirs of Sundry Transactions from the World in the Moon*. Translated from the Lunar Language, by the author of The True-Born English Man. London, 1705.

The Family Instructor, Part II. Oxford: Thomas Tegg, 1841.

The Fortunate Mistress, or, a History of the Life... of the Lady Roxana, ed. John Mullan. Oxford: Oxford University Press, 1996.

The Fortunes and Misfortunes of the Famous Moll Flanders, ed. Edward Kelly. New York: Norton, 1973.

The History of the Devil, as Well Ancient as Modern. London, 1727.

The History and Remarkable Life of the truly honourable Col. Jacque, ed. Samuel Holt Monk. London: Oxford University Press, 1965.

A Journal of the Plague Year, ed. Louis Landa, intro. by David Roberts. Oxford: Oxford University Press, 1990.

A Letter to the Dissenters. London, 1719.

Robinson Crusoe, ed. Michael Shinagel. 2nd edn. New York: Norton, 1994.

Serious Reflections of Robinson Crusoe, ed. G. H. Maynadier. New York: Sproul, 1903.

DePorte, Michael V. *Nightmares and Hobbyhorses: Swift, Sterne, and Augustan Ideas of Madness*. San Marino: Huntington Library, 1974.

Dewhurst, Kenneth. *Dr. Thomas Sydenham*. Berkeley: University of California Press, 1966.

Digby, Anne. *Madness, Morality and Medicine: a Study of the York Retreat, 1796–1914*. Cambridge: Cambridge University Press, 1985.

Doederlein, Sue Warrick. "Clarissa in the Hands of the Critics." *Eighteenth-Century Studies* 16 (1983), 401–14.

Doody, Margaret. *Frances Burney: the Life in the Works*. New Brunswick: Rutgers University Press, 1988.

"Heliodorus Rewritten: Samuel Richardson's *Clarissa* and Frances Burney's *Wanderer*." *The Search for the Ancient Novel*, ed. James Tatum. Baltimore: Johns Hopkins University Press, 1994, 117–31.

The True Story of the Novel. New Brunswick: Rutgers University Press, 1996.

A Natural Passion: a Study of the Novels of Samuel Richardson. Oxford: Clarendon Press, 1974.

Downie, J. Alan. "Mary Davy's 'Probable Feign'd Stories' and Critical Shibboleths about 'The Rise of the Novel.'" *Eighteenth-Century Fiction* 12: 2–3 (January-April 2000), 309–26.

"The Making of the English Novel." *Eighteenth-Century Fiction* 9 (1997), 249–266.

Dryden, John. "An Essay of Dramatic Poesy." *The Works of John Dryden*, ed. George Saintsbury. London: Paterson, 1892.

Duckworth, Alistair M. "Michael McKeon and Some Recent Studies of Eighteenth-Century Fiction." *Eighteenth-Century Fiction* 1 (1998), 53–66.

Dwyer, John. "A 'Peculiar Blessing': Social Converse in Scotland from Hutcheson to Burns." *Eighteenth Century Life* 15, n.s. # 1 & 2 (1991), 1–22.

The Age of the Passions. East Linton: Tuckwell Press, 1998.

Ebels-Hoving, B., and E. J. Ebels. "Erasmus and Galen." *Erasmus of Rotterdam: the Man and the Scholar*, eds. J. Sperna Weiland and W. Th. M. Frijhoff. Leiden: E. J. Brill, 1988, 132–42.

Edgeworth, Maria. *Belinda*, ed. Eva Figes. London: Pandora Press, 1986.

Edelstein, Ludwig. *The Meaning of Stoicism*. Cambridge: Harvard University Press, 1966.

Ancient Medicine, eds. Owsei Temkin and C. Lilian Temkin. Baltimore: Johns Hopkins University Press, 1967.

Epstein, Julia. *The Iron Pen: Frances Burney and the Politics of Women's Writing*. Madison, 1989.

"Writing the Unspeakable: Fanny Burney's Mastectomy and the Fictive Body." *Representations* 16 (1986), 131–166.

Erickson, Robert A. *The Language of the Heart, 1600–1750*. Philadelphia: University of Pennsylvania Press, 1997.

Mother Midnight: Birth, Sex, and Fate in Eighteenth-Century Fiction. New York: AMS Press, 1986.

"Starting over with *Robinson Crusoe*." *Studies in the Literary Imagination* 15 (1982), 51–63.

Erlam, H. D. "Alexander Monro, *primus*." *University of Edinburgh Journal* (1954), 77–105.

Falconer, W. *Dissertation on the Influence of the Passions upon Disorders of the Body*. 3rd edn., London, 1796.

Faller, Lincoln. *Crime and Defoe: a New Kind of Writing.* Cambridge: Cambridge University Press, 1993.

Fausett, David. *The Strange Surprizing Sources of "Robinson Crusoe."* Amsterdam: Rodopi, 1994.

Ferguson, Rebecca. *The Unbalanced Mind: Pope and the Rule of Passion.* Philadelphia: University of Pennsylvania Press, 1986.

Fielding, Henry. *Amelia*, ed. Martin C. Battestin. Middletown: Wesleyan University Press, 1983.

Joseph Andrews, ed. Martin C. Battestin. Middletown: Wesleyan University Press, 1967.

The History of Tom Jones, a Foundling, ed. Fredson Bowers, with introduction and commentary by Martin C. Battestin. Middletown: Wesleyan University Press, 1975.

Miscellanies by Henry Fielding, Esq., ed. Henry Knight Miller. 2 vols. Oxford: Wesleyan University Press, 1972.

Fielding, Sarah. *The Adventures of David Simple*, ed. Peter Sabor. Lexington: University Press of Kentucky, 1998.

Flynn, Carol Houlihan. *The Body in Swift and Defoe.* Cambridge: Cambridge University Press, 1990.

Fortuna, James Louis Jr. *"The Unsearchable Wisdom of God": a Study of Providence in Richardson's "Pamela."* Gainesville: University Presses of Florida, 1980.

Foster, James O. *"Robinson Crusoe* and the Uses of the Imagination." *Journal of English and Germanic Philology* 91 (April 1992), 179–202.

Foucault, Michel. *The History of Sexuality: Volume I, An Introduction*, trans. Robert Hurley. New York: Pantheon, 1978.

Madness and Civilization: a History of Insanity in the Age of Reason. New York: Random House, 1965.

Fox, Christopher, ed. *Psychology and Literature in the Eighteenth Century.* New York: AMS Press, 1987.

Locke and the Scriblerians: Identity and Consciousness in Early Eighteenth-Century Britain. Berkeley: University of California Press, 1988.

Frank, Robert G. Jr. *Harvey and the Oxford Physiologists.* Berkeley: University of California Press, 1980.

"Thomas Willis and his Circle: Brain and Mind in Seventeenth-Century Medicine." *The Languages of Psyche: Mind and Body in Enlightenment Thought*, ed. G. S. Rousseau. Berkeley: University of California Press, 1990.

Franklin, Benjamin. *Writings.* New York: Library of America, 1987.

French, Roger. "Sickness and the Soul: Stahl, Hoffmann and Sauvages on Pathology." *The Medical Enlightenment of the Eighteenth Century*, eds. Andrew Cunningham and Roger French. Cambridge: Cambridge University Press, 1990, 88–110.

Freud, Sigmund. *Totem and Taboo.* trans. James Strachey. London: Routledge and Kegan Paul, 1950.

Friedman, Jerome. *Michael Servetus: a Case Study in Total Heresy.* Genève: Librarie Droz, 1978.

Frye, Northrop. *The Anatomy of Criticism*. Princeton: Princeton University Press, 1957.

Fulton, John F. "Michael Servetus and the Lesser Circulation of the Blood through the Lungs." *Autour de Michel Servet et de Sebastien Castellion*. B. Becker, ed. Haarlem: H. D. Tjeenk Willink and Zoon, 1953.

Michael Servetus, Humanist and Martyr. New York: Herbert Reichner, 1953.

Furbank, P. N. and W. R. Owens. *Defoe De-Attributions*. London: Hambledon Press, 1994.

Galen. *Galen on the Passions and Errors of the Soul*, trans. Paul W. Harkins, introduction by Walther Riese. Columbus: Ohio State University Press, 1963.

Galen on Respiration and the Arteries, eds. David J. Furley and J. S. Wilkie. Princeton: Princeton University Press, 1984.

Galen on the Therapeutic Method, ed. R. J. Hankinson. Oxford: Clarendon Press, 1991.

Galen on the Usefulness of the Parts of the Body (De Usu Partium), trans. with introduction and commentary by Margaret Tallmadge May. 2 vols. Ithaca: Cornell University Press, 1968.

Gay, John. *John Gay: Poetry and Prose*, ed. Vincent A. Dearing. 2 vols. Oxford: Clarendon Press, 1974.

Glover, Susan. "'One Universal Act of Solitude'? Figuring the Female in *Robinson Crusoe*." Unpublished manuscript.

Golden, Morris. *Fielding's Moral Psychology*. Amherst: University of Massachusetts Press, 1966.

Richardson's Characters. Ann Arbor: University of Michigan Press, 1963.

Golden, Samuel A. *Jean LeClerc*. New York: Twayne, 1972.

Gomperz, Theodore. *Greek Thinkers: a History of Ancient Philosophy*. 4 vols. London: John Murray, 1901.

Gracián y Morales, Baltasar. *El Criticón* (1653), published in English as *The Critick*, trans. Paul Rycaut. London, 1681.

Greig, J. Y. T. *The Letters of David Hume*. Oxford: Clarendon Press, 1932.

Guerrini, Anita. "Case History as Spiritual Autobiography: George Cheyne's 'Case of the Author.'" *Eighteenth-Century Life* 19 (1995), 18–27.

"The Hungry Soul: George Cheyne and the Construction of Femininity." *Eighteenth-Century Studies* 32 (1999), 279–91.

Hagstrum, Jean H. *Sex and Sensibility: Ideal and Erotic Love from Milton to Mozart*. Chicago: University of Chicago Press, 1980.

Harris, C. R. S. *The Heart and the Vascular System in Ancient Greek Medicine, from Alcmaeon to Galen*. Oxford: Clarendon Press, 1973.

Harrison, Bernard. *Henry Fielding's Tom Jones: the Novelist as Moral Philosopher*. London: Sussex University Press, 1975.

Harvey, William, M.D. *Exercitatio Anatomica: De Motu Cordis et Sanguinis in Animalibus*, trans. Chauncey D. Leake. Springfield: Charles C. Thomas, 1930.

Healey, George. *The Letters of Daniel Defoe*. Oxford: Clarendon Press, 1955.

Heidenreich, Helmut, ed. *The Libraries of Daniel Defoe and Phillips Farewell: Olive Payne's Sales Catalogue*. Berlin: W. Hildebrand, 1970.

Hemlow, Joyce. *The History of Fanny Burney*. Oxford: Clarendon Press, 1958.

Hobbes, Thomas. *Leviathan*. Oxford: Clarendon Press, 1909.

Hunter, J. Paul. "Fielding and the Modern Reader: the Problem of Temporal Translation," in J. Paul Hunter and Martin Battestin, *Fielding in His Time and Ours*. Los Angeles: UCLA (1987), 1–28.

The Reluctant Pilgrim: Defoe's Emblematic Method and the Quest for Form in "Robinson Crusoe." Baltimore: Johns Hopkins University Press, 1966.

Before Novels: the Cultural Contexts of Eighteenth-Century English Fiction. New York: Norton, 1990.

Hutcheson, Francis. *An Essay on the Nature and Conduct of the Passions and Affections*. London, 1728.

Illustrations on the Moral Sense, ed. Bernard Peach. Cambridge: Belknap Press, 1971.

An Inquiry Concerning Beauty, Order, Harmony, Design, ed. Peter Kivy. The Hague: Martinus Nijhoff, 1973.

Thoughts on Laughter, and Observations on 'The Fable of the Bees' in Six Letters, ed. John Price. Bristol: Thoemmes Antiquarian Books, 1989.

Huxley, Thomas. "On Certain Errors Respecting the Structure of the Heart Attributed to Aristotle." *Nature* 21 : 523 (November 6, 1879).

Inglis, John Alexander. *The Monros of Auchinbowie and Cognate Families*. Edinburgh, 1911.

Irwin, William Robert. *The Making of "Jonathan Wild": a Study in the Literary Method of Henry Fielding*. Hamden: Archon Books, 1966.

James, Susan. *Passion and Action: the Emotions in Seventeenth-Century Philosophy*. Oxford: Clarendon Press, 1997.

Johnson, Samuel. *Lives of the English Poets*, ed. Peter Cunningham. 3 vols. London: John Murray, 1854.

The Rambler, eds. W. J. Bate and Albrecht B. Strauss. *Works of Samuel Johnson*, vols. III–V. New Haven: Yale University Press, 1969.

Jones, W. H. S., trans. *Hippocrates*. 3 vols. Cambridge: Harvard University Press, 1923.

Kaplan, Barbara Beigun. *"Divulging of Useful Truths in Physick"*: the Medical Agenda of Robert Boyle. Baltimore: Johns Hopkins University Press, 1993.

Kay, Carol. *Political Constructions: Defoe, Richardson, and Sterne in Relation to Hobbes, Hume, and Burke*. Ithaca: Cornell University Press, 1988.

Keynes, Geoffrey. *The Life of William Harvey*. Oxford: Clarendon Press, 1966.

King, Helen. "Once upon a Text: Hysteria from Hippocrates." *Hysteria Beyond Freud*, eds. Sander L. Gilman, Helen King, Roy Porter, G. S. Rousseau, and Elaine Showalter. Berkeley: University of California Press, 1993.

King, Lester S. *The Philosophy of Medicine: the Early Eighteenth Century*. Cambridge: Harvard University Press, 1978.

The Medical World of the Eighteenth Century. Chicago: University of Chicago Press, 1958.

Kinkead-Weekes, Mark. *Samuel Richardson, Dramatic Novelist*. Ithaca: Cornell University Press, 1973.

Klibansky, Raymond, Erwin Panofsky, and Fritz Saxl. *Saturn and Melancholy: Studies in the History of Natural Philosophy, Religion and Art*. London: Thomas Nelson and Sons, 1964.

Knapp, Lewis Mansfield. *Tobias Smollett: Doctor of Men and Manners*. Princeton: Princeton University Press, 1949.

Lacan, Jacques. *The Language of the Self: the Function of Language in Psychoanalysis*, trans. Anthony Wilden. Baltimore: Johns Hopkins University Press, 1968.

Lawrence, Christopher. "Joseph Black: the Natural Philosophical Background." *Joseph Black, 1728–1799: a Commemorative Symposium*, ed. A. D. C. Simpson. Edinburgh: Royal Scottish Museum, 1982.

LeClerc, Daniel. *The History of Physick, or, an Account of the Rise and Progress of the Art*. Paris, 1696; English trans. Dr. Drake and Dr. Baden, London, 1699.

LeClerc, Jean. *Bibliotheque Ancienne et Moderne* 24: 2 (1725), 421–37; 26: 1 (1727), 102–115.

The Life of the Famous Cardinal, Duke de Richlieu, trans. T. Brown. London, 1695.

Lee, William. *Daniel Defoe: his Life, and Recently Discovered Writings*. 3 vols. London: Hotten, 1869.

Lennox, Charlotte. *The Female Quixote*, ed. Margaret Dalziel. Oxford: Oxford University Press, 1989.

Levine, Joseph M. *The Battle of the Books: History and Literature in the Augustan Age*. Ithaca: Cornell University Press, 1991.

Lindeboom, G. A. *Herman Boerhaave: the Man and his Work*. London: Methuen, 1968.

Lewis, John. *The Church Catechism explain'd by way of Question and Answer, and confirm'd by Scripture Proofs*. London, 1700; 5th edn., 1710.

A Brief History of the Rise and Progress of Anabaptism in England. To which is prefixed, some account of the learned Dr. Wiclif, and a defence of him from the false charge of his, and his followers, denying infant baptism. London, 1738.

Locke, John. *An Essay Concerning Human Understanding*, ed. A. C. Fraser. 2 vols. New York: Dover, 1959.

Lodge, David. *Jane Austen's "Emma."* Nashville: Aurora Casebook, 1969.

Long, A. A., and D. N. Sedley, *The Hellenistic Philosophers*. 1. Cambridge: Cambridge University Press, 1987.

Lund, Roger D. "The Modern Reader and the 'Truly Feminine Novel' 1660–1815." *Fetter'd or Free?*, eds. Mary Anne Schofield and Cecilia Macheski. Athens: Ohio University Press, 1986, 398–425.

Luyendijk-Elshout, Antonie. "Of Masks and Mills: the Enlightened Doctor and his Frightened Patient." *The Languages of Psyche*, ed. G. S. Rousseau. Berkeley: University of California Press, 1990.

Mackall, L. L. "A Manuscript of the *Christianismi Restitutio* of Servetus." *Proceedings of the Royal Society of Medicine* 17 (1924), 35–38.

"Servetus Notes." *Contributions to Medical and Biological Research, dedicated to Sir William Osler*. 2 vols. New York: Paul B. Hoeber, 1919.

Maddox, James H. Jr. "Interpreter Crusoe." *ELH* 51 (1984), 33–52.

Malebranche, Nicholas. *Father Malebranche; his Treatise Concerning Search after Truth.* London, 1700.

Mandeville, Bernard. *The Fable of the Bees: or, Private Vices, Publick Benefits.* ed. F. B. Kaye. 2 vols. Oxford: Clarendon Press, 1924.

A Treatise of the Hypochondriack and Hysterick Diseases, ed. Stephen H. Good. Delmar: Scholars' Facsimiles and Reprints, 1976.

Mautner, Thomas, ed. *Francis Hutcheson: Two Texts on Human Nature.* Cambridge: Cambridge University Press, 1993.

Mayer, Robert. *History and the Early English Novel: Matters of Fact from Bacon to Defoe.* Cambridge: Cambridge University Press, 1997.

McBurney, W. H., ed. *Four before Richardson: Selected English Novels, 1720–1727.* Lincoln: University of Nebraska Press, 1963.

McKenzie, Alan T. *Certain, Lively Episodes: the Articulation of Passion in Eighteenth-Century Prose.* Athens: University of Georgia Press, 1990.

McKeon, Michael. "Generic Transformation and Social Change: Rethinking the Rise of the Novel." *Cultural Critique* 1 (1985), 159–81, rep. *Modern Essays on Eighteenth-Century Literature,* ed. Leopold Damrosch Jr. New York: Oxford University Press, 1988, 159–80.

Origins of the English Novel, 1600–1740. Baltimore: Johns Hopkins University Press, 1987.

Mead, Richard, M.D. *The Medical Works of Richard Mead,* M.D. Edinburgh, 1775. New York: AMS, 1978.

Melville, Lewis. *The Life and Letters of Tobias Smollett.* London: Faber and Gwyer, 1926.

Miller, Henry Knight. *Essays on Fielding's "Miscellanies": a Commentary on Volume One.* Princeton: Princeton University Press, 1961.

Monro, Alexander *primus. The Anatomy of the Humane Bones. To which are added, An Anatomical Treatise of the Nerves; an Account of the Reciprocal Motions of the Heart; and, a Description of the Humane Lacteal Sac and Duct.* 2nd edn. Edinburgh, 1732.

The Anatomy of the Human Bones and Nerves: with an Account of the reciprocal Motions of the Heart, and a Description of the Human Lacteal Sac and Duct. 3rd edn. Edinburgh, 1741.

The Anatomy of the Human Bones, Nerves, and Heart, 6th edn. Edinburgh, 1758.

Monro, Alexander *secundus. Experiments on the Nervous System, with opium and metalline substances; made chiefly with the view of determining the Nature and Effects of Animal Electricity.* Edinburgh, 1793.

Observations on the Structure and Functions of the Nervous System. Edinburgh, 1783.

Three Treatises on the Brain, the Eye, and the Ear. Edinburgh, 1797.

Moon, R. O. "Van Helmont, Chemist, Physician, Philosopher, and Mystic." *Proceedings of the Royal Society of Medicine* 25 (1932).

Moore, James. "The Two Systems of Francis Hutcheson: on the Origins of the Scottish Enlightenment." *Studies in the Philosophy of the Scottish Enlightenment,* ed. M. A. Stewart. Oxford: Clarendon Press, 1990.

"Hume and Hutcheson." *Hume and Hume's Connexions*, eds. M. A. Stewart and John P. Wright. Edinburgh: Edinburgh University Press, 1994, 23–57.

Morris, David B. *Alexander Pope: the Genius of Sense.* Cambridge: Harvard University Press, 1984.

Mossner, E. C. *The Life of David Hume.* Austin: University of Texas Press, 1954.

Mulford, Carla. "Booth's Progress and the Resolution of *Amelia*." *Studies in the Novel* 16 (1984), 20–31.

Nelson, T. G. A. *Children, Parents, and the Rise of the Novel.* Newark: University of Delaware Press, 1995.

Novak, Maximillian E. *Defoe and the Nature of Man.* Oxford: Oxford University Press, 1963.

———. "Defoe as an Innovator of Fictional Form." *The Cambridge Companion to the Eighteenth Century Novel*, ed. John J. Richetti. Cambridge: Cambridge University Press, 1996, 41–71.

———. "Crime and Punishment in Defoe's *Roxana*." *Journal of English and Germanic Philology* 65 (1966).

———. "Defoe and the Disordered City." *PMLA* 92 (1977), 241–52.

———. *Economics and the Fiction of Daniel Defoe.* Berkeley: University of California Press, 1962.

———. "Fiction and Society in the Early Eighteenth Century." *England in the Restoration and Early Eighteenth Century*, ed. H. T. Swedenberg, Jr. Los Angeles: University of California Press, 1972.

———. *Realism, Myth, and History in Defoe's Fiction.* Lincoln NE: University of Nebraska Press, 1983.

Nussbaum, Martha C. "Therapeutic Arguments: Epicurus and Aristotle." *The Norms of Nature*, eds. Malcolm Schofield and Gisela Striker. Cambridge: Cambridge University Press, 1986, 31–74.

———. *The Therapy of Desire: Theory and Practice in Hellenistic Ethics.* Princeton: Princeton University Press, 1994.

Nuttall, Geoffrey F. *The Holy Spirit in Puritan Faith and Experience.* Chicago: University of Chicago Press, 1992.

O'Malley, Charles Donald. "The English Physician in the Earlier Eighteenth Century." *England in the Restoration and Early Eighteenth Century: Essays on Culture and Society*, ed. H. T. Swedenberg Jr. Berkeley: University of California Press, 1972, 145–60.

———. *Michael Servetus, a Translation of his Writings.* Philadelphia: American Philosophical Society, 1953.

Overton, John H., and Frederick Relton. *The English Church from the Accession of George I to the End of the Eighteenth Century.* London: Macmillan, 1906.

Pagel, Walter. *William Harvey's Biological Ideas: Selected Aspects and Historical Backgrounds.* Basel: Karger, 1967.

Paulson, Ronald. *The Life of Henry Fielding, a Critical Biography.* Oxford: Blackwell, 2000.

Phillips, E. D. *Greek Medicine.* London: Thames and Hudson, 1973.

Plotkin, Mark J. *Tales of a Shaman's Apprentice.* New York: Penguin Books, 1993.

Pocock, J. G. A. *The Machiavellian Moment: Florentine Political Thought and the Atlantic Republican Tradition*. Princeton: Princeton University Press, 1975.

Pope, Alexander. *The Correspondence of Alexander Pope*, ed. George Sherburn. Oxford: Clarendon Press, 1956.

Porter, Roy. "*Barely Touching*: a Social Perspective on Mind and Body." *The Languages of Psyche: Mind and Body in Enlightenment Thought*, ed. G. S. Rousseau. Berkeley: University of California Press, 1990, 45–80.

Mind-Forg'd Manacles: a History of Madness in England from the Restoration to the Regency. Cambridge: Harvard University Press, 1987.

Posidonius. *Posidonius: the Fragments*, eds. Leon Edelstein and I. G. Kidd. Cambridge: Cambridge University Press, 1972.

Posidonius: the Commentary, ed. I. G. Kidd. 2 vols. Cambridge: Cambridge University Press, 1988.

Preston, John. "*Tom Jones*: Irony and Judgment." *Modern Essays on Eighteenth-Century Literature*, ed. Leopold Damrosch Jr. New York: Oxford University Press, 1988, 282–309.

Primer, Irwin. "Bernard Mandeville." *Dictionary of Literary Biography: British Prose Writers, 1660–1800*, CI, ed. Donald T. Siebert. Detroit: Gale Pub. Co., 1991.

Purchas, Samuel. *Microcosmus, or The Historie of Man*. London: 1619; facsimile ed. Amsterdam: Da Capo Press, 1969.

Purviance, Susan M. "Intersubjectivity and Sociable Relations in the Philosophy of Francis Hutcheson." *Sociability and Society in Eighteenth-Century Scotland*, eds. John Dwyer and Richard B. Sher. *Eighteenth Century Life* 15, n.s. 1. and 2 (1991), 23–38.

Ravitch, Norman. *Sword and Mitre: Government and Episcopate in France and England in the Age of Aristocracy*. The Hague: Mouton, 1966.

Relihan, Joel C. *Ancient Menippean Satire*. Baltimore: Johns Hopkins University Press, 1993.

Richardson, Samuel. *Clarissa, or the History of a Young Lady*. Harmondsworth: Penguin, 1985.

The History of Sir Charles Grandison, 7 vols. London, 1810.

Pamela; or, Virtue Rewarded, ed. Peter Sabor. London: Penguin, 1980.

Richetti, John J., ed. *The Cambridge Companion to the Eighteenth-Century Novel*. Cambridge: Cambridge University Press, 1996.

Defoe's Narratives: Situations and Structures. Oxford: Clarendon Press, 1975.

The English Novel in History, 1700–1780. London: Routledge, 1999.

Philosophical Writing: Locke, Berkeley, Hume. Cambridge: Harvard University Press, 1983.

Popular Fiction before Richardson: Narrative Patterns 1700–1739. Oxford: Clarendon Press, 1969.

Rodman, Jeffrey. "Defoe and the Psychotic Subject." *Ethics and the Subject*, ed. Karl Simms (Amsterdam: Rodopi, 1997), 245–251.

Rogers, Pat. *The Text of Great Britain: Theme and Design in Defoe's "Tour."* Newark: University of Delaware Press, 1998.

Rosner, Lisa. *Medical Education in the Age of Improvement: Edinburgh Students and Apprentices, 1760–1826*. Edinburgh: Edinburgh University Press, 1991.

Rothstein, Eric. *Systems of Order and Inquiry in Later Eighteenth-Century Fiction.* Berkeley: University of California Press, 1975.

"Virtues of Authority in *Tom Jones.*" *Critical Essays on Henry Fielding*, ed. Albert J. Rivero (New York, 1998), 141–163.

Rousseau, G. S. *Enlightenment Crossings: Pre- and Post-modern Discourses.* Manchester: Manchester University Press, 1991.

"Nerves, spirits, and fibres: towards an anthropology of sensibility." *Enlightenment Crossings: pre- and post-modern discourses: anthropological.* Manchester: Manchester University Press, 1991, 122–41.

"Pineapples, Pregnancy, Pica, and *Peregrine Pickle.*" *Tobias Smollett: Bicentennial Essays presented to Lewis M. Knapp* eds., G. S. Rousseau and P.-G. Boucé. New York: Oxford University Press, 1971.

"'A Strange Pathology': Hysteria in the Early Modern World, 1500–1800." *Hysteria Beyond Freud*, eds. Sander L. Gilman, Helen King, Roy Porter, G. S. Rousseau, and Elaine Showalter. Berkeley: University of California Press, 1993, 91–221.

Rush, Benjamin. *Benjamin Rush's Lectures on the Mind.* eds. Eric T. Carlson, Jeffrey L. Wollock, and Patricia S. Noel. Philadelphia: American Philosophical Society, 1981.

Medical Inquiries and Observations, upon the Diseases of the Mind. Philadelphia, 1812, rep. Birmingham, AL: The Classics of Medicine Library, 1979.

Sixteen Introductory Lectures. Philadelphia, 1811.

Sandbach, F. H. *The Stoics.* New York: Norton, 1975.

Santesso, Aaron. "A Note on Goats: Defoe on Crusoe's 'Devil.'" *The Scriblerian* 30: 2 (Spring, 1998), 48–49.

Sarton, George. *The Appreciation of Ancient and Medieval Science during the Renaissance.* Philadelphia: University of Pennsylvania Press, 1955.

Galen of Pergamon. Lawrence: University of Kansas Press, 1954.

Scarborough, John. *Roman Medicine.* Ithaca: Cornell University Press, 1969.

Schofield, Robert E. *Mechanism and Materialism: British Natural Philosophy in an Age of Reason.* Princeton: Princeton University Press, 1970.

Scott, Sir Walter. *Waverley*, ed. Andrew Hook. Harmondsworth: Penguin, 1972.

Scott, William Robert. *Francis Hutcheson: his Life, Teaching and Position in the History of Philosophy.* 1900; reprinted New York: Augustus M. Kelley, 1966.

Seidel, Michael. "The Man Who Came to Dinner: Ian Watt and the Theory of Formal Realism." *Reconsidering the Rise of the Novel*, ed. David Blewett. *ECF* 12: 2–3 (Jan.–April 2000), 193–212.

Servetus, Michael. *The Two Treatises of Servetus on the Trinity*, trans. Earl Morse Wilbur. Cambridge: Harvard University Press, 1932.

Shuttleton, David E. "'Pamela's Library': Samuel Richardson and Dr. Cheyne's 'Universal Cure.'" *Eighteenth-Century Life* 23 (1999), 59–79.

Siegel, Rudolph E., M.D. *Galen's System of Physiology and Medicine, an Analysis of his Doctrines on Bloodflow, Respiration, Humors, and Internal Diseases* Basel: Karger, 1968.

Galen on Psychology, Psychopathology, and Function and Diseases of the Nervous System. Basel: Karger, 1973.

Sill, Geoffrey M. "The Authorship of *An Impartial History of Michael Servetus*." *PBSA* 87 (1993), 303–18.

"Crusoe in the Cave: Defoe and the Semiotics of Desire." *Eighteenth-Century Fiction* 6 (1994), 215–32.

Defoe and the Idea of Fiction, 1713–1719. Newark: University of Delaware Press, 1983.

"*Roxana*'s Susan: Whose Daughter Is She Anyway?" *Studies in Eighteenth-Century Culture* 29 (1999), 261–72.

"A Source for Crusoe's Tobacco Cure," *English Language Notes* 32: 4 (June 1995), 46–48.

Singer, Charles. *A Short History of Anatomy from the Greeks to Harvey*. New York: Dover, 1957.

"A Study in Early Renaissance Anatomy." *Studies in the History and Method of Science*, ed. Charles Singer. London: Dawson and Sons, 1955.

Skinner, Quentin. *Reason and Rhetoric in the Philosophy of Hobbes*. Cambridge: Cambridge University Press, 1996.

Smith, LeRoy W. "Fielding and Mandeville: The 'War against Virtue.'" *Criticism* 3 (1961), 7–15.

Smollett, Tobias. *The Expedition of Humphry Clinker*, ed. James L. Thorson. New York: Norton, 1983.

Solomon, Robert C. *The Passions*. Garden City: Anchor Press, 1977.

Sontag, Susan. *Illness as Metaphor*. New York: Farrar, Straus and Giroux, 1978.

Spackman, I. J., W. R. Owens, and P. N. Furbank. *A Kwic Concordance to Daniel Defoe's "Robinson Crusoe."* New York: Garland, 1987.

Spacks, Patricia Meyer. *Desire and Truth: Functions of Plot in Eighteenth-Century Novels*. Chicago: University of Chicago Press, 1990.

"The Dangerous Age." *Eighteenth-Century Studies* 11 (1978), 417–38.

Spencer, Jane. *The Rise of the Woman Novelist from Aphra Behn to Jane Austen*. Oxford: Basil Blackwell, 1986.

"Women writers and the eighteenth-century novel." *The Cambridge Companion to the Eighteenth-Century Novel*, ed. John J. Richetti. Cambridge: Cambridge University Press, 1996, 212–35.

Starr, G. A. *Defoe and Spiritual Autobiography*. Princeton: Princeton University Press, 1965.

Defoe and Casuistry. Princeton: Princeton University Press, 1971.

Stauffer, Donald A. *The Art of Biography in Eighteenth Century England*. Princeton: Princeton University Press, 1941.

Steensma, Robert C. *Dr. John Arbuthnot*. Boston: Twayne, 1979.

Stephanson, Raymond. "Defoe's 'Malade Imaginaire': the Historical Foundation of Mental Illness in *Roxana*." *Huntington Library Quarterly* 45 (1982), 99–118.

Stephen, Sir Leslie. *History of English Thought in the Eighteenth Century*, 2 vols. New York: Putnam's, 1876.

Stevens, Scott Manning. "Sacred Heart and Secular Brain." *The Body in Parts: Fantasies of Corporeality in Early Modern Europe*, eds. David Hillman and Carla Mazzio. New York: Routledge, 1997, 263–82.

Straub, Kristina. *Divided Fictions: Fanny Burney and Feminine Strategy.* Lexington: University Press of Kentucky, 1987.

Sykes, Norman. *Edmund Gibson, Bishop of London.* London: Oxford University Press, 1926.

Swift, Jonathan. *The Correspondence of Jonathan Swift,* ed. Sir Harold Williams. 5 vols. Oxford: Clarendon Press, 1963–65.

Taylor, D. W. "The Manuscript Lecture-Notes of Alexander Monro *secundus* (1733–1817)." *Medical History* 22 (1978), 174–86.

"The Manuscript Lecture-Notes of Alexander Monro *primus* (1697–1767)." *Medical History* 30 (1986), 444–67.

"'Discourses on the Human Physiology' by Alexander Monro *primus* (1697–1767)." *Medical History* 32 (1988), 65–81.

Temkin, Owsei. *Galenism: Rise and Decline of a Medical Philosophy.* Ithaca: Cornell University Press, 1973.

Thomas, Donald. *Henry Fielding.* New York: St. Martin's Press, 1990.

Thompson, H. S. "Sir Peter Thompson's Library," rep. from "Notes and Queries for Somerset and Dorset," March 1925. British Library, 11902.c.53.

Thornbury, E. M. *Henry Fielding's Theory of the Comic Prose Epic.* New York: Russell and Russell, 1966.

Todd, Janet. *Sensibility: an Introduction.* London: Methuen, 1986.

The Sign of Angellica: Women, Writing, and Fiction, 1660–1800. New York: Columbia University Press, 1989.

Tomkins, Martin. *The Case of Mr. Martin Tomkins. Being an account of the Proceedings of the Dissenting Congregation at Stoke-Newington, upon Occasion of a Sermon preach'd by him July 13, 1718.* London: John Clark, 1719.

Underwood, E. Ashworth. *Boerhaave's Men: at Leyden and After.* Edinburgh: Edinburgh University Press, 1977.

Van Sant, Ann Jessie. *Eighteenth-Century Sensibility and the Novel: the Senses in Social Context.* Cambridge: Cambridge University Press, 1993.

Veith, Ilza. *Hysteria: the History of a Disease.* Chicago: University of Chicago Press, 1965.

Venner, Tobias. *Via Recta ad Vitam Longam, or, A Plain Philosophicall Demonstration of the Nature, Faculties, and Effects of all such things as by way of nourishments make for the preservation of health.* London, 1637.

Vickers, Ilse. *Defoe and the New Sciences.* Cambridge: Cambridge University Press, 1996.

Voitle, Robert. *The Third Earl of Shaftesbury.* Baton Rouge: Louisiana State University, 1984

Watt, Ian. *The Rise of the Novel: Studies in Defoe, Richardson and Fielding.* Harmondsworth: Penguin Books, 1963.

Myths of Modern Individualism: Faust, Don Quixote, Don Juan, Robinson Crusoe. Cambridge: Cambridge University Press, 1996.

Watts, Isaac. *The Doctrine of the Passions, Explain'd and Improv'd: or, a brief and comprehensive scheme of the natural affections of mankind . . . to which are subjoined, moral and divine rules for the regulation and government of them.* London: 1732; 3rd edn. 1739.

Watts, Michael R. *The Dissenters.* 2 vols. Oxford: Clarendon Press, 1978.
Weiner, Dora B. "Mind and Body in the Clinic: Philippe Pinel, Alexander Chrichton, Dominique Esquirol, and the Birth of Psychiatry." *The Languages of Psyche: Mind and Body in Enlightenment Thought,* G. S. Rousseau, ed. Berkeley: University of California Press, 1990, 331–402.
Wellman, Kathleen. *La Mettrie: Medicine, Philosophy, and Enlightenment.* Durham: Duke University Press, 1992.
West, Robert H. *Milton and the Angels.* Athens: University of Georgia Press, 1955.
Whitteridge, Gweneth. *William Harvey and the Circulation of the Blood.* London: Macdonald, 1971.
Whytt, Robert. *An Essay on the Vital and other Involuntary Motions of Animals.* Edinburgh, 1751.
Observations on the Nature, Causes, and Cure of those Disorders which have been commonly called Nervous, Hypochondriac, or Hysteric, to which are prefixed some remarks on the sympathy of the Nerves. Edinburgh, 1765.
Williams, George Huntston. *The Radical Reformation.* Philadelphia: Westminster Press, 1962.
Willis, Robert. *Servetus and Calvin.* London: Kegan Paul and Co., 1877.
Wotton, William. *Reflections Upon Ancient and Modern Learning.* London, 1694, rep. Hildesheim: George Olms Verlagsbuchhandlung, 1968.
Reflections upon Ancient and Modern Learning, 2nd edn. London, 1697.
Wright, Thomas. *The Passions of the Mind in General,* ed. William Webster Newbold. New York: Garland, 1986.
Wright-St. Clair, Rex E. *Doctors Monro: a Medical Saga.* London: Wellcome Historical Medical Library, 1964.
Yates, Nigel, Robert Hume, and Paul Hastings. *Religion and Society in Kent, 1640–1914.* Kent County Council: Boydell Press, 1994.
Yolton, John W. *Thinking Matter: Materialism in Eighteenth-Century Britain.* Minneapolis: University of Minnesota Press, 1983.
Zilboorg, Gregory. *A History of Medical Psychology.* New York: Norton, 1967.
Zimmerman, Everett. *Defoe and the Novel.* Berkeley: University of California Press, 1975.
Zweig, Stefan. *The Right to Heresy,* trans. Eden and Cedar Paul. London: Souvenir Press, 1979.

Index

C
(11)
1
£3.00

Printed in the United Kingdom
by Lightning Source UK Ltd.
119995UK00002B/33